Human-Computer Interaction Series

Human-Computer Interaction is a multidisciplinary field focused on human aspects of the development of computer technology. As computer-based technology becomes increasingly pervasive – not just in developed countries, but worldwide – the need to take a human-centered approach in the design and development of this technology becomes ever more important. For roughly 30 years now, researchers and practitioners in computational and behavioral sciences have worked to identify theory and practice that influences the direction of these technologies, and this diverse work makes up the field of human-computer interaction. Broadly speaking, it includes the study of what technology might be able to do for people and how people might interact with the technology.

In this series, we present work which advances the science and technology of developing systems which are both effective and satisfying for people in a wide variety of contexts. The human-computer interaction series will focus on theoretical perspectives (such as formal approaches drawn from a variety of behavioral sciences), practical approaches (such as the techniques for effectively integrating user needs in system development), and social issues (such as the determinants of utility, usability and acceptability).

For further volumes:
http://www.springer.com/series/6033

Ahmed Seffah · Jean Vanderdonckt ·
Michel C. Desmarais
Editors

Human-Centered Software Engineering

Software Engineering Models, Patterns and Architectures for HCI

Editors
Ahmed Seffah
Concordia University
Montreal QC H3G 1M8
Canada

Michel C. Desmarais
Ecole Polytechnique de Montreal
Montreal QC H3C 3A7
Canada

Prof. Dr. Jean Vanderdonckt
Université catholique de Louvain
1348 Louvain-la-Neuve
Belgium

ISSN 1571-5035
ISBN 978-1-84996-803-4 e-ISBN 978-1-84800-907-3
DOI 10.1007/978-1-84800-907-3
Springer Dordrecht Heidelberg London New York

British Library Cataloguing in Publication Data
A catalogue record for this book is available from the British Library

Printed on acid-free paper

Springer is part of Springer Science+Business Media (www.springer.com)

CONTENTS

List of Figures

List of Tables

To my mentors, professors and friends Dr Rabia Khaled and Pr Bertrand Tim David For their support, advice and guidance.
Ahmed

To my wife Teodora and our daughter Marina.
Jean

To those aging loved ones,
may we comfort them as well as
they nurtured us.
Michel

Contributing Authors

Marc Abrams serves as Harmonia's President and CTO. In the past, Dr. Abrams has been with the former U.S. Army Concepts Analysis Agency, a post-doc in the Distributed Operating Systems group in Stanford's Computer Science Department, a Visiting Scientist in the network protocol group at IBM's Zurich Research Laboratory in Switzerland, and an Associate Professor with Tenure in Computer Science at Virginia Tech in Blacksburg, Virginia. He has been the Principal Investigator for almost \$20M in research and development projects with IBM, MDA, NAVAIR, NAVSEA, NSF, ONR, OSD, Raytheon, and SAIC. He received his Ph.D. from the University of Maryland at College Park in Computer Science. Before Harmonia, Dr. Abrams was a tenured associate professor at Virginia Tech, where his research on Human-Computer Interfaces led to the creation of UIML and later the co-founding of Harmonia. UIML forms the basis for Harmonia's LiquidApps® product. At Virginia Tech, he also co-founded the Center for Human Computer Interaction, and worked with faculty in HCI in fields ranging from cognitive psychology to human factors on scenario-driven HCI design.

Gaëlle Calvary has been an assistant professor at UJF since 1999, and a member of the HCI research group headed by Joëlle Coutaz. Her research area is UI plasticity. She aims at providing models, methods and tools for supporting the engineering of plastic UIs capable of overcoming multiple, dynamic, and unforeseeable contexts of use. Her approach combines MDE and AI techniques.

Jim A. Carter is a Professor and Director of the Usability Engineering Research Lab (USERLab) of the Computer Science Department, University of Saskatchewan. His research investigates methods and methodologies for improving usability and accessibility and for incorporating these concerns within traditional software engineering methods and methodologies. Jim is involved as a Canadian expert in the development of ergonomic, software engineering, user interface, and accessibility standards within ISO and ISO/IEC JTC1.

Larry L. Constantine is Chief Scientist Constantine & Lockwood, Ltd, as well as an ACM Distinguished Engineer and one of the pioneers of software design whose current work in usage-centered design continues a long tradition of technical innovation and professional leadership. In a career spanning four decades, he has contributed numerous concepts and techniques forming the foundations of modern practice in software engineering and applications development. Constantine has keynoted numerous major international conferences and has taught in 20 countries around the world. He is a prolific writer and a widely read columnist. Among his publications in both the computer sciences and human sciences are over 150 articles and papers (see bibliography) plus 17 books, including the award-winning *Software for Use* (Addison-Wesley, 1999), written with Lucy Lockwood; The *Peopleware Papers* (Prentice Hall, 2001); and the software engineering classic, *Structured Design* (Prentice Hall, 1979), written with Ed Yourdon. His books and papers have been translated into Chinese, Danish, Dutch, German, Italian, Japanese, Portuguese, Russian, and Spanish. Constantine is a professor in the Department of Mathematics and Engineering at the University of Madeira, Funchal (Portugal) where he is also Director of LabUSE: the Laboratory for Usage-centered Software Engineering. He also served on the faculty of the University of Technology, Sydney (Australia), where he was Professor of Information Technology. He is a graduate of the Massachusetts Institute of Technology, Sloan School of Management.

Joëlle Coutaz has been professor at UJF since 1973 and the founder (in 1990) and head of the HCI research group (Ingénierie de l'Interaction Homme-Machine) at Laboratoire d'Informaitque de Grenoble. In April 2007, she was elected to the SIGCHI Academy for "leadership in the profession in Computer Human Interaction." In June 2007, she received the Honorary Degree of Doctor of Science from the University of Glasgow.

Adrien Coyette recently earned his Ph.D. in HCI at Université catholique de Louvain. His thesis work won him the Brian Schackel 2007 award for the most outstanding contribution with international impact in HCI. He is currently a member of the research staff at UCL Unité de systèmes d'information in Louvain School of Management.

Bertrand David is a Full Professor of Computer Science at the Ecole Centrale de Lyon (ECL) in Lyon working in the area of human-computer interaction, cooperative systems and wearable computer use in pervasive environments. He was cofounder and director for 8 years of a multidisciplinary research lab ICTT, working on cooperative systems design and evaluation. He is coeditor in chief of RIHM: Francophone Journal of Human-Machine Interaction.

Alexander Deichman is a graduate student with the Human-Centered Software Engineering Group, including the Usability and Empirical Studies Lab, in the Department of Computer Science and Software Engineering at Concordia University. He holds a

Bachelor of Engineering (Computer) from Concordia University, and is now pursuing his studies in Human-Computer Interaction. His research interests lie in designing novel tools that can support the UI design process. He is currently working on a tool called P2P Mapper, which helps designers in building pattern-oriented designs based on user specifications. Alex has been involved in a number of usability projects, mostly for web-based and biomedical applications.

Michel C. Desmarais has been an associate professor of Computer Engineering at École Polytechnique de Montréal, Canada, since 2002. He was the head of the HCI group at the Computer Research Institute of Montreal from 1990 to 1998, and was manager of software engineering teams in a private software company for 4 years afterwards. Besides user-centered engineering, his research interests are in artificial Intelligence and user modeling. `http://www.professeurs.polymtl.ca/michel.desmarais/desmarais_michel_c.html`

Mohammad El-Ramly completed his Ph.D. studies at Alberta University (Canada). He is a lecturer in Computer Science at the University of Leicester (UK). His research activities include software systems evolution, maintenance, reverse engineering, and reengineering. He is also investigating the applications of data mining to software data.

Daniel Engleberg earned a master's degree in cognitive sciences from the University of Michigan and bachelor of science from McGill University. He is a senior user experiences and usability professional with Nuange Technogies, a Montreal-based IT company. Daniel is active with the Usability Professional Association and has organized several workshops on HCI and Software Engineering Integration.

Houcine Ezzedine is a maître de Conférences at the Université de Valenciennes. He earned his Ph.D. in 1985 and his "Habilitation" in 2002 from the Université de Valenciennes et du Hainaut-Cambrésis. He is the author of over 60 scientific publications and an active member of the Laboratoire d'automatique de Mécanique et d'Informatique industrielles et Humaines et au sein du groupe de recherche RAIHM : Raisonnement Automatique et Interaction Homme-Machine.

Jean-Marie Favre is a Software Explorer and a Language Archaeologist practicing XFOR. He serves as an Assistant Professor at UJF. His research work aims at (1) understanding phenomenon that arises during the long-term evolution of very large scale software products, and (2) to improve software engineering techniques accordingly.

James Helms currently serves as a Software Engineer focused on usability and UI development for Digital Receiver Technology, Inc. Before that, he was responsible for ensuring that Harmonia, Inc. maintained a rigorous usability engineering ethic. He is the Chair of the OASIS UIML standardization committee and served on the original LiquidUI® product development team. His research background includes the development of a new usability engineering process model (the Wheel), in-depth analysis of usability issues associated with deploying training documents and interfaces to PDAs, and the field evaluation of a distributed, multiuser virtual science laboratory. Mr. Helms received his master's degree in Computer Science and Applications from Virginia Tech in 2001.

Fei Huang is an M.Sc.¡ student majoring in usability engineering. She also has expertise in databases and in accessibility engineering. Fei is a member of the USERLab of the Computer Science Department, University of Saskatchewan.

Ebba Thora Hvannberg is a professor of computer science. She has a B.S. in computer science from the University of Iceland, and an M.S. and a Ph.D. from Rensselaer Polytechnic Institute, New York. Her research interests include human-computer interaction and software engineering.

Homa Javahery is a researcher and project manager with the Human-Centered Software Engineering Group, including the Usability and Empirical Studies Lab, in the Department of Computer Science and Software Engineering at Concordia University. She holds a Ph.D. in Computer Science (Human-Computer Interaction) from Concordia University, and a Bachelor of Science degree from McGill University. She is combining different design approaches from human sciences and engineering disciplines to develop novel design frameworks which effectively address the user's needs and experiences. She has managed a number of large-scale usability studies and participated in collaborative projects at the INRIA Research Institute in France and the Daimler-Chrysler Research Institute in Germany. Her main areas of expertise are biomedical applications and multiple user interfaces.

Christophe Kolski has been a professor in computer science at the Université de Valenciennes et du Hainaut-Cambrésis since 1995. He earned his Ph.D. in 1989 and his "habilitation" in 1995. He is the author of over 200 publications and a member of the Laboratoire d'automatique de Mécanique et d'Informatique industrielles et Humaines et au sein du groupe de recherche RAIHM : Raisonnement Automatique et Interaction Homme-Machine.

Quentin Limbourg earned a Ph.D. in Management Sciences from the Management School (IAG) of the University of Louvain (UCL). His dissertation topic was "Multipath Development of User Interfaces." Currently he is an IT consultant at the R&D unit of SmalS-MvM, a Scientific collaborator at the Management School (IAG) of the University of Louvain (UCL), as well as a temporary invited lecturer (only for 2005-2006) at the Computer Science Department of the Université Libre de Bruxelles. His is investigating the application of software engineering to user interface development including Model-Driven Architecture, Conceptual modeling and Languages for user interface specification (e.g., UsiXML).

Martha J. Lindeman is president of Agile Interactions, Inc. in Columbus, Ohio. She has over 20 years of experience in the design and evaluation of how people process information in interactions with other people and technology.

Kris Luyten is working in the area of Human-Computer Interaction, focusing on advanced techniques and technologies that support the design, development, and deployment of traditional and non traditional user interfaces. These include context-sensitive, collaborative, and embedded/ubiquitous user interfaces. He is Assistant Professor at Hasselt University in Belgium and Adjunct group-leader HCI research group, Expertise Centre for Digital Media. He has authored and coauthored over 80 scientific papers and has participated in 25 conference and workshops program committees.

Atif M. Memon is an Associate Professor in the Department of Computer Science, University of Maryland. He received his B.S. in Computer Science in 1991 from the University of Karachi, his M.S. in Computer Science in 1995 from the King Fahd University of Petroleum and Minerals, and his Ph.D. in Computer Science from the University of Pittsburgh. He was awarded a Gold Medal during his undergraduate education, and received fellowships from the Andrew Mellon Foundation for his Ph.D. research. His research interests include program testing, software engineering, artificial intelligence, plan generation, reverse engineering, and program structures. He is a member of the ACM and the IEEE Computer Society and serves on the editorial boards of the *Journal of Software Testing, Verification, and Reliability*, *The Open Software Engineering Journal*, and the *Canadian Journal of Pure and Applied Sciences*. He has served on numerous National Science Foundation panels. He is currently serving on a National Academy of Sciences panel as an expert in the area of Computer Science and Information Technology, for the Pakistan-U.S. Science and Technology Cooperative Program, sponsored by the United States Agency for International Development (USAID).

David Navarre is a Lecturer in Computer Science Human Computer Interaction and Software Engineering at the University Toulouse 1. The main area of his research activities is defining methods and techniques dedicated to real-time safety critical interactive systems.

Nuno J. Nunes is an Associate Professor in the Mathematics and Engineering Department of the University of Madeira where he lectures in the fields of software engineering, programming languages and human-computer interaction. He holds a degree in Software and Computer Engineering (LEIC) from the Instituto Superior Tecnico (1994) of the Technical University of Lisbon, an MPhil in Software Engineering from the University of Madeira (1997), and a Ph.D. (Doctor of Engineering Degree in Systems and Computer Science) in Software Engineering from the University of Madeira (2001). In 1993 and 1994 he worked at INESC in the areas of telematic systems and services and advanced computer architecture.Since 1995 he shifted his research interests to software engineering and human-computer interaction. He was involved in the organization of several international conferences (IUI/CADUI2004, UML2004 and CAISE2005) and workshops (Wisdom99, Tupis00, DSV-IS2003). He is also the leading author of the Wisdom (Whitewater Interactive System Development with Object Models) lightweight software engineering method, a UML method specifically tailored for small software developing companies. Currently his research interests include User-centered Development, User Interface Design, Object-Oriented Methods, Agile Software Development, and Organizational Engineering. He is a member of the ACM, SIGCHI, SIGSOFT, and the IEEE Computer Society.

Philippe Palanque is full professor of computer science, University of Toulouse III (France). He is the Head of Master 2 Professional in HCI at Toulouse University. His interests cover a broad range of topics at the intersection of HCI and software engineering including critical safety systems.

Tamer Rafla holds a master's degree in software engineering from École Polytechnique de Montréal with his research nominated for the Best Thesis Award. His research interests include HCI, requirements engineering, software architecture and software process. He is currently working as a business consultant for a leading provider of SAP consulting services. He is a member of the Usability Professionals Association, the Worldwide Institute of Software Architects, and the Québec Order of Engineers.

Pierre-N. Robillard is a full professor of software engineering at École Polytechnique de Montréal. He leads the Software Engineering Research Laboratory whose research interests include software process, software cognition, software quality assurance and software applications to bio-informatics. He contributed to over 120 research papers, conference proceedings and three books on software engineering related topics. The latest book is *Software Engineering Process with the UPEDU*, Addison-Wesley, 2003. He is a licensed professional engineer in the province of Quebec and in Canada, and a member of the IEEE, ACM, EACE, and CIPS.

Kinan Samaan received his master's degree in "computer science for the society service." In 2002 he was awarded a Ph.D. in the area of adaptation of human-computer interface and software engineering from the Ecole Centrale de Lyon (France). He is currently the executive manager of Mamoun International Corporation—Aleppo branch, an international institute of higher education.

Robbie Schaefer received his doctoral degree at Paderborn University in 2007, where he has been working as a research assistant since 2001. There, he worked on several European projects with a focus on the challenges of user interface development for ambient intelligence. During this time he has authored about 30 publications in this field. His dissertation is titled "Model-Based Development of Multimodal and Multi-Device User Interfaces in Context-Aware Environments." He is active in the standardization of the User Interface Markup Language and a member of the OASIS UIML technical committee. Currently he works for Mettenmeier, a company which focuses on geographical information systems and asset management for gas, water, and electricity suppliers.

Kevin Schneider is Professor, Director of the Software Engineering Lab and Department Head of the Computer Science Department, University of Saskatchewan. His research investigates models, notations, and techniques to support collaborative software evolution. He is an elected member of the IFIP working group 2.7/13.4 on user interface engineering and the Prairie representative for the Canadian Association of Computer Science.

Ahmed Seffah is currently professor of Information and Software Technology at Ecole Hotelière Lausanne. He was previously an associate professor in the Department of Computer Science and Software Engineering. From 2000 to 2008 he has been the Concordia research chair on human-centered software engineering, a term he coined. His research interests are at the intersection of human-computer interaction, psychology, and software engineering, with an emphasis on usability and quality in use metrics and measurement, human experiences modeling as well as patterns as a vehicle for capturing and incorporating empirically valid best human-centric users and developers' experiences into software engineering processes. He is the cofounder of the Usability and Empirical Studies Lab which provides an advanced facility to support research and development in the field of human-centered software. Dr. Seffah is the vice chair of the IFIP working group on user-centered systems design methodologies and the cochair of the first working conference on Human-Centered Software Engineering.

Jean-Sébastien Sottet is doing a Ph.D. in Computer Science under the supervision of Gaëlle Calvary and Jean-Marie Favre. He is exploring Model Driven Engineering for plastic User Interfaces (UIs), i.e., UIs capable of adapting to their context of use ("User, Platform, Environment") while preserving usability.

Eleni Stroulia is an associate professor, Department of Computer Science (University of Alberta, Canada). Her recent research focuses on two major themes: (a) software understanding and reengineering and (b) reflective agent-based architectures for service-oriented Web-based applications.

Mohamed Taleb is a Ph.D. candiate at Concordia University and Ecole de Technologie Superieure de Montreal. He has more than 15 years' experience as a senior software engineer and HCI expert. His main interests include pattern driven, model based and architecture-centric development approaches for interactive systems engineering.

Jean-Claude Tarby is a maître de Conférences at the Université des Sciences et Technologies de Lille. He earned his Ph.D. in computer science at the Université de Toulouse. He is a member of Equipe NOCE at Laboratoire TRIGONE.

Franck Tarpin-Bernard is an Assistant Professor of Computer Science at the National Institute of Applied Sciences (INSA) in Lyon working in the area of human-computer interaction adaptation. He completed his Ph.D. in 1997 in the area of computer supported-collaborative work and software engineering. In 2000, he cofounded Scientific Brain Training, the current world-leader company of cognitive training software.

Jon Titus is a Database Analyst for the Potash Corporation and a member of the USERLab of the Computer Science Department, University of Saskatchewan.

Jean Vanderdonckt is a Full Professor in Computer Science at Université catholique de Louvain (Belgium), Louvain School of Management (IAG-LSM) where he leads the Belgian Laboratory of Computer-Human Interaction (BCHI, http://www.isys.ucl.ac.be/bchi). This laboratory is conducting research, development, and consulting services in the domain of user interface engineering, a domain that is located midway between software engineering, human-computer interaction, and usability engineering. Jean Vanderdonckt is the founder and the coordinator of the UsiXML Consortium (www.usixml.org) that structures activities towards the definition and the usage of UsiXML (User Interface eXtensible Markup Language) as a common User Interface Description Language. He is the coordinator of HCI activities within the Similar network of excellence (www.similar.cc, The European research taskforce creating human-machine interfaces SIMILAR to human-human communication). He is also a member of the European COST n°294 Action MAUSE (www.cost294.org) on usability engineering. He is a senior member of IEEE, ACM, and SIGCHI. He is a professor within the Faculty of Economical, Social and Political Sciences (ESPO), School of Management (IAG), Universite Catholique de Louvain La Neuve (Belgium). He also leads the BCHI Laboratory. He has coauthored and edited several books and published over 100 publication in the fields of software engineering and HCI.

Jo Vermeulen is a researcher at the Expertise Centre for Digital Media (EDM), a research institute of Hasselt University. He obtained his M.Sc. in computer science from Hasselt University in 2005 and joined EDM. Jo has been working with the User Interface Markup Language (UIML) since 2004, when he did an internship under the supervision of Kris Luyten to improve the open source Uiml.net renderer. For his M.Sc. thesis, he extended UIML with a declarative, platform-independent layout specification based on spatial constraints. He has been participating in the UIML Technical Committee since 2005. His research interests lie at the intersection of human-computer interaction and ubiquitous computing. He is currently pursuing a Ph.D. in this topic.

Marco Winckler completed his Ph.D. studies in 2004, focusing on the navigation modeling of complex Web applications. Since then, he has been a senior lecturer at University Toulouse III. His current research mingles Human-Computer Interaction methods and Software Engineering methods applied to the development of Web-based interactive systems.

Allan Wolinski is a Web Developer for Point2 and a member of the USERLab of the Computer Science Department, University of Saskatchewan.

1 HUMAN-CENTERED SOFTWARE ENGINEERING: SOFTWARE ENGINEERING ARCHITECTURES, PATTERNS, AND MODELS FOR HUMAN COMPUTER INTERACTION

Ahmed Seffah*,
Jean Vanderdonckt**, and Michel C. Desmarais***

*Human-Centered Software Engineering Group, Concordia University, Canada
**Université catholique de Louvain, Belgium
***École Polytechnique de Montréal, Canada

1.1 SCOPE

The Computer-Human Interaction and Software Engineering (CHISE) series of edited volumes originated from a number of workshops and discussions over the latest research and developments in the field of Human Computer Interaction (HCI) and Software Engineering (SE) integration, convergence and cross-pollination. A first volume in this series (CHISE Volume I – Human-Centered Software Engineering: Integrating Usability in the Development Lifecycle) aims at bridging the gap between the field of SE and HCI, and addresses specifically the concerns of integrating usability and user-centered systems design methods and tools into the software development lifecycle and practices. This has been done by defining techniques, tools and practices that can fit into the entire software engineering lifecycle as well as by defining ways of addressing the knowledge and skills needed, and the attitudes and basic values that a user-centered development methodology requires. The first volume has been edited as Vol. 8 in the Springer HCI Series (Seffah, Gulliksen and Desmarais, 2005).

1.2 SPECIFIC OBJECTIVES OF THE CHISE VOLUME II

In CHISE Volume I, we looked at means of integrating HCI and usability engineering techniques into the well-established software engineering lifecycles which, many of us claim, often lack the human-centered quality required for the development of highly interactive systems. In this volume, we look at the converse side of this issue. A development process may be dominated by HCI concerns and we may fail to integrate SE method into it. We also look at means of bringing more formal and systematic methods, and better tools for the HCI design and development of interactive systems.

A good example of how SE methods can have a positive impact in the design and development of interactive systems is in the transformation of the Web development process, from a print paradigm of online brochureware, to complex and highly interactive Web-based systems. Web user interfaces (UIs) and HCI designers have to consider new challenges such as content management, security versus usability, information architecture and navigation support, etc. Besides Web engineering, there has also been significant progress in terms of development approaches including component-based engineering, separation of software concerns, model-driven architecture, formal specification methods, and reengineering techniques. Such methods are certainly useful and needed by HCI researchers and practitioners. They help design the user interaction with the system and build more usable interfaces.

However, these methods are not sufficient yet. New methods and ideas are needed to address the particular issues of interaction engineering. They will borrow many of the software engineering's fundamental concepts and principles of SE emphasizing the same technical and management activities.

1.3 OVERVIEW

This second volume aim to establish a meaningful dialog between the HCI community and SE practitioners and researchers on the results (both good and bad), obstacles, and lessons learned associated with applying software development practices in the field of UI. The book will provide accounts of the application of SE practices (which may be principles, techniques, tools, methods, processes, etc.) to a specific domain or to the development of a significant interactive system.

This second volume includes 16 chapters organized in four sections. They provide a roadmap for the future of UI SE especially how emerging SE techniques can help HCI. The emphasis is put on the following topics:

- Software engineering models, methods and tools for challenging HCI issues such as adaptability, universal usability and accessibility
- Software architectures for HCI
- Model-driven architectures and engineering (MDA, MDE)

- Reengineering models and techniques
- Formal specifications methods and notations
- Software for supporting the UI development lifecycle: requirements, analysis, design, implementation, evaluation and traceability, and maintenance

1.4 CHAPTER SUMMARIES

We provide the summary of each of the 16 chapters that follow this introductory chapter.

In Chapter 2, Nunes presents two important avenues for incorporating SE techniques in usability engineering. The first issue addressed is use case driven development. He discusses the importance of describing use cases through technology-free and implementation-independent descriptions of user intentions and system responsibilities. He provides examples that demonstrate innovative tools support for multiple representations of essential use cases. The second issue is the architecture-centric nature of modern software development. Nunes discusses the importance of identifying usability aspects at the architectural level and describes an extension of the boundary-control-entity UML-based pattern that supports dialogue and presentation elements at the conceptual architectural level. This chapter presents and contrasts several examples that describe how the approach can be used to bridge software and usability engineering and some innovative developer-centric tools that support this approach.

In Chapter 3, Constantine introduces human activity modeling as a systematic approach to organizing and representing the contextual aspects of an interactive tool. Activity theory provides the vocabulary and conceptual framework for understanding the human use of tools and other artifacts. Simple extensions to the models of usage-centered design are introduced that together succinctly model the salient and most essential features of the activities within which tool use is embedded.

In Chapter 4, Javahery et al. highlight the challenge of combining individual design patterns to create a conceptual UI design that reflects user experiences and behaviors. They propose a user-centered design (UCD) framework that exploits the novel idea of using personas and software design patterns together. Personas, an emerging concept in HCI, are used initially to collect, analyze and model user experiences including their characteristics and tasks. UI design patterns are selected based on persona specifications; these patterns are then used as building blocks for constructing conceptual designs. Through a case study, they illustrate how personas and patterns can act as complementary techniques in narrowing the gap between two major steps in UCD. As a result of lessons learned from the study and by refining the UCD framework, they define a more systematic process called UX-P (User Experiences to Pattern).

In Chapter 5, Huang et al. suggest a set of XML-based and XMI-based tools for creating usability engineering requirements and automatically transforming them into SE specifications. Each of these tools is data-driven and uses XML to maximize flexibility, accessibility and translatability. These tools are primarily intended for use by usability engineers to create usability engineering (UE) requirements, analyze accessibility issues, and automatically transform UI requirements into SE specifications.

By transforming usability requirements into SE specifications, usability engineers can help software engineers design systems that satisfy the applicable usability requirements. Additionally these tools can be used by researchers investigating usability engineering methodologies.

In Chapter 6, Limbourg and Vanderdonckt investigate transformational development, a SE technique that aims at developing software systems by transforming a coarse-grained specification of a system to its final code through a series of transformation steps. Transformational development is known to bring benefits such as: correctness by construction, explicit mappings between development steps, and reversibility of transformations. Transformational development, applied to the development of UIs of interactive systems, allows reusability of design knowledge used to develop UIs and fosters incremental development of UIs by applying alternative transformations. A mathematical system for expressing specifications and transformation rules is introduced. This system is based on graph transformations. The problem of managing the transformation rules is detailed, e.g., how to enable a developer to access, define, extend, restrict or relax, test, verify, and apply appropriate transformations. A tool supporting this development paradigm is also described and exemplified.

In Chapter 7, Helms et al. summarize the efforts devoted to the definition and usage of UIML 4.0, which also covers dialog modeling. The User Interface Markup Language (UIML) consists of a User Interface Description Language aimed at producing multiple UIs from a single model for multiple contexts of use, in particular multiple computing platforms, thus addressing the need for multichannel UIs. The chapter describes the main parts of the UIML structure, i.e., structure, presentation style, contents, behavior, connectivity, and toolkit mappings, and the integrated development environment that supports the development lifecycle of multichannel UIs based on UIML.

In Chapter 8, Sottet, Calvary, and Favre address the challenge of engineering *Plastic UIs*, i.e., UIs capable of adapting to their context of use (User, Platform, Environment) while preserving usability. This chapter focuses on usability and proposes a mega and meta model-driven approach. The first Megamodel was used to make explicit the relations between the core concepts of MDE: *System*, *Model*, *Metamodel*, *Mapping*, and *Transformation*. When transposed to HCI, the Megamodel gives rise to the notion of *Mega-UI* that makes it possible for the user (designer and/or end-user) to browse and/or control the system from different levels of abstraction (e.g., user's tasks, workspaces, interactors, code) and different levels of genericity (e.g., model, metamodel, meta-metamodel). A first prototype has been implemented using general MDE tools (e.g., EMF, ATL).

In Chapter 9, Hvannberg suggests that a richer model of evaluation be created that is built concurrently with the design activity. The evaluation model should describe the implications work models have on design and record the cause/effect relationship between design and the problem domain. It also suggests that the distinction between elicitation and evaluation be diminished. The author presents two case studies from air traffic control that are meant to support and motivate the need for such a model.

In Chapter 10, Taleb et al. take a look at traditional interactive system architectures such as MVC and PAC. Such architectures decompose the system into two sub-

subsystems that are relatively independent, thereby allowing the design work to be partitioned between the UIs and underlying functionalities. They extend the independence assumption to usability, approaching the design of the UI as a subsystem that can be designed and tested independently from the underlying functionality. As highlighted in this chapter, such Cartesian dichotomy can be fallacious, as functionalities buried in the application's logic can sometimes affect the usability of the system. The authors propose a pattern-based approach for dealing with minimizing the effect of functionalities on UI usability.

In Chapter 11, Rafla, Desmarais, and Robilllard build upon a recent software architecture perspective on the usability of software systems which states that making software more usable is a lot easier to do if the high-level architecture was designed with usability in mind. However, there is a scarcity of methods and guidelines with the scope to ensure that software developing corporations consider usability requirements in their architectural design activities. This chapter addresses this need and provides a more elaborate approach for architecting usable systems. A non-formal exercise reveals that this proposed methodology was well-received by participants with different knowledge of usability. They found the process not too demanding as it guided them in discerning the concerns that could have a real impact on the architecture.

In Chapter 12, Tarby et al. address the issue of evaluating how people use interactive applications. They describe two innovative evaluation approaches that exploit the concept of traces as a way of capturing the usage of the system. The first approach uses Aspect-Oriented Programming; the second proposes an explicit coupling between agent-based architecture and evaluation agents. These two approaches are compared.

In Chapter 13, Tarpin-Bernard et al. an architectural framework for adapting interactive applications to different contexts while ensuring its usability. After a brief overview of the existing strategies for adaptation, they detail the different models that are at the core of the framework. This includes task, concept, platform, and user models as well as an interaction model. All these models are linked via an underlying architecture: the AMF which ensures the relationships between all the other models. AMF encapsulates the key usability attributes.

In Chapter 14, Lindeman describes a user interaction software design process created and used by a consultant to solve two challenges: (1) how to decrease the need for changes in the UI by subsequent system releases without doing big design upfront, and (2) how to apply a structured user-interaction design process no matter when brought into a project or what software methodology was being used. The four design levels in the process parallel Beck and Fowler's four planning levels described in their book *Planning Extreme Programming*. The design process is called "GAINS" because the user-interaction designer has only Attraction, Information and Navigation to connect users' Goals with the project sponsors' criteria for Success. Thus there are five questions, one for each letter of the acronym GAINS, asked at each of four levels of design: The first two design levels, Rough Plan and Big Plan, focus on business-process actions and objects that define users' goals. The next two levels, Release Planning and Iteration Planning, focus on the UI objects that support the tasks necessary to achieve those goals. Release Planning identifies the displays the user sees for each goal included in that release, and the across-display navigation for the proposed functionality. Iteration Planning focuses at a lower level of interaction, such as the within-display navigation among controls. For a voice system, the word "sees" would be changed to "hears," but the design process and the levels of focus are the same for UIs that are vision output (e.g., GUIs), voice output (e.g., IVRs) or multimodal.

In Chapter 15, El-Ramly et al. present a lightweight approach for reengineering the HCI and/or interaction with other software systems. While interaction reengineering can be achieved by changing the source code and design (e.g., library replacement, refactoring, etc.) resulting in a different UI, they look at interaction reengineering methods that do not involve changing the source code or internal design of the system. Instead, they focus on methods and techniques for wrapping and packaging the existing interaction layer to reproduce it in a different format, e.g., on a different platform or to integrate the legacy system services in another application possibly under a different architecture paradigm, e.g., service-oriented architectures (SOA).

In Chapter 16, Memon reinforces the fact that while manual evaluation is resource intensive, performing automatic usability evaluation usually involves the creation of a model of the GUI, a resource intensive step that intimidates many practitioners and prevents the application of the automated techniques. He presents GUI Ripping, a new process that automatically recovers models of the GUI by dynamically traversing all its windows and extracting all the widgets, properties, and values. The usefulness of this process is demonstrated by recovering a structural model called a GUI forest and dynamic models called event-low graphs and integration trees. Results of case studies show that GUI Ripping is effective and requires very little human intervention.

In Chapter 17, Navarre et al. address one of the major weaknesses of task modeling, a largely used method in HCI. Task modeling does not contain sufficient and necessary information to permit automatic generation of interactive systems. They propose a set of tools supporting the development of an interactive system using two different notations. They suggest supplementing Concur Task Tree (CTT) for task modeling with Interactive Cooperative Objects (ICO) for system modeling. Task and systems models represent two different views of the same system (a user interacting with an interactive system). They are built by different people (human factors specialist for the task models and software engineer for the system models) and are used independently. In particular, they introduce scenarios as a bridge between these two views. In task modeling, scenarios are seen as a possible trace of user's activity. In system modeling, scenarios are seen as a trace of user's actions. A case study from Air Traffic Control is presented. As both CTT and ICO notations are supported by tools (environments are respectively CTTE and PetShop), an integration tool based on scenarios is presented.

References

Seffah, A., Gulliksen, J., and Desmarais, M. C., editors (2005). *Human-Centered Software Engineering: Integrating Usability in the Development Process*. New York: Springer-Verlag.

I User Experiences, Usability Requirements, and Design

2 WHAT DRIVES SOFTWARE DEVELOPMENT: BRIDGING THE GAP BETWEEN SOFTWARE AND USABILITY ENGINEERING

Nuno J. Nunes

University of Madeira and LabUSE

Abstract. This chapter presents two important issues integrating software and usability engineering. The first issue is use case driven development, we discuss the importance of describing use cases through technology-free and implementation independent descriptions of user intentions and system responsibilities. We provide examples that demonstrate innovative tools support for multiple representations of essential use cases. The second issue is the architecture-centric nature of modern software development. Here we discuss the importance of identifying usability aspects at the architectural level and describe an extension of the boundary-control-entity UML-based pattern that supports dialogue and presentation elements at the conceptual architectural level. In this chapter we present and contrast several examples that describe how our approach can be used to bridge software and usability engineering and also supported by innovative developer-centric tools.

2.1 INTRODUCTION

The integration of software and usability engineering is increasingly becoming an important problem in modern software development. In a recent article Seffah and Metzker (2004) discuss five major obstacles and myths that prevent harmonious integration between the two disciplines. Here we will discuss three major obstacles identified by Seffah and Metzker: i) that user-centered-design (UCD) techniques are decoupled from the software development lifecycle and how they could be more easily integrated, ii) the communication problems between usability and software engineering specialists and how we could extend standard notation like the UML to overcome the communication barrier, and finally iii) how we could create computer-assisted usability engineering tools that are not only more usable for software developers but that also foster the integration of UCD techniques into modern software development.

User-centered design (UCD) is currently defined in the ISO 13407 standard and typically entails involving users in the design and evaluation of the system so that feedback can be obtained. Therefore, UCD produces software products that are easier to understand and use; improves the quality of the life of users by reducing stress and improving satisfaction; and improves the productivity and operational efficiency of individual users and the overall organization.

Activities required to achieve UCD are well known: understand and specify the context of use, specify users and their organizational requirements, produce designs and prototypes, and carry out user-based assessment.

Despite the fact that principles and activities behind UCD were identified during the 1980s (if not earlier) there is still discussion about the integration of UCD practices in modern software development (Seffah et al., 2005). One of the main activities of the IFIP working group on user interface engineering is bridging the SE and HCI communities (`http://www.se-hci.org`). Conversely, careful inspection of modern lifecycle models (for instance, the Unified Process (UP) and its commercial counterpart, the Rational Unified Process, RUP) clearly reveals that some UCD principles and activities are an integral part of modern software development.

- The UP is use case driven to denote the emphasis on knowing and understanding what real users want and need to accomplish with the envisioned system.

- The UP is architecture-centric, meaning that it focuses on the architecturally significant static and dynamic aspects of the system and the architecture grows out of the needs of the business and users reflected in the use cases.

- The UP is also iterative and incremental, meaning that development evolves in terms of mini-projects that correspond to controlled and planned iterations that result in increments to the end product.

One can argue that those characteristics of UP are not sustained in specific process activities. However, the same argument could be used to discuss the practical applicability of UCD. In essence, both UCD and UP (or RUP) are high-level models that define a set of principles and activities. Thus, discussing their practical applicability in terms of those high-level characteristics is an interesting but controversial (and perhaps pointless) exercise. Moreover, while UP and RUP define specific and well-documented workflows, activities and roles, UCD (at least at the standard level) lacks such a fine-grained description.

At the other extreme of modern software development, we have the so-called agile movement. Again we can find similarities between UCD principles and, for instance, the principles behind the Agile Manifesto (Agile Alliance, 2003).

- Agile methods promote that their highest priority is to satisfy customers through early and continuous delivery of valuable software.
- Agile methods welcome changing requirements and deliver working software frequently.
- Finally the agile movement promotes that business people and developers must work daily throughout the project.

Again one could argue that agile methods are just another buzzword for chaotic development. But evidence exists that lightweight techniques—such as small and continuous releases, refactoring, pair-programming and on-site customers—contribute to promote communication, simplicity and feedback.

2.2 USE CASE DRIVEN SOFTWARE DEVELOPMENT

The use case driven nature of the UP (and RUP) is grounded on two basic assumptions. On the one hand, the use case strategy forces developers to think in terms of real value to the users and not just in terms of internal functionalities. On the other hand, use cases drive the development process because they are used to understand the requirements. Use cases drive the development and review of the analysis and design level models, and they also facilitate testing of the implementation components for conformance with the requirements (Jacobson et al., 1999).

The adoption of use cases in the UML acknowledges this importance of identifying the different roles users play when interacting with an application supporting their tasks. However they are still mainly used to structure the application internals and do not provide an efficient way to support the usability aspects of interactive systems.

The major problems with these descriptions of user behavior are related to the system-centric nature of use cases. Constantine and Loockwood (1999) argue that "conventional use cases typically contain too many built-in assumptions, often hidden and implicit, about the form of the user interface that is yet to be designed." Such argument led the authors to propose the essential use case narrative, a technology-free, implementation-independent, structured scenario expressed in the language of the application domain and end-users. As the original authors discuss in Constantine and Lockwood (1999) this problem is evident in many examples from the leading promoters of the UP (Kruchten, 1998).

Figure 2.1 presents an example of multiple representations of essential use cases supported in the TaskSketch tool (`http://dme.uma.pt/tasksketch`). The TaskSketch tool is an example of a new generation of computer-assisted usability engineering tools that promote bridging between SE and HCI (Constantine and Campos, 2005). A conventional CASE tool would typically provide developers with the capability of storing the use case description in the form of structured text. In contrast, the TaskSketch tool enables developers to create and manipulate the use case description in different notations that are synchronized and semantically stored as a UML activity diagram. The three views supported by the TaskSketch tool are the participatory view, which is a typical result of a participatory session with end-users (obtained by manipulation of sticky notes); the use case narrative proposed by Constantine that can also be printed in index cards for stacking and ordering by the different stakeholders; and the activity diagram which could include additional details relevant to developers but that are not depicted in the other views. The activity diagram view is also UML compliant, thus it can easily be exported into XMI and interchanged with other tools.

The previous example demonstrates why conventional use cases are not user-centered and do not express the requirements in a way that maximizes value towards end-users and business. Although this distinction seems marginal at the notational level, the impacts at the requirement level are considerable. Conventional use cases (and in particular their descriptions) are complex and not suitable for cooperative participatory development. On the other hand, since use cases drive development, a user-centered perspective is clearly fundamental to reduce the complexity of software systems. Driving development from a system-centric use case perspective usually leads to the well-known problem of "featurism" (or "fatware"), that is, development is driven by functionalities that are not necessarily adding value to users and business.

The same arguments could be applied to agile development methods. Even though agile methods do not endorse modeling, there is a specific reference to the role of "user stories" or similar requirement specification strategies in approaches like XP. There are important similarities with use cases and their role in the UP and user-stories and their role in XP. On the one hand, both use cases and user stories are used to prioritize development (user stories are used in XP to drive release planning). On the other hand, user stories are inherently user-centered, they are produced by XP customers and used throughout the lifecycle to drive the creation of acceptance tests (Beck, 2000).

There is, however, an important distinction between UP and XP at this level. In UP, use cases drive the architecture, or in other words the architecture realizes the use cases. In XP, the architectural spike (and the system metaphor) are developed in parallel before release planning. Again careful inspection is required to analyze these subtle but important distinctions. Since XP does not promote modeling, user stories are usually captured in natural language in the form of what is usually known as scenarios in the HCI field.

Scenarios are an important technique to increase communication and discuss requirements. However, scenarios are the opposite of essential descriptions of use cases. Scenarios are inherently full of assumptions and details, which increase their communication effectiveness. However, those same characteristics obstruct the creativity required to generate simple and essential descriptions of requirements. Moreover, maintaining requirements in the form of natural language user stories is recognizably an overwhelming activity, in particular in agile environment and iterative development lifecycles.

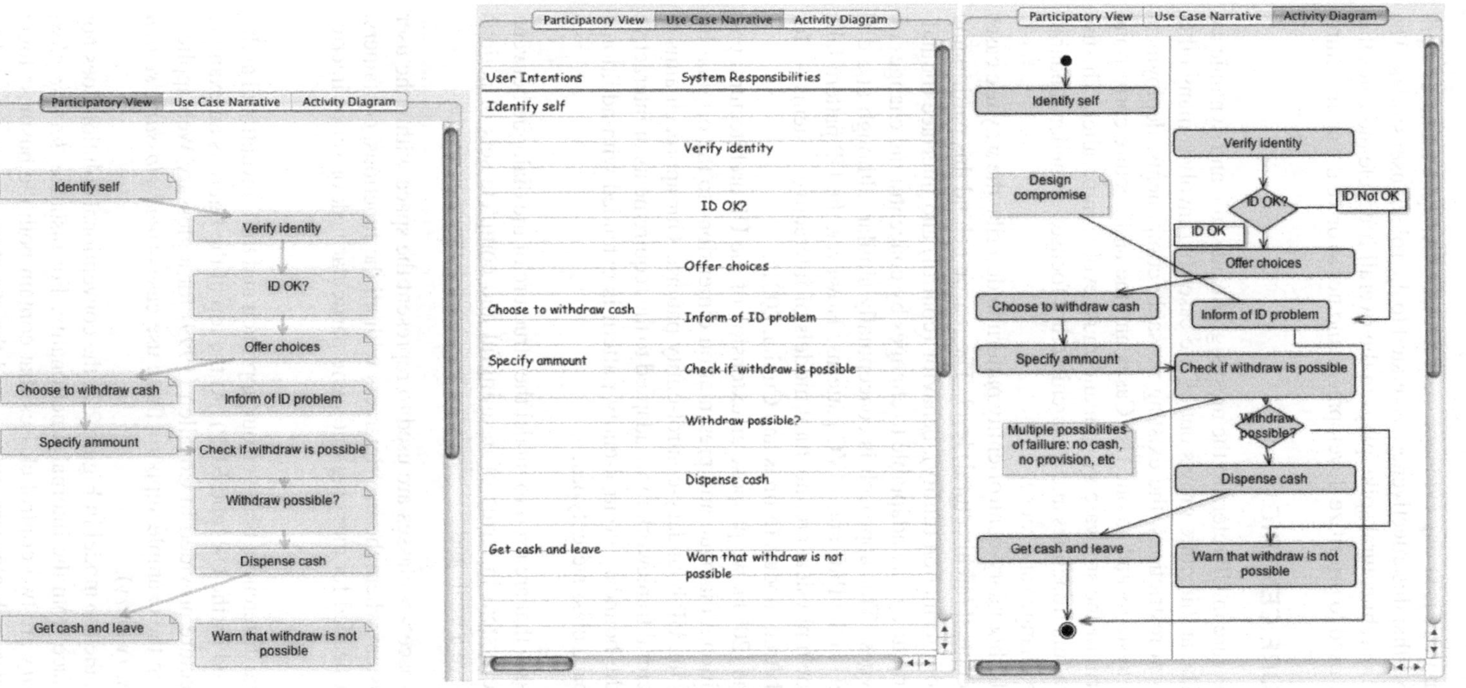

Figure 2.1 Multiple use case descriptions for the withdraw money use case in the TaskSketch tool

Despite the fact that there is strong evidence that XP and other agile methods work in practice, it is arguable that this effectiveness is related to the role of user stories. The important role that XP's architectural spike plays in the overall lifecycle indicates that user stories are mainly used to prioritize development and not to drive the architecture.

2.3 ARCHITECTURE CENTRIC

The conceptual architecture in UP refers to the most significant static and dynamic aspects of the system. The architecture grows out of use cases but involves many other factors, such as platform restrictions, the existing reusable components, deployment considerations, legacy systems and so on. Use Cases and the architecture correspond to the function and form of the software system and must evolve in parallel. The use cases define the system functionalities and the architecture focuses on understandability, resilience to future changes and reuse.

The UP promotes the boundary-control-entity pattern to describe the way use cases are realized at the conceptual (architectural) level. The reason behind this partitioning of analysis classes into information (entity), behavior (control) and interface (boundary) is to promote a structure more adaptable to changes by concentrating changes on different class stereotypes. This approach is conceptually similar, although at a different granularity level, to the PAC and MVC patterns. However, the UP pattern fails to map to the well-known physical architectural models of interactive systems — for instance, Seeheim and Arch models (Nunes and Cunha, 2001).

In Nunes and Cunha (2001), we propose an extension of the UP architectural pattern that includes additional dialogue and presentation dimensions to the original information structure of the UP boundary-control-entity pattern. Our approach aims at creating a new architectural framework more adapted to the requirements of interactive systems. Therefore, the boundary-control-entity pattern is extended with additional task and interaction space class stereotypes:

- <<task>> classes that are used to model the structure of the dialogue between the user and the system in terms of meaningful and complete sets of actions required to achieve a goal; and

- <<interaction space>> classes are used to represent the space within the user interface of a system where the user interacts with all the functions, containers, and information needed for carrying out some particular task or set of interrelated tasks.

Figure 2.2 illustrates the differences between our approach and the conventional architectural descriptions used by the UP (and RUP). At the top of the figure is an example of a conceptual architecture provided in Conallen (1999) for a glossary Web application. The architecture in the example supports three use cases (*read glossary*, *search glossary* and *edit glossary entry*).

As we can see from the top model in Figure 2.2, the conventional solution does not separate the user interface from the internal functionality. For instance, *browse glossary* and *search glossary* are two control classes that contain both the business logic required to browse and search glossary entries, and the structure of use required to

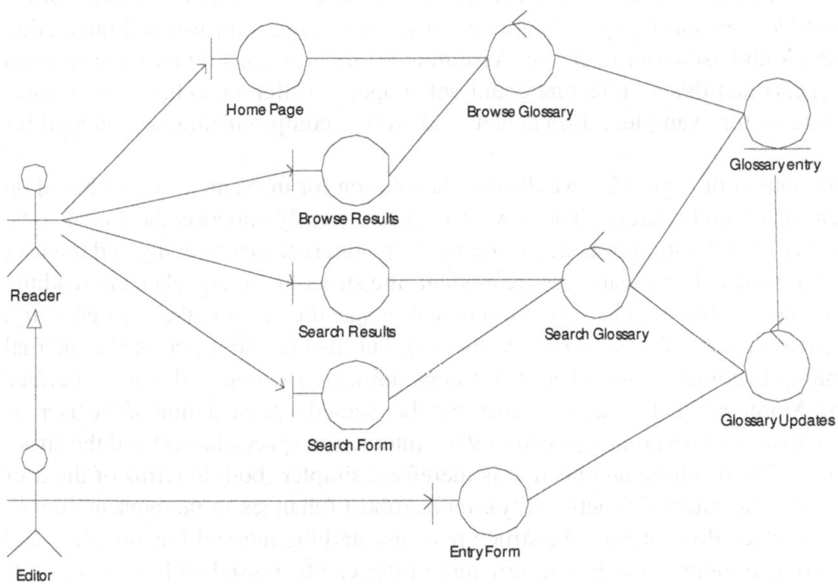

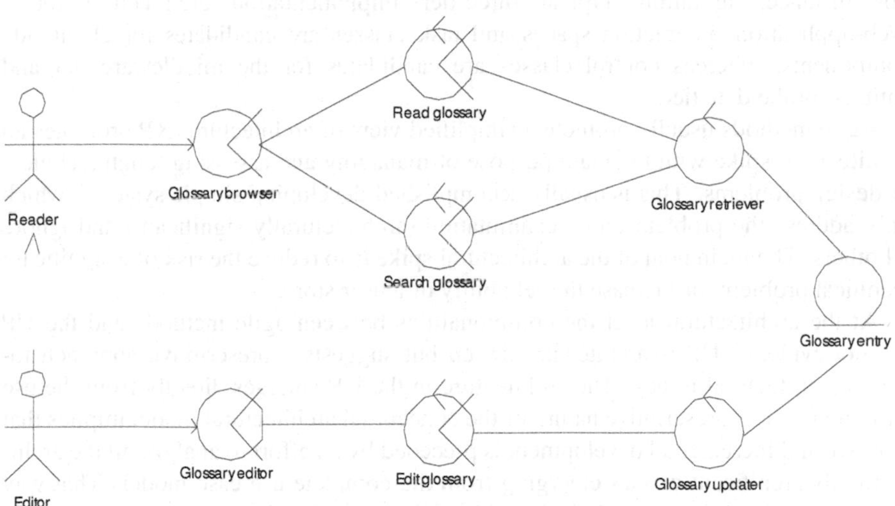

Figure 2.2 Application example of the UP architecture versus a revised proposal for interactive systems: top — transcription of a solution provided in Conallen (1999); bottom — the new solution based on Nunes and Cunha (2000)

perform those tasks. Furthermore, the conventional model contains built-in assumptions about the user interface technology and the interaction styles used to implement the user interface of the glossary application. For instance, the boundary classes *Home Page*, *Search form* and *Entry form* are obviously indicating a form-based interaction style and a Web-based user interface. Assuming technology constraints at the analysis level suggests that this architecture could not support a different technology or interaction style — for example, a Java applet — therefore compromising the potential for reuse.

At the bottom of Figure 2.2 we illustrate a solution for the same problem based on the extended UI architecture. The new architecture clearly supports the well-known best practice of separation of concerns between the internal functionality and the user interface specifics. The advantages are evident: the structure of use related to reading, searching and editing the glossary is contained in specific classes (the *read glossary*, *search glossary* and *edit glossary* task classes), but also the structure of the internal functionality becomes simpler because it does not have to contain the user interface behavior. Moreover, there is a clear separation between the presentation of the user interface (*glossary browser* and *glossary editor* interaction space classes) and the structure of use. The resulting architecture is therefore, simpler (both in terms of the user interface and the internal functionality), more robust (changes in the presentation of the user interface don't impact the structure of use and the internal functionality, and vice versa), and more reusable (the structure of use can be reused with respect to different implementation technologies).

Finally our approach seamlessly maps different implementation architectures. For instance, assuming typical three-tier implementation architecture for a Web-application, interaction spaces and task classes are candidates for client-side components, whereas control classes are candidates for the middleware tier and entities for the data tier.

Agile methods usually promote a simplified view of architecture. XP promotes an architectural spike with the main purpose of managing and assessing tough technical or design problems. This is usually accomplished developing simple systems, which only address the problem under examination (architecturally significant) and ignore all others. The main goal of the architectural spike is to reduce the risk of a significant technical problem, or increase the reliability of a user story.

At the architectural level the commonalities between agile methods and the UP are not evident. UP is architecture-driven but suggests a prescriptive approach towards architectural issues. The architecture in the UP emerges directly from the use case model. The prescriptive nature of the conceptual architectural model implies that iterative and incremental development is preceded by an effort to analyze all the architecturally significant classes emerging from the complete use case model. That way UP aims to detect major technical problems a priori. Furthermore, there is no specific effort in trying to use the architecture to increase the reliability of requirements, something XP emphasizes.

There are two important issues contrasting XP and UP at the architectural level. XP relies on vertical throwaway prototyping techniques to test potential architectural problems, both non functional (technical problems) and functional (misconceptions emerging from user stories). The major problem with this approach is that foremost architectural problems emerge late during development when the different components of the system are integrated or implemented incrementally. XP assumes that developers can "guess" the main architectural problems, while also relying on refactoring techniques to simplify design as development progresses. This "wild guess" approach clearly contrasts the prescriptive architecture-centric nature of the UP. The second issue is related to the way both lifecycle models cope with architectural problems associated with misconceptions of user requirements. XP emphasizes this second issue, and relies on user stories, fast release cycles, refactoring and user evaluation to quickly identify and correct problems. On the contrary, UP relies on defining a conceptual architecture model, based on prescriptive descriptions of requirements (the use case model). Since conventional use cases are system-centric (and therefore the conceptual architecture — as we discussed previously), the UP practice assumes that architectural problems can only be identified when developers can argue over an orthogonal view of the foremost system components.

There are increasing concerns about supporting usability through software architecture. Bass and John isolated 26 usability facets that require software architectural support other than separating the user interface (Bass and John, 2001). Those facets provide important usability benefits and most of them are related to user tasks that are not separated in the boundary-control-entity pattern. By introducing user tasks and interaction spaces at the architectural level, our approach increases the support for well-known implementation models like Seeheim and Arch. We also believe that our proposal will foster increased architectural support for usability facets such as those identified by Bass and John.

2.4 FROM ESSENTIAL USE CASES TO THE CONCEPTUAL ARCHITECTURE

An important aspect regarding the system architecture is the way architecturally significant classes are identified from the requirements descriptions. Both UP and XP encourage a clear connection between the requirements (use cases or user stories) and the conceptual architecture of the system. However, none of the approaches proposes a simple mapping between the two models.

In Figure 2.3 we illustrate how our approach supports the transition and traceability between task flows and the (extended) UML-based conceptual architecture described in the previous section. At the left-hand side of Figure 2.3 is a use case diagram and the corresponding essential task flows taken from the TaskSketch tool (depicted as UML activity diagrams). The model expresses three use cases for a simplified bank system: *check account balance*, *transfer money* and *check card transactions*. To the right-hand side of the figure is a tentative conceptual architecture expressed in terms of <<entity>>, <<control>>, <<task>> and <<interaction space>> stereotyped classes that realize the essential use cases. The dashed arrows between those two diagrams represent mappings used to identify stereotyped classes from the essential task flows (which are in fact traceability dependencies).

As we can see from this example, activities corresponding to the *user intentions* are candidates to <<task>> classes. Conversely, activities corresponding to the *system*

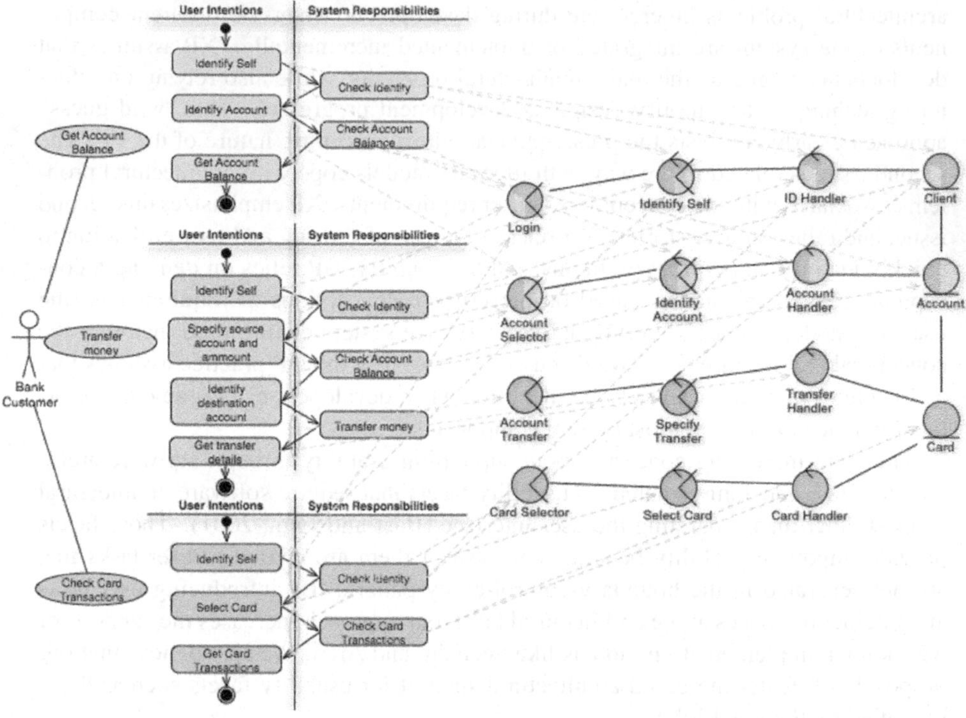

Figure 2.3 From task flows to the system architecture: an example for a simplified bank system

responsibilities are candidates to <<entity>> and <<control>> classes. Finally, control flows that traverse the *swimlanes* involve an interaction between the user and the system, thus correspond to <<interaction space>> classes. Although the mappings described previously are not completely straightforward, they provide developers with a more seamless way of connecting the conceptual architecture of the system to the requirements. This connection is supported in a semi-automatic way by the TaskSketch tool. Using a special cursor tool, developers can drag and drop activities to the architectural model therefore creating new traceability dependencies between the description of the essential use cases (task flows) and the class model depicting the conceptual architecture. Figure 2.4 illustrates the TaskSketch tool support for this traceability mechanism. At the far left of the screen is the list of supported essential use cases and in the middle the multiple view task flows that describe the selected use case. Through simple drag and drop of the activities in the task flow, developers can create the architectural model and even manage multiple dependencies depicted by a color schema. In the example illustrated, each use case corresponds to one color and each class exhibiting the same color in the right-hand pane represents a traceability dependency.

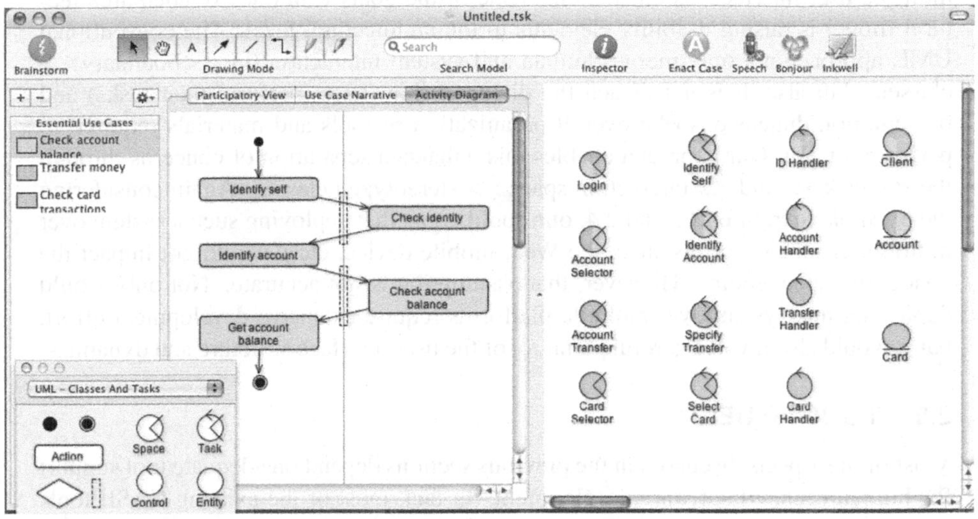

Figure 2.4 Semi-automatic traceability support in TaskSketch

The use case driven nature of modern software development relies on the assumption that systems are built in terms of iterations (or increments) that correspond to the implementation of the different use cases. The classes of the conceptual architecture realize the use cases, meaning that in order to implement a specific use case developers are required to implement all the classes that realize that use case. Figure 2.4 demonstrates this principle through a color schema. For instance, the *identify self* <<task>> class realizes the three use cases in the example. In other words, to deliver any of the three use cases it is mandatory that the *identify self* <<task>> class is fully implemented. At the other extreme are the *account transfer* or the *card selector* <<interaction space>> classes.

The enhanced traceability provided with our approach leverages crucial development activities, like requirements negotiation, release planning and estimation of development cost and effort. A simple inspection of the models in Figures 2.3 and 2.4 provides developers a broad idea of the development effort required to implement each use case. Although development effort is not a direct function of the number of classes to implement, one can clearly infer that implementing the account transfer use case will require an increased development effort over the other use cases in the example.

Finally, our approach brings user interface elements to the conceptual architectural level. Even though it is not our remit here to discuss the impact of the user interface at the architectural level (see Bass and John, 2001) for a list of usability facets), this issue is ultimately important, since a significant part of today's software development effort is devoted to the user interface (Myers and Rosson, 1992). With the advent of multiplatform development, the issue of deploying software systems that require multiple user interfaces is outstanding. One of the goals with our extended architectural model is raising usability elements to the architectural level. The conventional UML approach not only merges human and system interaction (in <<boundary>> classes), but also does not detach the dialogue (how users perform their tasks) and presentation dimensions (the overall organization of tools and materials required to perform a task). Our approach enables this enhanced separation of concerns through the <<task>> and <<interaction space>> stereotyped classes. Again considering the example in Figures 2.3 and 2.4, one could argue that deploying such a system over multiple channels (for instance, the Web, mobile device, etc.) would not impact the conceptual architecture. However, that assumption is not accurate. Not only would deploying that system over multiple platforms require extensive development effort, but it would also involve careful planning of the user interface structure and dynamics.

2.5 TOOL ISSUES

Most of the aspects discussed in the previous sections depend on adequate tool support for human-centered software development. In fact, most of the existing CASE tools are either not used (Iivari, 1996) or simply fail to support practitioners in their own development needs. This question is not new but certainly very timely, ACM Queue's "What's on your hard drive?" and IEEE Software "Tools of the Trade" columns, present testimony of how tools influence the work of practitioners to the point that they hate or love their tools. Not surprisingly the case for user-centered CASE tools is already on the agenda (Jarzabek and Huang, 2004).

We argue that bridging HCI and SE will not only require specific techniques, but also developer-centric tools. Our own investigation about tool usage, based on a survey of 370 practitioners that answered questions about their tool usage and workstyle transitions, presented some concluding results.

Regarding which tools are being used to perform interaction design activities, the respondents, perhaps not surprisingly, clearly referred paper and pencil as the most used tool. Figure 2.6 summarizes the results of tool usage.

Apart from analysis and modeling tools, the most frequent tools reported by practitioners are low-tech and informal (paper and pencil, whiteboards, Post-It notes, etc.). One could argue that this is clearly due to the processes underlying the software shops surveyed. However, when asked about the organizational development process, only roughly one third of the practitioners classified their process as agile or lightweight. Even a crosstab between development process and tool usage shows that interface builders are more used with formal development processes, such us waterfall and spiral models (Campos and Nunes, 2007a).

It is interesting to note that Visual Interface Builders was ranked in 7 out of 12 classes of tools. This is surprising, since the survey specifically asked for the most used tools for UI-related activities. We argue that these results contradict the idea, behind the XP and agile methods, that practitioners urge to work with the low-level artifacts like code and concrete widget layout.

However, we believe that these results should be considered with caution, thus our research also investigated developer workstyles and workstyle transitions (Campos and Nunes, 2005). This research was conducted by Pedro Campos who studied the

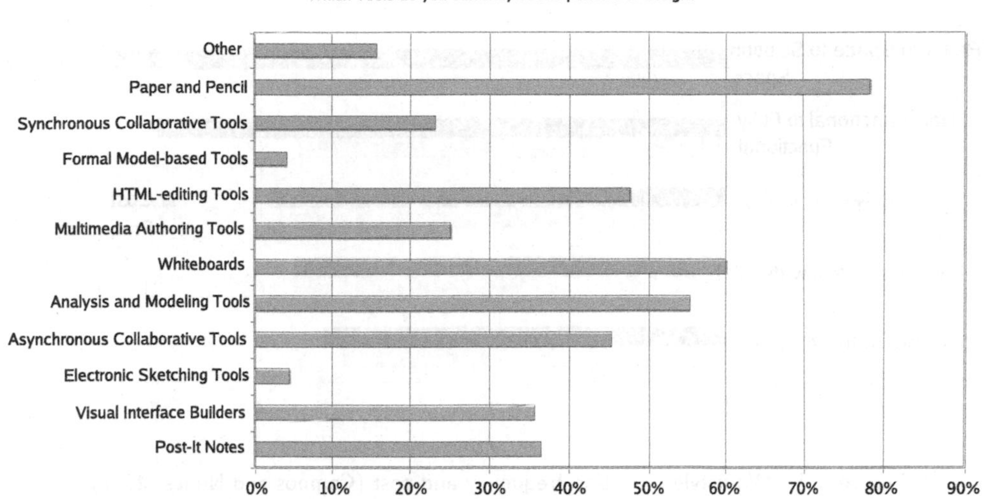

Figure 2.5 Tool usage based on a survey of 370 practitioners (Campos and Nunes, 2007a)

way developers perform different activities and transition between them. The survey asked developers to rate the frequency and cost of those transitions. By frequency we meant "how many times [they] engage and transition between activities and workstyles," by cost we meant "how difficult [they] believe the transitions are." For instance, in UI-related activities the interaction and software engineers are frequently interrupted by colleagues and emails or they are asked to change from low-tech card sorting to high-tech UML modeling.

When confronted with several concrete scenarios of workstyle transitions, the respondents were asked to rank them on a seven-point Likert scale. Figure 2.6 summarizes some of those results.

The above results corroborate the empirical evidence that moving from problem/solution and high/low detail are the two most frequent workstyle transitions in interactive software development. We believe that these results contrast the activities supported by the mainstream development tools and show there is a long road of research and improvement to reach development-centric tools.

It is not our remit here to discuss the research on developer workstyles, our point here is that the issues related to bridging SE and HCI are closely related to tool support — research and practice need to go hand-to-hand on this. The TaskSketch examples provided in this chapter to illustrate the bridging issues that drive software development are already a step towards this direction. For instance, semantic drag-and-drop of modeling constructs (activities in essential use cases and architectural elements) illustrates how traceability could be supported in a new class of innovative developer-centric tools. Together with the color-coding of modeling constructs (see Figs. 2.3 and 2.4) the tool can immediately help practitioners to take design decisions or perform complex prioritizing of development iterations.

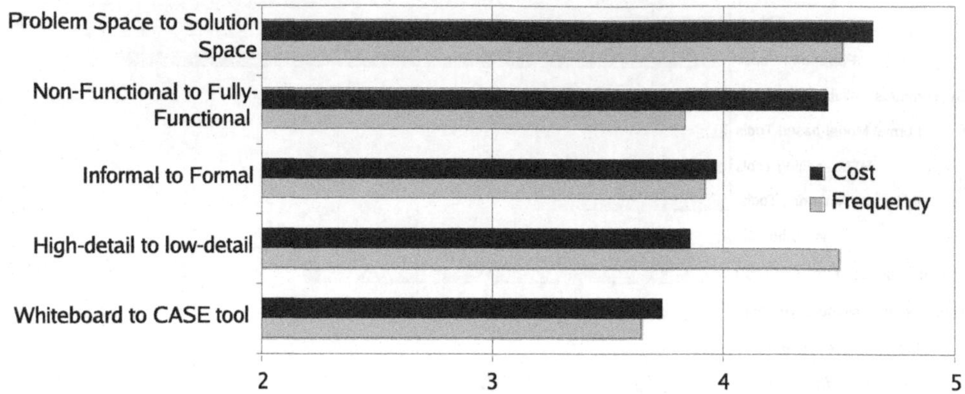

Figure 2.6 Workstyle transition frequency and cost (Campos and Nunes, 2007)

Another example of workstyle support was already illustrated in Figure 2.1. The TaskSketch tool allows editing of task flows at three different — but synchronized — views: the participatory view, which is a typical result of a participatory session with end-users (obtained by manipulation of sticky notes); the use case narrative proposed by Usage-Centered Design that can also be printed in index cards for stacking and ordering by the different stakeholders; and the activity diagram which could include additional details relevant to developers but that are not depicted in the other views. Further research with logging mechanisms in TaskSketch shows the effectiveness and implications of this feature. Figure 2.7 illustrates the distributed frequency of the different views support in TaskSketch for the essential use cases.

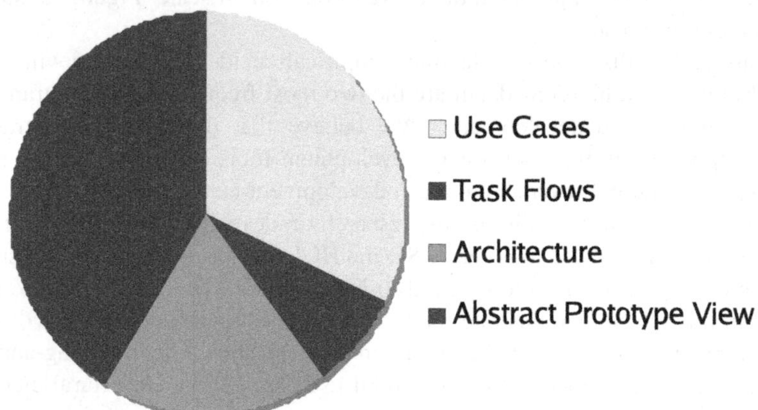

Figure 2.7 Frequency distribution of the several views in TaskSketch (recorded through automatic logging)

These results carry important implications for the design of interaction design tools: use cases and abstract prototype views exhibited the largest time share of usage, which means more attention should be devoted to the UI supporting these views. Conversely, if users spend most of the time modifying model elements (79% according to the logging tool's measurements), then it is clear that this activity is the most frequent, and therefore it should be carefully supported by the design tool at stake.

The TaskSketch tool was developed as a research proof-of-concept used to test and validate some ideas that quickly proved to be an effective instructive tool teaching usage-centered development and some related key techniques. The fact that it is essentially a research prototype supporting some innovative techniques that are not widespread in the mainstream software development shops did not prevent that in just 8 months it had more than 3000 downloads. The "sister" tool CanonSketch reached more than 2000 downloads in the same period, and they are both only available for the MacOS X platform. Free versions of the tools, including video demos and examples, are available at `http://dme.uma.pt/tasksketch` and `http://dme.uma.pt/canonsketch`.

2.6 CONCLUSION

Modern software development methods (such as UP and XP) are currently promoting some well-known UCD and HCI practices as a way to identify and manage requirements, drive and prioritize development and recognize architectural problems. In this chapter we tried to look closer at the application of those UCD and HCI techniques in SE. We argue that discussing those issues at the lifecycle level is a pointless exercise — one that unfortunately has dominated the SE and HCI integration agenda for too long. In order to promote the integration of both fields we need to work closer and carefully examine how SE is using UCD and HCI techniques.

Here we presented the issue of driving software development from a UCD perspective. Both the UP and XP promote the UCD practice of involving users in the design and evaluation of the system. However, careful inspection of how that principle is achieved reveals important misconceptions. We illustrate those problems by contrasting examples from the SE field with a new proposal that tries to selectively incorporate HCI techniques in a way that is not disruptive with current SE practice. The fact that the UML and UP promote use case modeling is not *per se* a solution consistent with the UCD and HCI best practices. On the other hand, we cannot ignore that UML is a de facto standard. Therefore we present an approach that tries to incorporate participatory design and essential task flows in a way that can be successfully translated to UML constructs and efficiently managed by innovative developer-centric tools. We have also discussed that XP user stories are misleading as an effective way to model user requirements. Scenarios play an important but focused role in HCI that is usually disastrous when applied indiscriminately as a general requirements discovery technique. Moreover, natural language scenarios are particularly difficult to manage, above all with iterative methods and tools that currently proliferate in software shops.

In this chapter we have also discussed why software architecture plays an important role in modern SE. Although both UP and XP concentrate heavily on the architecture, there are substantial differences in the way those approaches tackle and convey the conceptual system architecture. UP relies heavily on use cases to drive the architecture, whereas XP promotes independent and concurrent creation of user stories and the architecture spike. The specific examples provided here reflect that UP promotes a system-centric view of the conceptual architecture that is clearly more complex and inconsistent with HCI practice. Contrasting the UP approach does not provide separation of concerns between internal functionality and the user interface, lacks support for multiple platforms and usually leads to more complex analysis models. In addition, conventional use case descriptions don't provide guidance towards extracting architectural significant classes from user requirements. At the other extreme, XP relies on prototyping to test potential architectural problems. By combining refactoring techniques, with frequent releases and user testing of story estimates, XP tries to tackle architectural problems but does not provide a high-level view of the system architecture. The main problem with XP's approach is that there is no artifact that represents the conceptual system architecture and the connection between that architecture and the user tories. Relying on code and refactoring as the sole representation for the system architecture is neglecting the importance of architecture at all.

Finally in this chapter we presented some ideas and research results about developer-centric tool support. The examples provided in this chapter are drawn from the TaskSketch tool, which illustrates our research efforts trying to understand how developers perform interaction design, and what are the underlying workstyles. Jointly with an extensive research survey we investigated developer styles of work, their frequency and cost. The TaskSketch and CanonSketch tools support some key activities that we believe are crucial to bridge SE and HCI. Of particular importance is the support for multiple views, different abstraction levels and problem/solution space transitions. The examples provided here simply confirm that bridging the gap is not an easy task but both SE and HCI could benefit from CHISE efforts.

Acknowledgments

The author would like to thank Pedro Campos for the TaskSketch examples provided in this chapter.

References

Agile Alliance (2001). Manifesto for agile software development. Technical report, Agile Alliance. `http://www.agilealliance.org`.

Bass, L. and John, B. E. (2001). Supporting usability through software architecture. *Computer*, 34(10):113–115.

Beck, K. (2000). *Extreme Programming Explained: Embracing Change*. Addison-Wesley, Reading: MA.

Campos, P. and Nunes, N. J. (2005). Galactic dimensions: A unifying workstyle model for user-centered design. In Costabile, M. F. and Paternò, F., editors, *Human-Computer Interaction - INTERACT 2005, IFIP TC13 International Conference, Rome, Italy, September 12-16, 2005, Proceedings*, volume 3585 of *Lecture Notes in Computer Science*, pages 158–169. Springer.

Campos, P. and Nunes, N. J. (2007a). Practitioner tools and workstyles for user interface design. *IEEE Software*, 24(1):73–80.

Campos, P. and Nunes, N. J. (2007b). *Towards Useful and Usable Interaction Design Tools: CanonSketch, Interacting with Computers*. Amsterdam: Elsevier.

Conallen, J. (1999). *Building Web Applications with UML*. Addison-Wesley, Reading: MA.

Constantine, L. L. and Campos, P. (2005). Canonsketch and tasksketch: innovative modeling tools for usage-centered design. In Johnson, J. and Gabriel, R. P., editors, *Companion to the 20th Annual ACM SIGPLAN Conference on Object-Oriented Programming, Systems, Languages, and Applications, OOPSLA 2005, October 16-20, 2005, San Diego, CA, USA*, pages 162–163. ACM Press.

Constantine, L. L. and Lockwood, L. A. D. (1999). *Software for Use: A Practical Guide to the Models and Methods of Usage-Centered Design*. Addison-Wesley, Reading: MA.

Iivari, J. (1996). Why are case tools not used? *Commun. ACM*, 39(10):94–103.

Jacobson, I., Booch, G., and Rumbaugh, J. (1999). *The Unified Software Development Process*. Addison Wesley, Reading: MA.

Jarzabek, S. and Huang, R. (2004). The case for user-centered case tools. *Commun. ACM*, 41(8):93–99.

Kruchten, P. (1998). *The Rational Unified Process — An Introduction*. Addison-Wesley, Reading: MA.

Myers, B. A. and Rosson, M. B. (1992). Survey on user interface programming. In *CHI '92: Proceedings of the SIGCHI Conference on Human Factors in Computing Systems*, pages 195–202. ACM Press.

Nunes, N. J. and Cunha, J. F. (2000). Wisdom: A software engineering method for small software development companies. *IEEE Software*, 17(5):113–119.

Nunes, N. J. and Cunha, J. F. (2001). Whitewater interactive system development with object models. In Harmelen, M., editor, *Object Modeling and User Interface Design*. Addison-Wesley, Reading: MA.

Seffah, A., Gulliksen, J., and Desmarais, M. C., editors (2005). *Human-Centered Software Engineering: Integrating Usability in the Development Process*. Springer, Boston.

Seffah, A. and Metzker, E. (2004). The obstacles and myths of usability and software engineering. *Commun. ACM*, 47(12):71–76.

3 HUMAN ACTIVITY MODELING: TOWARD A PRAGMATIC INTEGRATION OF ACTIVITY THEORY AND USAGE-CENTERED DESIGN

Larry L. Constantine

Chief Scientist, Constantine & Lockwood, Ltd., IDSA
Director, Laboratory for Usage-centered Software Engineering
University of Madeira, Funchal, Portugal

Abstract. Human activity modeling is a systematic approach to organizing and representing the contextual aspects of tool use that is both well-grounded in an accepted theoretical framework and embedded within a proven design method. Activity theory provides the vocabulary and conceptual framework for understanding the human use of tools and other artifacts. Usage-centered design provides the methodological scaffolding for applying activity theory in practice. In this chapter, activity theory and usage-centered design are outlined and the connections between the two are highlighted. Simple extensions to the models of usage-centered design are introduced that together succinctly model the salient and most essential features of the activities within which tool use is embedded. Although not intended as a tutorial, examples of Activity Maps, Activity Profiles, and Participation Maps are provided.

3.1 INTRODUCTION

Activity theory is a way of describing and characterizing the structure of human activity of all kinds. First introduced by Russian psychologists Rubinshtein, Leontiev, and Vigotsky in the early part of the last century, activity theory has more recently gained increasing attention among interaction designers and others in the human-computer interaction and usability communities (see, for example, Gay and Hembrooke, 2004). Interest was given a significant boost when Donald Norman suggested activity-theory and activity-centered design as antidotes to some of the putative ills of "human-centered design" (Norman, 2005). Norman, who has been credited with coining the phrase "user-centered design," suggested that too much attention focused on human users may be harmful, that to design better tools designers need to focus not so much on users as on the activities in which users are engaged and the tasks they seek to perform within those activities.

Although many researchers and practitioners claim to have used or been influenced by activity theory in their work (see, for example, Nardi, 1996), it is often difficult to trace precisely where or how the results have actually been shaped by activity theory. In many cases, even detailed case studies report results that seem only distantly related, if at all, to the use of activity theory.

Contributing to the lack of precise and traceable impact is that activity theory, despite its name, is not truly a formal and proper theory. Better characterized as a conceptual framework, activity theory comprises a collection of concepts and categories for communicating about activity coupled to diverse assertions—posited but largely untested—about the nature of human activity. Rich in vocabulary but somewhat lacking in rigor, it is perhaps better described as a philosophy of analysis and design, a philosophy that emphasizes understanding the larger context of activities within which designed artifacts are and will be used.

For designers, the great potential of activity theory is to provide an organized and consistent way to investigate, describe, and understand the larger context of activity within which use of a software tool or other artifact is embedded. For this potential to be fully realized, however, the somewhat vague formulations and expressions of activity theory need to be made more precise and accessible.

Some attempts have been made to systematize and operationalize activity theory for purposes of informing the design process. For example, the Activity Checklist originally developed by Kaptalinin, Nardi, and Macaulay (1999) has recently been transformed into a somewhat more precise form as an Activity Interview (Duignan, Noble, and Biddle, 2006). Nevertheless, even its most ardent proponents acknowledge the problems of putting activity theory into practice: "These general principles help orient thought and research, but they are somewhat abstract when it comes to the actual business of working on a design or performing an evaluation" (Kaptalinin, Nardi, and Macaulay, 1999).

The purpose of this paper is to introduce human activity modeling, a systematic approach to representing activities that is intended to make it easier for practicing designers to capture essential insight and understanding about the context of activity and to reflect this understanding in their designs. Specifically, human activity modeling provides a link between activity theory and essential use cases (Constantine, 1995), a widely used task modeling technique and one of the core models of usage-centered design (Constantine and Lockwood, 1999). Usage-centered design itself has been viewed as providing already established and effective methods for putting activity-centered design into practice and for overcoming some of the stated shortcomings of human-centered design (Norman, 2006).

The development of human activity modeling was spurred by recognized limitations in both activity theory and usage-centered design. Activity theory has generated little in the way of systematic modeling techniques or straightforward methods connecting activity to interaction design. Usage-centered design has, for its part, lacked clear, concise constructs for representing the contextual or collective aspects of work. In undertaking to overcome these weaknesses, the aim has been to create an easily grasped modeling language anchored in a consistent, coherent vocabulary of well-defined concepts that link task modeling based on essential use cases to the established conceptual foundation of activity theory.

Human activity modeling is intended as a tool to capture and succinctly represent the salient information regarding activities that is most relevant to interaction design. The goal is first and foremost a practical design tool to serve practicing designers, rather than a comprehensive framework for research or academic analysis. As such, the focus is on pragmatics over rigor, on systematic rather than completely formal techniques.

Before elaborating the technique of activity modeling, it is appropriate to briefly review activity theory from a design perspective and to provide an overview of usage-centered design.

3.2 ACTIVITY THEORY

Activity theory in its most elaborate and fully articulated forms can be rather daunting, but the basic tenets are fairly straightforward. The essentials of activity theory can be summarized by a couple of simple diagrams supported by brief explanations.

In a formulation that has been widely replicated, the structure of human activity is represented schematically as in the diagram of Figure 3.1. The original perspective, represented by the upper triangle in the diagram, was that human activity is performed by agents (subject) motivated toward solution of a problem or by a purpose (object or motive) mediated by tools (artifacts) within a transformational process yielding a result (outcome). Engeström, Metitenen, and Punamäki (1999) elaborated this perspective by adding the elements in the bottom half of the diagram, implying that all activity takes place in a social context (community) with differentiated responsibilities (roles or division of labor) constrained by socio-cultural and procedural factors (rules).

Activity theory further characterizes human activity as hierarchical. As suggested by Figure 3.2, activity can be understood at three levels of analysis: activity, action, and operation. Activity consists of collections of actions directed toward goals that contribute to or are related to the purpose of the activity. Actions in turn comprise operations, conscious or non conscious, adapted to emerging conditions in service of the goals of the actions.

Activity theory sees all human activity as mediated by tools and, whether significantly or fortuitously, places tools at the very apex of the structure of activity. This is

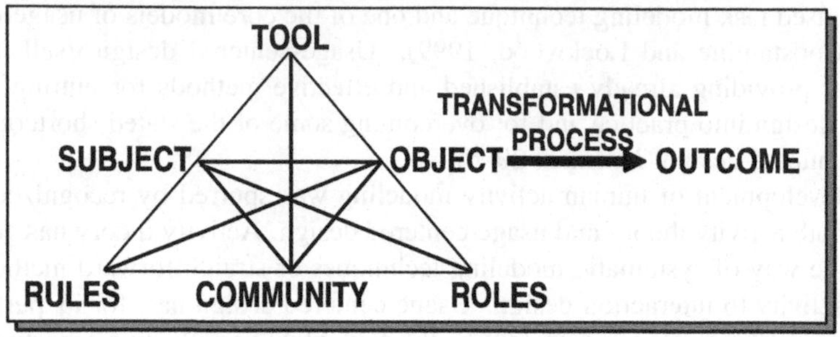

Figure 3.1 The structure of human activity (adapted from Engeström, 1999)

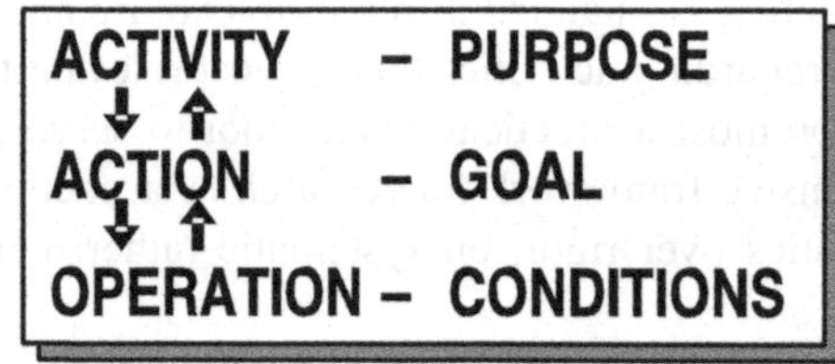

Figure 3.2 Hierarchical nature of activity (adapted from Engeström et al., 1999).

precisely the perspective of usage-centered design (Constantine and Lockwood, 1999). For designed artifacts to be most effective as tools, they must be suited to the operational context in which they are actually used and deployed. Most importantly, this requires that the design fit with the purpose(s) of the activities within which the use by subjects takes place. At a more detailed level, it also requires that designed artifacts effectively support the combined actions by which these purposes are advanced. Third, a well-designed artifact takes into account the community of participants, their roles, and the rules regulating their activity. These are arguably among the most important aspects of the immediate context of activity.

This brief synopsis does not, of course, do full justice to the richness of activity theory. Elucidating the conflicts among activities and among competing goals are considered to be essential to understanding how activity takes place and evolves. Activity theory also posits that of repeated actions gradually become operationalized to become automatic or partially automatic operations. For design purposes, it is useful to highlight some additional aspects of activities that, while not being obvious from the more compact formulations of activity theory, can have strong design implications. In particular, activities take place in and over time, within a particular physical and social setting, and are performed in characteristic manners, styles, or patterns. These are useful considerations for the designer to take into account in designing tools to support activity.

3.3 USAGE-CENTERED DESIGN

Because usage-centered design is probably more widely known among software engineers than in the HCI community (where it is sometimes confused with *user*-centered design), a brief review is appropriate. More detailed descriptions can be found elsewhere (Constantine and Lockwood, 1999; 2002)

Usage-centered design is a model-driven process for user interface and interaction design that takes its name from its primary focus on use or usage rather than on users per se. It is a systematic process for deriving a user interface design from a series of interrelated abstract models representing user roles, tasks, and interface contents. In this process, the content and organization of a user interface are derived more or less directly from a fine-grained task model, which in turn is grounded in a well-defined model of the relationships between users and the system being designed. What distinguishes usage-centered design from most mainstream user-centered approaches is a matter of emphasis and focus, but collectively these differences in degree can add up to substantial and significant differences in practice and in results (Constantine, 2004).

While it is certainly common for designers and design processes to compile information about users, tasks, and the content of user interfaces, usage-centered design is distinguished by the high level of abstraction of its models and the straightforward way in which these are interconnected. The most popular techniques for compiling and conveying information about users, for instance, are, in contrast, concrete and realistic rather than abstract; personas (Cooper and Reimann, 2003) and user profiles (Hackos and Redish, 1998) are probably the best known examples. In the case of personas, the pursuit of realism even includes construction of a hypothetical personal history, background, personality, and frequently even augmentation with photographs (Pruitt and Aldin, 2006). In contrast, *usage*-centered design carries salient information about users in the highly condensed form of user roles representing abstract relationships between users and the system being designed (Constantine, 2006).

Similarly, in *user*-centered design, tasks are often modeled using scenarios (Carroll, 1995), most commonly expressed in the form of plausible story narratives. In contrast, *usage*-centered design models user tasks as use cases (Cockburn, 2001; Jacobson et al., 1992), a construct originating in software engineering. A special form of use case, the so-called task case or essential use case (Constantine, 1994, 1995), was invented to serve the needs of user interface and interaction design by distilling interaction to its simplest, abstract essence. Task cases became the core of the model-driven process that is now known as usage-centered design.

Most designers rely heavily on paper prototypes, mockups, or other more or less realistic sketches or drawings of actual user interfaces (Snyder, 2003) to express and develop user interface designs. Usage-centered design relies on abstract prototypes to model the organization and functional content of user interfaces without regard to details of appearance or behavior (Constantine, 1998, 2003).

The use of abstraction has many advantages for designers. It makes it easier to defer decisions and avoid premature preoccupation with details. It helps focus the designer's attention on essentials, promoting resolution of large-scale or architectural issues before becoming immersed in low-level details. Experience has also shown that such abstract models encourage inventive, creative thinking about solutions to design problems. Most crucially, highly abstract models allow complex problems to be described more succinctly without sacrificing critical information.

Because of their connection with activity theory, the core models of user roles and task cases will be described in somewhat greater detail.

3.3.1 User Roles

Users who interact with a system are referred to as actors, a term borrowed from software engineering. Actors play roles. A user role is an abstraction representing a relationship between users and a system. In its simplest form, a role can be described by the context in which it is performed, the characteristic manner in which it is performed, and by the evident design criteria for effective support of performance of the role (Constantine, 2006). An example is shown below for a user working in the ticketing window reserved for "today's performances only" at a performing arts center.

R01 - Current-Sales-and-Ticketing Role

context (of role performance): isolated in booth, likely facing queue of customers; final step in performance promotion and sales

characteristics (of role performance): relatively simple task performed repeatedly with some training, prior experience likely; performed under some time pressure, which increases as show time approaches

criteria (for support of role performance): simplified, highly efficient interaction; foolproof means of identifying customer, guarantee that all the right tickets are dispensed and received by the customer

A typical application will involve a number of distinct roles representing the various relationships a user can assume in interaction with the application. Roles can, of course, be shared by any number of different occupants or incumbents, and a given user may occupy different roles at different times, even sometimes shifting rapidly between roles. For example, a visitor to a Web site may begin in the role of Indifferent-Curious-Information-Seeker and switch to the role of Engaged-Potential-Purchaser.

Usage-centered design models roles rather than users for two reasons. First, the characteristics of the role, the relationship to the system, have a more immediate and direct relevance for interaction design than do characteristics of the person playing the role. Second, the relationship to any given system represents a small subset of all possible aspects of the user. Interaction with the system takes place over a channel with relatively limited bandwidth which is restricted to a small subset of user behaviors that take place in specific settings. Because of its narrow focus on the most salient issues, a user role model can thus be substantially more compact than many alternative user models (Constantine, 2006). This simplicity has contributed to the popularity of usage-centered design for the streamlined and accelerated processes known as agile development (Constantine, 2002; Constantine and Lockwood, 2002; Patton, 2002).

3.3.2 Task Cases

A task case represents a single, discrete user intention in interaction with a system that is complete and meaningful to a user in some role. A task case is a specially structured form of a use case, one that is expressed in so-called essential form (Constantine, 1995; McMenamin and Palmer, 1984), that is, abstract, simplified, and independent of assumptions about technology or implementation. Task cases are written as an abstract dialog representing user intentions and system responsibilities. This form focuses on the essence of a task stripped of assumptions about how it might be performed with or supported by a particular user interface design. For example, a task supporting the Current-Sales-and-Ticketing Role described earlier might be:

T01 - Issuing-Held-Ticket(s) for Performance(s) **USER INTENTIONS**	SYSTEM RESPONSIBILITIES
	1. request customer identification
2. provide customer identification	3. provide confirming details
4. confirm by selection	5. print tickets with in-process and completion notification

Task cases are typically small and focused on a highly specific user goal, yielding a fine-grained model of user activity. A complete task model comprises a collection of such task cases interrelated in a variety of ways. For example, a task case can include or make use of other task cases to form more complex combinations, a task case can be extended by others that alter or interrupt its performance, or a task case can express a specialized variation of another.

More complex scenarios or workflow can be expressed by constructing composite task cases that include (by reference) any number of other task cases in the structured narrative. These so-called workflow task cases can be useful for modeling relatively predictable, orderly tasks that are well understood in detail but are not well suited to expressing combinations of individual tasks that may be performed in many different, largely unpredictable ways.

3.4 TOWARD INTEGRATION

Activity theory and usage-centered design are clearly connected at more than one point. The participation of actors in activities and the hierarchical nature of performance of activities represent the most important points of intersection. Activity theory provides a coherent way of understanding and modeling actors as tool users engaged with other participants and artifacts.

Perhaps most importantly, activities constitute an elegant scheme for aggregation of task cases into larger, loosely structured collections related by common purposes rather than by explicit or detailed interconnections. This approach to aggregation of task cases is particularly appealing because it is not an ad hoc modeling mechanism introduced to solve a problem in task modeling but comes already embedded in a larger body of knowledge and insight about human action.

The integration of activity theory with usage-centered design is less a matter of adding new concepts to the method than one of providing a stronger and more coherent organization to existing ones. The foundations of usage-centered design rest firmly on the bedrock of activity and action, but in practice over time environment and context became the backdrop for a focus on tasks as central to a model-driven design process. As originally conceived, operational context was represented by an operational model, a loosely bound collection of so-called operational profiles: the incumbent profile, proficiency profile, interaction profile, information profile, environment profile, and others (Constantine and Lockwood, 1999). Gradually, some of this information migrated into the user role model, but otherwise it remained largely unconnected with the other models of usage-centered design. Activity theory offers a single, simple framework capable of tying all this information together coherently.

3.4.1 Vocabulary

Both activity theory and usage-centered design have established vocabularies of specialized terminology. Unfortunately, the terminology is incompatible and can be confusing at points. For example, activity theory typically uses the term *object*, rather than *objective*, to refer to the motive for or purpose of an activity. Although semantically correct, this less common usage conflicts with the software engineering lexicon, in which object is a software component defined by attributes and operations.

In building a bridge between activity theory and usage-centered design, every attempt has been made to keep original vocabulary intact as much as possible while avoiding confusion and conflict. One way to smooth the linguistic integration is by allowing alternative terms for the same concept used from different perspectives. Thus the three levels of analysis can still be referred to in the traditional way as activity, action, and operation when speaking generically, but when focusing specifically on interactive activity, that is, activity in interaction with a system being designed or analyzed, the three levels are referred to as activity, *task*, and operation to maintain consistency with usage-centered design.

For design purposes it is also important to distinguish participants who actually interact directly with the user interface from those who are not engaged with the system or whose interaction is indirect, that is, mediated by other participants who do have direct contact with the user interface. Participants who are direct users are called *actors*, the well-established term in both usage-centered design and software engineering, while other participants are referred to as *players*. Clearly, whether a participant (subject) is an actor (user participant) or a player (other participant) can depend on the choice of the system of reference (the system to be designed or analyzed), the defined boundary of that system, and the activity frame of reference. For example, a customer on the telephone is an actor (direct user) with respect to the voice menu for initial contact but a player (indirect, mediated user) when speaking with a sales agent who has direct access to an ordering system. Players can, of course, be actors with respect to other systems.

3.4.2 Notation

The purpose of a notation is to enable the construction of compact representations that serve as repositories of insight and understanding and that facilitate rapid comprehension, clear and efficient communication, and detailed analysis. The notation introduced here for human activity modeling is an extension of the notation long used in usage-centered design, which, in turn, is related to the Unified Modeling Language (UML) widely used in software engineering (Fowler and Scott, 1997). The objective is a simple notation that expresses clear distinctions where needed with minimal elaborations or additions. The notation for human activity modeling summarized in Table 3.1 adds four new symbols for activities, actions, artifacts, and non actor participants to the established notation already employed in usage-centered design.

It is important to keep in mind that these models are being introduced to maximize utility and efficiency in representing activity context for interaction design purposes rather than for software engineering. The notation has not, therefore, been forced to fit, however awkwardly, within the constraints of UML at the expense of facile expression. An artifact, for example, could be argued to be an object in the object-oriented software engineering sense and, therefore, could bc represented by the extant (and much overworked) UML symbol for an object. However, an artifact is not a software object but an actual real-world physical entity of interest not for its modeling in software but for its part in some human activity. Making all objects, whether modeled in software or existing in the real world, look alike does not serve the purpose of facile expression and easy comprehension.

3.5 HUMAN ACTIVITY MODELING

In as much as usage-centered design is an already proven design method that has been widely and successfully practiced (see, for example, Constantine and Lockwood, 2002; Strope, 2003; Windl, 2002) for more than a decade, the objective in introducing systematic modeling of human activity is refinement rather than wholesale replacement. In particular, every effort has been made to add value without sacrificing the economy of expression of the established usage-centered models.

Human activity modeling is incorporated into usage-centered design through a three-part Activity Model consisting of an Activity Context Model, a Participation Model, and a Performance Model.

- The Activity Context Model, which is completely new, defines and describes human activities and their salient interrelationships.
- The Participation Model is a straightforward elaboration of the User Role Model that embeds User Roles explicitly within the context of the activities within which they are played.
- The Performance Model is a simple elaboration of a Task Model to incorporate actions in relation to other participants and artifacts and to connect task cases explicitly to activities.

The Activity Context Model itself consists of two parts: an Activity Map, which identifies activities of interest and their interrelationships, and a collection of Activity Profiles describing the salient aspects of the relevant activities.

Table 3.1 Extended usage-centered design notation for activity modeling

Symbol	Name	Description
	actor, user actor	activity participant interacting with the system of reference
	role, user role	relationship between an actor and the system of reference
	system actor	non human system (software or hardware) interacting with the system of reference
	player*	activity participant not interacting with the system of reference (but often an actor with other systems)
	artifact, tool*	any artifact employed within an activity
	activity*	collection of actions or tasks undertaken for some purpose
	task, task case	action by an actor in interaction with the system of reference for some goal within an activity
	action*	action by a player for some goal within an activity

*New notation introduced for activity modeling.

3.5.1 Activity Map

An Activity Map represents activities relevant to the design problem and the interrelationships among them. The most relevant are, of course, those activities that include interaction with the system of reference, which are referred to as proximate activities. Proximate activities define the immediate context of use, how individual tasks are combined into larger, more complex, interdependent collections. For example, telephone ticket sales is an activity that may involve a complex and changing mix of answering simple questions, helping customers find events of possible interest, responding to requests for specific tickets, taking credit card information, and the like.

Activities can contain or include other activities. Thus, for example, the larger activity of telephone sales might be clarified by breaking it down into two more focused activities: ticket selling and inquiry handling.

Even activities that do not involve interaction with the system of reference may in some cases impact a design and be relevant for defining and understanding the context of use. If, for example, actors are involved in activities with other participants that compete for their time and attention, this has implications for presentation and interaction design. In such cases, the ability to suspend or interrupt interaction at any arbitrary point might be required, and presentation design may need to make it easy for actors to recognize where they are and where they left off in a process.

Activities that are connected in time can be related in a number of different ways. They may be either independent or coordinated in some way. They may be concurrent or consecutive. If concurrent, they may be coordinated (or synchronized), independent, or interleaved, that is, alternated. (This last relationship is particularly common because a single actor can seldom engage in more than one activity at a time, which results in otherwise independent activities becoming coordinated in time.) If consecutive, activities may or may not overlap in time. An activity can compete with another activity because it shares common participants or resources. More indirectly, an activity can be affected by an adjacent activity with which it has no relationship other than both activities take place within the same setting.

The most commonly meaningful relationships among activities in an Activity Map are listed in Table 3.2. This is not intended as a complete listing but only to offer examples of the kinds of relationships that have proved useful for modeling real-world problems.

In considering whether to include an activity in an activity model or to define a relationship between activities, the sole issue is relevance: Does it make a demonstrable difference or have an arguable impact on the design? The objective is not to be exhaustive or all encompassing but to model what matters. In general, activities can be rank ordered on the relevance for interaction design. From most relevant to least, these are:

1. Proximate activities (the immediate activity context within which use occurs)
2. Competing activities also involving the same actor(s)
3. Competing activities involving shared resources in common with proximate activities

4. Adjacent activities in the same setting but otherwise unrelated to proximate activities

Activities are represented in an Activity Map by the block shape shown in Table 3.1. A line or arrow connecting one activity to another represents a relationship. Relationships can be labeled with qualifiers to specify the relationship more precisely. An example of an Activity Map using this notation is shown in Figure 3.3. This map represents some of the core activities for a retail sales context within the appliance department of a large retailer. As seen here, braces (curly brackets) can be freely used to visually simplify representation of relationships.

Table 3.2 Relationships between activities

Relationship Qualifier	**Explanation***
contains	[includes] activity is composed of other subactivities
coordinated	[synchronized] activities are coordinated/synchronized by some means
concurrent	activities occur over common time span, not further qualified
synchronized	[coordinated]
unsynchronized	independent, concurrent but not coordinated
interleaved	alternating
consecutive	sequential activities, not further qualified
precedes	strictly sequential
overlaps	activity finishes after another starts
competing	activities conflict or interfere, not further qualified
common participants	participant(s) (optionally identified) overlap
shared artifacts	some resources (optionally identified) are shared
adjacent	activities occur within same setting (place and time)

* Alternate terms are shown in brackets.

In addition to the qualifiers listed in Table 3.2, other terms or descriptions appropriate to the context can be used as needed. For example, the flow of information, participants, or artifacts between activities can be modeled where known and where relevant using small arrows running alongside the line or arrow for the relationship. An Activity Map can also be expanded into a combined Activity-Task Map that in-

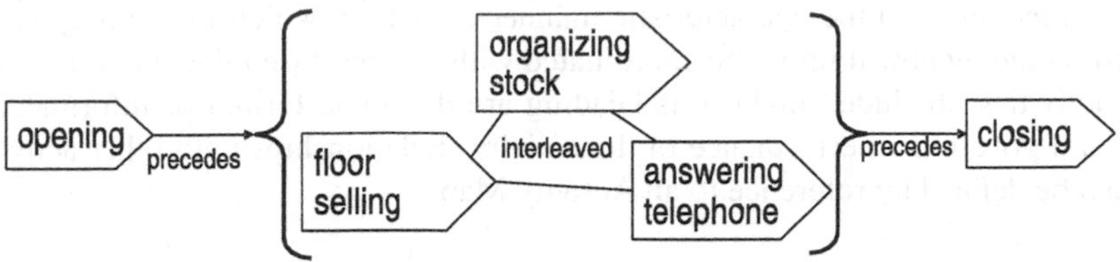

Figure 3.3 Example of an Activity Map in a retail sales context

cludes the aggregation of task cases into activities. An example of this can be found in Figure 3.6, to be discussed later.

3.5.2 Activity Profiles

For purposes of informing interaction design, activities are described by Activity Profiles. An Activity Profile is not intended to capture in fullest detail everything known or knowable about an activity but rather to organize in compact form the salient aspects of an activity that are most likely to be relevant to shaping the user interface design. This condensed formulation is organized under four easily remembered headings: Purpose, Place and Time, Participation, and Performance. A fifth heading, Product, is not, strictly speaking, part of the activity description but serves as a holding place for any evident design implications that follow from the understanding of the activity. An Activity Profile can, of course, be augmented by additional narrative description or supporting documentation or models.

Purpose refers to the motives or objectives for the activity, what it is all about. An activity can have more than one purpose and the purpose may in some cases be different for different participants. The purpose of a soccer game may be different for players on the field and for fans in the stands, for example. Purpose may also differ depending on whether an internal or external view is taken.

Place and Time (the setting) refers to where, when, and under what conditions the activity takes place, which can include both the physical and the social setting of the activity as well as the duration, schedule, frequency or other temporal aspects of the performance. The setting within which activity takes place is not always known or easily described. On-line shopping, for example, might take place within an office cubicle, in the living room of a home, or in a WiFi-equipped coffee shop. Such variations in the setting can be included if they are of significance for design and can be described at an appropriate level.

Participation refers to those engaged in the activity and the artifacts with which they are involved. Participants include actors engaged with the system of reference along with the roles they play as well as other players not engaged with the system. Artifacts include the physical and conceptual tools employed in the activity, including information sources, references, and other resources. Relationships and interactions among participants and between participants and artifacts as well as the division of responsibilities among participants also fall under this rubric. Participation can also be defined by reference to a Participation Map (see below).

Performance refers to the characteristic manner or style in which the activity is performed including how it might be coordinated with or otherwise related to other identified activities. Included under this heading are the rules, formal or informal, that shape and govern the performance of the activity. Relationships with other activities can also be defined by reference to an Activity Map.

3.5.3 Participation Map

One of the most straightforward ways to model human activity is through a simple map of the "playing field," a representation of the participants and their relationships with each other and with the various artifacts involved in the activity. Such a Participation Map, as it is called, gives a quick overview of the context within which system use takes place. For design purposes, it is useful to distinguish participants who are engaged in interaction with the system of reference, the tool being designed, from other participants. Carrying over the already established terminology, the former are referred to as *user actors*, or more simply, *actors*. Other systems that interact with the system of reference are called *system actors*. The term *player* is introduced to refer to all other participants.

The Participation Map takes the form of a simple diagram, such as the one shown in Figure 3.4. The notation employs simple but distinctive iconic representations to distinguish actors, roles, players, system actors, and artifacts. Interconnecting lines identify the interrelationships and can be decorated to represent the flow of information or material.

The Participation Map would typically include only participants and artifacts having a salient connection with actors (or roles) within proximate activities, either directly or as mediated by artifacts. Where the information is relevant, the Participation Map can be supplemented by more detailed descriptions of artifacts or of participants.

The system-centered Participation Map shown in Figure 3.4 has proved the most versatile as it compactly represents an overview of the context of use for the system of reference. As the particular roles and artifacts involved may vary from one activity to another, this information when deemed important can be incorporated in several ways, either by grouping participants and artifacts or by footnoting.

System Actors and Artifacts (tools, resources) are, of course, closely related and can be easily confused. System Actors, like User Actors, interact with the system of reference but unlike Artifacts, they are not directly used by User Actors. In Figure 3.4, for example, the credit card network interacts with the sales support system but, unlike the telephone, is not itself a tool used directly by any of the actors or players. In some cases, a system might be modeled either way, depending on the purpose and the context of the model.

3.5.4 Role Profiles

From an activity theory perspective, User Roles are played by Actors within activities. User Roles are connected to activity theory by modifying the Role Profile to include information about activities. The content of this revised Role Profile is organized under three headings: Activity, Background, and Characteristics.

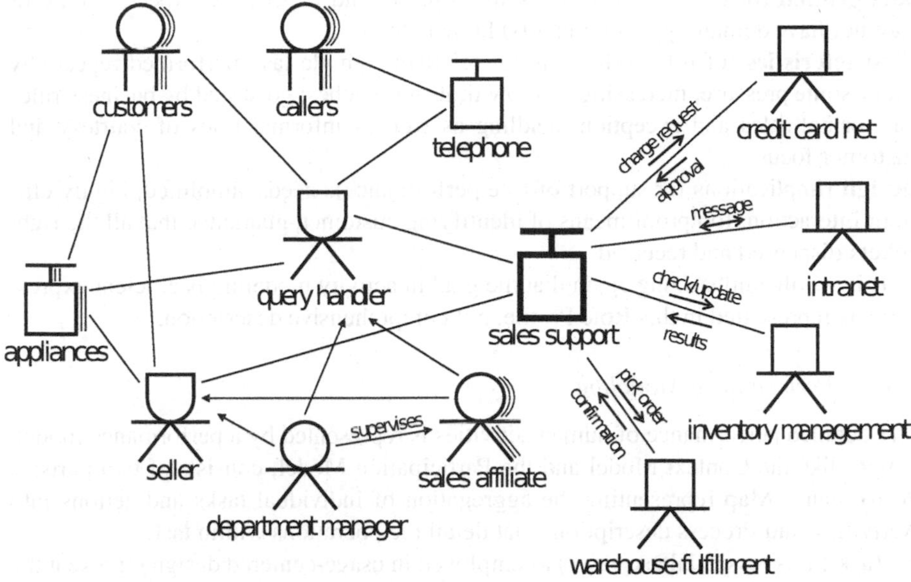

Figure 3.4 Example of Participation Map for retail selling situation

Activity refers, of course, to the activity within which the role is played. If the activity is defined elsewhere by an Activity Profile, then it can be referred to by name. Otherwise it is briefly described in terms of purpose, place (physical and social context) and time, and participation, including salient artifacts.

Background refers to the background characteristics of the performers of the role in terms of experience, training, education, system knowledge and domain knowledge, distribution of performance skills, and orientation or attitudes of performers

Characteristics refers to performance characteristics, such as frequency, regularity, intensity, complexity, and predictability of performance. In some cases this may overlap with or repeat aspects of the Activity Profile, particularly if there is only one Role for a single Actor in the activity.

A fourth rubric, *Design*, serves as a holding place for evident design implications for effective support of the role.

An activity-centered Role Profile for the Current-Sales-and-Ticketing Role resembles the description given earlier but places greater emphasis on the larger context within which the role is played:

R01 - Current-Sales-and-Ticketing Role

Activity (in which role is performed): selling and delivering tickets for today's events; part of performing arts promotion, sales, and presentation (purpose: sell and deliver tickets efficiently and accurately; place: isolated in booth outside main entrance, likely facing queue of customers; time: before show time, final step in activity; participants: seller, customer, queued customers, milling crowd, supervisor; artifacts: ticketing system, tickets in ticket printer, phone to supervisor)

Background (of role performers): some training and experience expected, may or may not have domain (performing arts) knowledge
Characteristics (of role performance): relatively simple task performed repeatedly under some pressure, increasing as show time approaches; governed by business rules for normal sales and exception handling as well as informal rules of courtesy and customer focus
Design (implications for support of role performance): needs simplified, highly efficient interaction, foolproof means of identifying customer, guarantee that all the right tickets dispensed and received

It is worth emphasizing again that the goal in activity modeling is efficient expression, as represented in this Role Profile, not comprehensive description.

3.5.5 Performance Modeling

The detailed performance of human activities is represented by a performance model, which, like the Context Model and the Participation Model, consists of two parts: a Performance Map representing the aggregation of individual tasks and actions into Activities, and Process descriptions that detail the operations within tasks.

Task cases (essential use cases) as employed in usage-centered design represent the second level of the activity hierarchy. A task model based on task cases provides a fine-grained view of user intentions and interactions within an activity. The traditional task model is extended to integrate with the activity model in two ways: by connecting tasks to the activities within which they are embedded and by elaborating the task model to incorporate non interactive actions. In this context, actions refer to goal-directed interactions among actors or players and between them and artifacts other than the system of reference. Actions are represented by a distinct symbol (the barred ellipse seen in Table 3.1), a variation of the symbol already generally used to represent task cases.

The Performance Map, a model used to represent the interrelationships among task cases in usage-centered design, can be extended to incorporate activities and actions. For complex problems, however, a single diagram combining activities, tasks, and actions along with lines representing all their relationships can become too complicated visually. The combined model can be simplified by omitting the relationships among tasks and actions to focus on the aggregation into activities, which in many cases is the primary interest. An example of such a Performance Map is shown in Figure 3.5. The aggregation of tasks and actions into activities can also be easily expressed in matrix form, with activities as columns and actions and tasks as rows. The choice of representation depends on the complexity of the problem and the goals of modeling.

The narrative body that defines a task case in detail can also, in turn, be extended to include, as appropriate, references to external actions involving other players. For example, in the ticket selling application, the interaction with the customer can be incorporated into the narrative as shown in the task case below. An external action is indicated by bracketing with vertical bars (as in the barred ellipse symbol), as for operations 2, 5, and 8 in the example below. Named actions, like tasks, are identified with underlined names. The former can be defined further with their own narratives or other description where warranted by the complexity and relevance of the action.

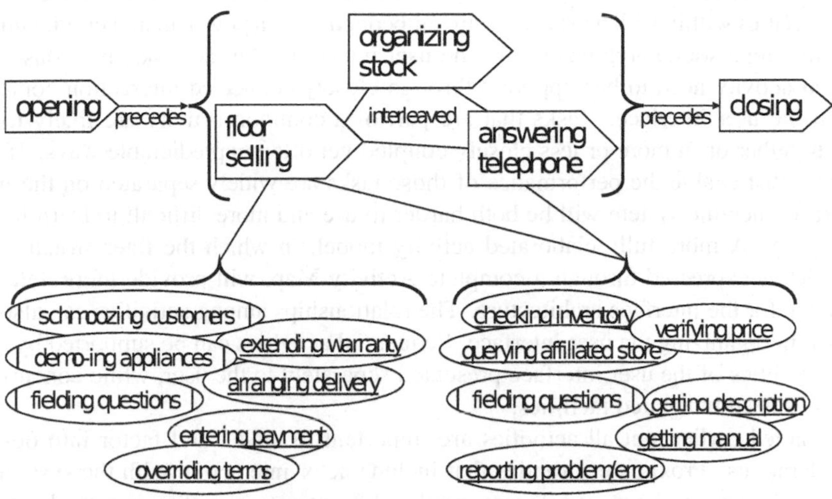

Figure 3.5 Example of partial Activity-Task Map for retail selling

Whether such attention to detail is worthwhile for a particular problem depends largely on whether there are potential interface design implications.

T01 - Issuing-Held-Ticket(s) for Performance(s) **USER INTENTIONS**	**SYSTEM RESPONSIBILITIES**
	1. request customer identification
2. |getting identification from customer|	
3. provide customer identification	4. provide confirming details
5. |confirming details with customer|	
6. confirm by selection	7. print tickets with in-process and completion notification
8. |give tickets to customer|	
9. confirm delivery	10. note as delivered

3.6 DESIGN IMPLICATIONS

The manifest design implications regarding activities and the roles played within them are captured and carried as part of the Activity Profiles and Role Profiles. Such implications, which are almost invariably idiosyncratic to the particular problem, can be expanded or altered whenever the need arises. In many cases, design implications will be clear when profiles are first constructed, but in others the significance for design may not become apparent until sometime later in the design and development process.

Some general implications of activity modeling have become clear from use so far. The activities within which task cases are embedded form a powerful and crucial guide to designing a sound architecture for the user interface. All the tasks that constitute a given activity need to be supported through closely connected interaction contexts within the user interface. Tasks that are part of a common activity are likely to be used together or in more or less closely coupled yet often unpredictable ways. If the features that enable the performance of those tasks are widely separated on the user interface, then the system will be both harder to use and more difficult to learn in the first place. A more fully elaborated activity model, in which the finer structure of activities is expressed through a complete Activity Map, will provide more detailed guidance for the interface architecture. The relationships among activities can also be helpful in organizing the user interface. Sequential activities can be supported by discrete facilities of the user interface presented separately to the user, while concurrent activities need integrated facilities.

As noted earlier, not all activities are important to model and factor into design considerations. Proximate activities that include actor interaction with the system of reference are apt to be most relevant, while adjacent activities that merely share the same setting are much less likely to be relevant.

In usage-centered design, the contents of the user interface derive more or less directly from the task model. Clusters of closely related tasks are initially assumed to require support through features in a shared interaction context, or a small set of closely connected ones. When externally directed actions are added into the mix, the derivation can change. The action-task formulation of Issuing Held Tickets for Performances shown above, for example, highlights the close connection between what identification information is requested by the system on the one hand and the exchange between the ticket agent actor and the customer player on the other, which is also true of the presentation of confirming details and the exchange to confirm with the customer. Planning or scripting the external exchanges and organizing the presentation design to correspond can contribute to efficient use and conformance to business rules. For example, business policies may favor using a purchase confirmation number because it uniquely identifies a particular set of tickets for a particular customer even though the customer is more likely to have other forms of identification or confirmation. This suggests a design that leads with a field for confirmation number coupled with a script that asks if the customer knows the confirmation number.

3.7 PROCESS IMPLICATIONS

The modest elaboration of usage-centered design to accommodate activity modeling does not radically alter the process. In overview, the process begins with a focus on users and other participants to clarify the immediate activity context. Actors, roles, players (other participants), and artifacts are identified and characterized, along with system actors. The immediate context is modeled by the Participation Map and Role Profiles. On the basis of those models, activities and their constituent actions and tasks are elaborated as an integrated model that includes an Activity-Task Map and Task Cases. The Activity Model guides the development of a Navigation Map to express the overall architecture of the user interface and the derivation of Abstract Prototypes expressing the content and organization of the parts of the user interface. Details of the presentation and interaction design are then determined to complete the design.

In outline, the logic of this process is represented in Figure 3.6. It conveniently breaks down into two focuses: activity modeling and solution modeling. The former expresses the problem from an activity-centered perspective while the latter expresses the design that follows from expression of the problem. The entire process is model-driven and linked end-to-end by common threads captured in the models. Thus, any given feature of the user interface design can be simply traced to some part of the abstract prototype that derived directly from some element of the task cases that, in turn, support some one or more user roles played by actors participating in modeled activities.

Although the logical connections suggest a straightforward sequential process, in practice the process is iterative and much more nonlinear. In particular, the models under activity modeling, owing to their strong interdependence, are often developed more or less concurrently, with the focus of attention repeatedly shifting among them.

3.8 APPLICATION

The purpose here is to provide a worked out example of human activity modeling for a real-world problem. The problem chosen for illustration is the design of the UInspect system, a software tool to support collaborative usability inspections (Constantine, 2005; Lockwood and Constantine, 2003), particularly the recording of defects during an inspection. A collaborative usability inspection is a structured review organized to identify usability defects in a design, prototype, or working system. Under the leadership of a Lead Reviewer, a User or User Surrogate following an inspection scenario collaborates with other Reviewers to identify usability problems according to a strict protocol. Each of the participants has an assigned role and responsibilities governed by explicit inspection rules. (For more details on collaborative inspections and the rules governing them, see Constantine, 2005; Lockwood and Constantine, 2003)

Activity Profile: Collaborative Usability Inspection Session

Purpose: to efficiently and effectively locate, describe, and categorize usability defects in a design, prototype, or working system

Place and Time: typically in a conference room or other isolated setting at a scheduled time, lasting 1–3 hours, typically under project schedule pressure; social setting mixes insiders (designers and developers) with outsiders (users or user surrogates, usability experts)

Participation: typically 6–12 people, 1–3 end-users or user surrogates, Lead Reviewer, Inspection Recorder, Reviewers (designers or developers), System Driver; optional Continuity Reviewer, Usability Specialist; see references for role responsibilities and rules of conduct (summarized by Lead Reviewer, optionally on poster). Artifacts include: design, prototype, or system being inspected; inspection scenario; UInspect tool with inspection record; optional projector or large-screen monitor, equipment to run prototype or system being inspected

Performance: intense, sometimes tense interaction, tending to come in bursts; process is carefully orchestrated and divided into distinct phases; location and multipart descriptions for as many as 100 defects per hour must be recorded accurately and in sufficient detail to support later review and correction; Recorder role particularly pressured; Lead Reviewer important to maintaining focus, preventing unproductive debate and discussion

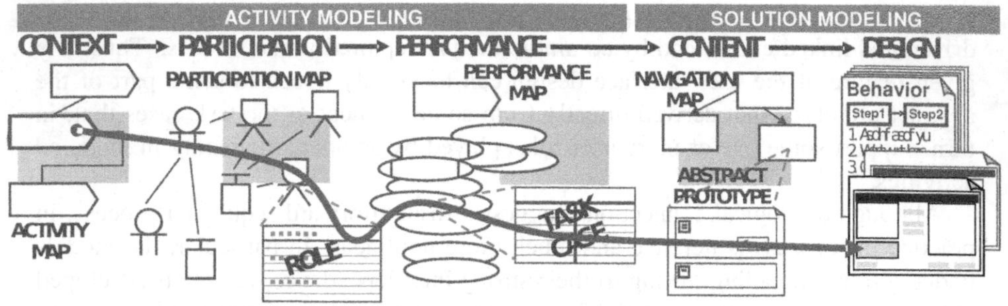

Figure 3.6 Logical overview of usage-centered design with activity modeling

The system-centered Participation Map in Figure 3.7 provides an overview of the activity context. The immediate context of the inspection proper is enclosed in the dashed line. This highlights the fact that all players are involved in identifying defects but that all defects flow through the inspection recorder. The unlabeled "couples" shown on some relationships represent the dominant flow of information. In this model, the same actor, the Recorder, is shown as playing three distinct roles: Prep/Configuring, Session Recording, and Record Refining. The first and last of these are associated with distinct activities represented in the Activity-Task Map of Figure 3.8, which shows the relationships among the activities connected with conducting a collaborative usability inspection, including both preparation and follow-up activities. For simplicity, this combined model shows the aggregation of tasks and actions into activities but not the relationships among actions and interactive tasks.

The pivotal role of session recorder can be described with a Role Profile.

R02 - Session-Recording Role

Activity (in which role is performed): Collaborative Usability Inspection Session. Purpose: quickly, accurately, and efficiently capture usability defects identified

Background (of role performers): trained and educated technical professional, probably member of design/development group (not non-technical or administrative); some familiarity with UInspect system and object being inspected (at least from Preparing for Inspection activity); some knowledge of basic user interface and usability concepts required, familiarity with inspection process desirable; role may be played repeatedly but infrequently, expert performance in using the UInspect tool is unlikely

Characteristics (of role performance): multipart repetitive recording task requiring rapid interaction and quick judgment under some pressure; close coordination with Lead Reviewer; competing attention between verbal reports, comments, and recording activity

Design (implications for support of role performance): speed and accuracy are foremost requiring maximum visibility of recording options and categories, simplified means for marking screenshots or design images; need ability to quickly navigate forward and back or to specific defect record, UI image, or scenario step; system must allow incomplete and blank entries with ability to edit on the fly

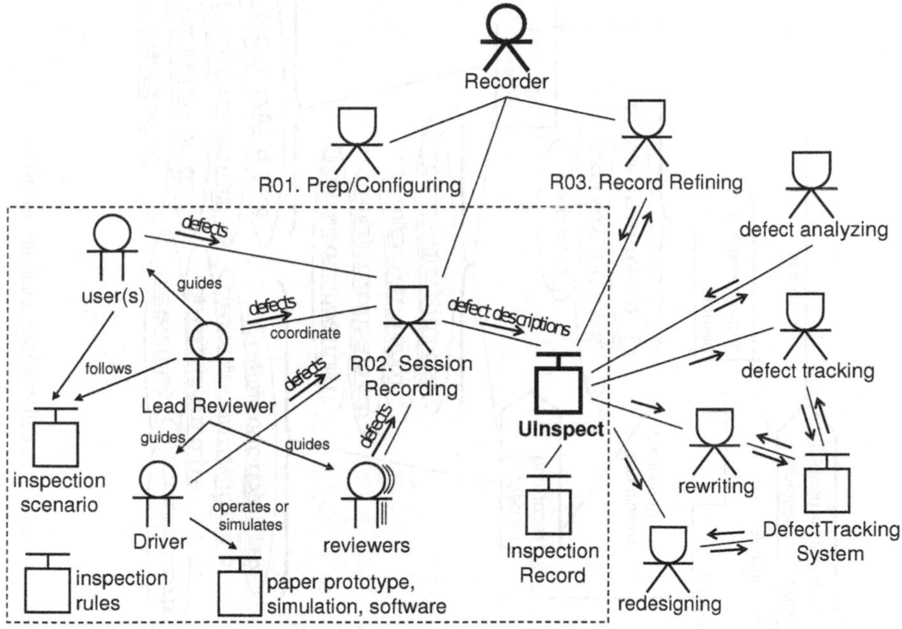

Figure 3.7 System-centered Participation Map for collaborative usability inspections

3.9 DISCUSSION

The integration provided by human activity modeling is unlikely to appeal to everyone. Longstanding activity theorists may disdain the distillation of an elaborate body of discourse into a few simple profiles and diagrams. Designers already working comfortably within a usage-centered perspective may object to complicating a straightforward process with additional models or elaborations of current models. Designers immersed in more elaborate ethnographic approaches to analysis and design may consider the models of human activity modeling too spare and simplistic.

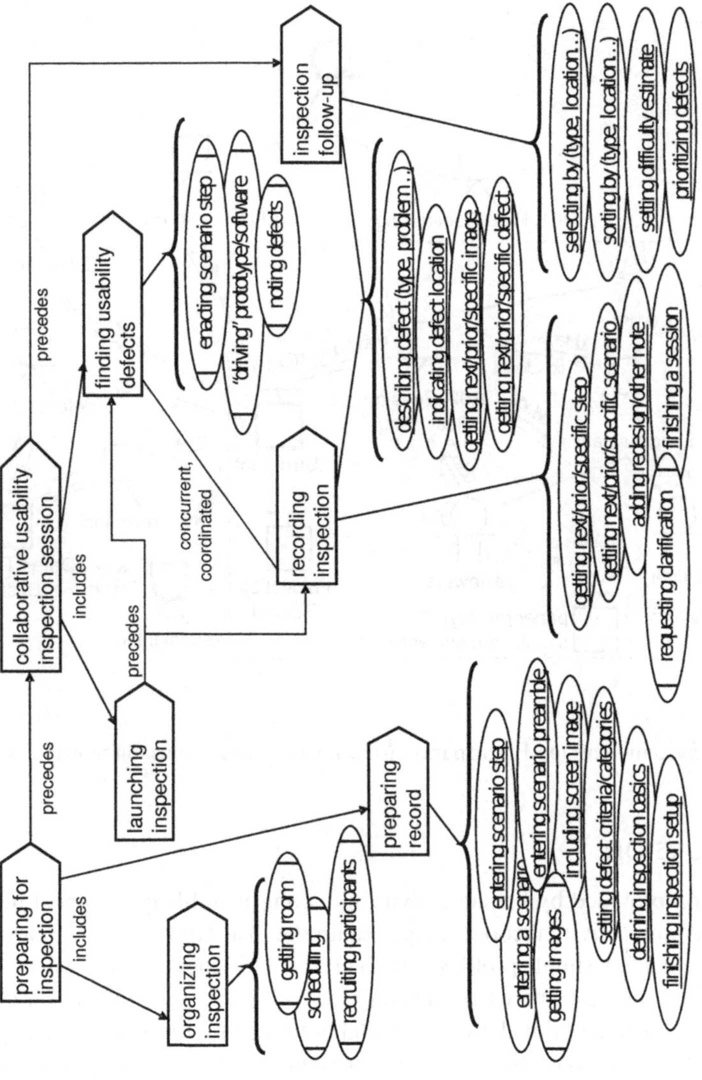

Figure 3.8 Performance Map for the UInspect collaborative usability inspections tool

Vocal objections to human activity modeling are likely also to come from the software engineering community, particularly that segment most closely tied to the Unified Modeling Language. Although it is no doubt possible to find ways to shoehorn human activity modeling into the procrustean bed of UML, this proposal makes no attempt to do so for two reasons. First, the purposes of human activity modeling and the professional constituency it is intended to serve are quite distinct from those of UML. Moreover, UML is particularly deficient in supporting visual and interaction design of user interfaces. Although it is possible to force fit user interface design problems and concerns into the UML, the results are rarely satisfying, particularly from the perspective of the interests and common practices of interaction designers and other related professionals, which is precisely the constituency targeted by activity modeling. Second, UML itself is objectionable from a human-factors perspective (Henderson-Sellers and Constantine, 1995a; 1995b), making it particularly inappropriate as a standard of reference for models directed toward human-factors professionals.

Human activity modeling bears some similarity to other techniques in current analysis and design practice, particularly business process modeling, and it might be argued that human activity modeling is already covered by such techniques. However, both the objectives and the targeted users of business process modeling and activity modeling are distinct. Business process modeling is intended to serve the needs of business analysts and requirements engineers capturing precise definitions of key business processes in terms of step-by-step workflow, well-defined decision criteria, and the exact flow of control, information, and resources that must be reflected in software that supports these business processes. For our purposes, then, business processes may be thought of as special cases of the broader construct of human activities. Activity modeling serves design professionals trying to capture the broad design implications of human activities as loose and relatively unconstrained and often unpredictable combinations of tasks toward the end of creating more useful and usable products. The differing needs and focuses of attention of these two analysis activities undertaken for differing purposes require different tools and techniques.

Regrettably, the term *activity* is also used in UML, where it refers to the behavior of a system expressed as a set of control and data flows. A UML activity diagram is used to represent the dynamic view of a system as the flow of control and data from activity to activity (Booch, Rumbaugh, and Jacobson, 2005). Business process modeling borrows the notation of UML activity diagrams to create business process diagrams which thus represent the workflow, inputs, and outputs of business processes (Penker and Eriksson, 2001).

The primary purpose of human activity modeling is to provide practicing designers of any ilk with a practical tool for expressing the most salient aspects of the human activity context within which use of a system is embedded. Through relatively modest extensions and minimal changes in process, the method of usage-centered design can be firmly anchored in activity theory, thereby improving the practice of interaction design and expanding the scope of application of activity theory.

No claim is made that human activity modeling in its present form is complete. Although the current formulation was developed through an extensive retrospective analysis of many projects and has been refined through generous feedback from early adopters and other colleagues, only long-term application in a variety of settings will expose weak or missing elements or reveal which elements are most often of significance in the design process. In putting this revised process to use, designers have the opportunity to contribute to the refinement of both theory and practice, both models and methods.

References

Booch, G., Rumbaugh, J., and Jacobson, I. (2005). *The Unified Modeling Language user guide*. Addison-Wesley, Reading: MA.

Carroll, J. M., editor (1995). *Scenario-Based Design: Envisioning Work and Technology in System Development*. New York: Wiley.

Cockburn, A. (2001). *Writing Effective Use Cases*. Addison-Wesley, Reading: MA.

Constantine, L. L. (1994). Essentially Speaking In *Software Development*, 2(11) Reprinted in L.L. Constantine, editor, *The Peopleware Papers*. Upper Saddle River, NJ: Prentice Hall, 2001.

Constantine, L. L. (1995). Essential modeling: use cases for user interfaces. *Interactions*, 2(2):34–46.

Constantine, L. L. (1998). Abstract prototyping. In *Software Development*, volume 6 (10). Reprinted in S. Ambler, and L. Constantine, editors, *The Unified Process Elaboration Phase*. San Francisco: CMP Books, 2000.

Constantine, L. L. (2003). Canonical abstract prototypes for abstract visual and interaction. In Jorge, J., Nunes, N., and Cunha, J., editors, *Interactive Systems: Design, Specification, and Verification, 10th International Workshop, DSV-IS 2003, Funchal, Madeira Island, Portugal, June 11-13, 2003, Revised Papers*, volume 2844 of *Lecture Notes in Computer Science*, pages 1–15. Springer-Verlag.

Constantine, L. L. (2004). Beyond user-centered design and user experience. *Cutter IT Journal*, 17(2):2–11.

Constantine, L. L. (2005). Peer reviews for usability. *Cutter IT Journal*, 18(1).

Constantine, L. L. (2006). Users, roles, and personas. In (Pruitt and Adlin, 2006), The Persona Lifecycle: Keeping People in Mind Throughout Product Design, San Francisco: Morgan-Kaufman, pages 87–110.

Constantine, L. L. (2002). Process agility and software usability: towards lightweight usage-centered design. In *Information Age*. http://www.foruse.com/articles/agiledesign.pdf.

Constantine, L. L. and Lockwood, L. A. D. (1999). *Software for Use: A Practical Guide to the Models and Methods of Usage-Centered Design*. Addison-Wesley, Reading: MA.

Constantine, L. L. and Lockwood, L. A. D. (2002). User-centered engineering for Web applications. *IEEE Software*, 19(2):42–50.

Cooper, A. and Reimann, R. (2003). *About Face 2.0: The Essentials of User Interface Design*. New York: John Wiley and Sons.

Duignan, M., Noble, J., and Biddle, R. (2006). Activity theory for design. In *HWID 2006*. University of Madeira.

Engeström, Y., Miettinen, R., and Punamäki, R. (1999). *Perspectives on Activity Theory*. London: Cambridge University Press.

Fowler, M. and Scott, K. (1997). UML distilled: applying the standard object modeling language. In Fowler, M., editor, *UML Distilled*. Addison Wesley, Reading: MA.

Gay, G. and Hembrooke, H. (2004). *Activity-Centered Design*. MIT Press.

Hackos, J. T. and Redish, J. (1998). *User and Task Analysis for Interface Design*. New York: Wiley.

Hendersons-Sellers, B. and Constantine, L. (1995a). Notation matters. part 1: Framing the issues. Technical Report 3.

Hendersons-Sellers, B. and Constantine, L. (1995b). Notation matters. part 2: Applying the principles. Technical Report 4.

Jacobson, I. (1992). *Object-Oriented Software Engineering: A Use Case Driven Approach*. Addison-Wesley, Reading: MA.: .

Kaptalinin, V., Nardi, B. A., and Macaulay, C. (1999). The activity checklist. *Interactions*, 6(4):27–39.

Lockwood, L. and Constantine, L. (2003). Usability by inspection: Collaborative techniques for software and Web applications. In Constantine, L., editor, *forUSE 2003 Performance by Design: Proceedings of the Second International Conference on Usage-Centered Design*, Focus on Computer Graphics. Rowley, MA: Ampersand Press.

McMenamin, S. and Palmer, J. (1984). *Essential Systems Analysis*. Englewood Cliffs, NJ: Prentice Hall.

Nardi, B., editor (1996). *Context and Consciousness*. Cambridge, MA: MIT Press.

Norman, D. (2005). Human-centered design considered harmful. *Interactions*, 12(4):14–19.

Norman, D. (2006). Private communication.

Patton, J. (2002). Hitting the target: adding interaction design to agile software development. In *OOPSLA '02: OOPSLA 2002 Practitioners Reports*, pages 1–ff. ACM Press.

Penker, M. and Eriksson, H., editors (2001). *Business Modeling with UML: Business Patterns at Work*. New York: Wiley.

Pruitt, J. and Adlin, T., editors (2006). *The Persona Lifecycle: Keeping People in Mind Throughout Product Design*. San Francisco: Morgan-Kaufman.

Snyder, C. (2003). *Paper Prototyping*. San Francisco: Morgan-Kaufmann.

Strope, J. (2003). Designing for breakthroughs in user performance. In Constantine, L., editor, *Performance by Design: Proceedings of forUSE 2003, the Second International Conference on Usage-Centered Design*. Rowley, MA: Ampersand Press.

Windl, H. (2002). Designing a winner: Creating STEP 7 lite with usage-centered design. In Constantine, L., editor, *forUSE 2002: Proceedings of the First International Conference on Usage-Centered Design*. Rowley, MA: Ampersand Press.

4 A USER-CENTERED FRAMEWORK FOR DERIVING A CONCEPTUAL DESIGN FROM USER EXPERIENCES: *LEVERAGING PERSONAS AND PATTERNS TO CREATE USABLE DESIGNS*

Homa Javahery,
Alexander Deichman, Ahmed Seffah, and Mohamed Taleb

Human-Centered Software Engineering (HCSE) Group,
Department of Computer Science and Software Engineering,
Concordia University,
1455 Maisonneuve Boulevard West, Montreal, Quebec, Canada H3G 1M8,
Website: http://hci.cs.concordia.ca/www

Abstract. Patterns are a design tool to capture best practices, tackling problems that occur in different contexts. A user interface (UI) design pattern spans several levels of design abstraction ranging from high-level navigation to low-level idioms detailing a screen layout. One challenge is to combine a set of patterns to create a conceptual design that reflects user experiences. In this chapter, we detail a user-centered design (UCD) framework that exploits the novel idea of using personas and patterns together. Personas are used initially to collect and model user experiences. UI patterns are selected based on personas pecifications; these patterns are then used as building blocks for constructing conceptual designs. Through the use of a case study, we illustrate how personas and patterns can act as complementary techniques in narrowing the gap between two major steps in UCD: capturing users and their experiences, and building an early design based on that information. As a result of lessons learned from the study and by refining our framework, we define a more systematic process called UX-P (User Experiences to Pattern), with a supporting tool. The process introduces intermediate analytical steps and supports designers in creating usable designs.

4.1 INTRODUCTION

User-Centered Design (UCD) has been proposed in the literature to provide designers with a general approach for interactive system design, by making end-users and their experiences a focal point of the design process. Based on UCD principles, different design methods have been developed. These include Scenario-based design (Carroll, 2000), Goal-directed design (Cooper, 1999), Contextual design, (Beyer and Holtzblatt, 1998) and Participatory design (Ehn, 1998). These methods introduce techniques for evolving and documenting the design at various steps of the process. If a designer would like to model user experiences, tasks, and the context of use—relevant techniques include personas, task analysis, scenarios, workflow modeling, and context analysis. Furthermore, if a designer would like to build a prototype, conceptual design, or detailed design—relevant techniques include design guidelines, principles, style sheets, and patterns.

Although these methods share a common user-focused tenet, there exists a significant gap between current user analysis and modeling techniques, and the process of deriving a UI conceptual design. Ethnographic and empirical techniques are generally used to collect relevant user data to describe user experiences. These experiences are then captured in narrative form, but the derivation of a conceptual design from them is ambiguous and based on guided principles rather than a reproducible systematic method. Even if some techniques like storyboarding try to "walk" designers through relevant user tasks, they only address a subset of user experiences. There is little reproducibility of solutions and traceability to user experiences. Often, the final design is only the result of the designer's background and knowledge rather than the result of following a well-established and standardized method (Preece et al., 2002).

In Seffah et al. (2005), the need to build a tighter fit between user experiences and design concepts is described as one of the main challenges in human-centered software engineering. To advance the state-of-the-art and narrow this existing gap, we require processes that support designers in deriving conceptual designs from user experience descriptions. Such a process should be systematic, traceable, and practical, but should also leave room for design creativity when appropriate. Figure 4.1 highlights the current lack of such a process.

In this chapter, we propose a design framework and associated process to tackle this problem. We investigate personas and patterns as two complementary artifacts which can be correlated for the purpose of narrowing this gap. More precisely, our research is tailored towards the definition of a systematic process that derives a pattern-oriented design from persona descriptions, through a set of intermediate steps. The research questions we have addressed are as follows: How can we systematically generate a conceptual design from the model we have of the user experiences? How much

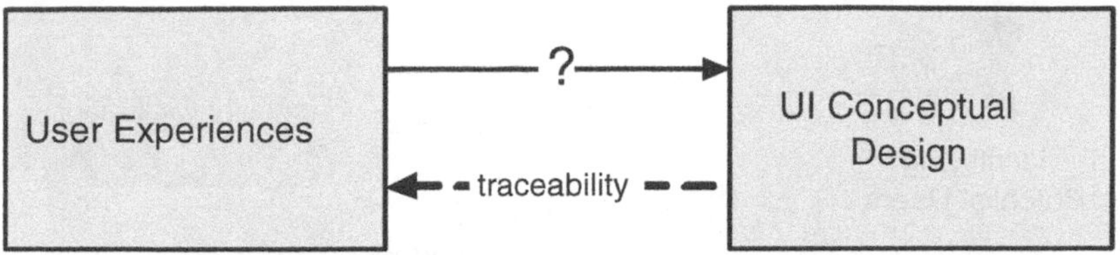

Figure 4.1 Current problem of deriving a design from user experiences

of this process can be automated or computer-supported? What are the major steps in this process? By defining such a process and with tool support, it is possible to empower UI designers with concrete design solutions that can be traced back to the user experiences. This is of great help in empirical or formal validations, as well as when design trade-offs are to be made.

In what follows, we will present the core UCD concepts applied relative to our framework, and illustrate it using a case study.

4.2 A FIRST LOOK AT THE PROPOSED FRAMEWORK

We have proposed and defined a framework to help narrow the gap between user experiences and conceptual design. The framework, illustrated in Figure 4.2, exploits two key UCD artifacts. Its starting point is an understanding of user behaviors and experiences, their tasks, and the context of their work.

Personas are the first key UCD artifact used. They are created iteratively to model user experiences. Initially, the personas help to identify actual users for predesign usability evaluation of the target application. Evaluation results from psychometric and heuristic assessment are used to categorize potential users into a set of personas, as well as to further enhance them—giving a clearer picture of user behaviors and experiences, their tasks, and the context of use. Other inputs, such as task analysis and scenario generation, are used to refine the persona set. Personas are represented by a set of persona elements (examples are age and computer experience) and textual descriptions (examples are general profile and interaction behavior).

Patterns, the second key UCD artifact used, are then selected based on personas. In HCI, design patterns and their associated languages are used to capture essential details of design knowledge. The presented information is organized within a set of predefined attributes, allowing designers, for example, to search rapidly through different design solutions while assessing the relevance of each pattern to their design. Every pattern has three necessary elements, usually presented as separate attributes, which are: a context, a problem, and a solution. Other attributes that may be included are design rationale, specific examples, and related patterns. Furthermore, our patterns include specific information about the user needs and usability criteria addressed.

The selected patterns are then used as "building blocks" and composed into a pattern-oriented design. By using personas, we are able to have a precise understanding of the user and context of use. During pattern composition, specific steps are followed which add structure to the design activity. This includes the use of a

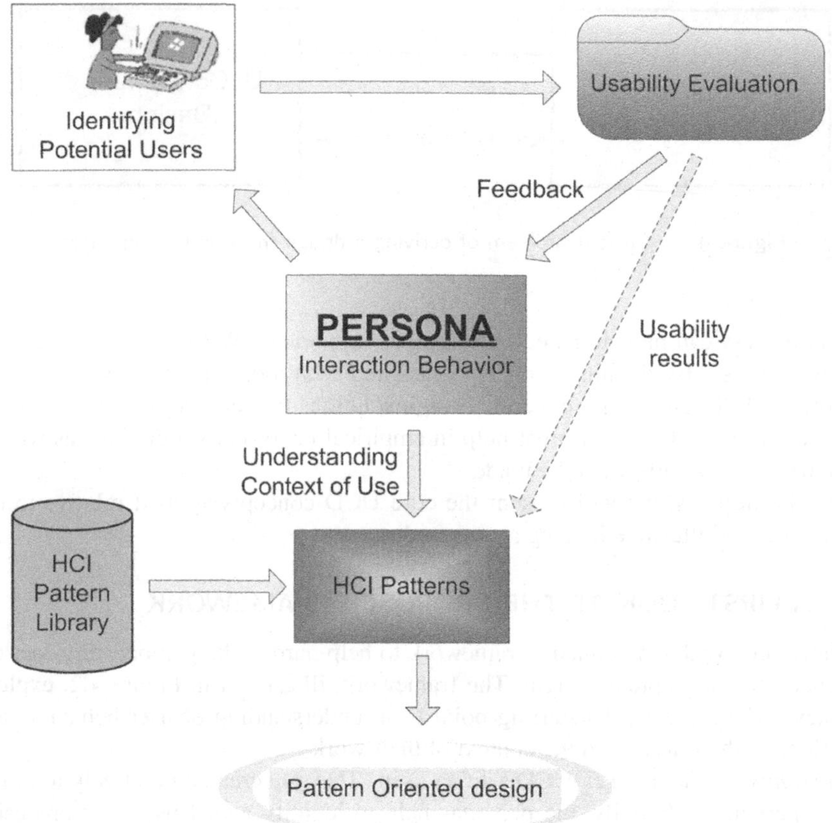

Figure 4.2 The proposed framework

pattern-oriented design model which addresses the logical organization of the entire application, as well as the use of pattern relationships. The latter exploits the generative nature of patterns, resulting in a network of patterns which can be combined in a design. As an example, certain patterns are subordinate to others, meaning that they can be composed within their super-ordinate pattern. Further details will be discussed later in this chapter.

4.3 MODELING USER EXPERIENCES WITH PERSONAS

Understanding user experiences is the starting crucial step in user-centered design. Several techniques have been proposed within the HCI community to understand users and to model their needs. This includes user profiles, stereotypes, and personas. In our UCD-based framework, we extend the concept of personas (Cooper, 1999) to model user experiences.

Alan Cooper, the father of Visual Basic, first proposed the use of personas in software design. His original work in 1999 brought the concept of personas from marketing to UCD; so as to redirect the focus of the development process towards end-users and their needs. His work emphasizes personas as being fictitious characters, based on composite archetypes, and encapsulating "behavioral data" gathered from ethnography and empirical analysis of actual users. Archetypes have been used in marketing research both as an alternative and as an extension of traditional market segmentation and user profiling. Instead of modeling only "average" users, personas also take into account boundary cases. The idea used is that all consumers are a mixture of certain types of users.

Each persona should have a name, an occupation, and personal characteristics such as likes, dislikes, needs, and desires. In addition, each persona should outline specific goals related to the application or project in question. These goals can be personal (e.g., having fun), work-related (e.g., hiring staff), or practical (e.g., avoiding meetings) (Tahir, 1997). Personas are intended to help developers better understand both the users and context of use for a planned tool or interactive system. Cooper (1999) argues that designing for any one external person is better than trying to design vaguely for everyone. He also believes that for each project, a different set of personas should be constructed. This is because each project targets different users in different contexts of use. An example of the kind of information contained in personas is illustrated in Table 14.1.

According to (Cooper, 1999), persona's imaginary, though realistic, representation of users' goals and skills is beneficial to designers, programmers, and managers at ending "feature debates." Personas eliminate the construct of "the user" and guide functional specifications. On the other hand, there are some pitfalls to avoid when using personas as an interaction design tool. The major risk, reported by both Pruit and Grudin (2003) and Mikkelson and Lee (2000) is the challenge to get the right persona or set of personas without stereotyping. Persona creation implies choices and biases that could overgeneralize or exclude users. Cooper would reply to this argument saying that it is better to design for any one person instead of ineffectively designing for the "masses." Figure 4.3, adapted from Whitney Queensberry's company website (Cognetics, 2005), illustrates an example of a persona.

Similar to Pruitt and Grudin (2003), we believe that personas should be based on empirical evidence and studies. Their approach encourages a more "global" use of personas. This includes attempts to integrate personas in the software development process by establishing relationships with other data sets through the use of artifacts such as feature–persona matrices, foundation documents, and task descriptions. A focus on ongoing qualitative and quantitative analysis is a central theme of their work. In our framework, we use empirical evidence to create our personas and extend their descriptions to include interaction details and scenarios. This will be illustrated in our case study.

4.4 CREATING A CONCEPTUAL DESIGN USING PATTERNS

A conceptual design is an early design of the system that abstracts away from presentation details. In this section, we will discuss how UI design patterns can be used as design "blocks" to build a conceptual design. To elaborate, UI design patterns have been introduced as a medium to capture, disseminate and reuse proven design knowl-

Table 4.1 Persona elements

Persona Elements	Description
Identity	Include a first and last name, age and other demographic information.
Status	Whether the user is a primary, secondary, tertiary, or anti-user of the application. Typically, only primary and in some cases, secondary users are included.
Goals	Besides goals related to the application, it includes personal and professional goals as well.
Knowledge and Experience	Knowledge and experience including education, training, and specialized skills. This should not be limited only to the application.
Tasks	Frequency, importance, and duration of most important tasks related to the application.
Relationships	Include information about user associates, since this could give insight on other stakeholders.
Psychological profile and Needs	Include information about cognitive and learning styles, as well as needs such as guidance and validation of decisions.
Attitude and Motivation	Include information about the user's attitude to information technology and level of motivation to use the system.
Expectations	Information about how the user perceives the system works, and how the user organizes information related to his/her task, domain, or job.
Disabilities	Any disabilities, such as color blindness, related to mobility, eyesight (wears contacts), etc.
Photograph	Include a photograph that fits with the persona's identity.

edge, and to facilitate the design of more usable systems. As a result, they are a key artifact for user-centered design, with interesting ramifications for designing across a variety of contexts. Patterns are toolkit-independent, presented in a specific format with defined attributes, and applicable at different levels of abstraction. These levels include the user-task model, navigation model, or the concrete presentation of the user interface (UI). They are a great source of interest not necessarily because they provide novel ideas to the software designer community, but because of the way that they package already-available design knowledge. This way of presenting information to designers promotes reusability of best design practices, and avoids reinventing the wheel each time we develop a design.

Based on the original work of Christopher Alexander (1979), some HCI practitioners have proposed to connect individual patterns to create pattern languages. Examples are patterns for Web page layout design (Welie, 2003), for navigation in large

Favorite Quote:	"A designer knows he has achieved perfection not when there is nothing left to add, but when there is nothing left to take away,"– St-Exupery
Company:	Cognetics Corporation
Name:	Linda
Title:	Interaction Designer
Age:	mid-30's
Membership:	SIGCHI, UPA and a local usability discussion group
Favorite Tool:	The whiteboard—or anything that lets me iterate the design quickly.
Education:	M.S. in HCI
Specialties:	Web, Intranet, Database Searching
Duties:	Interview Users, Define Requirements, Produce Visual Designs, Produce Specifications, Coordinate Usability Testing, and Produce UI Style Guide
Summary:	After initially graduating with a Computer Science degree, Linda spent several years as a Web administrator and programmer for two software companies. She then returned to school to complete an HCI degree and joined Cognetics upon completion of her degree. With the vision in place, she works with users to analyze their needs and requirements. She uses that data to produce a draft of a UI and manages an iterative design process, combining expert review with usability testing. She starts the design process in Visio, but she prefers to construct low-fidelity HTML prototypes as soon as possible for both review and testing. Once the design is stable, Linda typically delivers annotated specs for the full interface and the user interface style guide used to construct the prototype.
Constraints:	Linda is one of the few women who are red-green colorblind. Access to users for user analysis is not always feasible, so Linda must sometimes gather user data in more creative ways (tech support logs, surveys, remote interviews, etc.).

Figure 4.3 Example of persona (Cognetics, 2005)

information architectures (Engelberg and Seffah, 2002), as well as for visualizing and presenting information (Wilkins, 2003). Different pattern collections have been published including *The Design of Sites* (Duyne et alt., 2002) and *Designing Interfaces* (Tidwell, 2005). In addition, specific languages such as emphUser Interface Design Patterns (Laakso, 1993) and the *UPADE Web Language* (Javahery and Seffah, 2002) have been proposed.

However, to support pattern use as part of the design process, specific frameworks or methods are needed. To this end, Thomas Erickson (Erickson, 2000) proposed using pattern languages as a lingua franca for the design of interactive systems, with

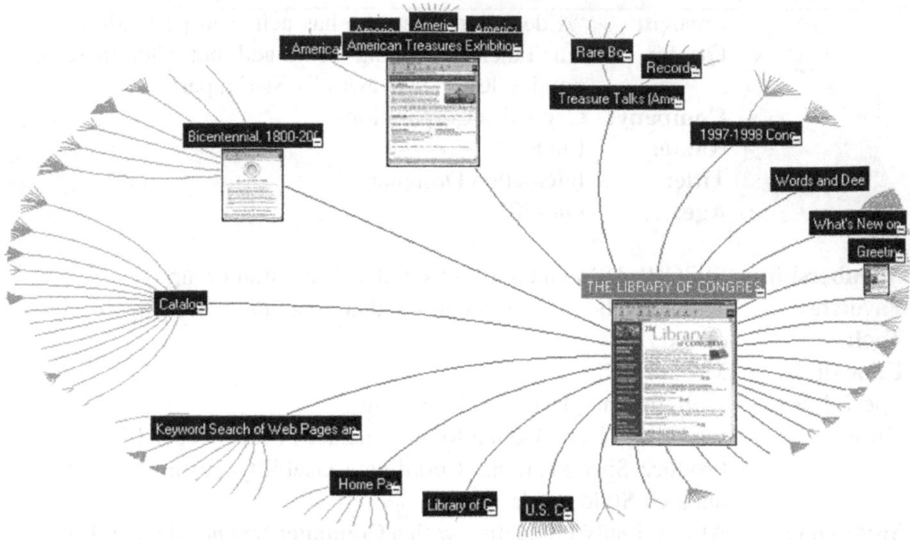

Figure 4.4 A Site Map page implemented using Tree Hyperbolic, a sophisticated visualization pattern

the purpose of disseminating the HCI body of knowledge. Such an approach assumes that several types of relationships exist between patterns. Pattern-Supported Approach (PSA) (Lafrenière and Granlund, 1999) links patterns with the purpose of supporting early system definition and the derivation of a conceptual design. In this direction, the set of design patterns that forms a language are also linked to the task model. As a consequence, during system definition and task analysis, appropriate design patterns are chosen for the design phase.

However, none of the above languages, frameworks or methods effectively leverages relationships *between* patterns. Relationships between patterns are key notions in the understanding of patterns and their use. In Taleb et al. (2006), we have defined five types of relationships between Web patterns. Pattern-Oriented Design (POD) (Javahery and Seffah, 2002) aims to exploit explicitly these relationships, as well as associate patterns and their languages to the design process. POD consists of understanding when a pattern is applicable during the design process, how it can be used, as well as how and why it can or cannot be combined with other related patterns.

Moreover, to be effective in a user-centered design setting, patterns need to be better associated with user experiences. Our framework tackles this problem by linking personas with patterns, allowing us to narrow the gap between user experiences and conceptual design. Patterns are chosen based on persona specifications, and then combined to create a pattern-oriented design. In essence, pattern-based designs are considered as design blocks that apply in particular situations, based on a description of the user experiences. Figures 4.4 and 4.5 portray examples of pattern-oriented designs.

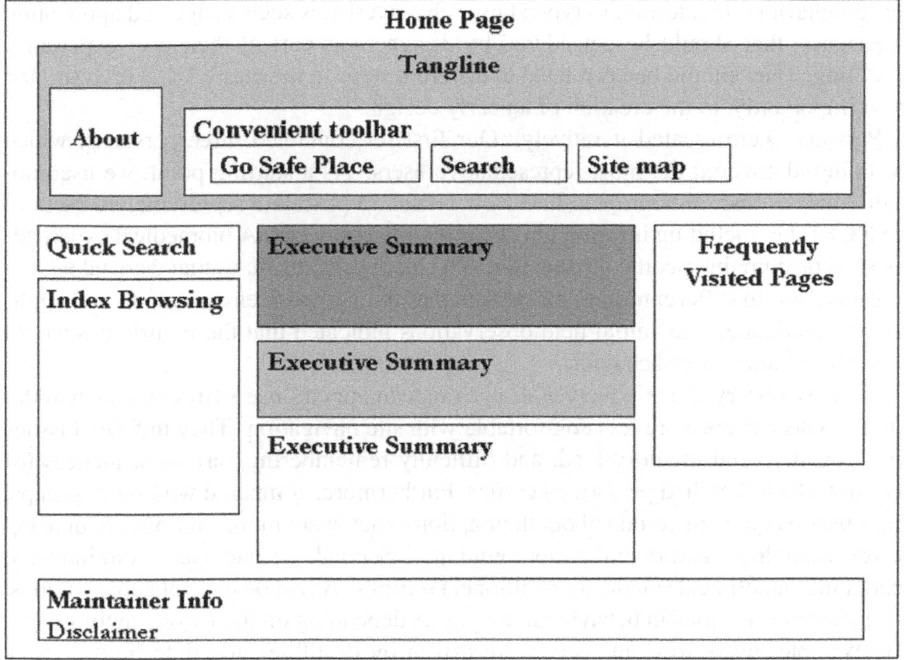

Figure 4.5 A Home Page Design combining several patterns

4.5 AN ILLUSTRATIVE CASE STUDY

We applied the proposed framework to a design project with a popular Web application, aimed at a specific user community—the National Center for Biotechnology Information (NCBI) site (NCBI, 2005). The goals of the study were to (1) evaluate whether the framework results in a more usable system, (2) evaluate the validity of correlating personas and patterns for designers, and (3) understand the limitations of the framework. It would lead us to conclude that we could either develop a more refined process leading from personas to patterns, or that our framework needs to be reworked.

The NCBI site is a well-established Bioinformatics website, with a large number of users and a vast amount of information. Some of the NCBI's specific aims include the creation of automated systems for storing and analyzing biological information, the facilitation of user access to databases and software, and the coordination of efforts to gather biotechnology information worldwide (Attwood and Parry-Smith, 1999). High user access and a great deal of content can often cause usability problems. Furthermore, the site acts as an information portal which aims to be a unique access point to diverse and specialized bioinformatics tools. Users accessing and interacting with the site and its tools have different behaviors ranging from simple information gathering, such as article searching, to more advanced molecular biology tool usage, such as sequence alignment and molecular visualization tools. It is these interaction and task-based behaviors, in addition to typical user characteristics such as age and application experience, that should be considered by designers as part of their user experience modeling. They should be correlated to different steps in the entire UCD process, and most importantly, to the creation of an early design.

Personas were created iteratively. Our first set contained three personas, which we believed covered the most representative users. As a starting point, we used domain analysis and ethnographic interview results to postulate representative users of the NCBI site, including information about their experiences. A biomedical expert advised us on domain-specific information. The main user attributes that were taken into consideration in differentiating our personas were age, work environment, and application experience. Our initial field observations indicated that these attributes would strongly influence user behavior.

First, we observed a relatively wide age range in our end-users (from young to older adults). Older users were less comfortable with site navigation. They indicated issues with cognitive and memory load, and difficulty remembering various sequences (of actions) which they had performed earlier. Furthermore, compared with other groups, older users seemed uncertain about their actions; they were more cautious about using newer technology, and required more guidance. Second, we had users from industry, academic, and clinical (medical practitioner) settings. Based on our field observations, we expected variations in behavior among users depending on their work environment. For example, users from industry were driven by deadlines and time limits. They demonstrated less patience, and were looking for task efficiency and more control over the system. Thirdly, application experience seemed to influence both the needs and satisfaction levels with the website. Basic users, who had just started to use the site within the past year, were dissatisfied. They demonstrated a sense of confusion about site structure and navigation, expressed information overload, and indicated that they needed more support. Intermediate users were more satisfied, but indicated that some of the tools they needed could "work better." Expert users were also quite satisfied, but indicated that the website was slow at times and they wanted to perform their tasks in a more efficient manner.

As highlighted previously, if constructed effectively, a persona should be sufficiently informative and engaging so that it redirects the focus of the development process towards end-users and their needs. However, constructing such an effective persona is not easy. Therefore, as a means to increase their effectiveness, a persona should be supported by user and empirical data (Pruitt and Grudin, 2003). To enhance and render our personas more informative, we decided to gather more specific user and behavioral information from usability evaluations with end-users and UI experts.

We had 39 participants in our study: 16 users for creating personas and predesign evaluation, and 23 users for post-design evaluation. Predesign evaluation consisted of psychometric and heuristic techniques to construct personas and identify usability issues with the current design. We then used these personas, as well as accrued usability results, to construct a UI design based on patterns. Post-design evaluation consisted of a comparative study between the new and current designs. This was to determine whether our framework added value to the design process, and helped with the overall usability of the application.

4.5.1 *Psychometric Evaluation to Quantify User Experiences*

Psychometric evaluation enables us to quantify user experiences with certain properties of an application or site. In our study, we dedicated part of the questionnaire with our NCBI users to collect this information; the other part was used to gather user characteristics such as demographic details. Similar to McKenzie (2000), heuristics were used to describe different facets or properties of the site, although the questionnaire was used for psychometric-based evaluation. In other words, each set of questions was correlated with a particular heuristic. Using a list of nine heuristics adapted from Nielsen (1994) and Nielsen et al. (2001), we were able to cover the most important aspects of usability by asking specific questions. For example, if we are to take the first heuristic, Visibility and Navigation, the following tailored questions were asked to assess user experiences with relation to the visibility and navigation of the site:

- Do you find it easy to navigate on the NCBI website, especially when performing a new task?
- Is it visually clear what is a link or a button?
- Do you receive feedback and requested information promptly, such as when you perform a BLAST search?
- Is it easy to get lost when looking for information?

When we analyzed the results of the administered questionnaire, results differed for users with varying application experience. Specifically, with relation to a number of properties of the site: (1) Visibility and Navigation, (2) Consistency and Standards, and (3) Help; two groups emerged (we have called them Novice and Expert users). The results can be found in Figure 4.6. The only property of the site that both user groups seemed to be satisfied with was Language and Communication. Other attributes which we had initially thought to also affect user experiences with the site did not demonstrate any significant differences.

4.5.2 *Heuristic Evaluation*

We carried out a second type of test with UI experts, who were asked to directly comment on a set of accepted principles, similar to the heuristics described above. However, in contrast to the psychometric evaluation, heuristic evaluation is an inspection method where UI experts evaluate a program's user interface against the heuristics. Nielsen introduced heuristic evaluation as a relatively low-cost method for identifying usability problems in an existing program (Nielsen, 1994). To reduce testing costs, Nielsen came up with a list of 10 heuristics that cover what he considered the most important aspects of usability.

We used a small number of UI experts (three) for heuristic evaluation. The number was small due to resource limitations of this project rather than to go with Nielsen's

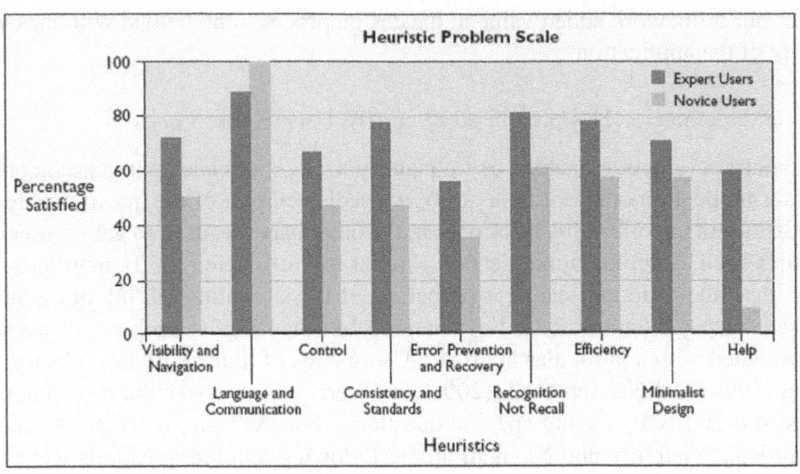

Figure 4.6 Questionnaire results of Novice and Expert users

claim that "3 to 5" evaluators is sufficient (Nielsen, 2001). One evaluator was a senior usability expert, whereas the other two were junior usability experts, with at least 2 years of experience in the field. The UI experts were asked to comment on the NCBI site with relation to nine heuristics (we found two to be redundant for our purposes, and therefore combined them), as well as to give comments and suggestions for improvement of navigation structure, home page, site map, and search tools. In addition, they were given space to write any other comments they deemed relevant that were not covered in the heuristics or specific items asked. A concise version of results is as follows: all heuristics, except for Language and Communication, were found to be problematic. Major problems found by UI experts were: (1) easy to get lost because path or current position is unclear, (2) difficult to get out of undesired or error states, (3) inconsistency amongst sites, such as with different menu structures, (4) information overload, (5) not enough help and guidance for novice users, (6) lack of efficient options for expert users, such as shortcuts. These results were similar to our earlier ethnographic interviews with users.

In addition, UI experts were asked to comment on the following specific items of the site: (a) navigation structure, (b) home page, (c) site map, and (d) search tools. The navigation structure was found to be big and fairly complex, so it is easy for users to lose their orientation on the site. The home page was found to be overloaded with links, low in visibility, and no guidance for first time users. 2 out of 3 UI experts suggested that it might be interesting to consider a different home page for different users, based on their experience with the site (i.e., Novice vs. Expert users). In practice, a site map is designed to give users who know what they are looking for, fast access to a certain subsite; and for new users, additional help in locating a page or topic. The site map for the NCBI site was found to be complicated and difficult to use for either of these groups of users. Search tools on the NCBI site were found to be relevant for more experienced users, but more explanation and control should be given to newer users.

4.5.3 Pattern Selection and Composition

We started off with three personas for NCBI site users. However, after refining the personas based on empirical results from our predesign evaluation, two predominant personas emerged. To stimulate the imagination of the designers, we defined them based primarily on application experience with the NCBI site and associated tools: (1) the Novice tool user, with less than 1 year experience, and (2) the Expert tool user, with more than 1 year experience. Furthermore, based on the different empirical tests described, our personas were enhanced with information about user behavior and experiences. Each persona was characterized by (a) personal characteristics, (b) computer and bioinformatics skills, (c) interaction behavior with the site, including tasks performed, and (d) scenario descriptions.

By using this newly gathered information, we applied pattern-oriented design to close the gap between actual user experiences and the features offered by such complex applications. We associated patterns with each type of desired task and user behavior, and combined them to design a more usable UI. The patterns used were from Web pattern languages—UPADE (Javahery and Seffah, 2002) and Welie's collection (Welie, 2003). As illustrated in Table 4.2, we selected applicable patterns based on information contained within our personas.

After pattern selection, we combined patterns into a comprehensive design. Pattern-oriented design may be used to create Web applications that customize the solution of common problems for different personas. Alternatively, they can guide designers in finding compromise solutions based on design trade-offs. One ideal design strategy in this case would be the implementation of separate home pages for novice and expert users. The two different home pages would actually be the result of using different types of patterns for each group of users. Although this strategy may be ideal for the user community, our context information revealed that its practicality and maintenance would be limited for such a large website, with a site architecture that is so multifaceted. It therefore made more sense to settle for a compromise, making the site usable for both types of users.

Taking into account earlier evaluation results, the two personas and the original NCBI site, one example of a design decision is as follows:

> The left navigation menu on the home page has important site links, however a textual description of the link is provided under each name; this is only useful for novice users who don't know what kind of information they can find from the links. This convenience for the novice user is a hindrance for an expert user as it contributes to more scrolling.

A solution would be implementation as rollovers (on-fly description pattern) to help new users. Using the selected patterns, we built a new design for a subset of the NCBI site—this included the portal home page, the main navigation elements, the site map, search tool, and some content pages. Selected pattern compositions are illustrated in Figure 4.7 (as a pattern skeleton) and in Figure 4.8 (the prototype).

4.5.4 Testing the Prototype

After applying the Persona to Pattern framework to the NCBI site, the resulting conceptual designs were used as a blueprint to build a test prototype. We evaluated the prototype in terms of usability, using principles of software usability measurement

Table 4.2 Pattern Selection based on persona

Persona 1		**Persona 2**	
Donna Smith (The Novice User) 24 years old; Master's student in Biochemistry; works daily in a lab Needs: Guidance, Simple Navigation		Xin Li (The Expert User) 37 years old; Molecular Biologist; researcher in a pharmaceutical company Needs: Control, Task Efficiency	
Attribute/behavior	**Patterns**	**Attribute/behavior**	**Patterns**
She recently started doing bioinformatics-based research, and has only been accessing the NCBI site for 6 months	Novice user patterns	He has been accessing the NCBI site for 2 years now, and is very familiar with tools related to his research	Expert user patterns
She is unfamiliar with all the menu options and functions and often needs guidance	On-Fly Description	English is his second language, and he is not always comfortable with spelling	Index Browsing Alphabetical Sitemap
She is still learning about the NCBI site, and wants general information about the site	Executive Summary	He uses the NCBI site for specific tasks, such as secondary structure prediction and wants to save results	Shortcut MySpace (customized)
She uses the site mainly for literature and article searches, information-gathering, and has only started to do sequence alignment searches	Index Browsing Simple Search	Likes to limit his searches to specific species and does not have patience to go through a long list of possibilities	Advanced Search
She gets lost looking for information after advancing more than 3 layers, and needs to go back to a safe place	Convenient Toolbar Dynamic Path	Likes to know about recent discoveries and advances in the field	Teaser Menu Executive Summary

based on ISO standards, and as indicated in (Msheik et al., 2004). We conducted a comparative study with the current NCBI site, which according to (NCBI, 2005), has been designed following "usability and user-friendly design guidelines."

Our participants this time included 23 users; 19 users who fit our novice persona and 4 users who fit our expert persona. The set of participants were selected initially based on a phone interview to assess whether they fit our study. Furthermore, these 23 users were different from the original set of users who participated in our predesign heuristic and psychometric evaluations. We primarily differentiated based on application experience, where novice users had limited or basic experience, and expert users had intermediate or advanced experience.

For novice users, we used a *between-subjects* (randomized) design, where each participant was assigned to a different condition (Dix et al., 1993): (1) the prototype built using our framework and (2) the current site. On one hand, by using a between-subjects protocol, we were able to control any learning effects which would have occurred if each user tested both conditions. On the other hand, this type of protocol required a greater number of participants and a careful matching of participants between the two conditions; the reason being that individual differences between users can bias the results.

Task duration, failure rates, and satisfaction ratings were collected and analyzed as usability indicators. Users were given four common tasks to perform on the website, with the purpose of calculating task duration and failure rates. A questionnaire was employed to rank their satisfaction. We used ANOVA (Analysis of Variance) tests to assess if the mean values were significantly different between the two conditions. We also computed effect size, eta-squared (η^2), which is a measure (of the magnitude)

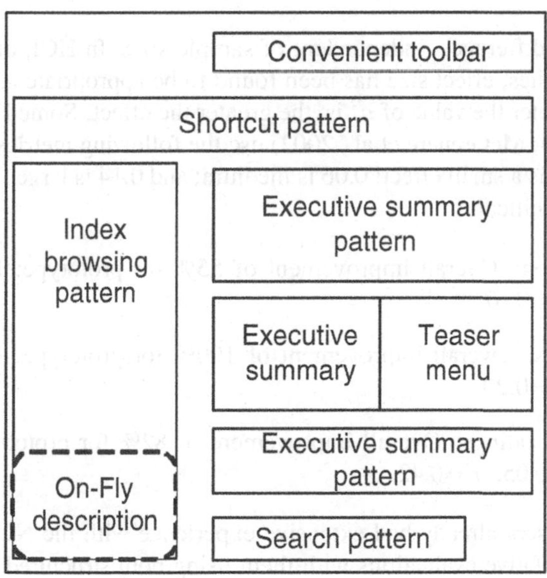

Figure 4.7 Pattern Skeleton of NCBI home page

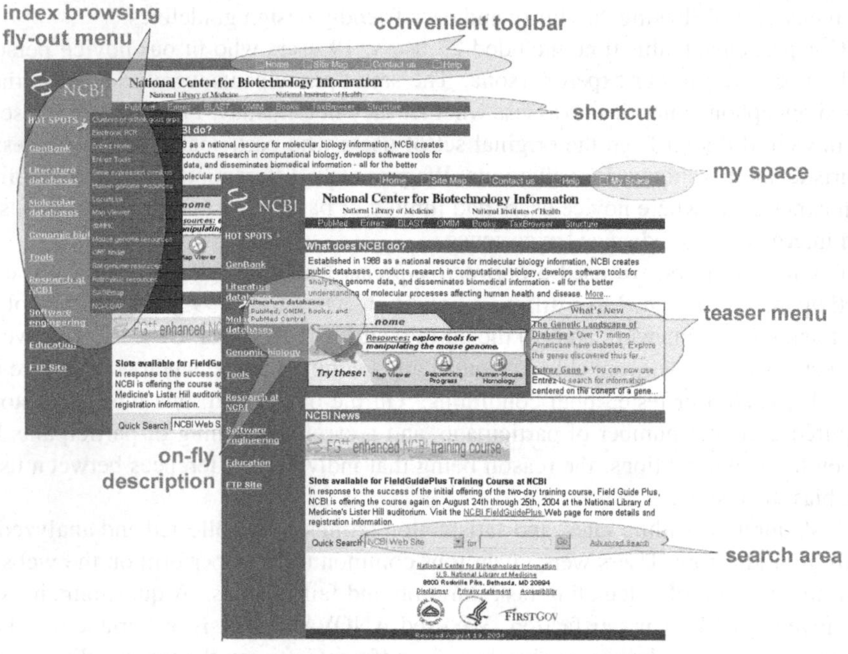

Figure 4.8 Pattern-Oriented Design of NCBI home page

of the effect of a difference, independent of sample size. In HCI, due to commonly small sizes of studies, effect size has been found to be appropriate (Landauer, 1997). In general the greater the value of η^2 is, the greater the effect. Some HCI practitioners (McGrenere, 2004; McGrenere et al., 2002) use the following metrics for interpreting eta-squared: 0.01 is a small effect; 0.06 is medium; and 0.14 is large. The results were all statistically significant:

- Task duration: Overall improvement of 55% for prototype; F (1, 14) = 6.4, $p<0.05$, $\eta^2=0.67$
- Failure rates: Overall improvement of 100% for prototype; F (1, 16) = 6.4, $p<0.05$, $\eta^2=0.29$
- Satisfaction ratings: Overall improvement of 82% for prototype; F (1, 16) = 11.53, $p < 0.05$, $\eta^2=0.42$

Since expert users already had extensive experience with the NCBI site, we performed only qualitative evaluations with them using both structured and open-ended interviews. They were given time to explore both the prototype and current site, and were asked a set of questions based on their experience. They were asked to give first impressions about both sites (likes/dislikes and any noticeable differences), as well as answer specific questions about individual Web pages (such as the portal home page), the overall site, and ease of navigation. Results varied in response. Two out of four users preferred the prototype, and noted that it was more "simplistic" and "lightweight." Other comments included that the prototype introduced less information overload and increased clarity. They also found it easier in terms of navigation, although they commented that they would need to get used to the new design. The other two users did not have an overall preference, but preferred different aspects of the two designs. Overall, the qualitative results with experts were what we expected. Expert users have been using the site for an extended amount of time; they are used to specific visual representations, habituated in performing tasks in a certain manner, and are comfortable with the current navigation path.

4.5.5 Lessons Learned

The results from the NCBI study were encouraging, and they led us to conclude that a more concrete process leading from personas to patterns was substantiated.

First, we found that applying the framework facilitated our design activities, allowed us to incorporate sound UCD principles into our design, and afforded guidance to an often ad-hoc process. The focus of the design activity was directed to the users early on. Since, personas are a relatively lightweight user model, we did not require a user or cognitive modeling specialist for their creation. By developing personas iteratively using empirical evidence, we were able to determine more precise interaction behavior and usability problems with the application; these points were essential in selecting HCI patterns. In this vein, the framework follows the reuse paradigm through the use of these patterns, enabling us to make design decisions based on best practices. Notably, in current practice, there exists no commonly agreed upon UI design process that employs patterns and their languages as first class tools. It was our intention to further develop the framework to overcome this problem.

Second, after applying the *Persona to Pattern* framework to the NCBI site, we carried out comparative usability studies with the current site and our prototype. We wanted to evaluate if the framework resulted in more usable systems. The results were positive for both quantitative and qualitative measures. In particular, our prototype indicated a statistically significant decrease in task duration and an increase in satisfaction with novice users. For total task time, we noted an overall improvement of more than 55%. Moreover, when we considered average satisfaction ratings of both designs, we found that users were almost two times more satisfied with our prototype as compared to the original design. As expected, our qualitative results with expert users were also positive but more mixed, since they have extensive experience with the current site.

Thirdly, there were some limitations we needed to address. The framework was a first step in using the techniques of personas and patterns together. We noted that links made between user experiences and design solutions were based on narrative and qualitative data, assessed manually where the "best" pattern within a specific context was selected. Any further development of our framework should include identifiable and discrete steps, and not be subject to extensive interpretation by the designer.

This would require some formalization of the information contained in both personas and patterns. We also realized early on that we would refer back to the personas for additional information both during the selection of appropriate patterns, and for pattern-oriented design. At times, the amount of additional information contained within personas was lacking. Therefore, an enhancement of persona descriptions with interaction behaviors, scenarios, and goals is an added value in guiding designers during design decisions.

4.6 A DETAILED DESCRIPTION OF UX-PROCESS

Based on the initial knowledge extracted from the NCBI study and refined by information collected from focus groups and interviews, we constructed a process following a natural flow as currently applied by design experts. The process is called UX-P, or User Experiences to Patterns. In this section, we will describe each phase of the process, its inputs, outputs, and artifacts produced. Figure 4.9 illustrates the process diagram, by depicting the flow of activities involved. The activities, which correspond also to the process steps, are grouped into three distinct phases: Persona Creation, Pattern Selection, and Pattern Composition. Persona Creation takes user data as input and is expected to produce a set of representative personas. Pattern Selection takes the personas and a pattern library as input, and produces an ordered set (based on importance and relevancy) of candidate patterns for design. Based on these candidate patterns, the Pattern Composition phase results in a conceptual design. It is important to note that context information serves as input during all phases of the design.

4.6.1 Persona Creation

Persona Creation consists of three steps and a decision point: clustering users, verifying that the clusters fit the context, modifying clustering parameters if needed and refining personas. In essence, clustering consists of grouping users based on their similarities and by analyzing a set of parameters. Once the users are grouped, it is important to ensure that the results produced fit the context of the current design. If the verification proves the clustering to be inadequate, the designer must modify the parameters used and repeat the clustering. In fact, clustering should be repeated as many times as required until the results are satisfactory. Once clusters are appropriate, each resulting cluster can be represented by a skeleton persona. Finally, these skeleton personas can be refined by completing the description based on real data from representative users.

Overall, the clustering step consists of grouping users based on their commonalities. Therefore, this step is a good candidate for automation allowing user involvement. In fact, k-means clustering or other statistical analysis techniques, when provided grouping parameters and a set of data, are capable of performing this task. Thus, the major difficulty is in presenting data in computer-readable format and producing flexible results.

The proposed solution is to describe a user by a set of variables grouped into categories. In order to assist the specialist, a finite amount of the categories and variables must be defined. Moreover, each variable must have a finite amount of values. There-

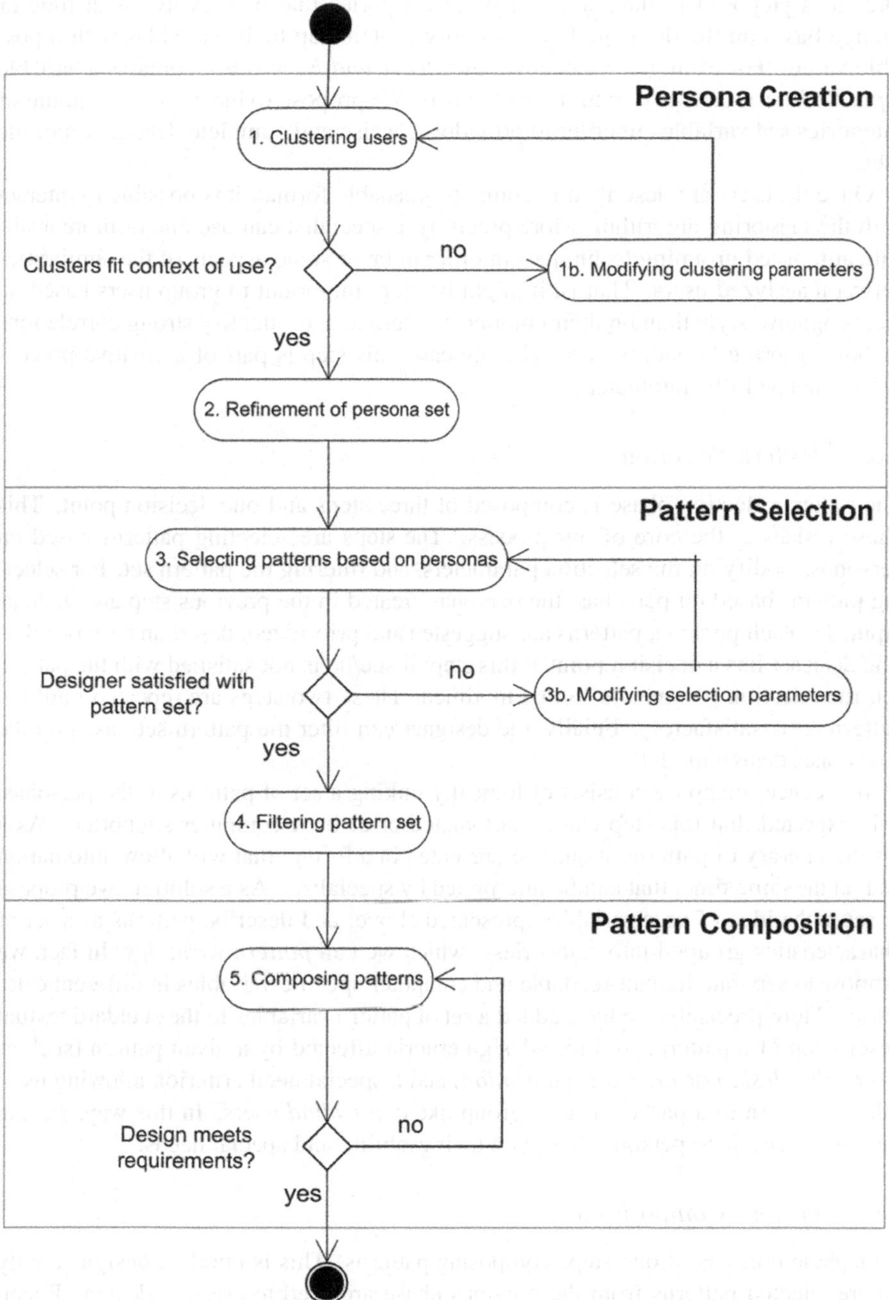

Figure 4.9 The UX-P Design Process

fore, it is proposed to have a set of basic categories that may evolve with time or change based on the domain. Each category contains up to 10 variables with 5 possible values. For example, a category *Knowledge and Experience* contains a variable *Input Skills* that can vary from none to expert. We propose to have a small amount of categories and variables in order to provide a concise and complete description of the user.

Once the users are described in computer-readable format, it is possible to interact with the clustering algorithm. More precisely, a specialist can use one or more available automated grouping techniques in order to favor some aspects of the similarities between analyzed users. That is, it might be more important to group users based on their cognitive style than on their computer experience, or identify strong correlations without ignoring boundary cases. In any case, this step is part of a creative process and cannot be fully automated.

4.6.2 Pattern Selection

The pattern selection phase is composed of three steps and one decision point. This phase resides at the core of our process. The steps are selecting patterns based on personas, modifying the selection parameters, and filtering the pattern set. For selecting patterns based on personas, the personas created in the previous step are taken as input. For each persona, patterns are suggested and prioritized, based on a set of rules. The designer has a decision point at this step; if she/he is not satisfied with the pattern set, the selection parameters can be modified. These two steps are repeated until the pattern set is satisfactory. Finally, the designer can filter the pattern set based on the envisioned design model.

In essence, mapping consists of logically linking a set of patterns to the personas. It is expected that this step can be automated or at least computer supported. As a result, a library of patterns should be presented in a format that will allow automation and, at the same time, that can be interpreted by specialists. As a solution, we propose to reuse the idea of user variables, presented above, and describe patterns as a set of characteristics grouped into categories—which we call *pattern variables*. In fact, we propose to separate human-readable and computer specific variables in different categories. More precisely, we have added a set of pattern variables to the standard textual description of a pattern: usability-design criteria affected by a given pattern (such as *minimalist design* or *logical organization*) and a special need criterion allowing us to relate a pattern to a particular user group like *color blind* users. In this way, we can link these criteria to personas based on their usability and special needs.

4.6.3 Pattern Composition

This phase consists of one step: composing patterns. This is purely a design activity where selected patterns from the previous phase are used to create a design. Recall that a valuable advantage of patterns and their associated languages is their generative nature, meaning that they can essentially be combined together as building blocks. However, design is an activity dependent on each designer's creativity, background, and expertise. Our goal is to simply provide some structure to the design activity,

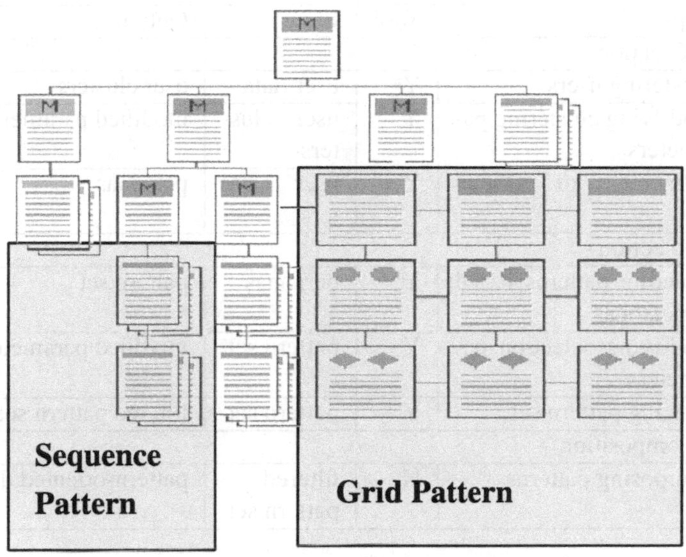

Figure 4.10 Website structure using three basic information patterns

by presenting designers with: (1) a Pattern-Oriented Design (POD) model, and (2) a means to exploit pattern relationships. Artifacts such as task and interaction models may be used during this step, although they are external to our process. The designer iterates through various compositions until a satisfactory pattern-oriented design is attained.

First, designers should follow a POD model. We have published literature on this model previously (Javahery et al., 2006). POD defines the overall design composition of a particular type of application, including a breakdown of this composition into different UI facets. The model acts as a guide for designers in making stepwise design decisions. To illustrate, for website design, we have defined four steps that designers should follow: (1) defining the architecture of the site with architectural patterns, where an example is illustrated in Figure 4.10, (2) establishing the overall structure of each page with page manager patterns, (3) identifying content-related elements for each page with information container patterns, and (4) organizing the interaction with navigation support patterns. Landay and Myers (2001) and Welie (2003) also propose to organize their Web pattern languages according to both the design process and UI structuring elements (such as *navigation*, *page layout* and *basic dialog style*).

Second, designers should exploit relationships between patterns. We have described five types of relationships between the UPADE patterns, published in (Taleb et al., 2006): Superordinate, subordinate, similar, competitor, and neighboring. The same relationships can easily be applied to other pattern libraries. This multicriterion classification is based on the original set of relationships used to classify the patterns

Table 4.3 UX-P Process steps and tool support

No.	Steps	Tool	Input	Output
Persona Creation				
1	Clustering users	Y*	user data	user clusters
1b	Modifying clustering parameters	Y	user clusters	modified parameters
2	Refinement of persona set	Y	user clusters	personas
Pattern Selection				
3	Selecting patterns based on personas	Y*	personas	pattern set
3b	Modifying selection parameters	Y	pattern set	modified parameters
4	Filtering pattern set	Y	pattern set	filtered pattern set
Pattern Composition				
5	Composing patterns	N	filtered pattern set	pattern-oriented design

* – automated.

proposed by (Gamma et al, 1995). The relationships are used to compose a UI design, allowing designers to make suppositions such as:

> For some problem P, if we apply Pattern X, then Patterns Y and Z apply as subordinates, but pattern S cannot apply since it is a competitor.

4.7 FURTHER INVESTIGATION: THE P2P MAPPER TOOL

As an attempt to better assist designers in using our process, we developed a supporting tool called the Persona to Pattern (P2P) Mapper. The proposed process involves a set of repetitive, tedious, and time-consuming tasks. In addition, some of the steps and artifacts described in the process have been constructed in a format which allows for automation. The general steps comprising our process are illustrated in Table 4.3. The persona creation and pattern selection phases were amenable for partial automation. In particular, we automated the following steps: clustering users (step 1) and selecting patterns based on personas (step 3). Moreover, we provided features for users to carry out the remainder of the persona creation and pattern selection phases.

The P2P Mapper provides the designer with three major features: (1) the data entry system, (2) the clustering utility, and (3) the pattern selection utility. The data entry system provides the user with an interface to enter, view, and modify user information. In particular, the designer provides a set of discrete user variables; optionally he/she may also include narrative text illustrating popular user scenarios and other textual descriptions.

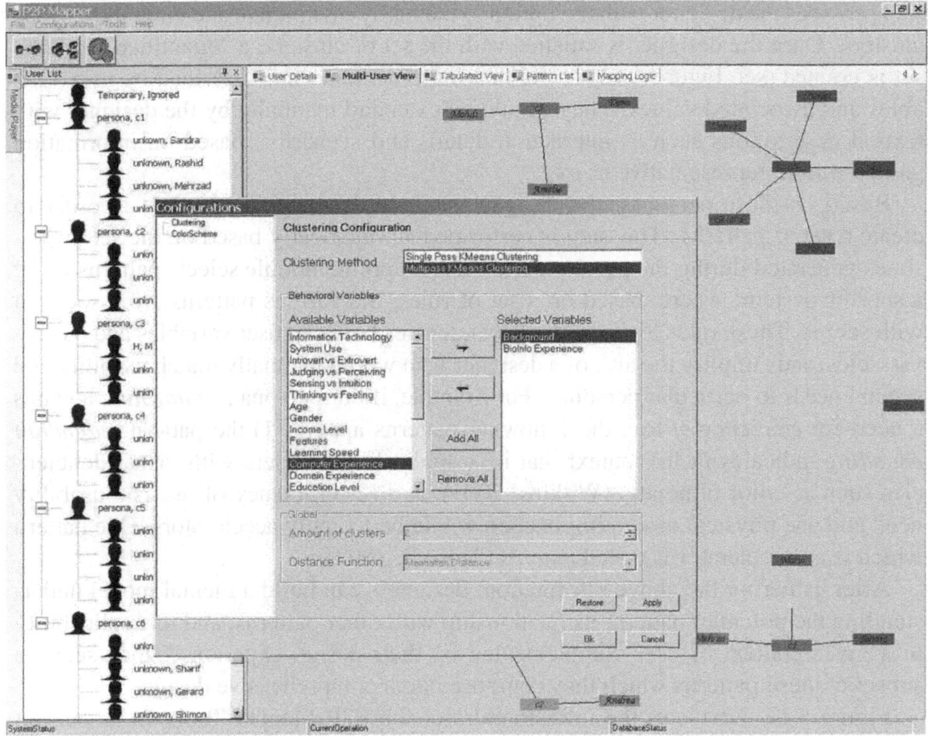

Figure 4.11 Clustering in P2P Mapper

Once the data is entered, the tool provides the designer with automatic and interactive clustering capabilities (see Figure 4.11) to derive quantified persona specifications. Clustering is performed based on the discrete user variables provided during the data entry phase. The tool provides the user with the choice between two clustering techniques, namely, k-means clustering and interactive clustering. The former technique is performed fully automatically but requires, apriori, an indication of the desired number of clusters. The latter technique is performed in an interactive manner, where the designer selects a subset of the user variables, on which the clustering should be based. The tool then returns a number of clusters, which can be iteratively refined and reduced by further constraining the allowed range of values of the selected user variables.

Automatic clustering is more suitable for novice designers as it can be used as a black box technique where the required designer intervention is minimal. It leaves, however, the designer with very little control to influence the outcome of the clusters. Iterative clustering is an interactive clustering method, which mimics the designer's strategy of manually building personas. Hence it provides the user with more influence on the outcome but requires advanced knowledge of the user variables and the domain on which the clustering will be based. If none of the previously described methods (automatic or interactive clustering) result in the desired set of clusters, the tool provides the designer with the option to manually manipulate and enter the various clusters. Once the designer is satisfied with the set of clusters, a "quantified" persona set is created (see Figure 4.12). Note that these personas are described by user variables and associated values. They should be extended manually by the designer with textual descriptions such as interaction details and scenarios, based on information gathered from representative users.

Based on these personas, the designer can use the mapping module in order to create a set of patterns. This step is performed automatically based on the set of personas generated during the previous step. The mapping module selects patterns using a scoring system; where, based on a set of rules, the various patterns are associated with scores. These rules leverage the dependencies between user variables and pattern variables, and simplify the task of a designer who would manually match usability and special needs to particular personas. For example, if our persona is *colorblind* and has a need for *efficiency of use*, the following patterns apply: (1) the pattern *redundant encoding* indicates in its context that it is applicable for users with visual deficiencies such as color blindness (Wilkins, 2003), and (2) efficiency of use is a usability need and one physical design implication would be to apply accelerators. One pattern which is an accelerator is called *macros* (Tidwell, 2002).

After gathering the above information, designers can build a mental model understanding the potential pattern, its relationship with other patterns, and its applicability in a given context of use. Supplemented by their design experience, they select a subset of these patterns which they compose into a comprehensive design.

Figure 4.12 overviews the infrastructure of the P2P Mapper Tool. In its current version, the tool supports the first two phases of the UX-P process, namely, Persona Creation and Pattern Selection. We also note that our tool comes with a prepopulated library containing the formalization of 83 patterns from the following pattern libraries: GUI (Tidwell, 2005), Web (Javahery and Seffah, 2002; Welie, 2003), visualization (Wilkins, 2003), and our own "special needs" patterns.

4.8 CONCLUSION

In current practice, the derivation of a conceptual design from user experiences is based on loosely defined guidelines, giving rise to a significant "gap" between user requirements and design outcomes. Typically, the outcome is reliant almost completely on the designer's intuition. This is especially problematic for novice designers who lack the background and training required to make trade-offs, judgments, and interpretations towards a usable design. In this chapter we propose a UI design framework to support designers in deriving a conceptual design from user experiences. Its starting point is an understanding of user behaviors and experiences, their tasks, and the context of their work. Using different usability methods, empirical studies on all aspects of the user's interaction with the target application are conducted. Only then can we perform a task analysis and scenario generation; followed by low-fidelity prototyping and rough usability studies; resulting in a high-fidelity product for more rigorous user testing.

The framework exploits two key UCD artifacts. Personas are created iteratively to model user experiences, giving a clearer picture of the user behaviors and experiences,

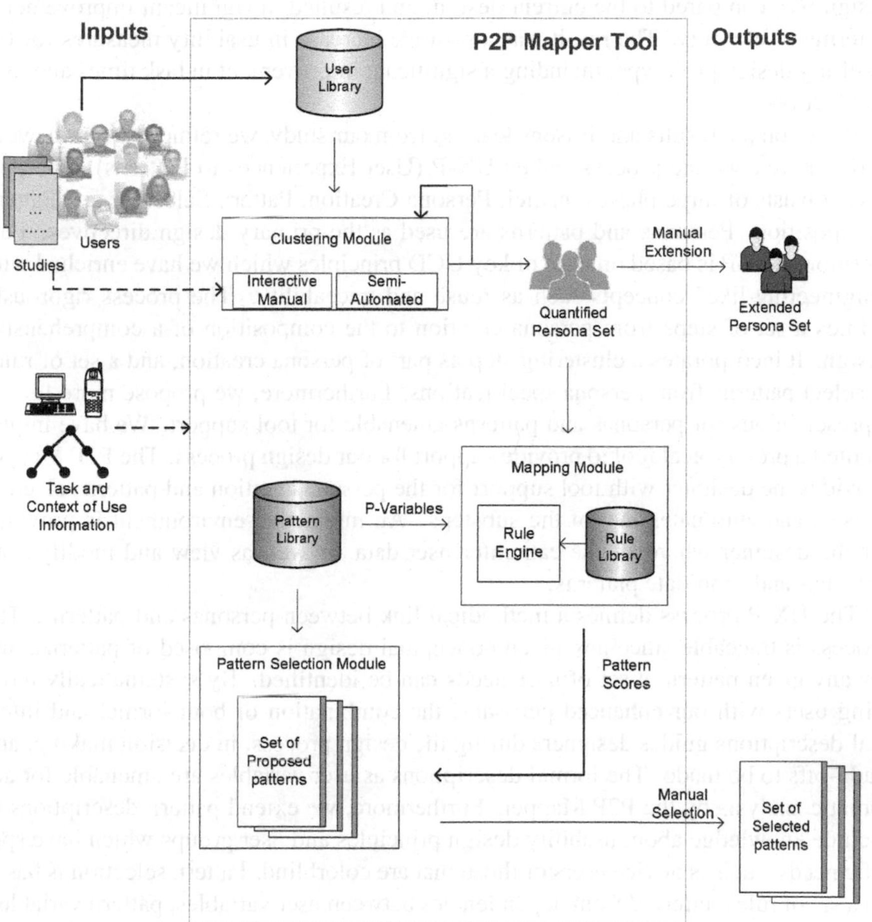

Figure 4.12 Overview of P2P Mapper Tool

their tasks and the context of use. Other inputs, such as task analysis and scenario generation, are used to refine the persona set. Information contained in personas is then used to select appropriate patterns—the second key UCD artifact used. In HCI and empirical software engineering, user-oriented studies are required both to motivate the research as well as to assess the validation and accuracy of the proposals. We therefore applied our framework in a proof-of-concept with a popular Bioinformatics website, which biologists use as a portal to access different analytical tools. The new design was compared to the current design, and resulted in significant improvements in terms of usability. The result was a positive increase in usability measures for the resulting design prototype, including a significant improvement in task times and user satisfaction.

Based on the results and lessons learned from our study, we refined our framework into a more concrete process, called UX-P (User Experiences to Patterns). The process consists of three phases, namel, Persona Creation, Pattern Selection and Pattern Composition. Personas and patterns are used as the primary design directives. Furthermore, UX-P is based on a set of key UCD principles which we have enriched with "engineering-like" concepts such as reuse and traceability. The process rigorously defines a set of steps from persona creation to the composition of a comprehensive design. It incorporates a clustering step as part of persona creation, and a set of rules to select patterns from persona specifications. Furthermore, we propose more formal representations for personas and patterns amenable for tool support. We have implemented a prototypical tool to provide support for our design process. The P2P Mapper provides the designer with tool support for the persona creation and pattern selection phases, and automates two of the substeps. An interactive environment is provided for the designer where she/he can enter user data, as well as view and modify both personas and candidate patterns.

The UX-P process defines a methodical link between personas and patterns. The process is traceable since any given conceptual design is composed of patterns, and for any given pattern, a set of user needs can be identified. By systematically modeling users with our enhanced personas, the combination of both formal and informal descriptions guides designers during the design process, in decision making, and trade-offs to be made. The formal descriptions as user variables are amenable for automatic analysis by the P2P Mapper. Furthermore, we extend pattern descriptions to include knowledge about usability design principles and user groups which have specific needs, such as novice users or those that are colorblind. Pattern selection is based on a set of rules, inferred from dependencies between user variables, pattern variables, and usability principles. The rules were implemented within a scoring system which takes user variables as input and outputs a list of patterns, ordered by their relevance.

Our research resulted in an initial design process to derive conceptual designs from user experiences; however, it led to additional research questions that can be avenues for further research. First, we described two types of associations between users and patterns, through their needs: a direct association with special needs, and an indirect association with usability needs. These associations allow designers to select a set of patterns appropriate to their design. An interesting possibility for investigation would be to further filter patterns based on task type. Recall that pattern descriptions make reference to typical tasks of the user-task model. Some patterns are only applicable for a particular task type (i.e., Advanced Search Pattern and tasks of type *search*). These task types could act as further input into pattern selection, rather than being manually assessed by designers.

Second, both our persona and pattern descriptions are a good starting point in standardizing the representation of personas and patterns, respectively. In current practice, personas are constructed based on general narrative guidelines and contain information which allows them to be little more than a communicative tool. Furthermore, pattern writers have few guidelines in constructing patterns. This results in little consistency in the structuring and definition of pattern descriptions for pattern libraries. It would be interesting to explore the use of both our descriptions as a standard representation of these two artifacts in HCI.

Thirdly, the associations discovered between user variables and pattern variables were based on knowledge elicited from HCI experts. It would be valuable to test each one of these through experimentation with end-users, to determine their precise impact. In this vein, we note that our scoring system is based on the heuristics elicited during expert consultation. Our knowledge elicitation activities concentrated on establishing associations between user experiences and design solutions attempting to satisfy user needs. A further improvement of our scoring system can be its enhancement with learning capabilities. Hence, the current implementation of the rules can be understood as an initial configuration of a future expert system or a neural network, which may be further adjusted and fine tuned based on the assessment of the quality of the results.

One of the major problems we found is that mastering and applying large collections as well as different types of patterns requires in-depth knowledge of both the problems and forces at play. As such, it is inconceivable that the mapping rules and ensuing pattern composition will evolve strictly from theoretical considerations. Practical research and industry feedback are crucial in determining how successful a pattern-oriented design framework is at solving design problems. It is therefore essential to build an "academia–industry bridge" by establishing formal communication channels between industrial specialists in UI design patterns, as well as pattern researchers. It is hoped that such collaboration will lead to a common POD framework that is essential in making the large diversity of patterns accessible to common UI designers. At this time, the POD approach including the list of patterns and relationships has been defined and illustrated for websites and Web applications. We can extend these ideas to other types of applications as well. In addition, further investigation is required to explore the scalability of the approach for multiple pattern-oriented designs and platforms; as well as strategies for providing heuristics and computer-support to designers during the pattern composition phase.

References

Alexander, C. (1979). *A Timeless Way of Building*. New York: Oxford University Press.

Attwood, T. and Parry-Smith, D. (1999). *Introduction to Bioinformatics*. Addison Wesley Longman Higher Education, Essex.

Holtzblatt, K. and Beyer, H. (1998). *Contextual Design: Defining Customer-Centered Systems*. San Francisco, CA: Morgan Kaufmann.

Carroll, J. M. (2000). *Making use: Scenario-based design of human-computer interactions*. Cambridge MA: MIT Press.

Cooper, A. (1999). *The Inmates Are Running the Asylum: Why High Tech Products Drive Us Crazy and How to Restore the Sanity*. Indianapolis, IN: Sams.

Corporation, C. (2005). Persona of a cognetics design specialist. http://www.cognetics.com/about/team/people4.html.

Dix, A., Findlay, J., Abowd, G., and Beale, R. (1993). *Human Computer Interaction*. Prentice Hall: New York.

Duyne, D. K. V., Landay, J., and Hong, J. I. (2002). *The Design of Sites: Patterns, Principles, and Processes for Crafting a Customer-Centered Web Experience*. Addison-Wesley, Reading: MA.

Ehn, P. (1998). *Work-Oriented Design of Computer Artifacts*. Ph.D. thesis. Stockholm: Arbetslivscentrum.

Engelberg, D. and Seffah, A. (2002). Design patterns for the navigation of large information architectures. In *11th Annual Usability Professional Association Conference*, Orlando, FL.

Erickson, T. (2000). Lingua francas for design: sacred places and pattern languages. In *Proceedings of DIS'00: Designing Interactive Systems: Processes, Practices, Methods, & Techniques*, Pattern Languages, pages 357–368.

Gamma, E., Helm, R., Johnson, R., and Vlissides, J. (1995). *Design Patterns: Elements of Reusable Object-Oriented Software*. Addison Wesley Professional Computing Series. http://www.aw.com.

Javahery, H. and Seffah, A. (2002). A model for usability pattern-oriented design. In Pribeanu, C. and Vanderdonckt, J., editors, *Task Models and Diagrams for User Interface Design: Proceedings of the First International Workshop on Task Models and Diagrams for User Interface Design - TAMODIA 2002, 18-19 July 2002, Bucharest, Romania*, pages 104–110. INFOREC Publishing House Bucharest.

Javahery, H., Sinnig, D., Seffah, A., Forbrig, P., and Radhakrishnan, T. (2006). Pattern-based UI design: adding rigor with user and context variables. In *Proceedings of TaMoDia 2006*, Hasselt.

Laakso, S. (1993). Collection of user interface design patterns. University of Helsinki, (September 16, 2003); http://www.cs.helsinki.fi/u/salaakso/patterns/.

Lafrenière, D. and Granlund, A. (1999). A pattern-supported approach to user interface design. *UPA 99 Workshop Report*; `http://www.gespro.com/lafrenid/Workshop_Report.pdf`.

Landauer, T. K. (1997). Behavioral research methods in human-computer interaction. In *Handbook of Human-Computer Interaction*. Amsterdam: North-Holland, 2nd edition.

Landay, J. A. and Myers, B. A. (2001). Sketching interfaces: toward more human interface design. *IEEE Computer*, 34(3).

McGrenere, J. (2004). Iterative design and evaluation of multiple interfaces for a complex commercial word processor. In Seffah, A. and Javahery, H., editors, *Multiple*

User Interfaces: Cross-Platform Applications and Context-Aware Interfaces. New York: Wiley.

McGrenere, J., Baecker, R. M., and Booth, K. S. (2002). An evaluation of a multiple interface design solution for bloated software. In *Proc. of SIGCHI, CHI'02*, pages 164–170. ACM Press.

McKenzie, K. (2000). 10 usability heuristics. `http://www.studiowhiz.com/_publications/10heuristics.php`.

Mikkelson, N. and Lee, W. (2000). Incorporating user archetypes into scenario-based design. In *UPA Workshop*.

Msheik, H., Abran, A., and Lefebvre, E. (2004). Compositional structured component model: Handling selective functional composition. In *EUROMICRO*, pages 74–81. IEEE Computer Society.

NCBI (2005). National Center for Biotechnology Information. http://www.ncbi.nlm.nih.gov/.

Nielsen, J. (1994). Heuristic evaluation. In Nielsen, J. and Mack, R. L., editors, *Usability Inspection Methods*. New York: Wiley.

Nielsen, J. (2001). How to conduct a heuristic evaluation. (November 2001); http://www.useit.com/papers/heuristic/heuristic_evaluation.html.

Preece, J., Rogers, Y., and Sharp, H. (2002). *Interaction Design: Beyond Human-Computer Interaction*. New York: Wiley. OCLC 48265540.

Pruitt, J. and Grudin, J. (2003). Personas: practice and theory. In *Proceedings of DUX'03: Designing for User Experiences*, number 6 in Informing DUX, pages 1–15, New York. ACM Press.

Seffah, A., Gulliksen, J., and Desmarais, M. C., editors (2005). *Human-Centered Software Engineering: Integrating Usability in the Development Process*. Wiley, Boston.

Tahir, M. (1997). Who's on the other side of your software: creating user profiles through contextual inquiry. In *Proceedings of Usability Professionals Association Conference UPA '97*, Monterey.

Taleb, M., Javahery, H., and Seffah, A. (2006). Pattern-oriented design composition and mapping for cross-platform Web applications. In *Proceedings of DSV-IS 2006*, Dublin.

Tidwell, J. (2002). Ui patterns and techniques. `http://timetripper.com/uipatterns/index.php`.

Tidwell, J. (2005). *Designing interfaces : Patterns for Effective Interaction Design*. Cambridge, MA: O'Reilly.

Welie, M. (2003). Interaction Design Patterns. http://www.welie.com/.

Wilkins, B. (2003). *MELD: A Pattern Supported Methodology for Visualization Design*. Ph.D. thesis, submitted to The University of Birmingham, School of Computer Science.

5 XML-BASED TOOLS FOR CREATING, MAPPING, AND TRANSFORMING USABILITY ENGINEERING REQUIREMENTS

Fei Huang, Jon Titus,
Allan Wolinski, Kevin Schneider, and Jim A. Carter

University of Saskatchewan, Saskatoon, SK, Canada

Abstract. This paper introduces a set of XML-based and XMI-based tools for creating usability engineering requirements and automatically transforming them into software engineering specifications. Each of these tools is data-driven and uses XML to maximize flexibility, accessibility, and translatability. These tools are primarily intended for use by usability engineers to create usability engineering (UE) requirements, analyze accessibility issues, and automatically transform UI requirements into software engineering specifications. By transforming usability requirements into software engineering specifications, usability engineers can help software engineers design systems that satisfy the applicable usability requirements. Additionally these tools can be used by researchers investigating usability engineering methodologies.

5.1 INTRODUCTION

There is a need for unifying the user interface development methodologies of software engineers, usability engineers, and other computer professionals (Carter et al.,

2005). The integration of usability engineering (UE) and software engineering (SE) can also aid in the development of systems that are universally accessible (Savadis and Stephanidis, 2004).

This chapter describes research under way in USERLab at the University of Saskatchewan that deals with developing UE methods and methodologies and integrating them with SE methodologies. In particular, this chapter discusses research integrating the USERLab's Putting Usability First (PUF) methodology and the USERLab's Common Access Profile (CAP) method with SE methodologies.

5.1.1 The Putting Usability First Methodology

The Putting Usability First Methodology (PUF) is a UE methodology that attempts to balance usability concerns for both end-users and the developers who create systems to serve them (Carter et al, 2005). It can be used to support the iterative evolution of the requirements of five types of entities (scenarios, tasks, user groups, content chunks, and tools) throughout a systems development lifecycle (possibilities identification, possibilities analysis, requirements analysis, design, construction, testing, and implementation). It can also be used as a means of creating usability requirements and integrating them with a software engineering development lifecycle.

5.1.2 The Common Access Profile

The Common Access Profile provides a method for identifying and dealing with accessibility issues in a standardized manner across multiple platforms (Fourney & Carter, 2006; ISO, 2007). The CAPs of users, systems, and environments can be compared to determine the potential for systems and system components (including assistive technologies) to meet the unique accessibility needs of an individual user or of a group of users with different needs.

5.1.3 Requirements, Tools, and Guidance

While it is important to develop methodologies and methods such as PUF and CAP, it is even more important to ensure that they can have an impact on actual software development. This involves recognition of the key role in project management played by software engineers. If UE methods do not integrate with SE methodologies, they may have little impact on actual development.

Software engineering tends to focus on "functional requirements" which are easy to translate into algorithms and data structures. This leaves the need to identify, integrate, and meet other, so-called "non-functional" requirements (Cortellessa and Pompei, 2004), throughout the development lifecycle, including those typically addressed by UE. Early identification and validation of these "non-functional" requirements is essential regardless of whether this is done by software engineers or other professionals who are more interested in these aspects of system analysis and design (Cysneiros and Sampaio do Prado Leite, 2001; Jerome and Kazman, 2005). In addition to project specific usability requirements, usability requirements should consider the user needs that support accessibility. As well, products are increasingly required to be localized for particular populations and cultures (Jagne and Smith-Atakan, 2006).

There is a need for development tools to better support UE (Carter, 1999) and requirements engineering (Zhang and Eberlein, 2003) and their integration with SE. The integration of the results and activities of UE and SE has been hampered by the different methods, notations, and tools that each specialty has developed (Seffah and Metzker, 2004). Metamodels for development methodologies (ISO, 2006c) are being developed to facilitate the comparison, integration, and customization of development methodologies. Various researchers (Cortellessa and Pompei, 2004; Cysneiros and Sampaio do Prado Leite, 2001; Jerome and Kazman, 2005) have focused on the integration of UE (UE) and other non-functional requirements into the set of UML diagrams that are used by SE (SE).

XML Metadata Interchange (XMI) provides a means "to enable easy interchange of metadata between application development lifecycle tools" (ISO, 2005). UML 2.1.1 XMI (Object Management Group, 2006b), which defines the content of an XML document that XMI creates, can be used to determine whether the UML metamodel data satisfies all of the UML metamodel's semantics constraints.

XML is used to represent the XMI interchange format and XML provides a good basis for recording specifications, for transforming specifications between methodologies, and for analyzing specifications to provide appropriate design guidance (Gaffar and Seffah, 2005; ISO, 2005). Nowadays, most UML CASE tools support XMI. Open source UML tools, such as ArgoUML (University of California, 2007), automatically generate XML files from UML diagrams, including: use case diagrams, class diagrams, and collaboration diagrams. The XML code in this paper is produced by ArgoUML.

There is a growing body of guidance developed by ISO TC159/SC 4 Ergonomics of Human-System Interaction and ISO/IEC JTC1/SC35 User Interfaces. There is also increasing international agreement in terms of high-level guidance (ISO, 2006a), and detailed guidance (ISO, 2006b) for making systems accessible. As this body of guidance grows, there is an increasing need for development tools to aid developers in identifying and applying this guidance (Carter, 1999). Tools can be developed to analyze XML-based requirements to identify guidance from applicable international standards; to identify accessibility issues (ISO/IEC, 2007); to extract, analyze user interface design patterns (Gaffar and Seffah, 2005); and to identify architecturally sensitive usability scenarios (Adams et al., 2006).

5.2 TOOLSET OVERVIEW

The primary goal of this research is to investigate and develop accessible methods, techniques, and tools for supporting development of accessible software systems. This is being accomplished by developing and using a data-driven workbench of tools for use by researchers and developers of interactive systems. XML provides a common basis for defining schema to support different development methodologies (including the PUF methodology and the CAP method).

Figure 5.1 shows the architecture of the main tools in the USERLab workbench. Basic support for UE will be provided by a combination of a Methodology Admin-

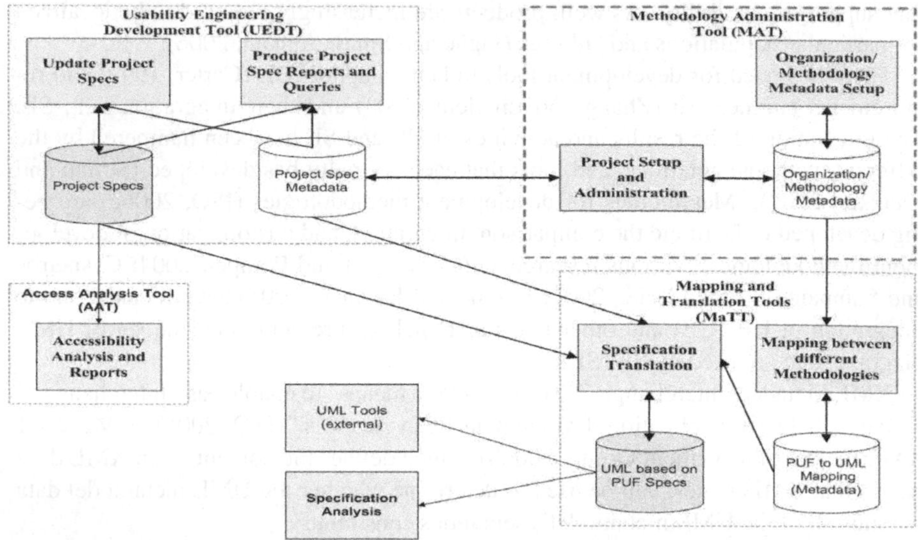

Figure 5.1 The structure of the USERLab toolset and its databases

istration Tool (that is used to specify the schema used to record requirements for a given methodology or method) and a UE Development Tool (that uses these schema to capture project specific requirements). This project is unique in that it separates out methodology administration (specification and modification of the record schema to support a given methodology) from using the methodology to capture requirements and to perform other lifecycle support processes. The resulting requirements and schema provide inputs to three sets of advanced tools: an Access Analysis Tool, a set of Mapping and Translation Tools, and a set of Specification Analysis Tools. The requirements specified in the analysis of the different tools within this project can be used as the basis for an initial evaluation of the usability of each of these advanced tools. The results of these evaluations will be used to identify improvements to one or more of the tools and their associated methods.

5.2.1 Methodology Administration

The Methodology Administration Tool (MAT) helps researchers and developers to investigate, develop, modify, and support various development methodologies without having to create separate development support tools for each one.

The MAT assists in creating a master schema for the requirements and specifications of multiple development methodologies and methods that will be used by a single UE Development Tool (Wolinski, 2005; Titus, 2006). The unique features of the MAT are discussed in Section 5.3 of this paper.

The MAT supports both defining a master version of individual methodologies and developing customized versions of methodologies to meet the needs of individual projects (including combining records from different methodologies and methods, such as PUF and CAP). This facilitates the investigation of alternate UE methodologies and variations of these. It also demonstrates a practical method of achieving cultural and linguistic adaptability by storing all headings and labels in a database, designed so that headings and labels in different languages can be substituted for each other.

5.2.2 *Usability Engineering Development*

The UE Development Tool (UEDT) helps usability engineers to create, manage, and query UE specifications at various stages within a project development lifecycle. The UEDT is a flexible tool driven by schemata produced by the MAT. This flexibility allows the UEDT to be used in researching and applying various UE methodologies.

The features of the UEDT are designed to meet the usability and accessibility needs of developers, including developers with disabilities. Extensive navigation is provided directly between interlinked specification records and between specification records and various types of management reports. Each successive lifecycle stage can involve adding more detailed information to existing information. The UEDT helps manage development activities by identifying which requirements have been completed by the usability engineer and which requirements have been approved by the user at each stage of the lifecycle.

The UEDT provides a means for prototyping different development methodologies and capturing UE requirements in a format that supports their analysis and their transformation into UML.

5.2.3 *Analyzing Accessibility*

The Access Analysis Tool (AAT) is used to compare CAPs of users, systems, system components (including assistive technologies), and their environments to identify issues that should be overcome to improve accessibility. It allows developers to consider possible configurations of assistive technologies that could eliminate or reduce accessibility obstacles.

The ATT (along with the previous two tools) supports accessibility assessment based on ISO/IEC 24756 (2007). The ATT can be used to identify access related issues in specific configurations of users, environments, and systems and can be used to help identify alternate configurations, including assistive technologies where necessary, that can reduce or eliminate these issues.

A CAP-specific version of the UEDT will be produced as a standalone tool to use in specifying CAPs, as defined in ISO/IEC 24756 (2007). It is expected that this may lead to the development of a registry of CAPs for various commercial hardware and software systems (including assistive technologies).

5.2.4 *Translating UE Requirements into SE Specifications*

The Mapping and Translation Tools (MaTTs) help integrate UE requirements into traditional SE (UML-based) specifications both in research and in development activities. They aid in defining the role and interactions of usability engineers within early stages of a development project. The MaTTs are usable with any methodologies that are XML-based.

The MaTTs supports analyzing and comparing semantics of different requirement specification schema, and translating between the source schema and the target schema components (Huang, 2006). This allows usability engineering requirements to be used as a starting point for the project's software engineers. These tools are also intended to support research into the unification of various development methodologies and models, especially the unification of UE and SE approaches to development.

The Methodology Mapping Tool (MMT) takes two XML-based specification schema, such as the PUF XML schema and the UML XML schema, helps the researcher analyze and compare semantics of these structures, and outputs a set of rules for producing a set of mappings between the source schema and the target schema components. It supports single tag mapping and multiple tag mapping and the specification of the type of relationship for each mapping (exact, inclusion, and non existing). The unique features of this mapping are discussed in Section 5.4 of this paper.

The Methodology Translation Tool (MTT) uses information from the mapping tool to transform a usability requirement instance from the source XML schema (e.g., PUF) into an instance of a different (e.g., UML) target XML schema. There are four inputs to the transformation: (a) the project specifications database containing the source XML document (the UE methodology-specific tags and data); (b) the project specifications metadata database containing the tag structure; (c) the target XMI schema; and, (d) the source to XMI mapping database. The inputs are transformed into a target XML document (e.g., a set of XMI records containing the PUF/CAP/other UE specifications) and an enhanced XMI schema (e.g., an XMI schema containing the PUF/CAP/other UE metadata). The tool creates both an improved XMI structure and initial requirements including the UE requirements captured by the flexible UE Development tool. The requirements are used as a starting point for the project's software engineers. Unique features of this translation are discussed in Section 5.5 of this chapter.

5.2.5 Analyzing UE Requirements and SE Specifications

The Specification Analysis Tools (SATs) analyze sets of UE/SE specifications, created by the UEDT or the MaTT, in terms of international standards and design patterns that can aid in developing systems to meet these usability and accessibility specifications. These tools support the development of a database of user interface design guidance (based on existing international standards and design patterns), the mapping of these standards and design patterns to different methodology schema components, and the use of the resulting information in analyzing specifications. The resulting design consistency can improve usability while reducing development costs.

The SATs will help to research possible UE contributions to the design of systems. In the long run, they will help to provide UE guidance to developers, regardless of whether the developers are usability engineers, software engineers, or other types of computer professionals.

5.3 USING XML TO STRUCTURE UE SPECIFICATIONS

The Methodology Administration Tool (MAT) provides a tool for a methodology developer or researcher to define metadata for a new or existing methodology and to create or modify requirement record templates to be used by this methodology. It uses XML to format and store methodology metadata and record template descriptions.

A methodology schema involves a methodology metadata record and zero, one, or multiple requirement template records. The methodology developer can view and edit: all data associated with a methodology, the methodology metadata record alone, and/or individual requirement record templates.

A methodology developer can create a new methodology schema either on its own or based on the schema from one or more methodologies already defined by the MAT. Copies may be made of a given methodology and modified to make them more suitable to the unique needs of individual projects. Each copy of an existing methodology is treated separately in the MAT database, to allow it to be modified without affecting the original methodology. Copies may also be made of individual requirement record templates from other methodologies at any time during the development of a new methodology. Each new copy is created as a unique record in the database and linked to the new methodology. This new copy is separate from the original and therefore changes to it are not reflected in the original record template

5.3.1 Methodology Metadata

MAT methodology metadata provides a starting point for defining methodology schema. It includes:

1. A unique methodology name
2. A unique abbreviated name
3. A unique id (for internal use only)
4. A short description of the methodology's purpose
5. A long description of the methodology's purpose, components, operations
6. Linkages to associated record template records

5.3.2 Methodology Requirements

Methodologies generally involve one or more templates used to record requirements identified by a project developer who is following the methodology. The MAT provides a powerful means of creating templates to be used in the UEDT by project developers.

All MAT requirement template records (RTRs) include the following associated descriptive information:

1. The name of the RTR
2. A short description of the purpose of the RTR

3. A full description of the purpose and use of the RTR

4. The RTR's frozen (or not frozen) status

5. Record management information consisting of: its designer proposed level and its user accepted level

Once a methodology schema is completed and put into production for use in the UEDT, it is important to freeze changes to it (using a frozen status flag in the RTRs), so that all project requirement data remains consistently described by the associated methodology schema.

Record management information is designed to aid a project developer using the UEDT to manage the collection of requirements for a given project. Levels of user acceptance correspond to the hierarchy of sections in the requirement record template. The project developer can propose a section is ready for user acceptance. A user is then able to accept or reject the section. If a project developer modifies a user accepted section, the section level the user has approved is reduced as is the section level the project developer had proposed for approval.

5.3.3 Requirement Template Building Blocks

The MAT provides "building block" components for a methodology developer to define a new record template. These components include: section headers, hierarchal header items, linkage items, and question items.

These components are supported by a hierarchal system where section headers are the top level component. Hierarchal headers, linkages, and questions belong to a 'parent' section header or item. The hierarchy is visually defined in the interface to the MAT by using indention and a numbering system. Figure 5.2 illustrates the use of MAT to develop a task requirement template for the PUF methodology.

Section header items include a section name and an abbreviation. The abbreviation must be unique to allow the project developer and user to use in proposing and approving the completeness of each section. A hierarchy header item only requires a header field for its name. A linkage item requires its name, type, the minimum and maximum number of times it may occur, and its related record type. A question item is to include its question and answer type and its minimum and maximum occurrences. Each component includes a comment field that may be viewed by the project developer or user or that may be hidden by the developer from the user.

When a methodology developer wants to add a new item, he is given a choice of the type of item to be added. The new item is added directly below the previous item. The methodology developer is then able to indent the item if necessary to create the desired hierarchy. An item cannot be indented more than one level under its parent. A developer can later decide to modify the hierarchy by moving an item out from its parent. If this is done, the moved item's children (if any) should move with it. A methodology developer is also able to delete an item. In the case where an item has children, a developer is given the choice of whether its children should also be deleted or whether they should join the deleted item's parent.

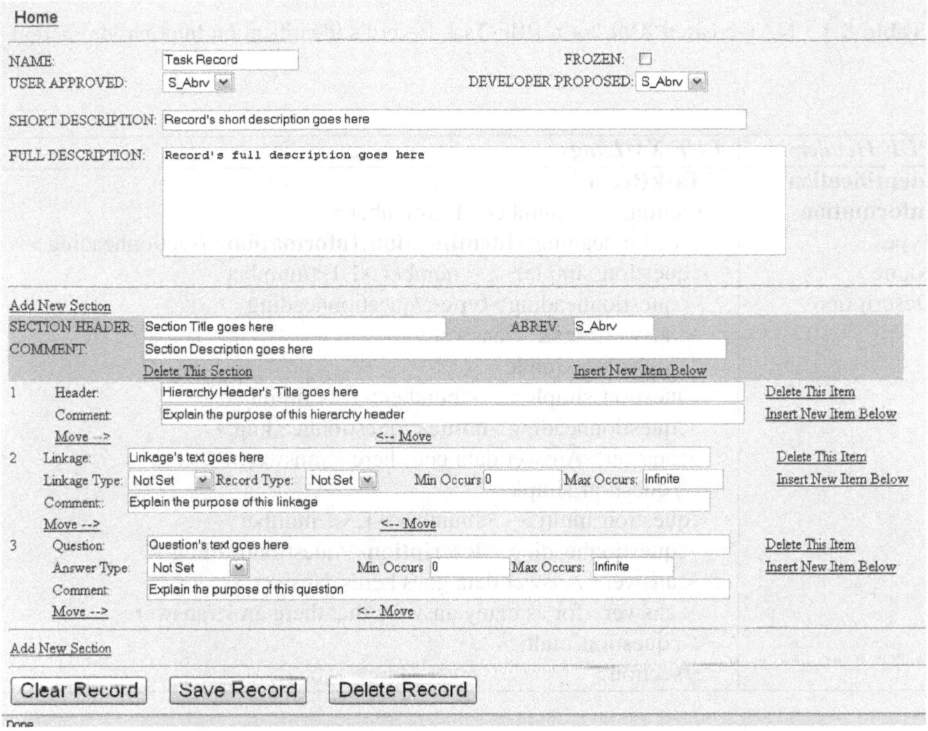

Figure 5.2 Creating a requirement template record with the MAT

5.3.4 *Using XML to Structure Task Requirement Records for PUF*

The MAT can be used to produce an XML schema for PUF, CAP, and other UE methodologies. An XML schema definition (XSD) shows a high-level abstract view of XML documents of that type which includes the XML tags and their interrelationships. XML schema can be used to create and use a type of XML document by imposing a set of rules and constraints on their structure and content.

Tables 5.1 and 5.2 provide partial examples of XML tags created using the MAT to define components of task requirement records for PUF. XML tag names come both from the methodology (e.g., "What" is used to identify a linkage to task requirement records in PUF) and from the type of structural element that is being used by the methodology (e.g., "linkquestion"). The overall structure of a requirement record is controlled using section numbers. Note that the MAT produces generic XML tags. The data of some of these tags actually acts as more specific tags.

While the complete PUF XML document contains a number of tags that are intended only for the use of a project developer using the UEDT, Table 5.3 contains a discussion of select XML tags that deal with requirements data and indicates how some of these tags and their data can be transformed into UML specifications.

Table 5.1 MAT-created XML for a PUF Task Record's Identification Information section

PUF Header	*PUF XML tags*
Identification	<**TaskRecord**>
Information	<section> <number>1</number>
Type	<sectionheading>**Identification_Information**</sectionheading>
Name	<question_simple> <number>1.1</number>
Description	<questionheading>**type**</questionheading>
	<answer>**task** </answer>
	< /question_simple>
	<question_simple> <number>1.2</number>
	<questionheading>**name**</questionheading>
	<answer>Answer data goes here </answer>
	< /question_simple>
	<question_multi> <number>1.3</number>
	<questionheading>**description**</questionheading>
	<answer>Answer data goes here</answer>
	<answer>for as many answers that there are</answer>
	< /question_multi>
	< /section>

5.4 MAPPING BETWEEN XML-BASED UE AND SE SPECIFICATIONS

Mapping is the first of the two-stage process that can transform UE specifications into SE requirements. Mapping only needs to be performed once for each pair of methodologies. It provides the logic to be used and reused in translating sets of project-specific requirements from one methodology to another.

Mapping is required for any pair of methodologies that generally contain differences in their defining XML schema, even in portions of the XML schema that both represent the same requirements/specifications. Its main use is to guide the transformation of UE requirements into SE specifications. It can also be used to guide the transformation of the UE requirements of one project into UE requirements for another project, where the two projects have their own customized methodology records/schema.

The Methodology Mapping Tool (MMT) is used by a methodology developer to analyze and compare semantics of a (UE) source XML schema (e.g., the PUF XML schema – PUF XSD) and the semantics of a target XMI schema (e.g., UML XSD), as illustrated in Figure 5.3. The MMT then produces a set of mapping rules that can be used by the Methodology Translation Tool (MTT).

There are a number of different mapping needs that the MMT handles. Mapping needs to occur both on an entity-to-entity basis and on an attribute-to-attribute basis.

Table 5.2 MAT-created XML for a PUF Task Record's Linkage Information Section

PUF Header	*PUF XML tags*
Linkage	<section> <number>2</number>
Information	<sectionheading>**Linkage_Information**</sectionheading>
Who	<question_link > <number>2.1</number>
What	<questionheading>**who**</questionheading>
How	<questionText>Who performs this task?</questionText>
With which	<linkage>Linkage data goes here</linkage>
(content)	<linkage>for as many linkages as there are. </linkage>
Scenarios	< /question_link>
	<question_link > <number>2.2</number>
	<questionheading>**what**</questionheading>
	<questionText>What subtasks does this task have?</questionText>
	<linkage>Linkage data goes here</linkage>
	<linkage>for as many linkages as there are. </linkage>
	< /question_link>
	not shown in this example:
	how *is done similar to structure for* ***who***
	with_which_content *also is done similar to structure for* ***who***
	scenarios *also is done similar to structure for* ***who***
	< /section>

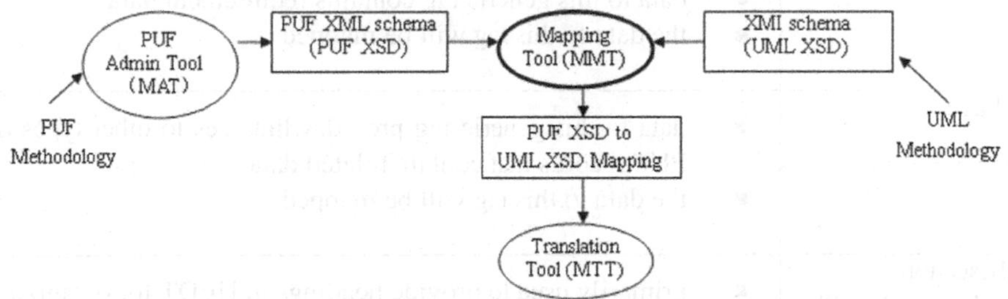

Figure 5.3 The interactions of the Methodology Mapping Tool

Table 5.3 PUF UML tags and their relationship to UML

PUF XML tag	Purpose
<section>	▪ allows mapping to consider one section at a time ▪ is not generally mapped into UML, but may help identify locations in UML where PUF data should be mapped to
<number>	▪ used to structure PUF, but not UML records ▪ is not mapped into UML
<question_simple>	▪ contains a single tag and piece of data to be mapped
<question_multi>	▪ contains a single tag and multiple pieces of data to be mapped
<question_link >	▪ contains a single tag and one or more links to additional data to be mapped
<questionheading>	▪ data to this generic tag provides semantics which can act as a tag for specific types of requirement data ▪ the data to this tag will be mapped ▪ this data may appear as a heading or subheading in a resulting UML diagram
<questionText>	▪ used only for UEDT
<answer>	▪ data to this generic tag contains requirement data ▪ the data to this tag will be mapped
<linkage>	▪ data to this generic tag provides linkages to other types of PUF records that contain related data ▪ the data to this tag will be mapped
<sub_section> (not illustrated in Tables 5.1 or 5.2)	▪ primarily used to provide headings in UEDT for organizing multiple questions ▪ is not generally mapped into UML, but may help identify locations in UML where PUF data should be mapped to ▪ the data to this tag could be mapped if this data should appear as a heading or subheading in a resulting UML diagram

5.4.1 *Entity and Attribute Mappings*

Specifications typically consist of a large number of instances of relatively few types of specification records (templates). For example, PUF contains multiple user, task, content, tool, and scenario records. Likewise, UML consists of a limited number of entities (including: use cases, object classes, attributes, operations, actors) that are then diagrammed in one or more diagrams. Mapping on an entity-to-entity basis is essential to preserving the individual instances of each entity. Table 5.4 contains some high-level mappings of PUF record types to UML entities that were identified in Carter et al. (2005).

Table 5.4 Some high-level mapping of entities from PUF to UML

For every *xxxx* identified in PUF . . .	**. . . there should be a *yyyy* created in UML**
user	actor
task	essential use case
scenario	use case
content	attribute
tool	operation

Entities in most methodologies are expected to have unique names. As illustrated in Table 5.1, the Identification Information section of PUF record templates (created by MAT) identifies the type of PUF record and contains a question designed to allow project developers to name individual records. These names can be used to direct the mapping, as described in Table 5.5.

The names of different types of specifications are also important when used as the answers to questions asking about links. For example, PUF content and tools correspond to attributes and operations in UML classes. The relationship between specific content and tool records needs to be mapped to the specific relationship between specific attributes and operations.

Attribute-to-attribute mapping occurs within the entities selected by entity-to-entity mapping. Attribute-to-attribute mappings can involve the attribute being mapped: directly to an existing target attribute, to a part of an existing target attribute, or as a new target attribute.

Where an attribute maps directly to an existing target element (within UML), it needs to have its data placed in that corresponding (UML) element. For example, PUF task names map to name attributes in UML Use Case tags as illustrated in Table 5.6.

Where an attribute maps directly to part of an existing element (within UML), it needs to have its data placed in a subelement of that corresponding (UML) element. For example, answers about what this task consists of in PUF task descriptions map to lower-level Use Cases, as illustrated in Table 5.7.

Table 5.5 High-level mapping of PUF tasks to UML actors

PUF XML	**Desired Result of Mapping**
<question_simple> <number>1.1</number> <questionheading>**type**</questionheading> <answer>**task** </answer> < /question_simple>	This requires mapping to (including the creation, where necessary) a UML **actor** record for each instance of a PUF **task** (**type** of) record.
<question_simple> <number>1.2</number> <questionheading>**name**</questionheading> <answer>Answer data goes here </answer> < /question_simple>	The **name** of the UML **actor** records will be taken from the answer to question 1.2 of the PUF task records. If no UML **actor** record exists with that **name**, then it will have to be created.

Table 5.6 Direct attribute-to-attribute mapping of PUF to UML

PUF XML	**UML XML**
(part of a PUF task record) <question_simple> <number>1.2</number> <questionheading> **name** < /questionheading> <answer> *paying for ordered items using e-Commerce* </answer></question_simple> <question_multi> <number>1.3</number> <questionheading> **description** < /questionheading> <answer> *paying for an order of items already selected and currently in the customer's virtual shopping cart.* < /answer> < /question_multi>	<UML:**UseCase** xmi.id="" **name** ="*paying for ordered items using e-Commerce*" isSpecification ="" isRoot="" isLeaf ="" isAbstract=""> ... <UML:**eAnnotations**> *paying for an order of items already selected and currently in the customer's virtual shopping cart.* </UML:**eAnnotations**> ... < /UML:**UseCase**>

Where an attribute does not correspond to an existing element (within UML), it needs to have its data placed at the appropriate location (within UML). For example, environmental data from PUF tasks needs to become a new type of constraint in UML, as illustrated in Table 5.8.

Table 5.7 Attribute-to-attribute part mapping of PUF to UML

PUF XML	**UML XML**
(continuing from example in Table 5.6) <question_link> <number>2.2</number> <questionheading> what </questionheading> <questionText> What subtasks does this task have? </questionText> <linkage> *enquiring about order status* </linkage> <linkage> *ordering selected items* </linkage> < /question_link>	(as in Table 5.6 with additions) <UML:**UseCase** xmi.id="" name =" *paying for ordered items using* *e-Commerce'* isSpecification ="" isRoot="" isLeaf ="" isAbstract=""> ... <UML:**ownedUseCase** xmi.id ="N" name="*enquiring about order* *status*"> </UML: ownedUseCase > <UML:**ownedUseCase** xmi.id = "M" name="*ordering selected items*"¿ < /UML: ownedUseCase > ... < /UML:**UseCase**>

5.4.2 *Multiplicity of Mappings*

Because different methodologies can involve very different structures of requirements/specifications, there are many possible mapping situations that may arise. The MMT is intended to handle a wide range of possible mapping situations.

When dealing with relationships between two types of data, it is important to consider the multiplicity involved in the relationships. Multiplicity denotes the number of source and target entities (or attributes) involved in the relationship. The relationships between two types of methodologies can involve at least four possible types of multiplicity: one-to-one, one-to-many, many-to-one, and many-to-many. The examples in Tables 5.6–5.8 demonstrate a few of these multiplicity types when mapping UE requirements to SE specifications.

One-to-one mappings are relatively simple to specify and implement since there is no ambiguity as to what is being mapped. Table 5.4 specifies some one-to-one mappings between PUF records and UML diagrams. Table 5.6 specifies a one-to-one mapping between a PUF task name and a UML use case name. There may be many individual answers to some PUF questions, each of which requires a one-to-one

Table 5.8 Attribute to new attribute mapping of PUF to UML

PUF XML	**UML XML**
(continuing from example in Table 5.5) <section> <number>2</number> <sectionheading> **Environmental_Information** < /sectionheading> <question_multi> <number>3.1</number> <questionheading> **when** < /questionheading> <questionText> When is this task performed? </questionText> <answer> *performed after ordering selected items* </answer> </question_multi> </section>	<UML:**Constraint** xmi.id="" name =""> <UML: constraintedElement> *paying for ordered items using e-Commerce* < /UML: constraintedElement> ... **<PUF: when>** *performed after ordering selected items* **</PUF: when>** ...

mapping. For example, the answers to the "what" question in Table 5.7 reference two PUF tasks. Redundant one-to-one mappings would occur if we naively created one-to-one mappings between every PUF task reference and its corresponding UML use case. To avoid this, it is important to consider the semantics involved when creating the mapping rules. For example, when a PUF task is referenced in a "what" answer, it denotes a structural relationship between tasks and this structural relationship needs to be maintained in the UML. A one-to-one mapping actually means that every instance of some type of data in the source maps to a unique instance of some other type of data in the target. Thus, the structural mapping of each answer to the question "what" is an example of a one-to-one mapping. The mapping of each line of a PUF task description to its own UML:eAnnotations is also an example of a one-to-one mapping.

Handling one-to-many mappings is also relatively straightforward, since the one-to-one mapping can be repeated many times, using the same source entity and identifying different target entities. While this increases the number of mapping rules, it does not increase the complexity of the mapping. Although no examples of one-to-many mappings occur for PUF and UML, the MMT can handle one-to-many mappings if instances of it are identified when relating other methodologies.

A many-to-one mapping is more complex to handle, since it can involve two different results, depending on whether the 'many' source entities are redundant or different. If two different source attributes are redundant (as in two different sources of task names both mapping to the name of a UML use case), then only a single one-to-one mapping is actually needed (unless, as discussed above, the different instances of task names have different purposes). When two sources containing different data are mapped to the same target attribute, it is important that both pieces of data are retained. It may also be useful to specify the ordering of how data from these two sources is placed into the target attribute. This ordering can easily be done within MMT, by selecting the exact location within target XML that any given mapping leads to.

Applying many-to-one mappings can lead to a target specification produced by the MTT containing conflicting specifications. In order to help the user of the resulting specifications, it may be useful that the source of each of the multiple requirements be identified as reference information along with the text. While this source information could clutter a UML diagram, the diagramming tool need not render this information as part of the diagram. It could, however, make this reference information available in interactive mode to the developer using the tool, either in a pop-up when scrolling over the associated specification or as a link into the UE requirements that have been translated as a basis for the UML diagram. However, if some reference information is to be included in the mapping, then all reference information should be included (since many-to-one mappings often start out as one-to-one mappings that are later added to by another one-to-one mapping to the same target attribute). In order to accommodate this information, the MMT can optionally create references for all source requirements using <UEref> tags in a manner similar to HTML <href> tags.

Many-to-many mappings can often be separated into sets of one-to-one, one-to-many, and/or many-to-one mappings. Since no examples of many-to-many mappings have been identified that cannot be separated, the MMT does not provide support for many-to-many mappings.

5.5 TRANSLATING BETWEEN XML-BASED UE REQUIREMENTS INTO SE SPECIFICATIONS

Translation makes use of mapping information to automatically transform UE specifications into SE requirements. The Methodology Translation Tool (MTT) is used by a project developer (either a usability engineer or a software engineer) to translate UE project data using the source XML schema (e.g., the PUF XML schema – PUF XSD), the target XMI schema (e.g., UML XSD), and the mapping between these schemas (e.g., the mapping of PUF to UML). The result of the mapping is both a version of the data that can be used by the target methodology (e.g., UML-PUF data) and an enhanced target XMI schema that describes how this data should be treated by the target methodology (e.g., PUF augmented XMI schema). This enhanced schema is necessary in order to explain how to interpret any new tags that have been added to accommodate attributes from the source methodology that did not directly translate into attributes of the target methodology. These interactions involving the MMT are illustrated in Figure 5.4.

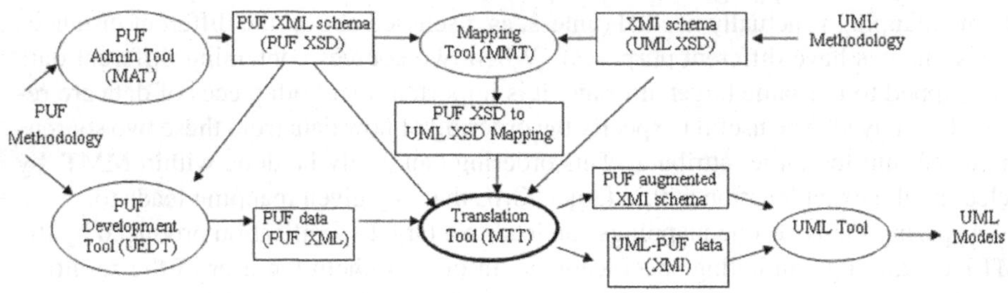

Figure 5.4 Basic interactions of the Methodology Mapping Tool

5.5.1 Adding Integration to Translation

The current MTT is designed to be used to translate PUF (UE) requirements that have been obtained at the start of a project into UML specifications that can be used as a starting point for software engineers developing a project. It is desirable to enhance the capabilities of the MTT so that it can be used to integrate UE requirements throughout the development lifecycle with various types of preexisting data.

The current MTT does not have to deal with any preexisting UML data. It creates new sets of SE specifications (UML-PUF data), involving UML tags, UML-PUF tags, and PUF data inserted within these tags. It also creates a new PUF augmented XMI schema that describes how to use these tags. Figure 5.5 illustrates an integration and translation tool (ITT) that could be used to deal with all combinations of preexisting XML-based requirements and specifications.

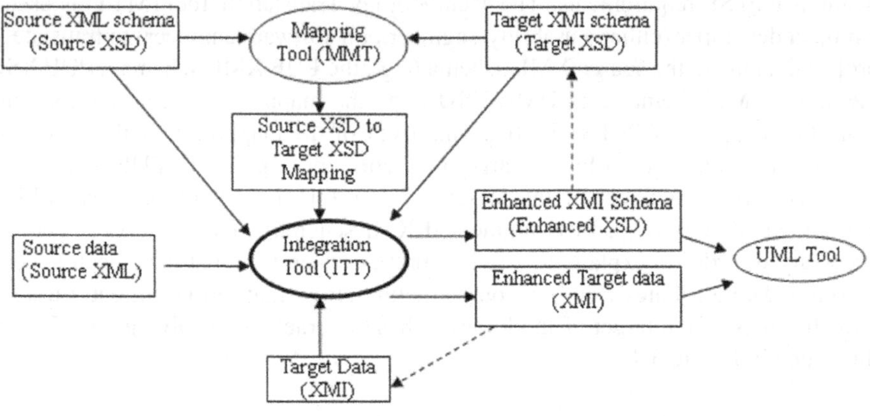

Figure 5.5 An integration and translation tool

There are two main situations where integration of UE requirements with existing SE specifications could occur: where only UML data exists and where UML-PUF data exists.

Both situations need to rely on matching high-level entity names in source and target data. For integration to be effective, UEs and SEs need to use a shared set of entity names (e.g., shared names for UE "users" and SE "actors"). Otherwise, the target data will contain multiple records, that each partially describes some entities. While the MTT provides automatic translation, it is likely that an ITT will require some level of developer interaction to ensure that these names are properly mapped.

UML data can be expected to already exist where UE is not the only activity done at the start of a project. Although Carter et al. (2005) advocate having UE create the initial set of requirements for SE, as a means of getting the value of UE accepted in project, this is not a usual occurrence in current projects. Thus, it is important that the enhanced ITT operations support the insertion of UE requirements in any point within the development lifecycle.

Integrating UE source requirements into an existing set of SE target specifications works like many-to-one mapping, in that it is based on whether or not a suitable target tag exists. Integration starts with creating an enhanced target XMI schema as is done when target specifications do not already exist (e.g., from a source (PUF) XML schema and a target (XMI) schema). Integration then copies existing target (e.g., UML) data to form the basis of the enhanced target data. The final, and most complex integration operation involves using this enhanced target data to determine the appropriate entities and appropriate locations within these entities for adding new (e.g., UML-PUF) tags and new source (e.g., PUF) data to the enhanced target data.

Once the target XMI document involves both UE and SE data, adding further UE source data becomes a more complicated operation. While iteration of both UE and SE data is important, it is likely that at this point the combined data is under the control of SEs using tools that focus on adding SE-related data.

The previously existing enhanced target XMI schema now becomes the target XMI schema used to create a new enhanced target schema. This target XMI schema may have most or all of the UE enhancements it already needs to accommodate new UE source data. However, there may need to be some enhancements to accommodate source XML that was not needed previously in translation and integrations.

Likewise, the existing enhanced target data now becomes the target data used with the source data, the schema, and mapping rules to create a new set of enhanced target data. Again, this may contain most of the data found in the source data (which has been iterated by the UE).

In order to accommodate new UE data, integration will have to compare the new set of UE source data with existing UE data in the set of enhanced target data. There are two possible types of source data that require different types of processing: partial source data and iterated source data.

UE requirements should not need to be complete sets of requirements that are merged together before being used as source data. Large projects may be divided in separate subprojects each of which has its own set of requirements. When dealing with partial requirements, integration should only process additions to the existing target data (making use of common data that already exists in both the target and source data).

Iterated source data contains the complete set of current UE requirements, and as such may require additions, modifications, and even deletions to this target data. Given the destructive nature of modifications and deletions, processing iterated source data should not be fully automated.

5.5.2 Visualizing and Working with the Results

The MTT currently uses Carlson's (2003) *hypermodel* modeling tool to generate UML object models from existing XMI documents or UML-PUF XSD. The generated UML object model showcases the structure of the XMI files using objects, attributes, operations, and relationships. To many people, a concise UML class diagram is the best way to get an overview of XML vocabulary models, which are most frequently published using the W3C XML Schema language (Carlson, 2001).

While the *hypermodel* tool does not meet the needs of integrating all UE requirements into SE specification and development, it does provide a proof of concept for our approach. However, it does not yet support diagram interchange, making exchanging files between UML modeling tools using XMI rarely possible. It is anticipated that in the future, more powerful UML tools will make use of XMI-based specifications. XMI has been adopted as the format for UML model interchange.

To address XMI's deficiency in modeling graphical information, UML 2.0 Diagram Interchange (Object Management Group, 2006a) extends the UML XMI format by allowing graphical elements to be expressed in an XMI representation of geometrical concepts such as node, edge, and connector. UML 2.0 Diagram Interchange allows the exchange of UML models with graphical diagrams via XMI. It supports presenting UML diagrams within a browser using SVG. To do so, EXtensible Stylesheet Language Transformations (XSLT) is adopted to transform the XML graphical elements into SVG format so that SVG-compliant tools can display the UML diagrams.

5.6 CONCLUSION

In this chapter we introduced research under way that deals with developing UE methods and methodologies, especially the PUF methodology and the CAP method. We described a set of XML-based and XMI-based tools for creating, mapping, transforming (translating and integrating) sets of UE requirements and SE specifications. These tools can be used to better integrate UE within software engineering controlled development projects, and to help develop accessible software systems. We also recognize a need for improvements to the SE tools that make use of XMI-based specifications, in order for this integration to be fully accomplished.

References

Adams, R., Bass, L., and John, B. (2006). Experience with using general usability scenarios on the software architecture of a collaborative system. In (Seffah et al., 2005), pages 87–110.

Carlson, D. (2001). *Modeling XML applications with UML : practical e-business applications*. Addison-Wesley, Reading: MA.

Carlson, D. (2003). http://www.xmlmodeling.com/.

Carter, J. A. (1999). Incorporating standards and guidelines in an approach that balances usability concerns for developers and end-users. *Interacting with Computers*, 12(2):179–206.

Carter, J. A., Liu, J., Schneider, K., and Fourney, D. (2005). Transforming usability engineering requirements into software engineering specifications: From PUF to UML. In (Seffah et al., 2005), chapter 9, page 391.

Cortellessa, V. and Pompei, A. (2004). Towards a uml profile for qos: a contribution in the reliability domain. In *Proc. Fourth International Workshop on Software and Performance (WOSP-04)*, pages 197–206.

Cysneiros, L. M. and Sampaio do Prado Leite, J. C. (2001). Using UML to reflect non-functional requirements. In *CASCON '01: Proceedings of the 2001 Conference of the Center for Advanced Studies on Collaborative Research*, Toronto, Ontario, Canada. IBM Center for Advanced Studies.

Fourney, D. and Carter, J. A. (2006). A standard method of profiling the accessibility needs of computer users with vision and hearing impairments. In *CVHI 2006 Conference and Workshop on Assistive Technologies for Vision and Hearing Impairment, EURO-ASSIST-VHI-4*, Kufstein, Austria.

Gaffar, A. and Seffah, A. (2005). An XML multitier pattern dissemination system. In Rivero, L. C., Doorn, J. H., and Ferraggine, V. E., editors, *Encyclopedia of Database Technologies and Applications*, pages 740–744. Idea Group, Montreal.

Huang, F. (2006). Method for translating and linking XML-based specifications between development methodologies. In *Proc. 2006 Graduate Symposium, Department of Computer Science*, University of Saskatchewan, Saskatoon, SK, Canada.

ISO (2005). Information technology—XML metadata interchange specification. ISO/IEC PAS 19503, 116 pages.

ISO (2006a). Ergonomics of human-system interaction—accessibility guidelines for information/communication technology (ICT) equipment and services. ISO DIS 9241-20, 22 pages.

ISO (2006b). Ergonomics of human-system interaction—guidance on software accessibility. ISO DIS 9241-171, 83 pages.

ISO (2006c). Software engineering—metamodel for development methodologies. ISO FDIS 24744, 78 pages.

ISO (2007). Information technology—framework for specifying a common access profile (CAP) of needs and capabilities of users, systems, and their environments. ISO/IEC FDIS 24756, 30 pages.

ISO/IEC (1998). *ISO/IEC 9241-14: Ergonomic requirements for office work with visual display terminals (VDT)s—Part 14 Menu dialogues*. ISO/IEC 9241-14: 1998.

Jagne, J. and Smith-Atakan, A. S. (2006). Cross-cultural interface design strategy. *Universal Access in the Information Society*. online-first version, DOI 10.1007/s10209-006-0048-6, 7 pages.

Jerome, B. and Kazman, R. (2005). Surveying the solitudes: An investigation into the relationships between human computer interaction and software engineering in practice. In (Seffah et al., 2005), chapter 6, page 391.

Object Management Group (2006a). Diagram interchange, v1.0. http://www.omg.org/technology/documents/formal/ diagram.htm.

Object Management Group (2006b). UML 2.1 XSD files. http://www.omg.org/cgi-bin/doc?ptc/2006-04-05.

Savadis, A. and Stephanidis, C. (2004). Unified user interface development: the software engineering of universally accessible interactions. *Universal Access in the Information Society*, 3:165–193.

Seffah, A., Gulliksen, J., and Desmarais, M. C., editors (2005). *Human-Centered Software Engineering: Integrating Usability in the Development Process*. New York: Springer-Verlag.

Seffah, A. and Metzker, E. (2004). The obstacles and myths of usability and software engineering. *Commun. ACM*, 47(12):71–76.

Titus, J. (2006) Building an Administration CASE Tool for CASE Tools, Department of Computer Science, University of Saskatchewan, Saskatoon, SK, Canada, unpublished report, 17 pages

University of California (2007). http://argouml.tigris.org/features.html.

Wolinski, A. (2003). Developing a CASE Tool for the Putting Usability First Methodology Department of Computer Science, University of Saskatchewan, Saskatoon, SK, Canada, unpublished report, 17 pages

Zhang, Q. and Eberlein, A. (2003). Architectural design of an intelligent requirements engineering tool. In *Proceedings of Canadian Conference on Electrical and Computer Engineering*, volume 2, pages 1375 – 1378, Montreal, Canada.

II Modeling and Model-Driven Engineering

6 MULTIPATH TRANSFORMATIONAL DEVELOPMENT OF USER INTERFACES WITH GRAPH TRANSFORMATIONS

Quentin Limbourg* and Jean Vanderdonckt**

*SmalS-MvM

Av. Prince Royal, 102 – B-1050 Brussels, Belgium.

**Belgian Laboratory of Computer-Human Interaction (BCHI),

Louvain School of Management (LSM),

Université catholique de Louvain

Place des Doyens, 1 – B-1348 Louvain-la-Neuve, Belgium.

Abstract. In software engineering, transformational development is aimed at developing computer systems by transforming a coarse-grained specification of a system to its final code through a series of transformation steps. Transformational development is known to bring benefits such as: correctness by construction, explicit mappings between development steps, and reversibility of transformations. No comparable piece exists in the literature that provides a formal system applying transformational development in the area of user interface engineering. This chapter defines such a system. For this purpose, a mathematical system for expressing specifications and transformation rules is introduced. This system is based on graph transformations. The problem of managing the transformation rules is detailed, e.g., how to enable a developer to access, define, extend, restrict or relax, test, verify, and apply appropriate transformations. A tool supporting this development paradigm is also described and exemplified. Transformational development, applied to the development of user interfaces of interactive systems, allows reusability of design knowledge used to develop user interfaces and fosters incremental development of user interfaces by applying alternative transformations.

6.1 INTRODUCTION

A recent survey of the area of Human-Computer Interaction (HCI) compared to the area of Software Engineering (SE) would find the former to be mainly empirical, experience-based, and relying on implicit knowledge and the latter to be notoriously and deliberately structured, principle-based, and relying on explicit knowledge. The development lifecycle of highly-interactive systems in general and of their User Interface (UI) in particular form the cornerstones of HCI, which has been observed to suffer from several shortcomings that are intrinsic either to the type of interactive systems being developed or to the existing practices used. Among these shortcomings are the following observations:

- *Lack of rigorousness*: on the one hand, the development lifecycle of interactive systems cannot be based on the same rigorous models that are typically used in SE (Brown 1997). On the other hand, HCI lifecycle is submitted to a high order of complexity that is neither reflected nor well supported in existing models and methods (Wegner 1997).

- *Lack of systematicity*: as SE aimed for a well-structured method for developing highly complex systems, so did HCI for developing interactive systems. However, the systematicity and the reproducibility found in SE methods cannot be transferred straightforwardly to HCI: the development lifecycle remains intrinsically open, ill-defined, and highly iterative (Sumner et al. 1997) as opposed to the domain of SE where it is structured, well-defined, and progressive (D'Souza and Wills, 1999).

- *Lack of a principle-based approach*: where SE proceeds in the development from one step to another according to well-established principles, in contrast HCI usually advances in a more opportunistic way when the current result is usable enough to proceed to the next step (Bodart et al., 1995; Puerta, 1997).

- *Lack of explicitness*: not only the knowledge required to properly conduct the development lifecycle of interactive systems is not as principled as in SE, but also it is implicitly maintained in the mind of experienced designers. This knowledge is therefore harder to communicate from one person to another, although initiatives exist that make this knowledge more explicit through design patterns, usability guidelines. Even more, when this knowledge is made more explicit, nothing can guarantee that it is applied uniformly and consistently within a same development project or across various development projects.

The aforementioned comparison holds as long as significant efforts toward structured, principle-based, and explicitly based process devoted in SE remain unparalleled with the area of HCI. This chapter seeks to contribute to reestablish a balance between HCI and SE regarding this aspect by providing an effort in the direction of a true development process for UI engineering with the same quality factors that are usually found in SE. For this purpose, it is expected that a model-driven approach of UI development could represent an engineering effort attempting to systematize UI development. It does so by constructing high-level requirements and, progressively, transforms them to obtain specifications that are detailed and precise enough to be rendered or transformed into code. This type of approach is referred to in the SE literature as the *transformational approach*. More recently, along with the Model Driven Architecture (OMG, 2006) proposal (Miller and Mukerij, 2003), model processing and transformation has gained a particular importance in the software engineering literature (Rensik, 2003; Kuske et al., 2002; Gerber et al., 2002).

Several ingredients are lacking in existing HCI methods to fully achieve a transformational approach in the development of UI. Conceptually, there is no systematic understanding of the relationships among all development artifacts (i.e., models) needed to build a UI. Furthermore, the design knowledge required to feed these models and to make them smoothly evolve over time from one development step to another is often implicitly maintained in the minds of developers and designers and/or hard-coded in supporting software. When such design knowledge exists, it is not always systematically, consistently, and correctly applied throughout the project or across projects.

Sumner et al. (1997) explain that the development process, as usually conducted in HCI, is a process that is eminently open (several development steps can be conducted or considered simultaneously), ill-defined (the initial requirements are usually largely incomplete, if not inconsistent), and mostly iterative (it seems impossible to conduct a development step in such a way that its outputs are definitive).

Nanard and Nanard (1995) report that the development lifecycle of an interactive application consists of a sophisticated Echternach process that does not always proceed linearly in a predefined way. It is rather an interwoven set of development steps, which alternate bottom-up and top-down paths, with selecting, backtracking, and switching among several actions. Thus any method and development tool is expected to effectively and efficiently support a flexible development lifecycle, which does not stiffen the mental process of expert designers in a fixed procedural schema. On the other end, when we consider the needs of moderately experienced designers, the method and its supporting tool should enforce a minimum number of priority constraints. These constraints should define which development artifacts must be specified before others, suggesting for example how and when to proceed from one development step to another.

The variety of the approaches adopted in organizations and the rigidity of existing solutions provide ample motivations for a UI development paradigm that is flexible enough to accommodate multiple development paths and design situations while staying precise enough to manipulate information required for UI development. To alleviate these problems, a development paradigm of **multipath UI development** is introduced that is characterized by the following principles:

- *Expressiveness of UI*: any UI is expressed depending on the context of use via a suite of models that are analyzable, editable, and manipulable by software (Puerta, 1997).

- *Central storage of models*: each model is stored in a model repository where all UI models are expressed according to the same UI Description Language (UIDL).

- *Transformational approach*: each model stored in the model repository may be subject to one or many transformations supporting various development steps (Eisenstein *et al.* 2001).

- *Multiple development paths*: development steps can be combined together to form development paths that are compatible with the organization's constraints, conventions, and context of use. For example, a series of transformations may derive a presentation from a task model.

- *Flexible development approaches*: development approaches are supported by following alternate development paths (Nanard and Nanard, 1995) and enable designers to freely shift between these paths depending on the changes imposed by the context of use (Calvary et al., 2003).

To address the above requirements, this chapter presents a method for expressing models that are relevant to HCI, but expressed in an SE way so that HCI development paths can be supported with a level of flexibility that is desired in HCI, while keeping the rigorousness brought by SE. For this purpose, the present chapter is structured as follows: Section 6.2 presents existing work that is related to the issue of structuring the HCI development process via the model-based approach similarly to what MDA is doing in SE. Section 6.3 introduces and motivates the choice of graph grammars and graph transformations to ensure a transformational approach guaranteeing expressiveness and flexibility. The methodology introduced in this chapter supports model transformation based on these concepts. Section 6.4 analyzes how traditional development approaches found in SE can be addressed in a parallel way in HCI by identifying a series of levels of abstractions between which transformations can be applied. Throughout this section, ample examples of design knowledge manipulated at each level are provided. Section 6.5 summarizes the main benefits brought by our methodology and perceived shortcomings.

6.2 RELATED WORK

Model-Based Approach of User Interface (MBAUI) has been around for many years, basing its power on models in order to develop interactive systems. MBAUI can be assimilated to a larger trend in software engineering called the transformational development paradigm. Its *modus operandi* resides in the performance of model-to-model transformations to support model engineering activities of UI development. To provide relevant concepts and a stepwise development cycle is essential in the definition of a development lifecycle. Support for a developer in accomplishing development steps is also highly desirable. In the context of MBAUI, the nature of the support provided to a developer can consist for multiple elements (Puerta, 1997): a simple syntax editor, a graphical model editor, a well-furbished and exemplified documentation system, a structured knowledge base, a model derivation module, a model analyzer, and a code generator. Such a methodology combining all these advantages does not exist today.

Historically, MBAUI has exploited models of various types and for various uses. MECANO (Puerta, 1996) automatically generates presentation and dialog models as intermediary steps toward a NeXT GUI from a domain model expressed in an object-oriented language. JANUS (Balzert et al. 1996) exploits relationships such as inheritance, aggregation and generalization of a domain model to deduce a UI structure. GENIUS (Janssen et al. 1993) derives UI code from an extended entity-relationship model and, so called, dialog nets based on Petri nets. MOBI-D (Puerta, 1997) uses as input scenarios, a task model and a domain model to automatically generate a GUI. MOBI-D is equipped with a module called TIMM learning from a designer's choices to sharpen a widget selection process.

TEALLACH (Griffiths et al., 2001) allows designing database UIs while allowing co-evolutionary design of a user's task model design is the first tool to integrate explicitly in the design process the concept of model mapping. More recently tools like ARTSTUDIO (Thevenin, 2001) or TERESA (Mori et al. , 2004) exploited the information contained in a user's task model, to derive context-specific presentation of a UI.

All of the above-cited tools and methods perform some model mapping and transformation, somehow. None of them provides an explicit mechanism to represent and manipulate heuristics (or patterns) governing the model transformation process. Some tools do involve some transformational mechanism, but it is built-in so that their modifiability is impossible.

MBAUI is suffering from a bottleneck in the consolidation and dissemination of the knowledge used to realize model transformation. From this statement we may define two requirements to fill our research agenda:

- *Core requirement 1*: an easy-to-understand and uniform description of models subject to transformation. This description would cover various viewpoints on a UI system.
- *Core requirement 2*: an explicit formalism to specify and perform UI model transformations.

6.3 EXPRESSING THE UI DEVELOPMENT CYCLE WITH GRAPH TRANSFORMATIONS

Developing a UI according to an MBAUI philosophy can be seen as an activity of transforming a high-level specification into a more concrete specification (or code). Unfortunately, no generic solution has been proposed to address the problem of defining a computational framework for expressing, manipulating, and executing model transformation involved in engineering approaches to UI construction. To achieve this goal, several requirements have been identified (Limbourg and Vanderdonckt, 2004a, 2004b):

- A definition of each manipulated artifact capturing different *viewpoints* necessary to UI development.

- A definition of relationships between different *viewpoints*. These relationships are essential in order to obtain an integrated view of a specification.
- A representation of the knowledge needed to perform model-to-model transformations.
- A mechanism to manipulate the knowledge to perform a derivation. UI model derivation is heuristic by nature. A satisfactory solution implies at least a possibility, for a developer, to choose between different derivation heuristics. Ideally, a developer should be able to alter or redefine these heuristics.
- A mechanism to check desirable properties on derived models. These properties might be consistency, correctness, or usability.

6.3.1 Approaches for Model Transformation

In the next paragraphs we survey a number of existing techniques and evaluate their relevance to our goal. Imperative languages provide a means to perform model transformation:

- Text-processing languages like Perl or Awk are popular for performing small text transformation. These tools cannot be considered to specify complex transformation systems as they force the programmer to focus on very low-level syntactic details.
- Several environments provide APIs to manipulate and transform models and, often, their corresponding to specific metamodels: Jamda (Boocock, 2003), UMLAUT (Ho *et al.*, 1999), dMof (Queensland University, 2002).

Relational approaches (Akehurst et al., 2003; Gerber et al., 2002) rely on the specification of mappings between source and target element types along with the conditions in which a mapping must be instantiated. Mapping rules can be purely declarative, and non executable, or executable thanks to a definition of an execution semantic. Relational approaches are generally implemented using a logic-based programming language and require a clear separation of the source and target model.

XSLT transformations are a good candidate as models have, generally, a syntactical representation in an XML-compliant format. The way XSLT proceeds is very appealing as it (1) searches for matches in a source XML document (2) executes a set of procedural instructions, when a match is found, to progressively construct a target XML file. Unfortunately, some experiences (Gerber *et al.*, 2002) showed that XSLT transformations are not convenient to compute model transformation for two main reasons (1) their verbosity has been identified as a major problem to manage complex sets of transformation rules (2) their lack of abstraction: progressively constructing a target XML file entails an inclusion, in transformation rules, of syntactic details relative to the target file.

Common Warehouse Metamodel (CWM) Specification (Object Management Group, 2003) provides a set of concepts to describe model transformation. Transformations can be specified using a black box or a white box metaphor.

Transformations are grouped in transformation tasks (some meaningful set of transformations), which are in turn themselves grouped in transformation activities. A control flow of transformation can be defined between transformation tasks at this level (with the concept of transformation step). Even if transformations allow a fine-grained mapping between source and target element, CWM does not provide a predefined language to specify the way these elements are transformed one to another.

Graph grammars and graph transformations have been used for many years to represent complex transformation systems. It has been used notably in the software engineering field for representing, for instance: software refactoring (Mens et al., 2001), software evolution (Heckel et al., 2002), multiagent system modeling (Depke et al., 2002), modeling language formalization (Varro *et al.*, 2002). Graph grammars have been proved an 'efficient in time' formalism for specifying and computing any model-to-model transformation (Agrawal et al., 2003). As main advantages to our approach, graph transformation specification: (1) are rather declarative (they are based on graph patterns expression) (2) provide an appealing graphical syntax which does not exclude the use of a textual one (3) are executable thanks to an grounded execution semantic based on push-out theory (4) offer modularity by allowing the fragmentation of complex transformation heuristics into small, independent chunks. In the context of UI development with graph transformations, two pioneering work can be mentioned (Freund et al., 1992; Sucrow, 1998). Both approaches make an interesting use of graph transformations but have a too narrow conceptual coverage to address a fully defined UI development cycle.

6.3.2 Our Methodology

Our methodology proposes a framework (Figure 6.1) coping with the development of UIs for single and multiple contexts of use. To achieve this goal, this methodology relies on a set of models structured in four levels of abstraction: (1) an implementation level contains UI code. The UI code is generated from models contained at the model level (2) a model level contains models developed for an actual system. A model at model level is an instance of a meta-model at meta-model level (3) a meta-model level contains a definition of all concepts needed to build UI models (4) a meta-meta model level contains the basic structure definition used to define the meta-model (and transitively, the model level), i.e., a directed, attributed, labeled graph structure.

In a model-based approach of UI development, a designer's task consists mainly in defining models and producing UI code according to these previously defined models. At each phase of the development cycle, specific artifacts are defined; these artifacts correspond to, so called, *viewpoints* on the system. We propose four viewpoints on UI systems:

1. *Computation-independent viewpoint* contains elements enabling the description of a UI system independently of any computer-related considerations. This viewpoint is composed of a *task model and domain model.* A task model is a hierarchical decomposition of the tasks to be carried out by a user to achieve her goal. After a comparison of a dozen task modeling techniques (Limbourg and Vanderdonckt, 2003), an altered version of ConcurTaskTree (CTT) (Mori

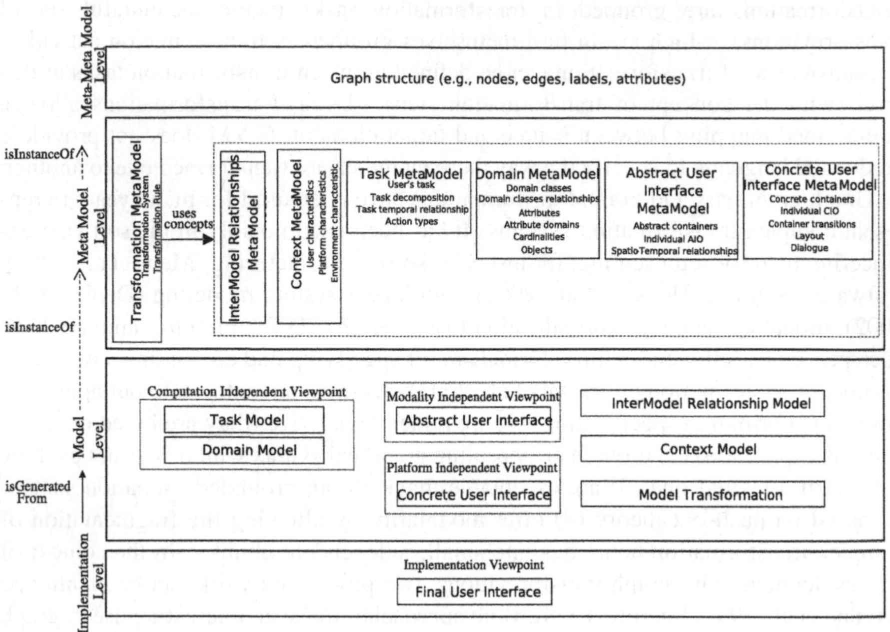

Figure 6.1 Overall framework of our methodology

et al., 2004) has been chosen to represent user's tasks and their logical and temporal ordering. CTT has been altered in the sense that a task taxonomy has been introduced to better describe the nature of a basic task, leaf of a task decomposition. This taxonomy facilitates a mapping between tasks and interaction objects supposed to support this task. A *domain model* contains domain-oriented concepts as they are required by the tasks described in a task model. A domain model describes the real-world concepts and their interactions as understood by users (D'Souza and Wills, 1999). Our domain model is a UML class diagram populated with classes, attributes, methods, objects (Larman, 2001). Concepts contained in a domain model are at a certain point manipulated by systems users. By manipulated, it is meant that domain concepts are at a certain point subject of an exchange (an input or/and an output) between the user and the system. Consequently, domain concepts can be mapped onto elements describing a UI structure and behavior (e.g., abstract UI, concrete UI).

2. *Modality-independent viewpoint* contains elements that are independent of the modality (e.g., graphical interaction, vocal interaction, speech synthesis and recognition, video-based interaction, virtual, augmented, or mixed reality) in which the UI they describe will be rendered. This viewpoint contains an *Abstract UI* (AUI) specification. An AUI defines abstract containers by grouping subtasks according to various criteria (e.g., task model structural patterns, cognitive load analysis, and semantic relationships identification), a navigation

scheme between the Abstract Containers (AC) and selects one or several *Abstract Individual Component* (AIC) for each basic user's task. Each "abstract individual component" is attached to one or several facets describing its function in a UI. We identify four types of facets: input, output, navigation, and control. Abstract interaction objects can be mapped onto: (i) a task or a set of tasks they support, (ii) a domain class or a set of attributes they represent, (iii) a concrete interaction object.

3. *Platform-independent viewpoint* contains a viewpoint that is (1) independent of the computing platform for which the system will be implemented and (2) dependent of a particular modality. This viewpoint contains a *Concrete UI* specification. A CUI concretizes an abstract UI for a given context of use. A CUI is populated with *Concrete Interaction Objects* (CIOs) (Vanderdonckt and Bodart, 1993).

4. *An implementation viewpoint* is a viewpoint containing a coded UI i.e., any UI running on a particular platform either by interpretation (e.g., through a browser) or by execution (e.g., after compilation of code).

Three other models are defined in our framework: (1) an inter-model relationship model, (2) a context model, and (3) a transformation model. These models do not define any particular viewpoint but rather are needed in a UI development process at every phase: (1) contains a set of mapping declarations linking elements belonging to different viewpoints, (2) contains a description of all the context considered during the development process, and (3) contains a set of rules enabling the transformation of one viewpoint into another or to adapt a viewpoint for a new context of use.

Our viewpoint structuring can be compared (Figure 6.2) with respect to the Model-Driven Architecture (MDA) proposal provided by the Object Management Group (Miller and Mukerij, 2003). MDA proposes a set of concepts and methodological recommendations to address the development of systems in a context characterized by a diversity of evolving computing platforms. MDA *viewpoints* are: (1) a Computation-Independent Model (CIM), sometimes called business model, shows a system in a way that is totally independent of technology (typically a business class diagram in OO methods). (2) A Platform-Independent Model (PIM) provides a view of the system independently of any details of the possible platform for which a system is supposed to be built. (3) A Platform-Specific Model (PSM) provides a view of a system that is dependent on a specific platform type for which a system is supposed to be built. (4) An implementation is a specification providing all details necessary to put a system into operation.

6.3.3 Transformation Is the Name of the Game

Our methodology enables expressing and executing model transformation based on UI viewpoints. Figure 6.3 illustrates the different kinds of transformation steps in our framework:

- *Reification* is a transformation of a high-level requirement into a form that is appropriate for low-level analysis or design.

Table 6.1 A comparison of terms used in MDA and our methodology

Model-Driven Architecture	Our methodology
Computing-Independent Model	Computation-independent viewpoint: task and domain models
Platform-Independent Model	(1) Modality-Independent viewpoint: Abstract UI model; (2) platform independent viewpoint: Concrete UI
Platform-Specific Model	Implementation viewpoint: UI Code
Platform Model	Context Model

- *Abstraction* is an extraction of a high-level requirement from a set of low-level requirement artifacts or from code.
- *Translation* is a transformation a UI in consequence of a context of use change. The context of use is, here, defined as a triple of the form *(E, P, U)* where E is an possible or actual environments considered for a software system, P is a target platform, U is a user category.
- *Reflection* is a transformation of the artifacts of any level onto artifacts of the same level of abstraction, but different constructs or various contents (Calvary et al., 2003).
- *Code generation* is a process of transforming a concrete UI model into a compilable or interpretable code.
- *Code reverse engineering* is the inverse process of code generation.

The different transformation types are instantiated by *development steps* (each occurrence of a numbered arrow in Figure 6.3). These development steps may be combined to form *development paths.* Development paths are detailed in Section 6.4. The content of Section 6.4 is detailed right of Figure 6.3).

While code generation and code reverse engineering are supported by specific techniques (not covered in this chapter), we use graph transformations to perform model-to-model transformations i.e., reifications, abstractions and translations.

The models have been designed with an underlying graph structure. Consequently any graph transformation rule can be applied to any UI specification. Graph transformations have been shown convenient formalism (Limbourg and Vanderdonckt, 2004a, 2004b). The main reasons are (1) an attractive graphical syntax, (2) a clear execution semantic, and (3) an inherent declarativeness of this formalism. Development steps

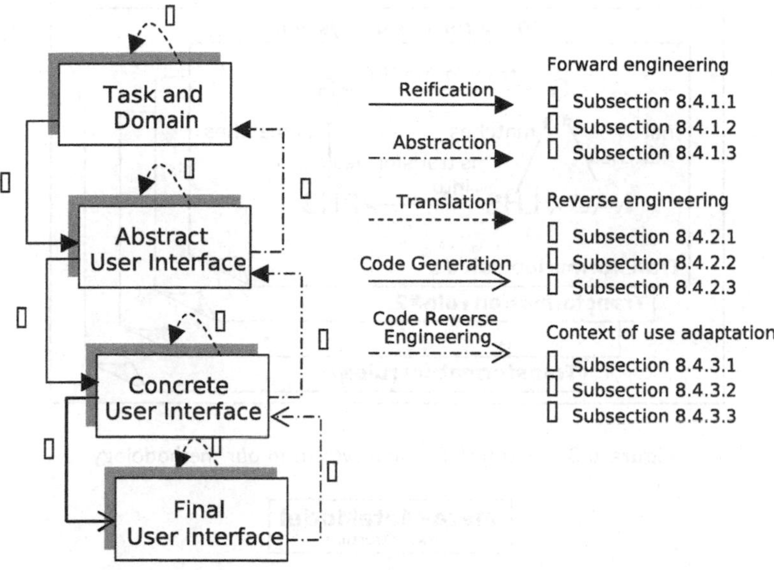

Figure 6.2 Transformations between viewpoints

are realized with transformation systems. A transformation system is a set of (individual) transformation rules. A transformation rule is a graph rewriting rule equipped with negative application conditions and attribute conditions (Rozenberg, 1997).

Figure 6.3 illustrates how a transformation system applies to a specification: let G be a specification, when (1) a Left-Hand Side (LHS) matches into G and (2) a Negative Application Condition (NAC) does not matche into G (note that several NAC may be associated with a rule), and (3) the LHS is replaced by a Right-Hand Side (RHS). G is resultantly transformed into G', a resultant specification. All elements of G not covered by the match are considered as unchanged. All elements contained in the LHS and not contained in the RHS are considered as deleted (i.e., rules have destructive power). To add to the expressive power of transformation rules, variables may be associated to attributes within an LHS. Theses variables are initialized in the LHS; their value can be used to assign an attribute in the expression of the RHS (e.g., LHS : button.name:=x, RHS : task.name:=x). An expression may also be defined to compare a variable declared in the LHS with a constant or with another variable. This mechanism is called *attribute condition*.

As shown in Figure 6.4, transformation rules have a common meta-model with our models. Furthermore, to preserve the consistency of transformed artifact, resultant UI models are checked upon their meta-model. Transformation rules resulting in a non-consistent resulting graph are just not applied.

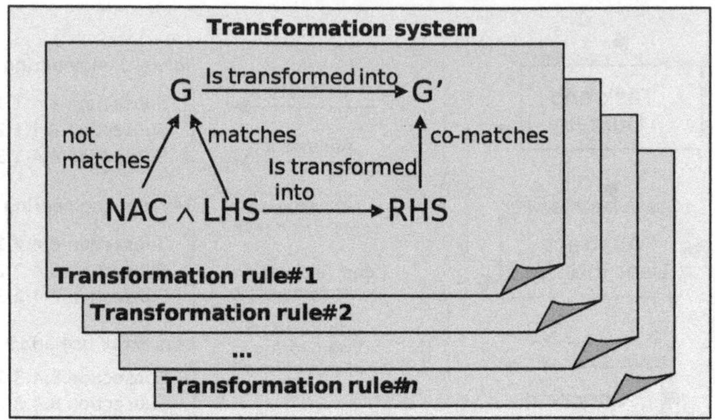

Figure 6.3 A transformation system in our methodology

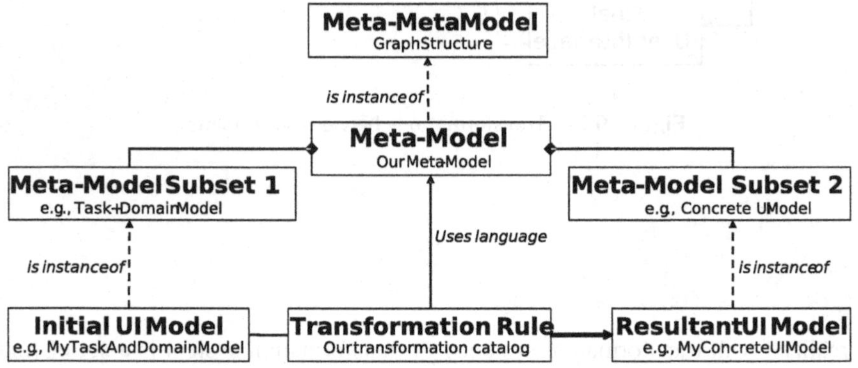

Figure 6.4 Framework for model transformations

6.4 DEVELOPMENT PATHS

Transformation types have been introduced in Section 6.3.3. These transformation types are instantiated into *development steps*. These development steps may be composed to form *development paths*. Several types of development paths are identified:

- **Forward engineering** (or **requirement derivation**) is a composition of *reifications and code generation* enabling a transformation of a high-level viewpoint into a lower-level viewpoint.

- **Reverse engineering** is a composition of *abstractions* and *code reverse engineering* enabling a transformation of a low-level viewpoint into a higher level viewpoint.

- **Context of use adaptation** is a composition of a *translation* with another type of transformation enabling a viewpoint to be adapted in order to reflect a change in the context of use of a UI.

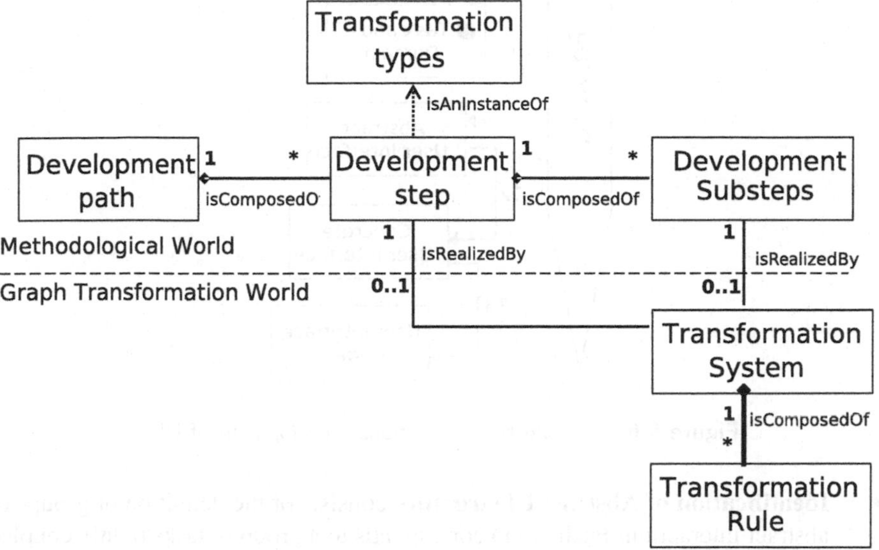

Figure 6.5 Transformation paths, step and substep

As show in Figure 6.5, development paths are composed of development steps. Development steps are instances of transformation types described in Section 6.3.3. Development steps are decomposed into development substeps. A development substep realizes a basic goal assumed by the developer while constructing a system. Some basic goals have been identified by Luo (1995). It may consist, for instance, of selecting concrete interaction objects, defining navigation, etc. Development steps and development substeps may be realized by transform system. In the remainder of this section, subsections 6.4.1, 6.4.2, and 6.4.3 respectively illustrate main development paths (forward, reverse engineering, and context of use adaptation). An example for each development step and substep is provided. All examples use the graphical formalism of the tool AGG (Ehrig et al., 1999).

6.4.1 Forward Engineering

As shown in Figure 6.6, the starting point of UI forward engineering is the construction of a task specification and a domain model. This initial representation is then transformed into an abstract UI which is then transformed into a concrete UI model. The concrete UI model is then used to generate UI code. A forward engineering process is fully illustrated hereafter.

From Task & Domain to Abstract User Interface. Step T1 (Figure 6.6) concerns the derivation of an AUI from models at the computation-independent viewpoint (e.g., a task, a domain, or task and domain model). This development step may involve the following development substeps:

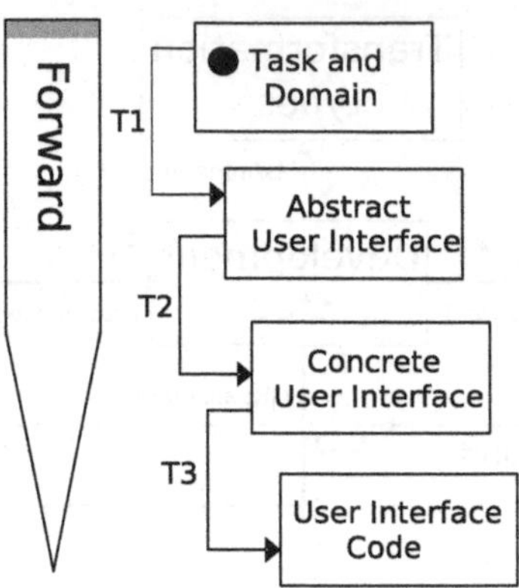

Figure 6.6 Forward transformational development of UIs

- **Identification of Abstract UI structure** consists of the definition of groups of abstract interaction. Each group corresponds to a group of tasks tightly coupled together. The meaning of "task coupling" may vary from one method to another. It goes from very simple heuristics like "for each group of task child of a same task generate an interaction space" to sophisticated heuristics exploiting temporal ordering and decomposition structure between tasks (e.g., enable task sets method followed by Mori et al. ,2004) or information flow between tasks e.g., TRIDENT method proposed by Vanderdonckt and Bodart (1993).

Example 1 is a transformation system composed of two rules enabling the creation of a simple hierarchical structure containing abstract individual components and abstract containers.

- Rule 1 (Figure 6.7): For each leaf task of a task tree, create an Abstract Individual Element. For each task, parent of a leaf task, create an Abstract. Link the abstract container and the Abstract Individual Element by a containment relationship.
  - Rule 2 (Figure 6.8): create an Abstract Container structure similar to the task decomposition structure.

- **Selection of abstract individual component** consists of finding the best abstract individual component type to support one or several user's tasks. Task type, attribute types and domain of value of domain concepts, structure of the domain model are notably important information to perform an adequate AIC selection.

Example 2 is composed of rule 3. It exploits information on task action types to attach appropriate facets to corresponding abstract individual components.

- Rule 3 (Figure 6.9): for each abstract individual element mapped onto a task the nature of which consists in the activation of an operation and this task is

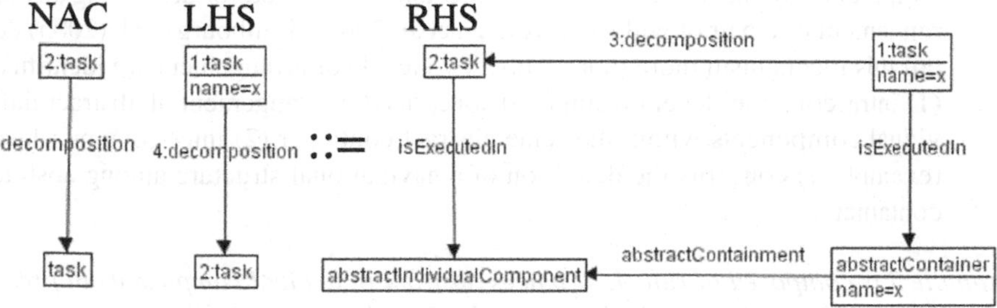

Figure 6.7 Creation of abstract individual components derived from task model leaves

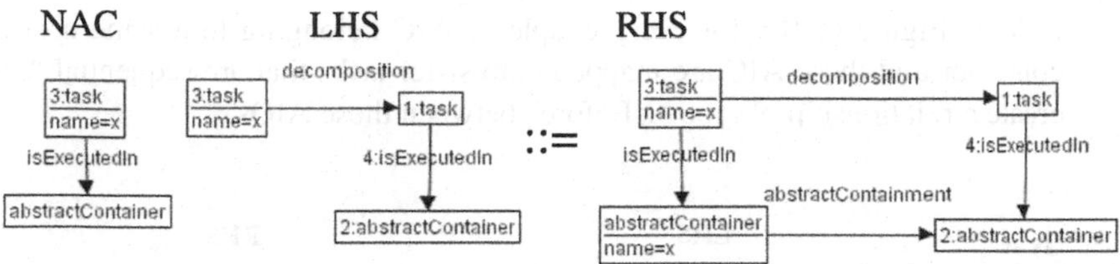

Figure 6.8 Creation of abstract containers derived from task model structure

mapped onto a class, assign to the abstract individual component an action facet that activates the mapped method.

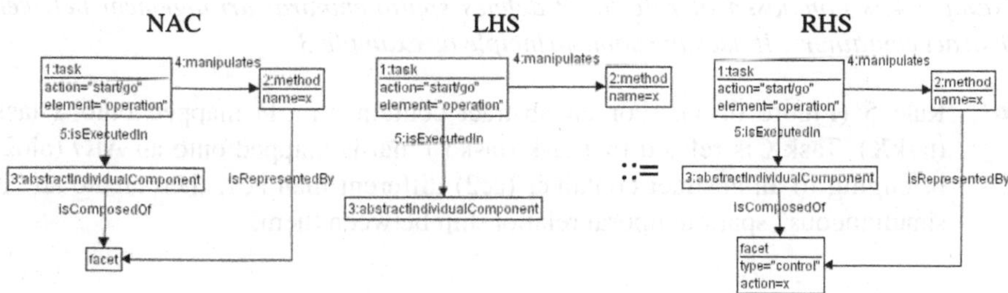

Figure 6.9 Creation of a facet for an abstract individual component derived from task action type

- **Identification of spatiotemporal arrangement of abstract individual components and abstract containers**. The structure of a task model is exploited to derive spatiotemporal arrangement of elements contained in an AUI. This, temporal relationships defined between tasks can be respected in the abstract specification. This is an essential guarantee of usability of the UI to be created. Spatiotemporal relationships between abstract elements are done using Allen temporal relationships generalized for 2D and specialized for describing any arrangement of a pair of widgets (Trevisan et al. 2002). Limbourg et al. (2005) detail this mechanism more thoroughly. Two levels of arrangement are identified: (1) intra-container level (example 3) concerns the arrangement of abstract individual components within the same abstract container (2) inter-container level (example 4) concerns the definition of a navigational structure among abstract containers.

Example 3 is composed of rule 4. It places abstract individual components in precedence relationship ("isBefore") based on the fact that the tasks they represent are sequential ("≫"). To perform a complete arrangement every type of task temporal relationship should be covered by a rule.

- Rule 4 (Figure 6.10): for every couple of AIC belonging to a same abstract container and these AIC are mapped onto sister tasks that are sequential "≫", create a relationship of type "isBefore" between these AIOs.

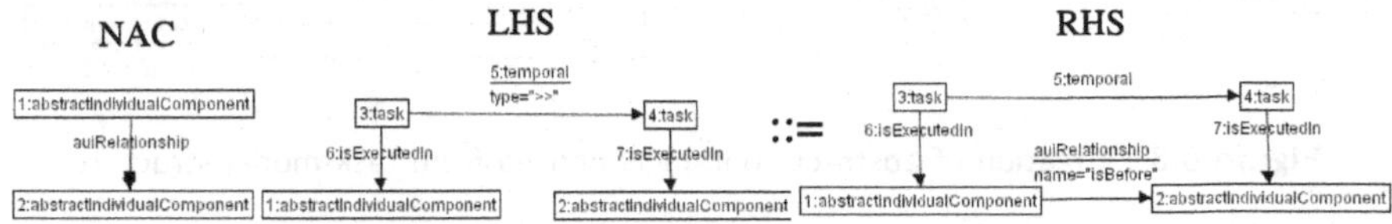

Figure 6.10 A sequentialization of abstract individual component derived from task temporal relationships

Example 4 is composed of rule 5. It defines spatiotemporal arrangement between abstract containers. It uses the same principle as example 3

- Rule 5 (Figure 6.11): For an abstract container (ac1) mapped onto a task (taskX). TaskX is related to a task (taskY) that is mapped onto an AIO (aio2) belonging to an abstract container (ac2) different than ac1, then create an "is simultaneous" spatiotemporal relationship between them.

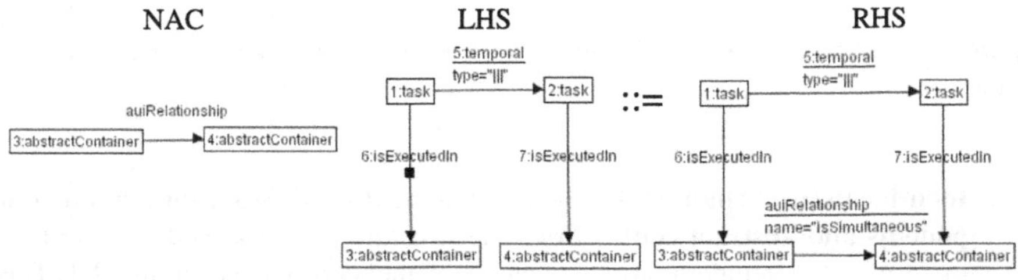

Figure 6.11 A placement of abstract container derived from task temporal relationships

From Abstract User Interface to Concrete User Interface . Step T2 consists of generating a concrete UI from an abstract UI. This development step may involve the following development substeps:

- **Reification of abstract containers into concrete containers.** An abstract container may be reified in different types of concrete containers. Factors influencing this transformation are: modality, context of use, interaction style, designer's preference. A major difficulty of this step resides in the problem of choosing an appropriate level to group abstract containers into a concrete container (typically a window for a graphical modality). A minimal choice would be to create a concrete container (e.g., a window) for each group of sibling leaf tasks. A maximal solution would be to group all abstract individual components and all abstract containers into a single concrete container (e.g., one window).

Example 5 is a transformation system composed of rules 6 and 7. This system transforms into window, abstract containers at a certain depth in the abstract container hierarchy. All abstract containers content is reified and embedded into the newly created window.

- Rule 6 (Figure 6.12): Each abstract container at level "leaf-l" is transformed into a window. Note that an abstract container is always reified into a, so called, box at the concrete level. This box is then embedded into a window.

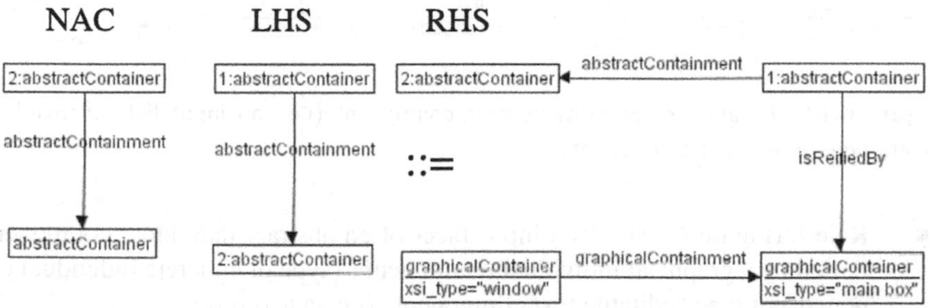

Figure 6.12 A creation of windows derived from containment relationships at the abstract level

- Rule 7 (Figure 6.13): Each abstract container contained into an abstract container that was reified into a window is transformed into a horizontal box and embedded into the window.

- **Selection of concrete individual components**. Functionalities of abstract individual component are identified with their facet. Selection of concrete individual components consists of choosing the appropriate concrete element that will support whole or a part of the facets associated with an abstract individual component.

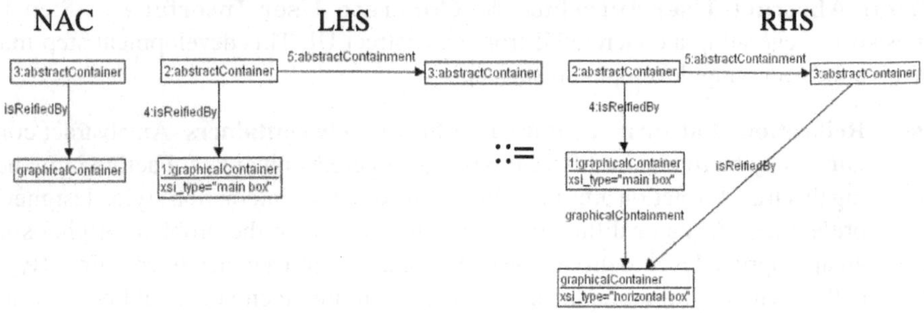

Figure 6.13 A generation of window structure derived from containment relationship at the abstract level

Example 6 is composed of rule 8. It creates an editable text component (i.e., a text box) to reify an AIO with an input facet.

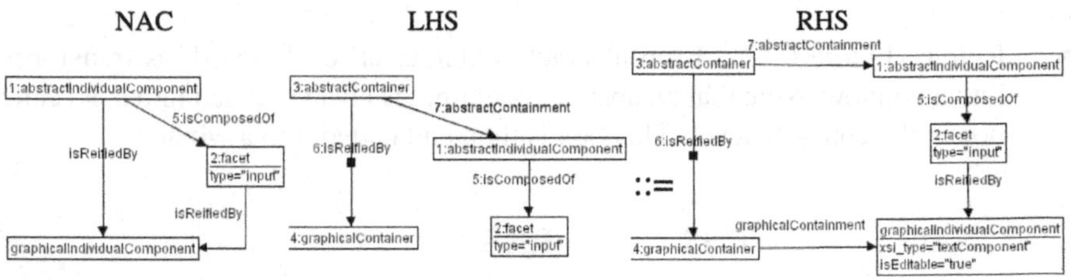

Figure 6.14 Creation of an editable text component (i.e., an input field) derived from facets type of abstract components

- Rule 8 (Figure 6.14): Each input facet of an abstract individual component is reified by a graphical individual component (a type of concrete individual component) of type "editable text component" (i.e., a text box).

  – **Arrangement of concrete individual component.** Allen relationships used to specify spatiotemporal relationships among abstract interaction objects are interpreted in order to provide information on the relative placement of a concrete individual component with respect to other elements of this type.

Example 7 is composed of rule 9. This example transforms an AUI into a concrete model for the graphical modality. It chains concrete individual components according to abstract individual component ordering.

- Rule 9 (Figure 6.15): For each couple of abstract individual components related by a "isBefore" relationship and reified into concrete individual components, generate a "isAdjacent" relationship between the concrete individual components.

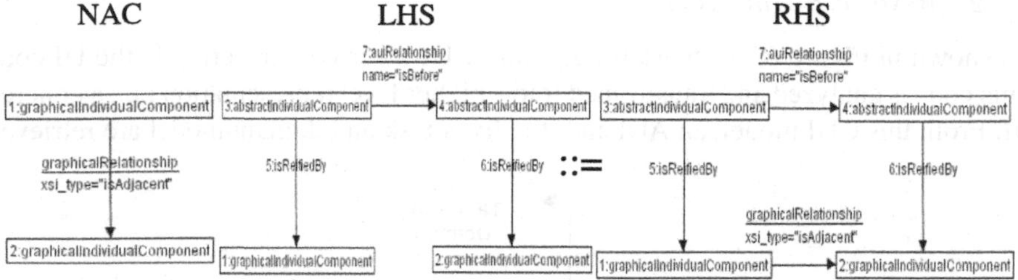

Figure 6.15 A placement of graphical individual components derived from spatiotemporal relationships at the abstract level

– **Definition of navigation**. Container transition relationships are transformed into navigation relationships. Ad hoc navigation objects may be created for this purpose (e.g., a menu, a tabbed dialog box bar may be created).

Example 8 is composed of rule 10. It generates a button to enable navigating between two windows.

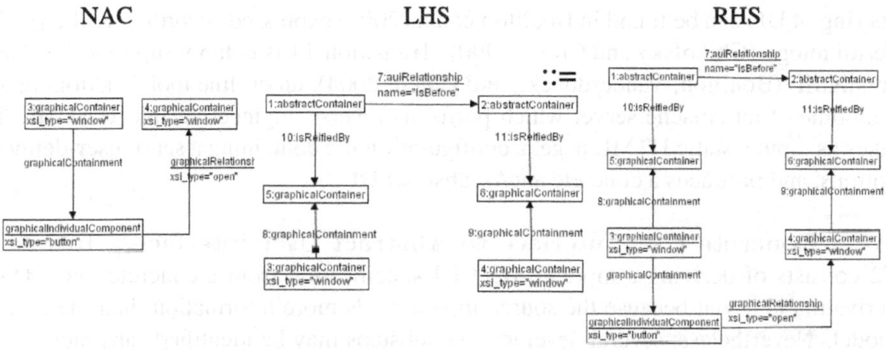

Figure 6.16 A window navigation definition derived from spatiotemporal relationships at the abstract level

- Rule 10 (Figure 6.16): For each container related to another container belonging to different windows and their respective abstract container related by a "is before relationship", generate a navigation button in source container pointing to the window of target container.

From Concrete User Interface to Code. Step T3 consists of code generation from a CUI. Code generation techniques for UI have been surveyed in various domains such as generative programming and model to code approach in Visitor-based approach and template based approach (Czarnecki and Eisenecker, 2000).

6.4.2 Reverse Engineering

As shown in Figure 6.17, the starting point of UI reverse engineering is the UI code. This code is analyzed and transformed into a higher level representation i.e., a concrete UI. From this CUI model, an AUI and, finally, a task and domain model are retrieved.

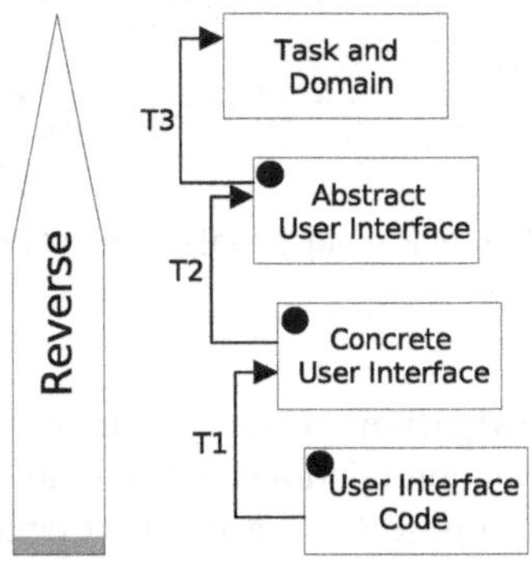

Figure 6.17 Reverse transformational development of UIs

From Code to Concrete User Interface . A state of the art in reverse engineering of UIs can be found in Bouillon et al., (2004) expressed according to the IEEE Terminology (Chikofsky and Cross, 1990). Transition T1 is notably supported by ReversiXML (Bouillon, Vanderdonckt, and Chieu, 2004), an on-line tool functioning as a module of an Apache server which performs reverse engineering into UsiXML. It takes as input a static HTML page, a configuration file containing a set of user-defined options, and produces a concrete and/or abstract UI.

From Concrete User Interface to Abstract User Interface. Transition T2 consists of deriving a more abstract UI specification from a concrete one. This derivation is trivial because the source model holds more information than the target model. Nevertheless, several development substeps may be identified: abstraction of CIO into AIO, abstraction of arrangement relationships, abstraction of navigation, etc. *Example 9 is composed of rule 11. It consists of obtaining an abstract individual component equipped with an input facet.*

- Rule 11 (Figure 6.18): For each editable graphical individual component create an abstract individual component equipped with an input facet.

From Abstract User Interface To Task & Domain. Transition T3 is the derivation of a task and concept specification. This transition has been considered very extensively in the area of reverse engineering where several techniques exist that contribute to recover a design model from existing information such as code. Indeed, the conceptual gap between AUI level and task and domain level is so important that little information may be extracted from an AUI model to retrieve a task or domain specification. Static analysis of Web pages examines the code of a Web page without

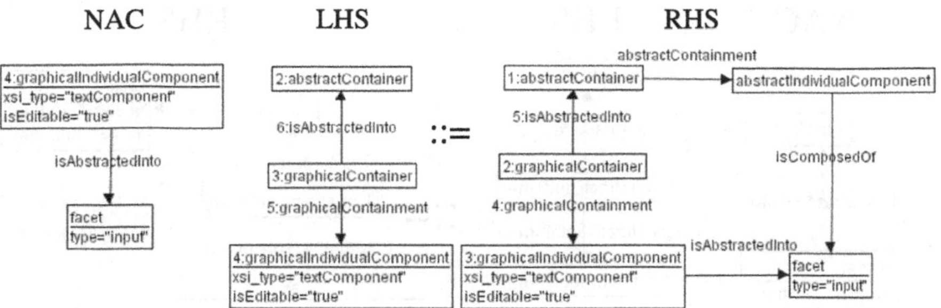

Figure 6.18 Creation of a facet at the abstract level derived from a type analysis of graphical individual components

interpreting or executing it in order to understand aspects of the website. Since static analysis has been successfully used in software testing and compiler optimization, it has been extensively used for analyzing the HTML code of Web pages. However, this technique leaves untreated all non-HTML parts of the Web page. Therefore other techniques need to be investigated such as the following methods. *Pattern matching* parses the code of a Web page to build a manipulable representation of it. Then slicing techniques are used to extract interface fragments from this representation, and a pattern matcher identifies syntactic patterns in the fragments. Using the code fragments as a basis, details about modes of interaction and conditions of activation are identified with control flow analysis. *Syntactic Analysis and Grouping* relies on a recognition algorithm that identifies input/output statements and attempts to incorporate them into groups. The grouping information is then used to define screens from the original user interface. This is particularly appropriate for scripting languages. *Cliché and Plan recognition* automatically identify occurrences of clichés, stereotyped code fragments for algorithms and data structures. The cliché recognition system translates the original code into a plan calculus, which is then encoded into a flow graph, producing a language-independent representation of the interpretation's flow that neutralizes syntactic variations in the code.
Example 10 is composed of rule 12. This example derives information on task action type from the abstract UI level.

- Rule 12 (Figure 6.19): For each abstract individual component equipped with a navigation facet create a task of action type "start/go" on an item of type "element".

6.4.3 Context of Use Adaptation

Context adaptation (illustrated in Figure 6.20) covers model transformations adapting a viewpoint to another context of use. This adaptation may be done at different levels.

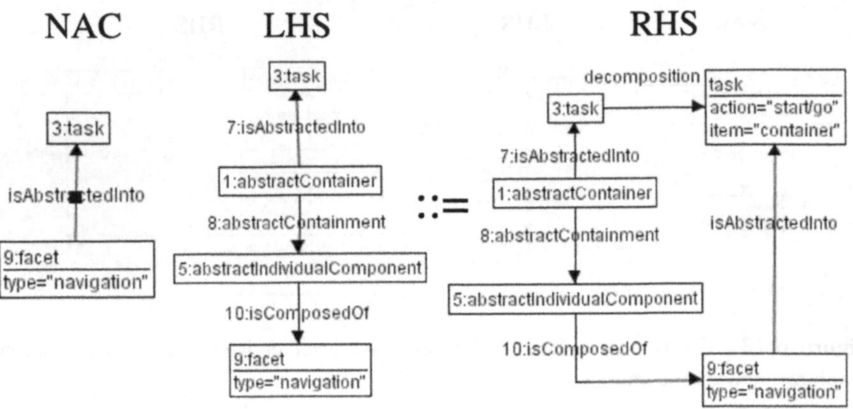

Figure 6.19 Definition of task action types derived from an analysis of facets at the abstract level

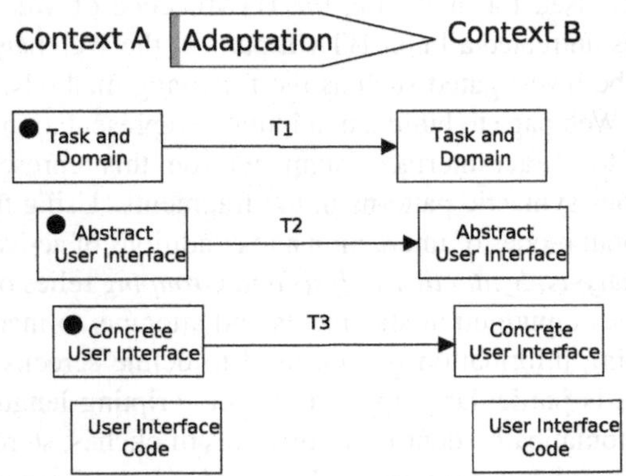

Figure 6.20 Context adaptation at different levels of our framework

From Task & Domain to Task & Domain. We propose one development substep type to exemplify adaptation at T1 level (Figure 6.20): Transformation of a task model.

- **Transformation of a task model:** Transformation of a task model may be useful to adapt a task specification to different categories of users, to different environments. For instance, an expert user needs less structuring in the accomplishment of a task than a novice user. This has an influence on the relationships between tasks. Another example is the management of user's permissions. Some users may not be allowed to perform certain tasks (e.g.,., editing a document), transformation rules may be defined to adapt a task specification to these constraints.

Example 11 is a transformation system composed of rule 13 and rule 14. A task hierarchy is "flattened" to allow an (expert) user to perform all tasks at the same time (i.e., concurrently).

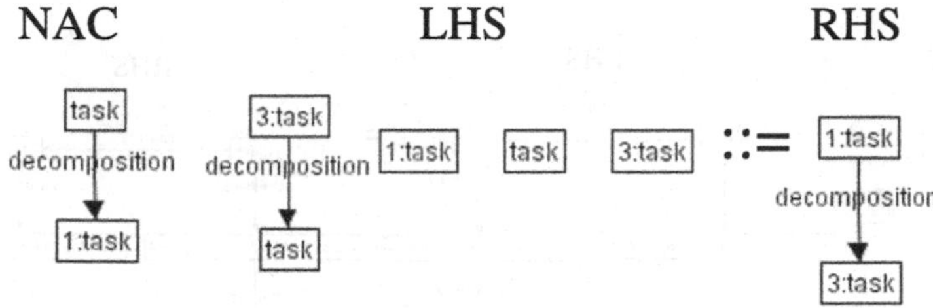

Figure 6.21 Flattening of a task tree structure

- Rule 13 (Figure 6.21): This rule (1) erases each intermediary task (i.e., non-leaf and non-root tasks) and (2) attaches every leaf task to the root.
- Rule 14 (Figure 6.22): For each sister tasks change their temporal relationship into concurrent.

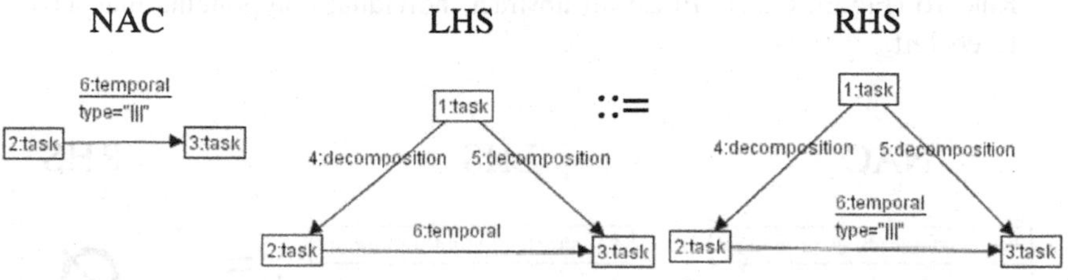

Figure 6.22 Transforming all temporal relationship to concurrent

From Abstract User Interface to Abstract User Interface Adaptation at this level. Adaptation at the abstract level concerns abstract container reshuffling and abstract individual component modification (e.g., facet modification, facet splitting, facet merging). We propose an example of abstract individual component modification.

- **Abstract individual component facet modification:** A modification of an abstract individual component affects its facets in their specification (e.g., an input facet is mapped onto a different domain concept) or their structuring (e.g., a facet is transferred onto another abstract component, a facet is erased).

Example 12 is a transformation system containing rules 15 and 16. It merges the facets of two abstract individual components mapped onto concurrent tasks. This example is based on the assumption that the tasks of a system must be concentrated into a lesser number of abstract components. This means that concrete components resulting from the abstract specification will have to assume more 'functionalities' than in the source version of the specification.

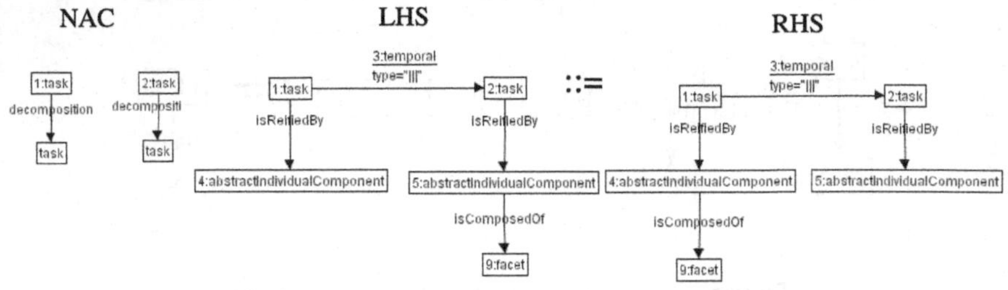

Figure 6.23 A merging of facets of abstract individual components

- Rule 15 (Figure 6.23): For each pair of abstract individual components mapped onto concurrent tasks. Transfer all facets of the abstract individual component that is mapped onto the task that is target of the concurrency relationship, to the other abstract individual component.
- Rule 16 (Figure 6.24): Erase all abstract individual components that have no facets left.

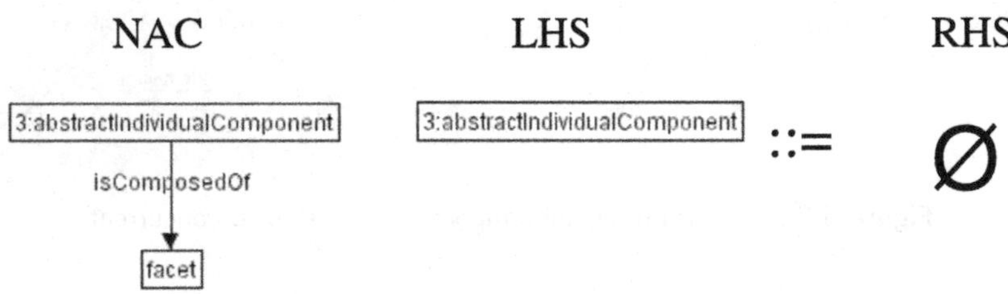

Figure 6.24 Erasing abstract individual components with no facets left

From Concrete User Interface to Concrete User Interface. Adaptation at the concrete level consist of several development substeps like container type modification (called concrete container reformation), modification of the types of concrete individual components (called concrete individual components reselection), layout modification (layout reshuffling), or navigation redefinition. We provide hereafter examples for these first three adaptation types.

- **Concrete container reformation:** Concrete container reformation may cover situations like container type transformation (e.g., a window is transformed into a tabbed dialog box) or container system modification (e.g., a system of windows are merged into a single window).

Example 13 is a transformation system composed of rules 17, 18 and 19. This transformation adapts a window into a tabbed dialog box and transfers window content into several "tabbed items".

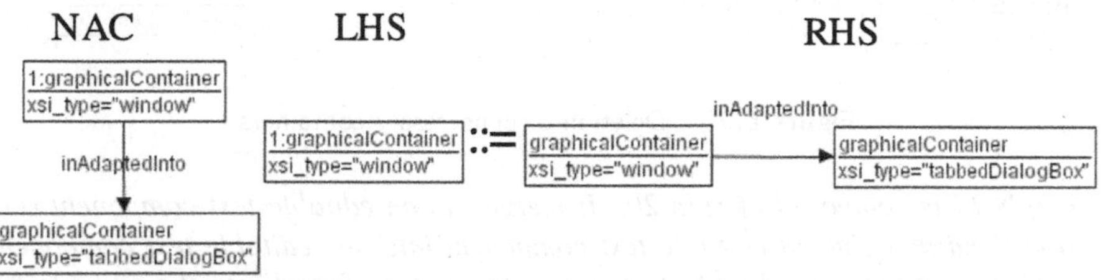

Figure 6.25 Initializing of the adaptation process by creating graphical component to adapt into

- Rule 17 (Figure 6.25): Each window is selected and mapped onto a newly created tabbed dialog box.
- Rule 18 (Figure 6.26): Transfers every first level box of the window to adapt into tabbed item composing a tabbed dialog box.
- Rule 19 (Figure 6.27): Cleans up the specification of remaining empty main boxes.

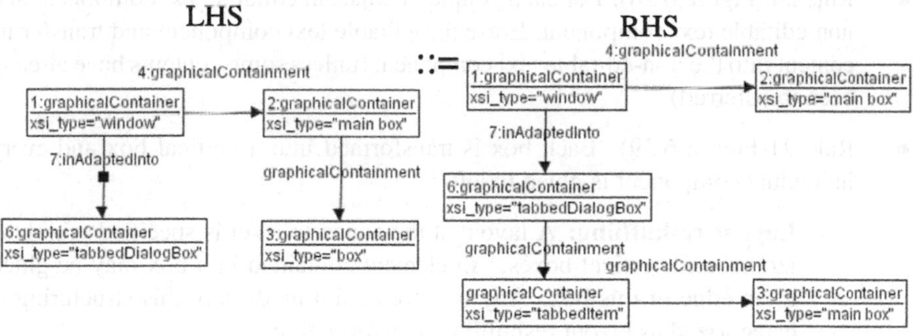

Figure 6.26 Creation of tabbed item and transfer of the content of the adapted window

- **Concrete individual component reselection:** Reselection transformations adapt individual component into other individual components. This covers individual component merging or slitting, or replacement.

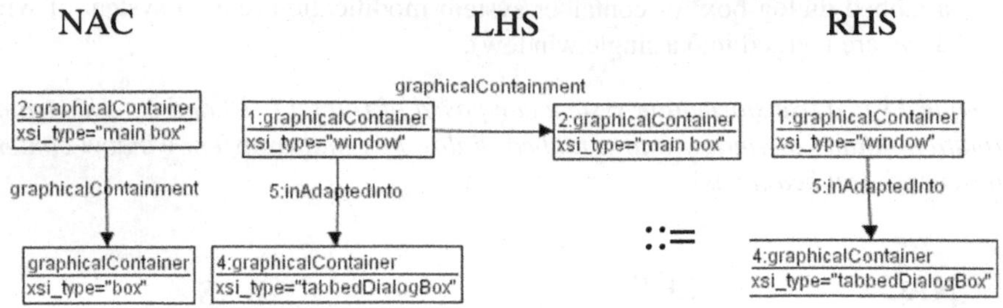

Figure 6.27 Deletion of unnecessary containers

Example 14 is composed of rule 20. It merges a non-editable text component (i.e., a label) and its adjacent editable text component into one editable text component. The content of the non-editable text component is transferred into the editable text component

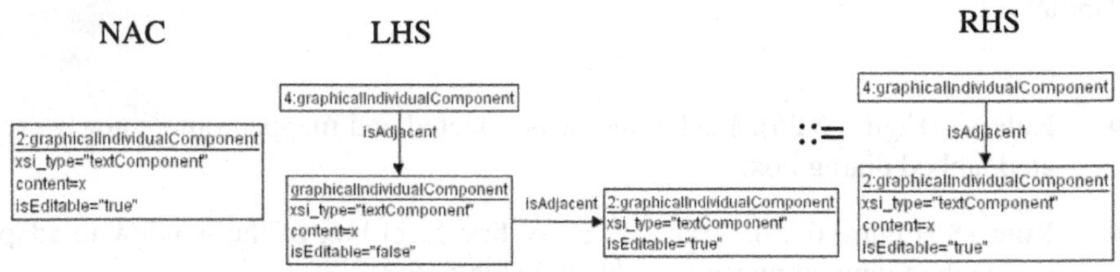

Figure 6.28 Merging of a non-editable text component (e.g., a label) and an editable text component (e.g., an input field) into one single editable text component

- Rule 20 (Figure 6.28): For each couple of adjacent editable text component and non-editable text component. Erase the editable text component and transfer its content into the non-editable text component (unless some contents have already been transferred).

- Rule 21(Figure 6.29): Each box is transformed into a vertical box and every individual component is glued to left.

  - **Layout reshuffling:** A layout at the concrete level is specified with horizontal and vertical boxes. An element contained in a box may be glued to an edge of this box. Any transformation modifying this structuring is categorized as layout reshuffling transformation.

Example 15 is composed of rule 21. It squeezes all boxes of a UI.

1. **Alternate and Composed development paths**

Other development paths could be equally expressed depending on their entry and exit points. Some of them are partially supported by various tools based on the UsiXML language (Vanderdonckt, 2005).

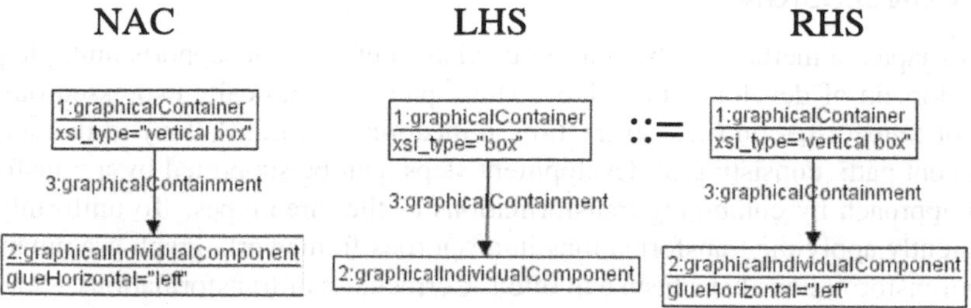

Figure 6.29 Squeezing of a layout structure to display vertically

- **Retargeting**: This transition is useful in processes where an existing system should be retargeted, that is, migrated from one source computing platform to another target computing platform that poses different constraints. Retargeting is a composition of reverse engineering, context adaptation, and forward engineering. In other words a UI code is abstracted away into a CUI (or an AUI). This CUI (or AUI) is reshuffled according to specific adaptation heuristics. From this reshuffled CUI (or AUI) a new interface code is created along a forward engineering process.

- **Middle-out development**: This term coined by Luo (1995) refers to a situation where a developer starts a development by a specification of the UI (no task or concept specification is priorly built). Several contributions have shown that, in reality, a development cycle is rarely sequential and even rarely begins by a task and domain specification. Literature in rapid prototyping converges with similar observations. Middle-out development shows a development path starting in the middle of the development cycle e.g., by the creation of a CUI or AUI model. After several iterations at this level (more likely until customer's satisfaction is reached) a specification is reverse engineered. From this specification the forward engineering path is followed.

- **Widespread development** (Hartson and Hix, 1989): In this development path, the designer may start wherever she wants (e.g., at any level of the development process), perform the rules that are relevant at this level, evaluate the results provided by these rules and proceed to other development steps as appropriate. This is a somewhat extreme position where everything is open and flexible, perhaps somewhat too much.

- **Round-trip engineering** (Demeyer et al. 1999): This development path is unique in the sense that it is a genuine path, but not directly for development. It results from applying manual modifications to code which has been generated automatically, after a model-to-code transformation. If a manual change has been operated on some piece of code generated automatically, then this change will be lost the next time a model-to-code transformation is applied. In order not to lose this effort, it is desirable to propagate the manual change into an abstraction which is relevant to the CUI.

6.5 CONCLUSION

In this chapter, a method has been introduced and defined that supports multiple paths in the domain of development of UIs. These paths are basically expressed on three types of transformation (i.e., abstraction, reification, and translation) so that any development path, consisting of development steps, can be supported by a transformational approach by combining transformations of the three types. To uniformly and consistently apply the transformations in a rigorous framework, graph grammars and graph transformations have been exploited. Correctness of transformations is an issue that may emerge when talking about model transformation. Two types of correctness may be considered.

Syntactic (structural) correctness stipulates that for any well-formed source model, and transformation rule enabled to provide a well-formed target model. While semantic correctness is hard to prove, syntactic correctness is easily guaranteed within our framework by two essential elements: Model type checking and consistency checks mechanism. Graph type checking ensures that a given transformation will not be applied if the resulting model it produces violates the meta-model it is supposed to conform to. Deriving a model to another may endanger consistency between different representations. For this purpose some basic consistency rules can be expressed with the technique of graph consistence rules. A graph of types may also be accompanied with the expression of specific consistency constraints inexpressible within the graph of types. OCL is used for this purpose in Agrawal et al. (2003), pre and post-condition with graph patterns (Akehurst et al., 2003).

Semantic correctness stipulates a semantic adequacy between a source and a target model. In our context, semantic correctness proving is hard to consider as by definition the domain of discourse of source model and target model are different.

Other important properties of interest that denote the powerfulness and the limitations of our method can be discussed equally.

Incompleteness of the method. There are few criteria to judge the quality of the method. It is also impossible to prove that a general solution is optimal. We can only prove sometimes formally, sometimes informally that a solution meets several quality criterias.

Seamlessness. This is a quality attribute attached to certain methodologies in the field of software engineering. It qualifies a small gap between concepts used at the analysis level and concepts relevant to implementation. Graph grammars, as used in this work, contribute to reach seamlessness of our method as manipulated structures from the requirements analysis to the design are graphs. Furthermore, the knowledge used to perform development steps are graphs.

Traceability. The identification and documentation of derivation paths (upward) and allocation or flow down paths (downward) of work products in the work product hierarchy. Important kinds of traceability include: To or from external sources to or from system requirements; to or from system requirements to or from lowest level requirements; to or from requirements to or from design; to or from design to or from implementation; to or from implementation to test; and to or from requirements to test (IEEE, 1998).

Consistency The degree of uniformity, standardization, and freedom from contradiction among the documents or parts of a system or component (IEEE, 1998).
Iterative development cycle. Iteration is well supported as graph productions supporting transitions in the development cycle may be undone to retrieve the source artifact as it was before transformation. This artifact may be modified by a developer and reused as source of a new derivation.

Last, and although empirical studies have already proven the advantages of using an MDA-driven approach for the development of software applications (Bettin, 2002), specific metrics should be precisely defined and applied to determine the effort and quality of the models and code obtained by using on the one hand any UI methodology on its own and on the other hand such methodologies like the one introduced in this chapter. A comparative analysis of several projects conducted through a traditional development method and through an MDA-driven method like the one presented here represents a huge amount of work, but would certainly be very interesting to establish.

Acknowledgments

The authors acknowledge the support of the CAMELEON European project and the SIMILAR network of excellence (`www.similar.cc`) on multimodal interfaces funded by European Commission.

References

Agrawal, A., Karsai, G., and Lédeczi, A. (2003). An end-to-end domain-driven software development framework. In Crocker, R. and Steele, G. L. Jr., editors, *Companion of the 18th Annual ACM SIGPLAN Conference on Object-Oriented Programming, Systems, Languages, and Applications, OOPSLA 2003, October 26-30, 2003, Anaheim, CA, USA*, pages 8–15. ACM.

Akehurst, D. H., Kent, S., and Patrascoiu, O. (2003). A relational approach to defining and implementing transformations between metamodels. *Software and System Modeling*, 2(4):215–239. On-line: http://www.cs.kent.ac.uk/pubs/2003/1764.

Bettin, J. (2002). Measuring the potential of domain-specific modeling techniques. In *Proceedings of the 2nd Domain-Specific Modeling Languages Workshop, Working Papers W-334, Helsinki School of Economics*, pages 39–44.

Boocock, P. (2003). The Jamda project. http://jamda.sourceforge.net/.

Bodart, F., Hennebert, A. M., Leheureux, J. M. and Vanderdonckt, J. (1995). A model-based approach to presentation: A continuum from task analysis to prototype. In F. Bodart, *Focus on Computer Graphics Series*, p. 77–94. New York: Springer-Verlag.

Bouillon, L., Vanderdonckt, J., and Chieu, K. (2004). Flexible reengineering of websites. In *Proceedings of the* 8th *International Conference on Intelligent User Interfaces*, Multiplatform interfaces, pages 132–139.

Brown, J. (1997). Exploring human-computer interaction and software engineering methodologies for the creation of interactive software. *ACM SIGCHI Bulletin*, 29(1):32–35.

Calvary, G., Coutaz, J., Thevenin, D., Limbourg, Q., Bouillon, L., and Vanderdonckt, J. (2003). A unifying reference framework for multitarget user interfaces. *Interacting with Computers*, 15(3):289–308.

Chikofsky, E. J. and Cross, J. H. (1990). Reverse engineering and design recovery: a taxonomy. *IEEE Software*, 7(1):13–17.

Czarnecki, K. and Eisenecker, U. W. (2000). *Generative Programming Methods, Tools, and Applications*. Addison-Wesley, Readign: MA.

Demeyer, S., Ducasse, S., and Tichelaar, S. (1999), Why Unified is not Universal. UML Shortcomings for Coping with Round-trip Engineering, *In Proceedings UML '99 (The Second International Conference on The Unified Modeling Language)*, Kaiserslautern, Germany, pages 630–644.

Depke, R., Heckel, R., and Küster, J. M. (2002). Formal agent-oriented modeling with UML and graph transformation. *Science of Computer Programming*, 44(2):229–252.

D'Souza, D. F. and Wills, A. C. (1999). *Objects, Components and Frameworks with UML: The Catalysis Approach*. Addison-Wesley, Readign: MA.

Ehrig, H., Engels, G., Kreowski, H.-J., and Rozenberg, G. (1999). *Handbook of Graph Grammars and Computing by Graph Transformation, Vol. 2: Applications, Languages and Tools*. Singapore: World Scientific.

Eisenstein, J., Vanderdonckt, J., and Puerta, A. (2001). Applying model-based techniques to the development of UIs for mobile computers. In *Proceedings of the 2001 International Conference on Intelligent User Interfaces*, pages 69–76, New York. ACM Press.

Freund, R., Haberstroh, B., and Stary, C. (1992). Applying graph grammars for task-oriented user interface development. In Koczkodaj, W. W., Lauer, P. E., and Toptsis, A. A., editors, *Computing and Information - ICCI'92, Fourth International Conference on Computing and Information, Toronto, Ontario, Canada, May 28-30, 1992, Proceedings*, pages 389–392, IEEE Computer Society.

Gerber, A., Lawley, M., Raymond, K., Steel, J., and Wood, A. (2002). Transformation: The missing link of MDA. In Corradini, A., Ehrig, H., Kreowski, H.-J., and Rozenberg, G., editors, *Graph Transformation, First International Conference, ICGT 2002, Barcelona, Spain, October 7-12, 2002, Proceedings*, volume 2505 of *Lecture Notes in Computer Science*, pages 90–105. Springer.

Griffiths, T., Barclay, P. J., Paton, N. W., McKirdy, J., Kennedy, J. B., Gray, P. D., Cooper, R., Goble, C. A., and Silva, P. P. (2001). Teallach: a model-based user interface development environment for object databases. *Interacting with Computers*, 14(1):31–68.

Hartson, H. R. and Hix, D. (1989). Toward empirically derived methodologies and tools for human-computer interface development. *International Journal of Man-Machine Studies*, 31(4):477–494.

Heckel, R., Mens, T., and Wermelinger, M. (2002). Workshop on software evolution through transformations: Towards uniform support throughout the software life-cycle. In Corradini, A., Ehrig, H., Kreowski, H., and Rozenberg, G., editors, *Graph Transformation, First International Conference, ICGT 2002, Barcelona, Spain, Oc-*

tober 7-12, 2002, Proceedings, volume 2505 of *Lecture Notes in Computer Science*, pages 450–454. Springer.

Ho, W. M., Jézéquel, J. M., Le Guennec, A., and Pennaneac'h, F. (1999). UMLAUT: An extendible UML transformation framework. In *14th IEEE International Conference on Automated Software Engineering*, pages 275–278. IEEE Computer Society Press.

IEEE, *IEEE 830: Recommended Practice for Software Requirements Specifications*. IEEE Computer Society Press.

Kuske, S., Gogolla, M., Kollmann, R., and Kreowski, H.-J. (2002). An integrated semantics for UML class, object, and state diagrams based on graph transformation. In Butler, M. and Sere, K., editors, *3rd Int. Conf. Integrated Formal Methods (IFM'02)*, pages 11–28, Springer-Verlag.

Larman, C. (2001). *Applying UML and Patterns: An Introduction to Object-Oriented Analysis and Design and the Unified Process*. Englewood Cliffs: Prentice Hall.

Limbourg, Q. and Vanderdonckt, J. (2003). Comparing task models for user interface design. In Diaper, D. and Stanton, N., editors, *The Handbook of Task Analysis for Human-Computer Interaction*, pages 135–154. Lawrence Erlbaum Associates.

Limbourg, Q. and Vanderdonckt, J. (2004a). Transformational development of user interfaces with graph transformations. In Jacob, R. J. K., Limbourg, Q., and Vanderdonckt, J., editors, *Proceedings of the* 5th *International Conference on Computer-Aided Design of User Interfaces CADUI*, pages 105–118. Kluwer.

Limbourg, Q. and Vanderdonckt, J. (2004b). UsiXML: A user interface description language supporting mul-tiple levels of independence. In Matera, M. and Comai, S., editors, *Engineering Advanced Web Applications*, pages 325–338. Rinton Press.

Limbourg, Q., Vanderdonckt, J., Michotte, B., Bouillon, L., and Lopez, V. (2005). UsiXML: a language sup-porting multipath development of user interfaces. In *Proc. of* 9th *IFIP Working Conference on Engineering for Human-Computer Interaction jointly with 11th Int. Workshop on Design, Specification, and Verification of Interactive Systems EHCI-DSVIS'2004*, volume 3425 of *Lecture Notes in Computer Science*, pages 200–220, Springer-Verlag.

Luo, P. (1995). A human-computer collaboration paradigm for bridging design conceptualization and implementation. In Paternó, F., editor, *Design, Specification and Verification of Interactive Systems '94*, Focus on Computer Graphics, pages 129–147, Springer-Verlag. Proceedings of the Eurographics Workshop in Bocca di Magra, Italy, June 8 – 10, 1994.

Mens, T., Van Eetvelde, N., Janssens, D., and Demeyer, S. (2001). Formalising refactoring with graph transformations. *Fundamenta Informaticae*, 21:1001–1022.

Miller, J. and Mukerij, J. (2003). MDA guide version 1.0.1. On-line: www.omg.org.

Mori, G., Paternò, F., and Santoro, C. (2004). Design and development of multidevice user interfaces through multiple logical descriptions. *IEEE Trans. Software Eng*, 30(8):507–520.

Nanard, J. and Nanard, M. (1995). Hypertext design environments and the hypertext design process. *Communications of the ACM*, 38(8):49–56.

Object Management Group (2003). Common warehouse specification version 1.1, vol. 1. http://www.omg.org/docs/formal/03-03-02.pdf.

Puerta, A. R. (1996). The MECANO project: Comprehensive and integrated support for model-based interface development. In Vanderdonckt, J., editor, *Computer-Aided Design of User Interfaces I, Proceedings of the Second International Workshop on Computer-Aided Design of User Interfaces CADUI'96, June 5-7, 1996, Namur, Belgium*, pages 19–36. Presses Universitaires de Namur.

Puerta, A. R. (1997). A model-based interface development environment. *IEEE Software*, 14(4):40–47.

Queensland University (2002). An OMG Meta Object Facility Implementation. The Corba Service Product Manager, University of Queensland, 2002, On-line: `http://www.dstc.edu.au/Products/CORBA/MOF/`.

Rensik, A. (2003). Proceedings of the 1st Workshop on Model-Driven Architecture: Foundation and Application MDAFA'03. CTIT Technical Report TR-CTIT-03-27, University of Twente, Twente. On-line: http://trese.cs.utwente.nl/mdafa2003/.

Rozenberg, G. (1997). *Handbook on Graph Grammars and Computing by Graph Transformation 1 (Foundations)*. World Scientific, Singapore.

Sucrow, B. (1998). On integrating software-ergonomic aspects in the specification process of graphical user interfaces. *Transactions of the SDPS Journal of Integrated Design & Process Science*, 2(2):32–42.

Sumner, T., Bonnardel, B., and Harstad, B. (1997). The cognitive ergonomics of knowledge-based design support systems. In *presented at Proceedings of the Conference on Human Factors in Computing Systems (CHI'97)*, Atlanta, GA.

Thevenin, D. (2001). *Adaptation en interaction homme-machine : le cas de la plasticité*. Ph.D. thesis, Universite Joseph-Fourier - Grenoble I, France.

Trevisan, D. G., Vanderdonckt, J., and Macq, M. (2002). Analyzing interaction in augmented reality systems. In Pingali, G. and Jain, R., editors, *roceedings of ACM Multimedia 2002 International Workshop on Immersive Telepresence ITP'2002*, pages 56–59, ACM Press.

Vanderdonckt, J. (2005). A MDA-compliant environment for developing user interfaces of information systems. In Pastor, O. and Cunha, J. F., editors, *Proceedings of the 17th International Conference on Advanced Information Systems Engineering CAiSE 2005, Porto, Portugal, June 13-17*, volume 3520 of *Lecture Notes in Computer Science*, pages 16–31. Springer-Verlag.

Vanderdonckt, J. and Bodart, F. (1993). Encapsulating knowledge for intelligent automatic interaction objects selection. In *Proceedings of ACM INTERCHI'93 Conference on Human Factors in Computing Systems, Amsterdam*, pages 424–429. ACM Press.

Varró, D., Varró, G., and Pataricza, A. (2002). Designing the automatic transformation of visual languages. *Science of Computer Programming*, 44(2):205–227.

Wegner, P. (1997). Why interaction is more powerful than algorithms. *Communications of the ACM*, 40(5):80–91.

7 HUMAN-CENTERED ENGINEERING OF INTERACTIVE SYSTEMS WITH THE USER INTERFACE MARKUP LANGUAGE

James Helms[1], Robbie Schaefer[2], Kris Luyten[3], Jo Vermeulen[3], Marc Abrams[1,4], Adrien Coyette[5], and Jean Vanderdonckt[5]

[1]Harmonia Inc. P.O. Box 11282 – Blacksburg, VA 24062-1282, U.S.A.

[2]Paderborn University, Fakultät für Elektrotechnik, Informatik und Mathematik, Institut für Informatik, Fürstenallee, 11 – D-33102 Paderborn Germany

[3]Hasselt University - tUL - IBBT
Expertise Center for Digital Media
Wetenschapspark 2, 3590 Diepenbeek, Belgium

[4]Department of Computer Science, Virginia Tech,
508 McBryde Hall – Blacksburg, VA 24061-0106, U.S.A.

[5]Belgian Laboratory of Computer-Human Interaction (BCHI),
Louvain School of Management (LSM), Université catholique de Louvain
Place des Doyens, 1 – B-1348 Louvain-la-Neuve, Belgium.

Abstract. The User Interface Markup Language (UIML) is a User Interface Description Language aimed at producing multiple user interfaces from a single model for multiple contexts of use, in particular multiple computing platforms, thus addressing the need for multichannel user interfaces. This chapter summarizes efforts devoted to the definition and usage of UIML 4.0, the latest version of this UIDL which also covers dialog modeling. It describes the main parts of the UIML language, i.e., structure, presentation style, contents, behavior, connectivity, and toolkit mappings, and the integrated development environment that supports the development lifecycle of multichannel user interfaces based on UIML.

7.1 INTRODUCTION

User Interface Description Languages (UIDLs) can bridge the gap between formal Human-Computer Interaction (HCI) models (e.g., with graphical representations) and concrete implementations of User Interfaces (UIs) (Abrams *et al.* 1999). As such, they are an integral part of human-centered engineering of interactive systems and can be applied at any stage of a human-centered design process (Hartson and Hix, 1989). In this chapter, we will give an overview on the User Interface Markup Language (UIML) and show, how the fundamental language concepts, tools and extensions as well as the new features of UIML 4.0 can be used to improve a human-centered software development process.

7.1.1 What Are UIDLs?

In general, any UIDL should fulfill a series of requirements such as: the ability to specify any target UI, the ability to process a UI specified in the terms of this UIDL, legibility of the resulting specifications, etc. Specifying a UI in a particular UIDL should not be viewed as just an exercise in specification. A UI should be specified as rigorously as possible for multiple purposes: capturing user requirements and turning them into a concrete UI, determining the attributes of a particular UI, describing a UI unambiguously so that this description could be passed to the developers, whether they use a software tool or not. A UIDL could be interpreted as a concrete syntax for UI specification similar to specification languages for the other areas of computer science (e.g., for data base management systems). As such, it could take any form. Expressing this concrete syntax in an XML format is nowadays particularly popular since XML-based technology has received enough attention to be widely used and effectively supported by appropriate software.

7.1.2 UIML and Software Engineering

In this chapter we focus on UIML, an open, standardized XML language to express user interface (UI) designs that are multidevice, multilingual, multimodal, independent of UI metaphor, and designed to interoperate with concepts and languages from OASIS, W3C, and other standards organizations. Using UIML, HCI best practices can be adopted more easily by viewing HCI design and implementation as a process of transformation from initial design model to an open standard XML UI implementation language and finally to target languages for deployment. UIML defines mappings between the abstractions used in the UI description and the underlying implementation, and UIML implementations make liberal use of transforms to convert from one set of abstractions to another. Note that the target languages can be XML languages (e.g., XHTML, SVG) or programming languages (e.g., C# and Java).

There are many XML-based UIDLs. In addition to languages from W3C (HTML, XHTML, XForms, and SVG), early efforts include UIML, the Alternate Abstract Interface Markup Language (Zimmermann et al., 2002), the eXtensible Interface Markup Language (XIML) (Puerta and Eisenstein, 2002) and the XML User Interface Language (XUL) (`www.mozilla.org/projects/xul/`). More recently we have seen the onset of DISL (7.3.4) and UsiXML.

One challenge in creating UIDLs is designing the language to support the software engineering aspects of HCI engineering over the entire range of user interfaces that people build, from simple personal applications to complex enterprise applications (e.g., a ship with tens of thousands of UIs); from throw-away software with a single version (e.g., a class project) to software that is used for decades in many different versions (e.g., a banking or hospital system); from UIs deployed to one device to UIs deployed to thousands of vastly different devices (e.g., 2D or 3D, virtual or augmented reality, voice or haptic), and for any UI metaphor.

We will explore how UIML supports software engineering by providing the following benefits:

- Reusability of HCI design components and modules (see section 7.2)
- Abstraction and domain-specific vocabularies to allow generalized use of the language (see section 7.2.3)
- Adaptability to implementation languages and display devices (see Section 7.3.1)
- Separation of HCI engineering concerns (see Section 7.2.1)
- Rapid prototyping for user-centered design (see Section 7.3.1)
- Tool support (see section 7.3)
- A unified language for representing UIs

In this chapter, we will show how the fundamental UIML concepts, tools, and extensions, as well as the new features of UIML 4.0 can be used to improve a human-centered HCI development process.

7.2 UIML: AN OVERVIEW

The User Interface Markup Language (UIML) is a declarative, XML-compliant meta-language for describing UIs. The design objective of the UIML is to provide a vendor-neutral, platform-independent, canonical representation of any UI suitable for mapping (rendering) to existing implementation languages, and as such an ideal candidate for human-centered engineering of interactive systems. Work on UIML was motivated by the following goals:

- Allow individuals to implement UIs for any device without learning languages and application programming interfaces (APIs) specific to the device.

- Reduce the time to develop UIs for a family of devices.
- Provide a natural separation between UI code and application logic code.
- Allow non-programmers to implement UIs.
- Permit rapid prototyping of UIs.
- Simplify internationalization and localization.
- Allow efficient download of UIs over networks to client machines.
- Allow extension to support UI technologies that are invented in the future.

UIML provides a puzzle piece to be used in conjunction with other technologies, including HCI design methodologies, modeling languages such as XIML (Eisenstein, Puerta and Vanderdonckt 2001) and UsiXML (Limbourg and Vanderdonckt, 2004b), authoring tools, transformation algorithms, and existing languages and standards (W3C and OASIS specifications). UIML is not a silver bullet that replaces human decisions needed to create UIs.

UIML is biased toward an object-oriented view and toward complementing other specifications (e.g., SOAP, XForms Models, XHTML, HTML, WML, VoiceXML). During the design of UIML an effort was made to allow interface descriptions in UIML to be mapped with equal efficiency to various vendors' technologies (e.g., UIML should efficiently map to both ASP .Net and JSP to further the goal of vendor-independence in Web Services).

Why is a canonical representation useful? Today, HCIs are built using a variety of languages: XML variants (e.g., HTML, XHTML, VoiceXML,), JavaScript, Java, C++, etc. Each language differs in its syntax and its abstractions. For example, the syntax in HTML 4.0 to represent a button is <button>, and in Java Swing "JButton b = new JButton;". The work on UIML asks the fundamental question, "Do we inherently need different syntaxes, or can one common syntax be used?" The benefit of using a single syntax is analogous to the benefit of XML: Software tools can be created for a single syntax (UIML), yet process UIs destined for any existing language. For example, a tool to author UIs can store the design in UIML, and then map UIML to target languages in use today (e.g., HTML, Java) or invented in the future. Progress in the field of UI design can move faster, because everyone can build tools that either map interface designs into UIML or map UIML out to existing languages. Tools can then be snapped together using UIML as a standard interchange language.

There is a second benefit of a canonical UI description. By using a single syntax to represent any UI, an interface is in a very malleable form. For example, one technique gaining popularity in the human computer interface community is transformation. With a canonical representation for any UI, someone that designs a transform algorithm can simply implement the algorithm to transform an input UIML document to a new output UIML document. Compare this approach to implementing the same transform algorithm only to transform HTML documents, then reimplementing the transform algorithm to only transform C++ interfaces, and so on.

In any language design, there is a fundamental trade-off between creating something general versus special-purpose. UIML is for general-purpose use by people who implement UIs and people who build tools for authoring UIs. It is envisioned that UIML will be used with other languages with a more focused purpose, such as UI design languages. Ultimately most people may never write UIML directly—they may instead use a particular design language suited to a certain design methodology, and then use tools to transform the design into a UIML representation that is then mapped to various XML or programming languages.

UIML is object-based, in that it describes both objects, classes, and the interactions among objects. UIML was designed to allow UI descriptions to be mapped with equal efficiency to different vendors' technologies. Reuse is a first class concept in UIML and is accomplished through a template mechanism. UIML templates can contain snippets of UIML that can then be inserted into other UIML documents. This capability allows designers to build up libraries of user interface components and style sheets that can be applied throughout their systems. UI style guidance can be directly enforced via this mechanism. Libraries defined in this way allow custom components to be defined once and reused, which can be very helpful for user-centered software engineering e.g., by adhering to usability patterns. Four key concepts underlie UIML:

1. *UIML is a metalanguage.* To understand this, consider XML. XML does not define tags, such as <p>. Instead, one must add to XML a specification of the legal tags and their attributes, for example by creating a document type definition (DTD). Therefore the XML specification does not need to be modified as new tag sets are created, and a set of tools can be created to process XML independent of the tag sets that are used. UIML defines a small set of powerful tags, such as <part> to describe a part of a UI, or <property> to describe a property of a UI part. UIML tags are independent of any UI metaphor (e.g., graphical UIs), target platform (e.g., PC, phone), or target language to which UIML will be mapped (e.g., Java, HTML). To use UIML, one must add a toolkit vocabulary (roughly analogous to adding a DTD to an XML document). The vocabulary specifies a set of classes of parts, and properties of the classes. Different groups of people can define different vocabularies, depending on their needs. One group might define a vocabulary whose classes have a 1-to-1 correspondence to HCI widgets in a particular target language (i.e., the classes might match those in the Java Swing API). Another group might define a vocabulary whose classes match abstractions used by a UI designer (e.g., Title, Abstract, BodyText for UIs to documents). UIML is eventually standardized once and tools can be developed for UIML, independently from the development of vocabularies. For more on vocabularies see Section 7.2.3.

2. *UIML "factors out" or separates the elements of a UI.* The design of UIML started with the question: what are the fundamental elements needed to describe any man-machine interaction? The separation in UIML identifies what parts comprise the UI, the presentation style for each part as a list of <property> elements, the content of each part (e.g., text, sounds, images) and binding of content to external resources (e.g., XML resources, or method calls in external

objects), the behavior of parts when a user interacts with the interface as a set of rules with conditions and actions, the connection of the UI to the outside world (e.g., to business logic), and the definition of the vocabulary of part classes. For a comparison of the separation in UIML to existing UI models, such as the Model View Controller, refer to Phanouriou (2000).

3. *UIML views the structure of an HCI, logically, as a tree of UI parts that changes over the lifetime of the interface.* There is an initial tree of parts, which is the UI initially presented to a user when the interface starts its lifetime. During the lifetime of the interface, the tree of parts may dynamically change shape by adding or deleting parts. For example, opening a new window containing buttons and labels in a graphical interface may correspond to adding a subtree of parts to the UIML tree. UIML provides elements to describe the initial tree structure (<structure>) and to dynamically modify the structure (<restructure>).

4. *UIML allows UI parts and part-trees to be packaged in templates.* Templates may then be reused in various interface designs. This provides a first-class notion of reuse within UIML, which is missing from other XML HCI languages, such as HTML.

Due to these concepts, UIML is particularly useful for creating multiplatform UIs and also personalized solutions for different users. To create multiplatform UIs, one leverages the metalanguage nature of UIML to create a vocabulary of part classes (e.g., defining class Button), and then separately defines the vocabulary by specifying a mapping of the classes to target languages (e.g., mapping UIML part class Button to class javax. swing.JButton for Java and to tag <button> for HTML 4.0). One can create a highly device-independent UI by creating a generic vocabulary that tries to eliminate bias toward particular UI metaphors and devices. By "device" we mean PCs, various information appliances (e.g., handheld computers, desktop phones, cellular or PCS phones), or any other machine with which a human can interact. In addition, because UIML describes the interface behavior as rules whose actions are applied to parts, the rules can be mapped to code in the target languages (e.g., to lines of Java code or JavaScript code).

UIML is currently being standardized in the Organization for the Advancement of Structured Information Standards (OASIS, `www.oasis-open.org`) by a technical committee comprised of UI definition language experts from across the globe. The technical committee's Web page can be accessed at `www.oasis-open.org/committees/tc_home.php?wg_abbrev=uiml`.

7.2.1 Generalizing the Model View Controller Pattern for UIs

UIML is modeled by the placeMeta-Interface Model (Phanouriou 2000) pictured in Figure 7.1.

UIML is designed to describe arbitrarily complex UIs on any device through a unique division of the UI definition into the following six elemental components:

1. *Structure*: the hierarchy of parts in the UI.

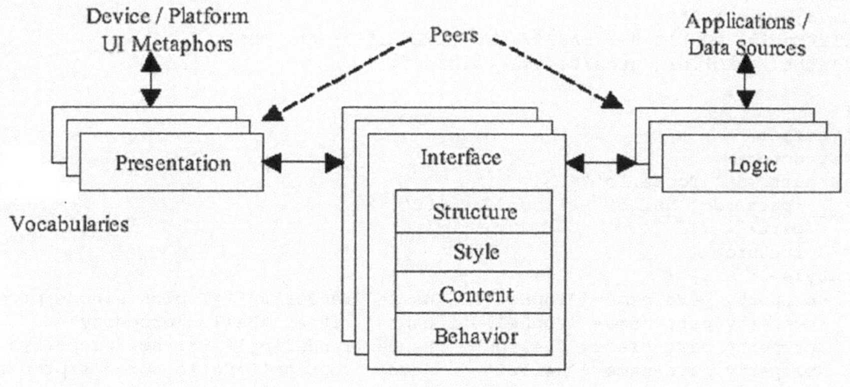

Figure 7.1 The Meta-Interface Model

2. *Presentation style*: the sensory characteristics of the parts in the UI.

3. *Content*: the words, images, etc. appearing or being spoken in the UI.

4. *Behavior*: a set of condition-action rules that define what happens when a user inters with an UI element, such as a button.

5. *Connectivity* (mappings to object methods in the application layer).

6. *Toolkit mappings* (mappings of the object class names in the hierarchy of parts to specific objects in the toolkit used to render the UI.

Each of these elements can be described independently to allow reuse and flexibility in creating UIs for widely different platforms. In addition, the separation of concerns inherent to UIML was developed to generalize the Model View Controller design pattern for use with UIs. In UIML, the Interface shown in Figure 7.1, serves as the model of the UI, describing the structure, style, content, and behavior of the HCI in a canonical way. The View is then generated from the presentation which maps concepts used in the interface (model) to concrete widgets on the screen. Finally the Logic acts as the controller bridge between the HCI and the model. This allows the UI to communicate with the application without defining specifics of the communication (protocols, syntax, etc.).

7.2.2 Hello World Example

The famous "Hello World" example in UIML is shown in Figure 7.2. It simply generates a non-interactive UI that contains the words "Hello World!". The example illustrates the typical structure of a UIML UI description. Notice how the interface definition is divided into a separate structure and style child. The structure child contains all the parts that define the user interface, in this case a container called "TopHello" and a label called "hello". The hierarchical nature of the structure definition implies that

```
<?xml version="1.0"?>
<!DOCTYPE uiml PUBLIC "-//OASIS//DTD UIML 3.1 Draft//EN''
    ''http://uiml.org/dtds/UIML4\_0a.dtd''>

<uiml>
  <interface>
    <structure>
      <part id=''TopHello''>
        <part id=''hello'' class=''helloC''/>
      </part>
    </structure>
    <style>
      <property part-name=''TopHello'' name=''rendering''>TopContainer</property>
      <property part-name=''TopHello'' name=''title''>Hello</property>
      <property part-class=''helloC''  name=''rendering''>String</property>
      <property part-name=''hello''    name=''content''>Hello World!</property>
    </style>
  </interface>
  <peers> ... </peers>
</uiml>
```

Figure 7.2 The UIML specifications for the "Hello World!" example

"hello" is a child of "TopHello" and is therefore contained within it. The style section enumerates the presentation properties on the two parts that will affect the appearance of the UI. For example, the "TopHello" container will have "Hello" as the title and the label will contain "Hello World!" as specified by the title and content properties, respectively. Properties are associated with parts through the *part-name* or *part-class* attribute. If a property is meant to apply to only one part, then we use *part-name* to specify by id the part that will exhibit this property. If *part-class* is used, then the property will be applied to all parts of that class.

7.2.3 Generalizing Through Vocabularies

The richness of the user interfaces that can be described with a UIDL is proportional with the expressive power of the presentation model. There are two extremes with regard to the expressive power of a UIDL: the *common denominator* and the *metawidget* set approach. On the one hand, the common denominator approach identifies a general set of abstract interactors that can be used on most platforms or devices. This set is used to create the UIDL: the language's syntax is limited to describing user interfaces composed out of elements from the general set. On the other hand, the metawidget set approach avoids including any widget-set specific information in the language. In this case, the UIDL is a metalanguage that describes different aspects of a user interface that are independent of any widget set, platform or device. UIML is such a canonical language that adheres the metawidget set approach.

The mapping vocabulary is the part of UIML that allows using a custom naming scheme while creating the user interface description. This implies the names used in UIML to describe the user interface can be domain-specific names and the nam-

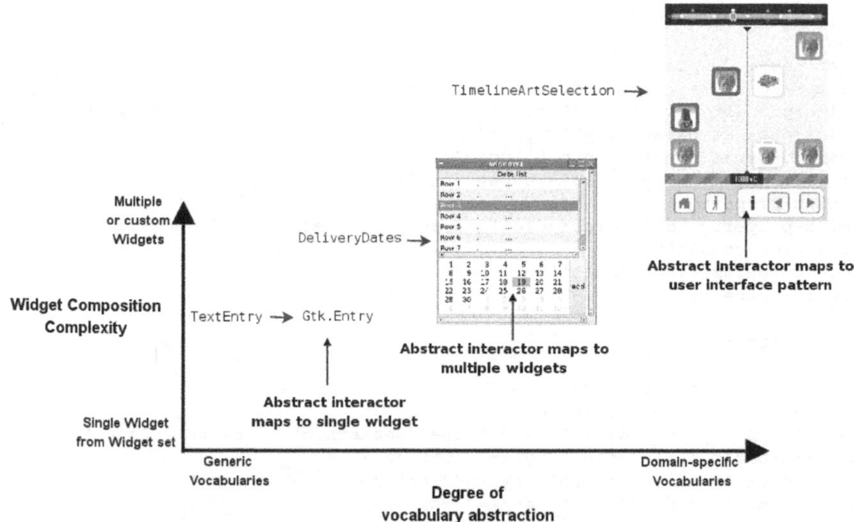

Figure 7.3 Graphical overview of abstraction by using vocabularies

ing scheme defined in the external vocabulary will map these names onto platform-specific names. For example, a UIML document for in-car navigation systems could use names as "route", "speed", "crossroad" and the vocabulary will tell how to present these domain specific names in a concrete widget set. Similar, a vocabulary for building music player user interfaces could define names as "playlist", "arrangement" and "track". Support for custom naming schemes allow creating vocabularies that abstract the problem domain and uses names known to the domain experts. Figure 7.3 provides a graphical overview of the vocabulary abstraction idea.

The standard UIML vocabulary allows mapping one domain object onto one *widget class* but does not allow mapping a domain object onto *a set* of widget classes or a *user interface pattern*. We are currently extending the mapping vocabulary with more semantics, of which an example is shown in the listing below. The listing shows how a date part could be mapped on different types of concrete widgets, or even on a template containing a user interface pattern. More on templates can be found in Section 7.4.3

Vocabularies can be used to tailor UIML to the needs of specific deployment platforms. For example, Harmonia has developed vocabularies for Java, C++/Motif, HTML, WML, and VoiceXML. Harmonia also developed a generic vocabulary that uses abstract component classes and properties to describe visual interfaces (Ali et al., 2002). Such a generic vocabulary allows mappings to be defined from the abstract class and property names to multiple platform-specific widget toolkits. This approach enables a single UIML file to be mapped to multiple platforms without rewriting it. To accommodate other user interface toolkits, one only needs to define an appropriate vocabulary.

```
<uiml:d-class id=''Date'' used-in-tag=''part'' maps-type=''class''>
 <xsl:choose>
  <xsl:when test=''expression1">
   <uiml:maps-to name=''Gtk:Label''>
     <uiml:d-property id=''date'' maps-type=''setMethod'' maps-to=''Text.Concat''>
       <uiml:d-param name=''day'' type=''int''/>
       <uiml:d-param name=''month'' type=''int''/>
       <uiml:d-param name=''year'' type=''int''/>
     </uiml:d-property>
     <uiml:d-property id=''selectable'' maps-type=''setMethod'' maps-\\
        to=''Selectable''>
       <uiml:d-param type=''bool''/>
     </uiml:d-property>
     ...
   </uiml:maps-to>
  </xsl/when>
  <xsl:when test=''expression2">
   <uiml:maps-to name=''Gtk:Calender''>
     <uiml:d-property id=''date'' maps-type=''setMethod'' maps-to=''Date''>
       <uiml:d-param name=''day'' type=''int''/>
       <uiml:d-param name=''month'' type=''int''/>
       <uiml:d-param name=''year'' type=''int''/>
   </uiml:d-property>
   <uiml:d-property id=''selectDay'' maps-type=''setMethod'' maps-\\
       to=''SelectDay''>
      <uiml:d-param type=''System.Int''/>
   </uiml:d-property>
   ...
  </uiml:maps-to>
 </xsl:when>
  ...
 <xsl:otherwise>
   <uiml:maps-to name=''mytemplate'' source="\#mytemplate1" how=''replace'' />
 </xsl:otherwise>
</xsl:choose>
...
```

Figure 7.4 Listing of mapping of a date part on types of concrete widgets

7.3 TOOLS FOR AND EXTENSIONS OF UIML

The benefits of a language cannot be realized without a set of tools designed to utilize the language. Therefore a set of commercial and non-commercial tools and applications based on UIML have been produced to serve different developer communities. These tools are all based on the UIML specification and are available for a wide range of markets and different types of end-users: this section describes UIML-based tools that range from high-quality commercial-level products on the one hand to highly experimental and open source software on the other hand.

7.3.1 LiquidApps™

Harmonia's LiquidApps™ product suite is a comprehensive development and deployment environment for the rapid assembly of applications. Using LiquidApps™, appli-

	Product Name	Capability
Integrate	**uReuse**™	Analyze legacy resources to expose interface; encapsulate for Flex
	uInventory™	Create and search module and transform library with metadata
	uGlue™	Create data transformations
Develop	**uDevelop**®	Design HCIs with library modules, hook up services, link to process
	uRender™	Implement graphic design of HCI to variety of target devices
	uTest™	Test automatically using scenario-driven regression testing across platforms
Manage	**uMeasure**™	Collect metrics on key/mouse movement; analyze human; estimate processing time
	uManage™	Manage versions; integrate with requirements, configuration. & project management
	uLearn™	Emit automatically training parts generated from & synchronized to business process, ready for flushing out; emit technical manuals

Table 7.2 Definition of LiquidApps™ components

cations are composed from an ecosystem of reusable application components. These components can be custom built, assembled from other more primitive components, or extracted from existing systems. LiquidApps™ utilizes UIML to describe all aspects of an application's interface and connection to the presentation logic. LiquidApps™ began life as LiquidAPPS™, a UI development environment based solely on UIML. Now, it retains its HCI focus while extending the lessons learned with UIML to the rest of the application development process.

LiquidApps™ serves as a testbed for the application of UIML in multiple facets of the UI design and development lifecycle. The product suite implements a forward-looking vision to provide comprehensive support for all aspects of rapid application development and integration into the software lifecycle, with a focus on the user's HCI experience. LiquidApps™ has been used for UI prototyping in major Defense applications. In addition, LiquidApps™ users include the US Navy, prime US Government contractors, the US Department of Energy, the automotive multimedia interface collaboration (AMI-C, `www.ami-c.org`), and European consumer electronics manufacturer Beko Elektronik. The LiquidApps™ suite consists of the products shown in Table 7.2.

Each product in the LiquidApps^{TM} suite provides a different avenue of exploration that helps to test the limits of UIML's utility and function. The individual tools generally fall into the following three categories:

1. *Integration Products*: products in this category focus on extracting reusable modules from existing software systems and allowing them to be assembled and reused in new UIs.

2. *HCI Development Products*: these tools provide mechanisms for creating UIML UI descriptions and synchronizing these descriptions to software engineering design artifacts. Deployment tools then take the UIML descriptions produced by other products and create deployable UIs from them. For example, products in this category could take a UIML file and automatically produce C++ source code for the UI.

3. *Management Products*: products in this category synchronize the UI description to training development, version control, and performance measurement. This helps to ensure that designs produced using the tool adhere to a user-centered methodology and provide the appropriate supplemental functionality to integrate into all aspects of the HCI design and software engineering process.

Trial versions of LiquidApps^{TM} can be requested from `http://www.harmonia-inc.com/products/index.php`.

7.3.2 SketchiXML

Among the various tools which are compliant with UIML, there also exists a sketching tool where a designer is able to sketch a graphical user interface (Figure 7.5) and to export it in UIML in order to automatically generate its code. This software is called SketchiXML (Coyette and Vanderdonckt, 2005) and can be downloaded from `http://www.usixml.org/`. Figure 7.5 reproduces a typical sketching sessions where various UI elements are provided. This sketching tool addresses the following requirements for quickly producing a very first UI prototype.

Indeed, designing "the" right UI is very unlikely to occur the first time, even with experience. Instead, UI design is recognized as a process that is intrinsically open (new considerations may appear at any time), iterative (several cycles are needed to reach an acceptable result), and incomplete (not all required considerations are available at design time). Consequently, means to support early UI design have been extensively researched to identify appropriate techniques such as paper sketching, prototypes, mock-ups, diagrams, etc. Most designers consider hand sketches on paper as one of the most effective ways to represent the first drafts of a future UI. This kind of unconstrained approach presents many advantages: sketches can be drawn during any design stage, it is fast to learn and quick to produce, it lets the sketcher focus on basic structural issues instead of unimportant details (e.g., exact alignment, typography, and colors), it is very appropriate to convey ongoing, unfinished designs, and it encourages creativity, sketches can be performed collaboratively between designers and end-users. When the sketch is close enough to the final UI, an agreement can be signed between the designer and the end-user, thus facilitating the contract and validation.

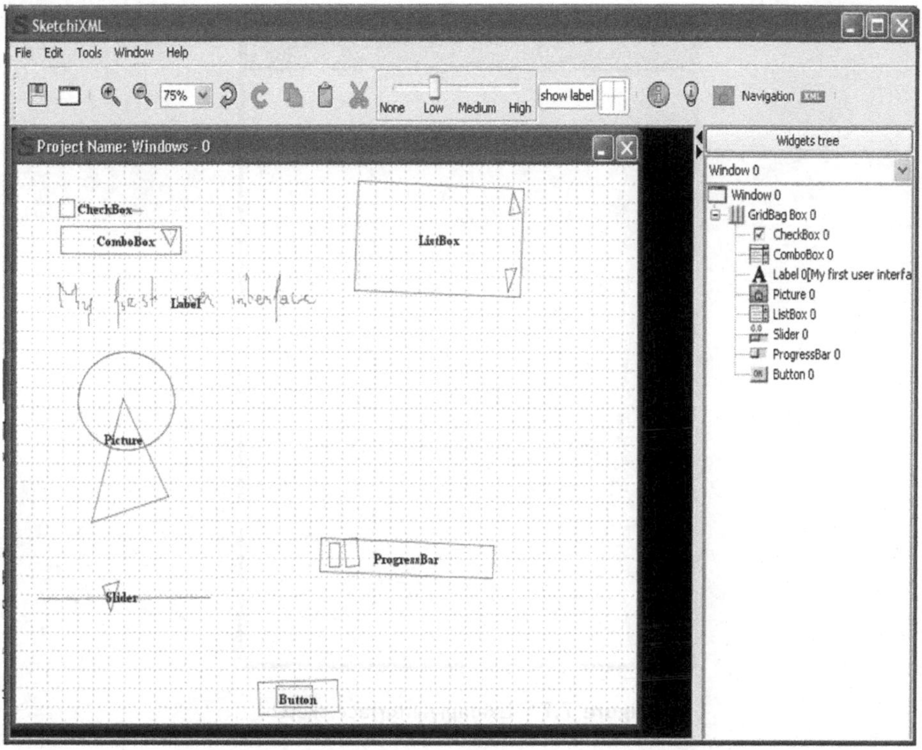

Figure 7.5 A general screen-shot of the sketching tool

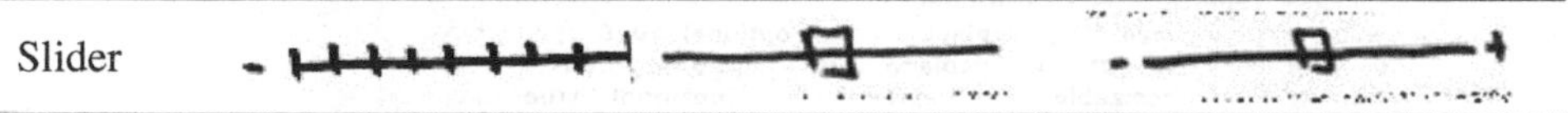

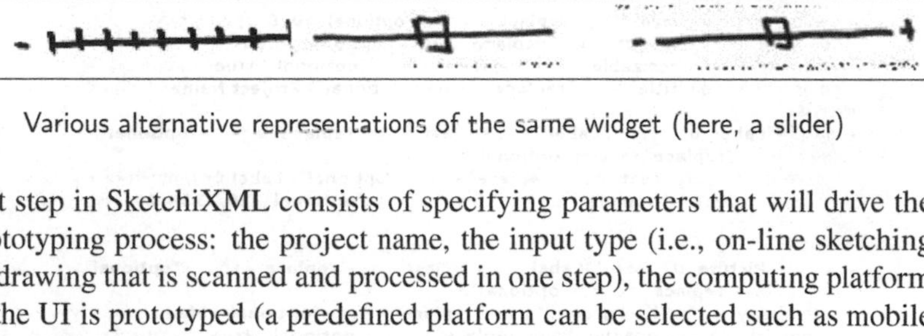

Figure 7.6 Various alternative representations of the same widget (here, a slider)

The first step in SketchiXML consists of specifying parameters that will drive the fidelity prototyping process: the project name, the input type (i.e., on-line sketching or off-line drawing that is scanned and processed in one step), the computing platform for which the UI is prototyped (a predefined platform can be selected such as mobile phone, PDA, TabletPC, kiosk, ScreenPhone, laptop, desktop, wall screen, or a custom one can be defined in terms of platform model), the output folder, the time when the recognition process is initiated, the intervention mode of the usability advisor (manual, mixed-initiative, automatic), and the output quality stating the response time vs. quality of results of the recognition and usability advisor processes. After that, the designer is free to naturally draw virtually anything on the sketching area. Depending on the parameters, what you sketched is all that you get (the sketch remains drawn as is, thus preserving the naturalness of its role) or what you sketched is what will be recognized (in this case, a shape recognition engine detects a familiar shape like a widget, an image, a frame, and transforms it into its real counterpart, thus producing more precise specifications). It is not mandatory to sketch only widgets which are recognized: another representation of the same widget could be accommodated or the initial one (Figure 7.6).

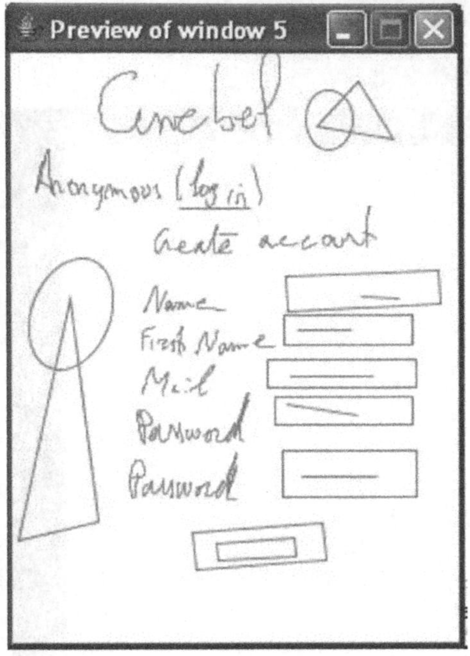

Figure 7.7 Example interface sketch

```
<?xml version="1.0" encoding="UTF-8" ?>
- <uiml>
 - <interface id="interface" how="replace" export="optional">
  - <structure how="replace" export="optional">
   - <part id="GridBag_Box_0" class="JFrame" where="last" how="replace" export="optional">
    - <style how="replace" export="optional">
       <property name="size" how="replace" export="optional">0, 0</property>
       <property name="layout" how="replace" export="optional">null</property>
       <property name="resizable" how="replace" export="optional">true</property>
       <property name="title" how="replace" export="optional">Project Name</property>
     </style>
   - <part id="Label_0" class="JLabel" where="last" how="replace" export="optional">
    - <style how="replace" export="optional">
        <property name="text" how="replace" export="optional">Label 0</property>
        <property name="bounds" how="replace" export="optional">29,23,74,20</property>
      </style>
     </part>
   - <part id="Picture_0" class="JLabel" where="last" how="replace" export="optional">
    - <style how="replace" export="optional">
        <property name="background" how="replace" export="optional">blue</property>
        <property name="opaque" how="replace" export="optional">true</property>
        <property name="bounds" how="replace" export="optional">136,8,41,27</property>
      </style>
     </part>
   + <part id="Label_1" class="JLabel" where="last" how="replace" export="optional">
   + <part id="Label_2" class="JLabel" where="last" how="replace" export="optional">
   + <part id="Picture_1" class="JLabel" where="last" how="replace" export="optional">
   + <part id="Label_3" class="JLabel" where="last" how="replace" export="optional">
   + <part id="Label_4" class="JLabel" where="last" how="replace" export="optional">
   + <part id="Label_5" class="JLabel" where="last" how="replace" export="optional">
   + <part id="Label_6" class="JLabel" where="last" how="replace" export="optional">
   + <part id="Label_7" class="JLabel" where="last" how="replace" export="optional">
   + <part id="Button_0" class="JButton" where="last" how="replace" export="optional">
```

Figure 7.8 An example of a UI for a PDA and its corresponding UIML code

7.3.3 UIML.net: a UIML Renderer for .NET Architecture

UIML.net is a highly dynamic open source UIML rendering engine that interprets and transforms a UIML document into a concrete working user interface. The UIML.net renderer was created to cope with a wide range of devices and to minimize the effort required to support new devices or platforms (Luyten and Coninx, 2004). To accomplish this, vocabularies (or peers) are loaded and processed at run-time by the renderer instead of preprogrammed in the renderer software. The rendering engine queries the vocabulary while rendering the user interface so no widget-set or platform-specific information needs to be included in the rendering software itself. Instead, the mappings defined in the vocabulary are interpreted at runtime and loaded on demand. If a vocabulary is changed, a user interface rendered with this vocabulary will be automatically adapted according to the altered mapping rules and presented using the appropriate concrete widgets. This approach allows for a more sustainable user interface over time: while platforms and devices evolve, a UIML document can be easily reused. However, the UI rendered from the UIML document also takes advantage of the changes.

A prerequisite for the renderer to work is the availability of a virtual machine on the target device. Although the original UIML.net implementation was developed for the Microsoft .Net framework (both the standard framework and the compact framework), there is also a Java implementation based on the .Net implementation. Since most mobile and embedded devices support a Java or .Net virtual machines, UIML.net is almost ubiquitous. Our implementation is built in such a way that there are no further dependencies on exactly which version or type of virtual machine, it simply relies on the virtual machine as a dynamic execution environment that allows loading new functionality on demand while running the user interface. This enables us to support multiple mapping vocabularies on-the-fly.

The architecture of UIML.net consists of a rendering core and multiple rendering backends that contain code that is only used by specific vocabularies. A rendering core can process a UIML document and builds an internal representation of the UIML document. Notice that the mappings from abstract interactors to concrete widgets are defined in the peers section (the vocabulary) of a UIML document. Since the mapping information is provided from outside of the renderer, it can be loaded dynamically and applied at runtime to the rendering core. The rendering backends have a very limited responsibility: they process the parts of a UIML document that can rely on widget-set specific knowledge. Although this seems to break with the promise of being a ubiquitous rendering engine, the specific rendering backends are not required to create a working user interface. They provide access to platform specific widgets which is often required to create an optimal user experience for a specific platform. The reflection mechanism allows using the information from the vocabulary to detect and load the required widgets at runtime without any platform-specific code. This approach overcomes the limitations of a generic vocabulary by allowing the designer to also use widget-set specific parts.

Once UIML.net has processed the UIML document, an internal representation of the document is built as a set of objects structured as an in-memory tree which can be rendered at any time without further transformations. This internal representation is similar to a Document Object Model tree, and is accessible by an internal API. We define a concrete instantiation of a UIML document as a set of objects that represent the in-memory tree of a UIML document where each object that represents a UIML part has a reference to a final widget on the target platform. A concrete instantiation is the result of executing the mapping rules included in the vocabulary without rendering the user interface on screen. A concrete instantiation can be used to perform post-processing operations that will be discussed in the following paragraphs.

The UIML.net renderer uses several stages, where each stage processes a certain aspect of the UIML document. UIML.net uses three different stages of processing that are required for a flexible ubiquitous rendering engine:

- **preprocessing:** during this stage a UIML document can be transformed into another UIML document. For example; the style properties of the user interface can be changed to avoid using green and red for users suffering from color blindness.
- **main processing:** during this stage a UIML document will be interpreted and a concrete instantiation of the document using the UI toolkits that are available on the target platform will be generated.
- **post-processing:** during this stage the runtime behavior strategies of the UI will be selected. For example; the instantiated layout can be changed to optimize the user experience.

The main processing stage is more specifically composed out of the following steps;

- The UIML-renderer takes a UIML document as input, and looks up the rendering backend library that is referred to in the UIML document.
- An internal representation of the UIML document is built. Every part element of the document is processed to create a tree of abstract interface elements.
- For every part element, its corresponding style is applied.
- For every part element, the corresponding behavior is attached and the required libraries to execute this behavior will be loaded just-in-time.
- The generated tree is handed over to the rendering module: for every part tag, a corresponding concrete widget is loaded according to the mappings defined in the vocabulary and linked with the internal representation. For the generated concrete widget, the related style properties are retrieved, mapped by the vocabulary to concrete widget properties and applied on the concrete widget.

7.3.4 DISL: A Modality-Independent UIML-Variant for Limited Devices

Within a project to develop an architecture that allows the provision and management of user interfaces for different devices and modalities—potentially in a multimodal setting—the Dialog and Interface Specification Language (DISL) has been established

(Mueller et al., 2004). DISL can be considered as a modified subset of UIML 4.0 and has been designed with the following two major goals in mind:

- The language should be generic enough to be independent of platforms, devices and even modalities.
- The language should be supportive of devices with limited processing and memory capabilities.

UIML itself could be modality independent, as the interface description itself can be done quite generic and the vocabularies are used to map the user interface to specific targets. However, either, a range of vocabularies is needed and the right target platform is selected at runtime as done for example in Luyten et al. (2006), see Section 7.3.3, or a multistage process to map abstract interfaces to more concrete instances is advisable like the process defined in (Ali et al., 2002).

Anyway both approaches require the definition of several mapping vocabularies. With DISL, the opposite strategy was selected, which means that DISL does not provide the mappings but relies either on an external transcoding process or a dedicated DISL renderer on the target device. So instead of assigning a class to a part which connects to the peers section, a fixed set of generic widgets (inspired by a generic vocabulary for graphical and speech-driven applications (Plomp and Mayora-Ibarra, 2002) and the concept of abstract interaction objects (Vanderdonckt and Bodart, 1993)) can be used with a special attribute of the part. The choice of generic widgets was mainly limited to those allowing input with and without data, output with or without data, confirmations, choices, and logical grouping.

In addition, the communication with the backend logic was simplified, so that only calls to a remote or local peer are supported within the action part, e.g., through HTTP or RMI. Again, the communication method relies on the implementation of the renderer and does not have to be modeled separately.

Through these means, the peers section is obsolete, which decreases the language complexity and the size of concrete instances dramatically. However, this was a design decision for DISL and the selected generic widgets could be implemented with a proper vocabulary in UIML just as well.

Even though DISL is as such simpler than UIML, UI descriptions in DISL still consume a lot of memory (at least from the limited device perspective) and parsing a complex tree structure can soon outrun the maximum stack- or heap size of the underlying system. For this reason a serialized format (S-DISL) has been devised, which reduces size and complexity of an original DISL document without losing information. The number of tags is reduced through following means:

1. Merging of child elements into the parent tag
2. Place union of tags that require the same evaluation semantic
3. Discarding structural tags with no semantic meaning

The first method can be applied to elements where the number of children is finite and static. In that case, the child elements can be converted to a set of attributes for the parent element. The second method applies the same principle as the first one but is used to combine those parts that belong together with respect to the evaluation but have been distributed for better human readability. Some very few tags may be discarded at all as they convey no semantic meaning but just provide information for the human editor of the DISL document (e.g., the part element for logical structuring of the user interface). The tags for which none of the previous methods can be applied are kept intact. The following listing shows for example a part of the collected conditions in the SDISL format.

```
<cl cs="44">
  <c uid="91" cid=''none'' exp=''equal'' n=''no'' tA=''variable'' oA="58"
     tB=''constant'' oB=''true''/>
  <c uid="92" cid=''none'' exp=''equal'' n=''no'' tA=''variable'' oA="58"
     tB=''constant'' oB=''false''/>
  <c uid="93" cid=''none'' exp=''equal'' n=''no'' tA=''variable'' oA="59"
     tB=''constant'' oB=''true''/>
  <c uid="94" cid=''none'' exp=''equal'' n=''no'' tA=''variable'' oA="59"
     tB=''constant'' oB=''false''/>
  . . .
</cl>
```

The element <cl> stands for condition list and is basically a table of all the conditions that exist in the user interface description, while its attribute "cs" reveals the number of the conditions in the list, so that the interpreter knows the size of the table it must set up. For each element of the UI specification a unique numerical identifier "uid" is assigned instead of the manually selected ids in DISL in order to avoid conflicts when sourcing templates or when dealing with several (sub) interfaces at once. Looking at the first condition in the list, one can see that it checks for the equality of the variable with the id "58" and the "true"-constant.

While this encoding and resorting makes the processing of the specification easier, the limitations of elements and restrictions with the assignment of ids provide a reduction of the complete interface specification, so that it is more suitable for limited memory and slow networks. A further compression is gained after the assignment of specific tokens for reserved words like "variable" or "constant". The latter step is a similar process as proposed with binary XML (Martin and Jano, 1999). With these concepts applied, an SDISL renderer has been successfully implemented on a first-generation J2ME-enabled mobile phone (Mueller et al., 2004) and currently 32k Smart Cards are employed to carry complete additionally gzipped SDISL UI descriptions, embedded in a secure architecture (Schaefer et al., 2007).

7.4 IMPROVEMENTS TO UIML FOR VERSION 4.0

Having shown the goals and properties of the different available UIML tools, it is now time to review the most recent enhancements to the UIML specification, which are particularly useful for a human-centered software engineering process, namely, variables, layout management, and parametrizable templates.

7.4.1 Variables and Arithmetic for Improved Dialogs

As UIML is designed to represent all possible user interfaces and provides a clear separation of concerns, a core part consists of the definition of the behavior, which is analog to the dialog model in the sense of a control model in model-based user interface development. From the first version of UIML, the behavior part provided the possibility to specify event-based dialogs, such as reacting on a "button-pressed" event. Furthermore the behavior could be used to define conditions which contain an event and some associated data. A prominent example is the selection of an item in a list box when an item-selected event fires and the value of the item can be extracted from a property. Only if the event hits, and the value is correct, such a condition evaluates to true and the action part can be executed. However events are transient by nature and properties are limited to their widgets they belong to. This can be a restriction for the UI developer in the sense that parts of the behavior which could belong to the UI have to be delegated to the application logic. Up to version 4.0, UIML had no means to capture and exploit information of the UI state, which allows for more powerful dialog models. For this purpose, variables have been introduced and together with simple arithmetic, the control model can be kept completely within the UIML document. As a most simple example for building a UI state machine, consider a dialog with only one button which toggles the state between on and off. The UIML code is illustrated in Figure 7.9.

Let us focus on the behavior part. First, a Boolean variable OnOffState has been defined, which is eventually used to capture the state of this little dialog. The following variables are constants for true and false which are used later for comparisons and assignments. The actual behavior of the dialog is defined with two rules, one for an even number of button operations and one for an odd number. Both check whether a button has been pressed and then check if the current state matches one of the Boolean constants (e.g., for the even case, the OnOffState variable should be equal to the EvenValue before the action can be executed). The action part then assigns to the OnOffVariable the inverse value in order to toggle the state. This example just employed comparison operations and assignments, but UIML 4.0 also supports some basic arithmetic which can be useful for several operations like counting the widget operations, comparison with timers, input validation etc. The latter use of variables is particularly useful in order to reduce communication with the backend logic, especially in a distributed case (e.g., client-server), and thus can add to the user acceptance, since systems can be designed to be more responsive already at a high level.

Consider for example a part of a hotel reservation form that checks the entered number of rooms with the policy of the hotel booking system. In this example, the hotel requires a minimum of one room and a maximum of four rooms to be booked by individuals.

Rooms can be entered directly in the text field or by using up- and down buttons, as illustrated in Figure 7.10. By pressing the buttons, the new room number is immediately checked and the value in the text field changed respectively. In the event the upper or lower bounds are reached, the value in the text field does not change. By pressing the "submit" button, the value in the text field will be submitted to the backend. The advantage of this method is evident when the User Interface is connected via

```
<uiml>
 <interface>
  <structure>
   <part id=''button'' class=''G:Button''/>
  </structure>
  <style>
   <property part-name=''button'' name=''g:text''>ON/OFF</property>
  </style>
  <behavior>
   <variable id=''OnOffState'' type=''boolean'' reference=''false''>
     false
   </variable>
   <variable id=''TrueValue'' constant=''true'' type=''boolean''
             reference=''false''>
    true
   </variable>
   <variable id=''FalseValue'' constant=''true'' type=''boolean''
             reference=''false''>
     false
   </variable>
   <!-- If state == true and button pressed then state = false -->
   <rule id=''buttonPushedEvent''>
     <condition>
       <op nam=''and''>
         <event part-name=''button'' class=''g:actionperformed''>
         <op name=''equals''>
           <variable id=''OnOffState''/>
           <variable id=''TrueValue''/>
         </op>
       </op>
     </condition>
     <action>
       <variable id=''OnOffState''>
         <variable id=''FalseValue''/>
       </variable>
     </action>
   </rule>
   <!-- If state == false and button pressed then state = true -->
   <rule id=''buttonPushedOdd''>
     <condition>
       <op nam=''and''>
         <event part-name=''button'' class=''g:actionperformed''>
         <op name=''equals''>
           <variable id=''OnOffState''/>
           <variable id=''FalseValue''/>
         </op>
       </op>
     </condition>
     <action>
       <variable id=''OnOffState''>
         <variable id=''TrueValue''/>
       </variable>
     </action>
   </rule>
  </behavior>
 </interface>
 <peers>
  <presentation base=''Generic\_1.2\_Harmonia\_1.0">
 </peers>
</uiml>
```

Figure 7.9 UIML code of the simple UI state machine example

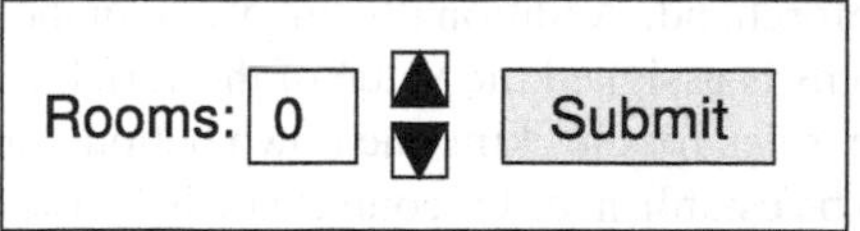

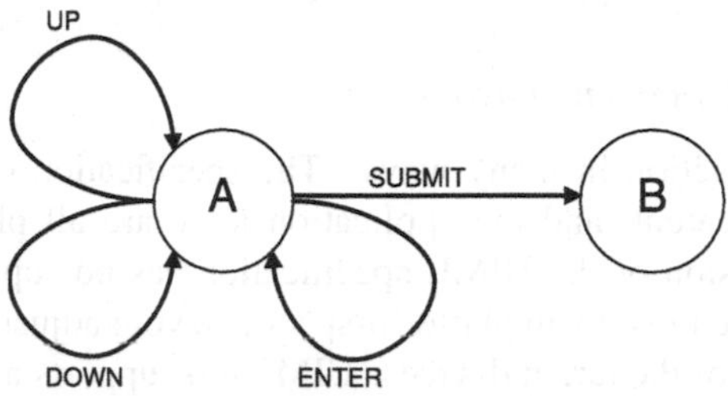

Figure 7.10 Room reservation form and corresponding state machine

```
<rule id=``upButtonPressed>
      <condition>
        <op name=``and''>
          <event part-name=``buttonUP'' class=``g:actionperformed''>
          <op name=``lessthan''>
            <variable id=``curNoRooms''/>
            <variable id=``maxNoRooms''/>
          </op>
        </op>
      </condition>
      <action>
        <op name=``add''>
          <variable id=``curNoRooms''/>
          <variable id=``step''/>
        </op>
        <property part-name=``editRooms'' name=``g:text''>
          <variable id=``curNoRooms''/>
        </property>
      </action>
</rule>
```

Figure 7.11 Part of the UIML code for the room reservation

a network to the backend logic. By checking valid values on the client side no retransmissions are required. This is equivalent to HTML-forms, where JavaScript would be used to check the input prior submission. The code fragment of Figure 7.11 shows how the input validation with the "up"-button works in UIML 4.0.

The condition checks if the "up"-button has been pressed and if the value of the variable curNoRooms is lower than the maximum allowed. Only if both is the case, the action-part can be processed in this case, simple arithmetic is used with the add operator which increments curNoRooms with the value of the variable step, which has been assigned to one beforehand. Additionally, the value in the text box is updated, as the property of editRooms is assigned the value of the variable curNoRooms.

Similarly to this rule, rules for checking the down button, direct text entry and submitting the data have to be established. Of course care has to be taken that this concept is not misused to move parts of the application logic into the UI description, but considering that building program structures with XML is quite cumbersome, the risk is low that UI developers and application developers will produce conflicting overlaps.

7.4.2 Platform-Independent Layouts

UIML achieves abstraction in many ways. The specification of user interface elements, interaction, content, and the application logic are all platform-independent. However, the 3.0 version of the UIML specification has no support for flexible layout management, which results in platform-specific layout adjustments to be made by the designer for each of the target devices. UIML 4.0 supports a flexible layout management technique that ensures consistent layouts in a wide range of circumstances. The layout can still adjust to more extreme conditions without loosing consistency however.

If only the common characteristics of existing layout managers were to be extracted, the resulting layout mechanism would be so general as to only be suitable for creating very simple layouts. Ideally, the general solution should support at least every layout that is possible by each of the layout managers that can be found for the individual specific widget sets. The generic layout extension we introduced for UIML 4.0 is based on the combination of spatial constraints and a constraint solving algorithm. Spatial constraints are sufficiently powerful to describe complex layouts (Badros et al., 2000) and allow us to offer several levels of abstractions. A spatial constraint is a mathematical relation concerning the location or size of different abstract interactors that needs to be maintained in the final user interface. The interface designer specifies the layout by defining constraints over the different user interface parts. This can be as simple as stating *buttonA left-of labelB* to indicate buttonA should appear on the left of labelB. *Left-of* is an abstraction of a one dimensional mathematical relation that indicates the right side of buttonA on the horizontal axis should have a lower value than the left side of labelB on the horizontal axis. Even simple constraint solvers can solve these kinds of constraints.

A constraint solver can find a solution in a two- or three-dimensional solution space that adheres to these constraints. If only a two-dimensional solution space is supported, the interactors can be laid out on a two-dimensional canvas, but cannot be put on top of each other (e.g., in ordered tab pages or partial overlaps). The UIML.net implementation includes Cassowary, an incremental constraint solver that efficiently solves systems of linear equalities and inequalities (Badros et al., 2000). The constraint solver is available in most of the programming languages that are used to implement UIML renderers and interpreters (Java, C++, C#, Python, etc. is distributed under a free software license. Future UIML implementations should have easy access to flexible constraint-based layout management.

Constraints are resolved on the level of the *abstract interaction objects*, so are *independent of the concrete representation* of the widgets. Constraints allow us to specify the layout in a declarative manner and integrate smoothly with UIML. The designer can focus only on *what* the desired layout exactly is, rather than *how* this layout is to be achieved. Furthermore, constraints allow partial specification of the layout, which can be combined with other partial specifications in a predictable way. For example, we can define that the container *selection* is *left-of* the container *content*. The selection and content containers can then each on their own specify the layout of their children. When a change in this layout requires the containers to grow, shrink or move, the upper-level layout constraints will be reevaluated. This allows us to define generic layout patterns (Luyten et al., 2006). These define the layout of a number of containers, which can afterwards be filled in with a specific widget hierarchy using its own layout specification.

Figure 7.12 shows a music player interface rendered from a UIML document. This user interface can be used on different platforms and with different screen sizes as shown in figure 7.13. Without the layout management extension the designer could reuse a great deal of the UIML document for different platforms except the parts of the UIML document concerning the layout of the final user interface. The constraint-based layout technique solves this problem and makes it possible to reuse the interface design completely with different widget sets for different screen sizes without any manual intervention. If other behavior is required, a designer can still add or remove a constraint to obtain the envisioned effect, and is no longer bothered by any platform-specific problems while designing the interface.

Previously, designers had to specify a platform-specific layout for every instantiation of the user interface. This process relied on the careful and precise manual work of the designer in order to keep the different layouts consistent. Furthermore, this process introduced a lot of work, because for every new target platform, the layout had to be almost completely redesigned. The layout extension enables designers to create new layout templates and reuse them whenever appropriate. A layout template is nothing more than a set of layout constraints that can be applied to a set of parts from the structure section.

7.4.3 Template Parametrization

UIML provides a *template* mechanism that allows defining reusable components. A *reusable component* is a reusable part of the user interface: a combination of structure, style, behavior and/or content written down in UIML. They enable interface implementers to reuse part or all of their UI through the UIML <template> element. For example, many UIs for electronic commerce applications include a credit-card entry form. If such a form is described in UIML as a template, then it can be reused multiple times either within the same UI or across other UIs. This reduces the amount of UIML code needed to develop a UI and also ensures a consistent presentation across enterprise-wide UIs.

The reusability of these components can still be improved however. In this section we describe a method to enhance the reusability of the template mechanism by allowing more flexible relations between a template and its *sourcing document*; the part of the user interface that embeds the template.

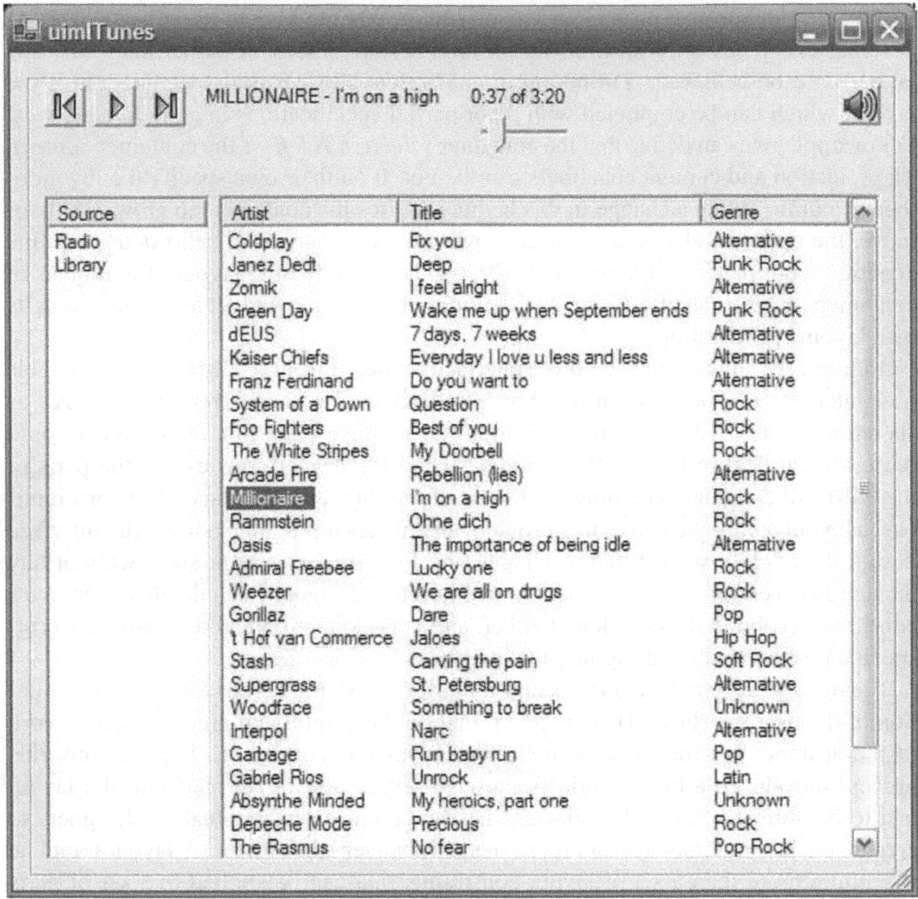

Figure 7.12 Fully functional music player interface rendered on desktop computer from UIML document

We increased the expressive power of a template definition by allowing parameters to be passed from the sourcing document to the template. This allows a user interface designer to create a reusable user interface component that supports variations in structure, style, content and/or behavior. The components vary according to the parameters that are passed to it. In contrast with non-parameterized templates that provide immutable user interface components, a *parameterized template* allows us to describe a user interface pattern (van Welie et al., 2000). A pattern captures design knowledge for a specific problem that can be reapplied in other contexts, such as the credit-card entry form. Parametrized templates are very useful for describing reusable layout patterns, which we discussed in the previous section. These have the same purpose as the XUL layout patterns described by Sinnig et al. (2004). Their approach uses the Velocity templating language to support variations in the patterns, while parametrized templates allow this to be built into UIML.

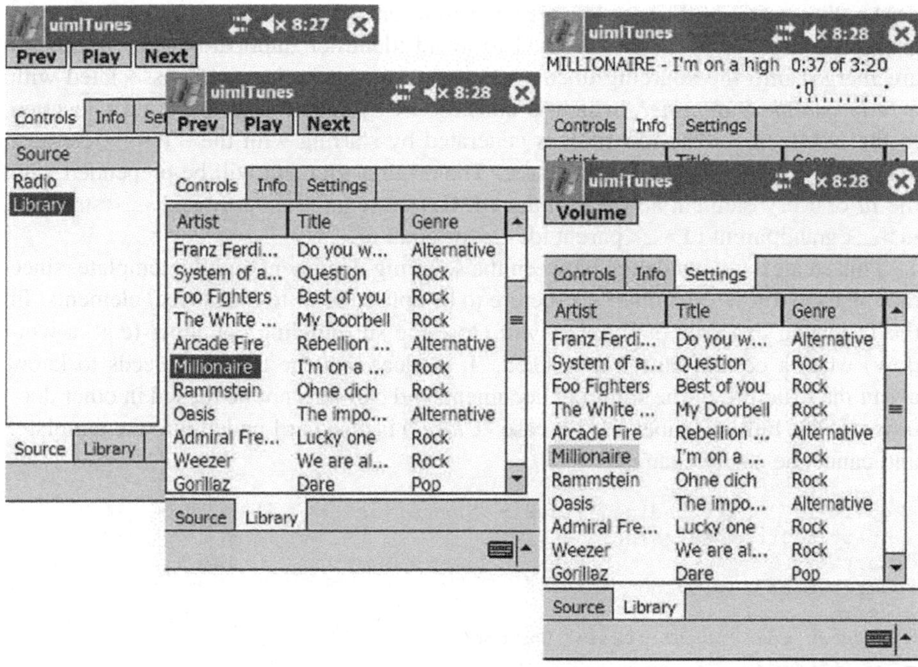

Figure 7.13 Fully functional music player interface rendered on PDA from UIML document

As a simple example, suppose we want to define the behavior of a calculator. When one of the buttons is pressed, the corresponding number is added to the display. The behavior rule for this would be:

```
  <rule>
  <condition>
    <event part-name=''Button1" class=''actionPerformed''/>
  </condition>
  <action>
    <property part-name=''Display'' name=''text''>
      <call name=''utils.concatenate''>
        <param>
          <property part-name=''Display'' name=''text''/>
        </param>
        <param>
          <property part-name=''Button1" name=''label''/>
        </param>
      </call>
    </property>
  </action>
</rule>
```

We would need ten similar rules (one for each button), only varying in the part-name of the button. Although this scenario seems to be ideal for a reusable template, the 3.0 version of UIML is not capable of defining a template for these rules because they were slightly different.

Another aspect of the template mechanism where the reusability could be improved is the naming schemes that are used to avoid identifier duplicates when templates are merged into the sourcing documents part tree. Each element is associated with a *fully qualified identifier*, which is constructed by identifying the child's location in the UIML tree. The identifier is generated by starting with the <uiml>-element and tracing downward through the tree. The original element will be prepended with the *id* of every element above it in the UIML tree (e.g., "<interface id>__<structure id>__<grandparent id>__<parent id>__<original id>").

This creates a dependency between the sourcing document and the template, since they need to know each other's structure to be able to refer to the correct elements. In the following example, a template will close the surrounding container (e.g., a window) when a certain button is clicked. It is clear that the template needs to know about the structure of the sourcing document, and can thus not be reused in other documents. The button's label (in this case "*Close*") is also hard-coded into the template, and cannot be easily changed.

```
  <part id=''surrounding'' class=''Container''>
  <part source="#closing'' .../>
</part>
<template id=''closing''>
  <part>
    <part id=''btn1" class=''Button''>
      <style>
        <property name=''label''>Close</property>
      </style>
      <behavior>
        <rule>
          <condition>
            <event class=''actionPerformed''/>
          </condition>
          <action>
            <property part-name=
               ''interf1_strct1_surrounding'' name=''visible''>
              false
            </property>
          </action>
        </rule>
      </behavior>
    </part>
  </part>
</template>
```

In order to solve these issues, we introduced some concepts of traditional programming languages into the template specification. By passing parameters to a template it should be possible to establish stable, yet flexible relationships between a template and any UIML document.

The next example shows a parametrized template for the calculator behavior rules:

```
<template id=''calculator_rule''>
  <d-template-parameters>
    <d-template-param>button</d-template-param>
 </d-template-parameters>
  <rule>
```

```
    <condition>
      <event part-name="$button'' class=''actionPerformed''/>
    </condition>
    <action>
      <property part-name=''Display'' name=''text''>
        <call name=''utils.concatenate''>
          <param>
            <property part-name=''Display'' name=''text''/>
          </param>
          <param>
            <property part-name="$button'' property=''label''/>
          </param>
        </call>
      </property>
    </action>
  </rule>
</template>
```

The template defines a parameter *button*, which will be used to fill in the correct reference in the label property and actionPerformed event. Note that if a parameter is used within a certain attribute, it is prefixed with a $-sign to distinguish it from normal references. To source this template, we pass the corresponding button as a parameter to it (in this case Button1):

```
<rule source=''calculator_rule'' how=''replace''>
  <template-parameters>
    <template-param id=''button''>Button1<template-param>
  </template-parameters>
</rule>
```

To parametrize the example where we want to close the surrounding container in the sourcing document, we introduce two parameters: one for the label of the button, and one for the surrounding container:

```
<template id=''closing''>
  <d-template-parameters>
    <d-template-param>label</d-template-param>
    <d-template-param>container</d-template-param>
  </d-template-parameters>
  <part>
    <part id=''btn1" class=''Button''>
      <style>
        <property name=''label''>
          <template-param id=''label''/>
</property>
      </style>
      <behavior>
        <rule>
          <condition>
            <event class=''actionPerformed''/>
          </condition>
          <action>
            <property part-name="$container'' name=''visible''>
              false
            </property>
          </action>
```

```
        </rule>
      </behavior>
    </part>
  </part>
```

The example shows that we can also use the parameters in any UIML tag (in this case, inside a property tag). Finally, to instantiate this template we provide values for the two parameters:

```
<part id=''surrounding'' class=''Container''>
  <part source="#closing'' ...>
    <template-parameters>
      <template-param id=''label''>Close</template-param>
      <template-param id=''container''>
           surrounding
      </template-param>
    </template-parameters>
  </part>
</part>
```

In conclusion, *parametrized templates* improve the existing template mechanism in UIML to allow for full reusability since they are completely independent of the sourcing document.

7.5 UIML-RELATED STANDARDS

UIML is an answer to the question of what a declarative language would look like that could provide a canonical representation of any UI suitable for multiplatform, multilingual, and multimodal UIs. This section describes the influences from W3C and other complimentary efforts on UIML, and comments on how UIML fits into these various technologies.

7.5.1 HTML, XML, CSS, WAI, and SOAP—Inspirations for UIML

Several W3C activities in 1997—XML, HTML, CSS, and WAI—formed a catalyst of ideas that inspired the development of UIML. At that time a group of HCI developers in Blacksburg, Virginia, who were frustrated with the difficulty of creating UIs in traditional imperative languages (e.g., C, C++) starting work on UIML using a number of insights from these W3C activities.

The success of HTML by 1997 in allowing non-programmers to design UIs with a rich user experience was a beacon of light to the team that designed the original UIML language: Could we start fresh, and design a new declarative language powerful enough to describe UIs that historically were built only in imperative programming languages and toolkits (e.g., C with X-windows, C++ with MFC, Java with AWT/Swing)? Doing so would bridge the gap between HTML, which allows easy design of UIs with limited interaction, and imperative languages, which allow design of rich UIs but only in the hands of experienced programmers.

In 1997, the first XML conference was held. XML is a metalanguage, to which a vocabulary of element and attribute names must be added. XML could be standardized once, and was extensible because many vocabularies could be created by different groups of people. In designing UIML we realized that if a UI language was a metalanguage, then it could potentially serve as a canonical representation of any UI. Hence UIML is a metalanguage. By separately creating vocabularies for UIML, UIML could be devoid of bias toward UI metaphors, target devices (e.g., PCs, phones, PDAs), UI toolkits (e.g., Swing, MFC), and could be translated to various target languages (e.g., Java, HTML, VoiceXML).

The world was clearly on a trend to untether users from the desktop computer, allowing them to use a plethora of devices via growing wireless technologies. UIML recognized that a metalanguage enables the creation of UI descriptions in a device-independent form.

Another influence by 1997 was Cascading Style Sheets, which could be viewed as the first step to creating UI descriptions that are separated, or factored, into orthogonal components. The factoring was again a key to device-independent descriptions of UIs. The design of UIML started by asking what fundamentally are the orthogonal parts of a UI. The Model-View-Controller paradigm is a three-way separation. UIML arrived at a six-way separation (structure, style, content, behavior, APIs to components outside the UI, and mappings to UI toolkits) (Phanouriou, 2000).

The W3C's Web Accessibility Initiative, which also started in 1997, influenced UIML as well. The key to making documents and UIs accessible, according to WAI, is to capture the author's intent. A language like HTML has ingrained into it a certain metaphor based on the printed page. What authors need is the ability to represent a UI using abstractions representing the semantic information they have, which cannot be rediscovered easily from markup like HTML. Again, a metalanguage appeared to be a key element for UIML, because an author could define and work with his or her own abstractions in a vocabulary that the author creates.

A second influence of WAI was the recognition that scripting in HTML pages presents an obstacle to making documents portable across devices. The lesson learned for UIML's designers was that the behavior of a user's interaction with a UI should clearly be a separable component in a UI description.

The original work on SOAP in 1998 also influenced UIML. When SOAP was first proposed, it suggested that remote calls to objects could be done using XML. Therefore the actions in UIML's syntax for behavior description were designed to allow invocation of SOAP or other XML-based remote calls.

7.5.2 HCI—Another Influence on UIML

Aside from W3C, there was one other key influence on UIML: the field of Human-Computer Interaction (HCI). The design of UIs that work across devices requires a good design methodology. Much work has been done in the HCI field in UI design. There is also a body of literature called UI Management Systems, which include notations to represent UIs, and these heavily influenced the design of UIML (especially the question of how to represent user interaction with a UI in a canonical form).

Our expectation is that work on design techniques for UIs will produce a number of tools and UI design languages. UIML was not necessarily intended as a UI design language (although it can be used as such), but rather as a language for UI implementation. Therefore UI design tools could represent a design in a design language, and then transform a UI in a design language to a canonical representation for UI implementation, namely, UIML. If Integrated Development Environments (IDEs) and Web page design tools could read UIML, then the world would have a complete path for computer-assisted design and implementation of multiplatform UIs.

7.5.3 How UIML Fits W3C Architecture Today

Dave Raggett in his talk at the W3C Workshop on Web Device Independence (Bristol, Oct. 2000) proposed that there was a need for a layer that can adapt a UI to the particular XML language used by a target device. UIML is an element of this device adaptation layer, but not a complete solution. For example, there may be transform algorithms that transform the interface description (e.g., in UIML) to take into account device characteristics.

Without a single canonical language to represent UIs at this layer (regardless of whether it is UIML), then one must create transforms for multiple languages. Obviously if it is possible to have one language at this layer, the construction of reusable transforms is simplified.

One way to apply UIML at this layer is to use multiple vocabularies with UIML, and transform from UIML using one vocabulary to UIML using another vocabulary. For example, one may start with a UI description using a generic vocabulary (e.g., a vocabulary whose abstractions can be mapped to a variety of devices). Perhaps the UI was authored with this generic vocabulary to facilitate accessibility. A transform algorithm, guided by a rule base that takes into account characteristics of different devices, can then be used to map UIML with the generic vocabulary to UIML with a vocabulary specific to a particular device. This technique has been implemented to adapt UIs to various versions of Web browsers (e.g., to give a similar appearance to UIs for HTML 3.2 vs. HTML 4.0 browsers). The UIML produced by the Device Adaptation layer can then be rendered to a particular XML language (e.g., by a rendering program that compiles UIML into XHTML, or UIML into VoiceXML).

7.5.4 The Path Toward Separation in User Interfaces

The evolution of W3C specifications in the UI area has followed a path of gradually separating a UI description into orthogonal parts:

Up until HTML 3.2, there was no separation.

In HTML4, the style was separated (via CSS and XSL-FO).

In XForms, the portion of a document that represents a form was separated.

In XML Events, events were separated.

As stated earlier, UIML separates a UI into six parts, answering these six questions:

1. What are the parts that constitute the structure of the UI?
2. What is the presentation style of the parts?
3. What is the content associated with the parts?
4. What is the behavior of the UI when a user interacts with the UI?
5. What is the API of components outside the UI with which the UI interacts?
6. What is the mapping of the vocabulary to a target UI toolkit or markup language?

These six questions are answered in UIML's structure, style, content, behavior, logic, and presentation elements, respectively.

Therefore this fundamental design decision in UIML is compatible with the path being followed by W3C. UIML should provide W3C working groups with an example of what will ultimately be reached as this path toward separation is followed in the future.

7.6 CONCLUSION

The User Interface Markup Language (UIML) is based on the concept of using transforms and mappings to extend its utility to any UI technology or toolkit. The goal of UIML is to remove the complexity of generating the UI description and to focus on defining the mappings and transforms that enable UIML to be converted into the appropriate deployment language. We have found that this approach improves the software engineering aspects of UI engineering by improving reusability through modular templates, enabling rapid prototyping by empowering the usability engineer to produce developer level code through automated tools, and separating both concerns within the UI design and platform idiosyncrasies from the abstract UI design.

Our experience indicates that adding layers of abstraction in the software engineering process can be especially beneficial when the systems and interfaces are complex. In these cases, the ability to quickly and easily modify and regenerate code becomes very important. Imagine two systems: one consists of a single dialog box while the other consists of hundreds of such windows. Now imagine the relative cost of modifying one property within each dialog of the systems. What becomes apparent is that while modifying one dialog at the source code level is practical, the opposite is true for trying to maintain a large system at this level. Here is where a UIML can be very effective. It provides a way for non-programmers to take part in the maintenance of the system at a lower overall cost to the development effort. It also opens the possibility of structuring the UI description in such a way that each can use centralized stylesheets and property definitions, further reducing the time required to modify the interface.

The set of computing platforms and devices is too diverse to be covered by a single UIDL that relies on platform-specific constructs to describe all possible platforms and devices. A metalanguage approach is essential to creating a viable, platform-independent representation. The primary goal of UIML's designers has been to create such a metalanguage as an open standard for UI definition. OASIS established a UIML Technical Committee (TC) that has examined UIML and is in the process of standardizing the language.

Acknowledgements

A. Coyette and J. Vanderdonckt acknowledge the support of the SIMILAR European network of excellence (`www.similar.cc`) on multimodal interfaces funded by European Commission. Part of the research at EDM is funded by EFRO (European Fund for Regional Development), the Flemish Government and the Flemish Interdisciplinary Institute for Broadband Technology (IBBT). Work on the most relevant products in the LiquidApps™ suite is supported by NAVAIR contracts N00421-04-C-0030, N68335-06-C-0010, and N68335-05-C-0029; NAVSEA contract N00164-06-

C-6093; Office of Naval Research contract N00014-06-M-0047; and Missile Defense Agency contract W9113M-06-C-0041.

References

Abrams, M., Phanouriou, C., Batongbacal, A. L., Williams, S. M., and Shuster, J. E. (1999). UIML: An appliance-independent XML user interface language. *Computer Networks*, 31(11-16):1695–1708.

Ali, M. F., Pérez-Quiñones, M. A., Abrams, M., and Shell, E. (2002). Building multi-platform user interfaces with UIML. In Kolski, C. and Vanderdonckt, J., editors, *CADUI Computer-Aided Design of User Interfaces III, Proceedings of the Fourth International Conference on Computer-Aided Design of User Interfaces, May, 15-17, 2002, Valenciennes, France*, pages 255–266. Kluwer.

G. J. Badros, J. Nichols, and A. Boming. SCWM-an intelligent constraint-enabled window manager. *In Proc. AAAI Spring Symposium on Smart Graphics*, Cambridge, MA, Mar.20-22 2000. (`http://scwm.mit.edu`).

Coyette, A. and Vanderdonckt, J. (2005). A sketching tool for designing anyuser, any-platform, anywhere user interfaces. In Costabile, M. F. and Paternò, F., editors, *INTERACT*, volume 3585 of *Lecture Notes in Computer Science*, pages 550–564. Springer.

Eisenstein, J., Vanderdonckt, J., and Puerta, A. (2001). Applying model-based techniques to the development of UIs for mobile computers. In *Proceedings of the 2001 International Conference on Intelligent User Interfaces*, pages 69–76, New York. ACM Press.

Hartson, H. R. and Hix, D. (1989). Toward empirically derived methodologies and tools for human-computer interface development. *International Journal of Man-Machine Studies*, 31(4):477–494.

Limbourg, Q. and Vanderdonckt, J. (2004). UsiXML: A user interface description language supporting mul-tiple levels of independence. In Matera, M. and Comai, S., editors, *Engineering Advanced Web Applications*, pages 325–338. Rinton Press, Paramus.

Luyten, K. and Coninx, K. (2004). UIML.NET: an open UIML renderer for the.net framework. In Jacob, R. J. K., Limbourg, Q., and Vanderdonckt, J., editors, *CADUI*, pages 257–268. New York: Kluwer.

Martin, B. and Jano, B. (1999). Wap binary xml content format. World Wide Web Consortium. W3C NOTE.

Mueller, W., Schaefer, R., and Bleul, S. (2004). Interactive multimodal user interfaces for mobile devices. In *HICSS*.

Phanouriou, C. (2000). *UIML: A Device-Independent User Interface Markup Language*. Ph.D. thesis, Vermont University. Available at `http://scholar.lib.vt.edu/theses/available/etd-08122000-19510051/unrestricted/PhanouriouETD.pdf`.

Puerta, A. R. and Eisenstein, J. (2002). XIML: a common representation for interaction data. In *IUI*, pages 216–217.

Schaefer, R., Mueller, W., López, M., and Sánchez, D. (2007). Device independent user interfaces for smart cards. Technical report, C-LAB Report.

Vanderdonckt, J. and Bodart, F. (1993). Encapsulating knowledge for intelligent automatic interaction objects selection. In *Proceedings of ACM INTERCHI'93 Conference on Human Factors in Computing Systems, Amsterdam*, pages 424–429. ACM Press.

Zimmermann, G., Vanderheiden, G. C., and Gilman, A. S. (2002). Universal remote console - prototyping for the alternate interface access standard. In Carbonell, N. and Stephanidis, C., editors, *User Interfaces for All*, volume 2615 of *Lecture Notes in Computer Science*, pages 524–531, Springer.

Vanderdonckt, J. and Bodart, F. (1993). Encapsulating knowledge for intelligent automatic interaction objects selection. In *Proceedings of ACM INTERCHI'93 Conference on Human Factors in Computing Systems Amsterdam*, pages 424–429. ACM Press.

Zimmermann, G., Vanderheiden, G. C. and Gilman, A. S. (2002). Universal remote console – prototyping for the alternate interface access standard. In Carbonell, N. and Stephanidis, C., editors, *User Interfaces for All*, volume 2615 of *Lecture Notes in Computer Science*, pages 524–531. Springer.

8 MEGAMODELING AND METAMODEL-DRIVEN ENGINEERING FOR PLASTIC USER INTERFACES: MEGA-UI

Jean-Sébastien Sottet,
Gaelle Calvary, Jean-Marie Favre, and Joëlle Coutaz

Laboratoire d'Informatique de Grenoble

Abstract. Models are not new in Human Computer Interaction (HCI). Consider all the Model-Based Interface Design Environments (MB-IDE) that emerged in the 1990s for generating User Interfaces (UI) from more abstract descriptions. Unfortunately, the resulting poor usability killed the approach, burying the models in HCI for a long time until new requirements sprung, pushed by ubiquitous computing (e.g., the need for device independence). These requirements, bolstered by the large effort expended in Model-Driven Engineering (MDE) by the Software Engineering (SE) community, have brought the models back to life in HCI. This paper utilizes both the know-how in HCI and recent advances in MDE to address the challenge of engineering Plastic UIs, i.e., UIs capable of adapting to their context of use (User, Platform, Environment) while preserving usability. Although most of the work has concentrated on the functional aspect of adaptation so far, this chapter focuses on usability. The point is to acknowledge the strength of keeping trace of the UI's design rationale at runtime so as to make it possible for the system to reason about its own design when the context of use changes. As design transformations link together different perspectives on the same

UI (e.g., user's tasks and workspaces for spatially grouping items together), the paper claims for embedding a graph that depicts a UI from different perspectives at runtime while explaining its design rationale. This meets the notion of Megamodel as promoted in MDE. The first Megamodel was used to make explicit the relations between the core concepts of MDE: System, Model, Metamodel, Mapping, and Transformation. When transposed to HCI, the Megamodel gives rise to the notion of Mega-UI that makes it possible for the user (designer and/or end-user) to browse and/or control the system from different levels of abstraction (e.g., user's tasks, workspaces, interactors, code) and different levels of genericity (e.g., model, metamodel, meta-metamodel). Yet, a first prototype (a rapid prototyping tool) has been implemented using general MDE tools (e.g., EMF, ATL). So far, the effort has been directed on the subset of the graph that links together different perspectives on the same UI including its mapping on the platform. Via an Extra-UI, the designer controls the UI's molding and distribution based on a library of self-explanative transformations. Extra-UIs were previously called Meta-UIs. But as Meta is confusing with the same Meta prefix in MDE, we prefer the prefix Extra to assess there is no change of level of genericity. By contrast, the Meta-UI manipulates upper levels of genericity (Meta levels in MDE) for making it possible for the user (designer and/or end-user) to observe and/or define languages for specifying UIs and Meta-UIs. Meta-UIs is the next step in our research agenda. Mega-UI is the overall UI that encompasses UIs, Extra-UIs, and Meta-UIs.

8.1 INTRODUCTION

"Bridging the gap between Software Engineering (SE) and Human Computer Interaction (HCI)" is an old and recurrent slogan that clearly points out the lack of integration between the two disciplines. The different backgrounds and concerns probably explain the two parallel roads that have been followed so far. Nevertheless, there is a shared agreement that a tighter coupling would favor the tuning of unifying and powerful methods and tools. It seems to be the case today with Model-Driven Engineering (MDE) which the two communities seem to adhere to. MDE is becoming increasingly popular, reaching the point where "model-driven" or "model-based" prefixes have become buzzwords. In SE, the MDE trend took root in 2000 with the publication of the Model Driven Architecture (MDA) standard from the Object Management Group (OMG). In fact, MDA is a complex set of industrial evolving standards, and at the same time a grand-vision for the decades to come. Current approaches try to depart from this very technological root and dependence from the OMG, some of the core ideas being retained and seeking more generality. In recent years, a balanced understanding has emerged among the MDE community, and techniques are now available to support the first steps of this long-term vision. In the meantime, the HCI community was waiting up, as modeling is there an old tradition but not always a good memory.

Models are not new in HCI. In the 90s, the dream was to automatically generate UIs from more abstract descriptions. Many tools appeared (such as ADEPT, Johnson et al., 1993, TADEUS, Elwert and Schlungbaum, 1995, FUSE, Lonczewski and Schreiber, 1996, and AME, Martin, 1996) but failed because of a series of drawbacks (Myers et al., 2000):

- Developers had to learn a new specification language.
- The connection between the specification and the resulting code was hard to understand and control.
- The generated UIs were constrained by the underlying toolkit, depriving designers of any originality.
- Generators were rigid "black boxes" without any tuning of the generation process. As a result, the usability of the generated UIs was unpredictable and quite low.

These failings killed the model-based approach definitively. Models were just appreciated for exploring design spaces (Luo et al., 1993) or for contemplatively supporting the design process. Experience shows that industry still remains code-centric and that models still fit in the contemplative category in HCI: of course models help in reasoning, of course they might look nice, nevertheless in practice developers love coding above all. So, "why would MDE succeed now where it has failed in the same domain in the past?"

When reconsidering model-based approaches in HCI, we must be vigilant not to reproduce past experience. Of course, new requirements have emerged, pushed by ubiquitous computing (e.g., the need for device independence). Nevertheless, if model-based approaches have failed on the simplest interactive systems, why would they succeed on more complex ones? Our answer is threefold: (1) take advantage of MDE arsenal of concepts and tools, (2) rebalance model-based approaches in considering Transformations as well, (3) put the user in the loop for mastering the resulting UIs.

This paper argues for these three principles on the specific case of Plastic User Interfaces. Plasticity is concerned with device independence that was one of the fields (Myers et al., 2000) pointed out as key for digging up models in HCI. Section 8.2 is devoted to plasticity. It elicits the SE issues on a small running example called HHCS (Home Heating Control System). HHCS supports the illustration all over the paper. Section 8.3 gathers MDE advances for addressing plasticity. The core concepts are put in practice in Section 8.4 giving rise to a taxonomy of UIs: UI, Extra-UI, Meta-UI and Mega-UI. This taxonomy opens new doors in HCI, shifting the horizon further. Section 8.5 is devoted to these perspectives and challenges.

8.2 PLASTICITY: CASE STUDY AND ENGINEERING ISSUES

The term plasticity is derived from the capacity of solids and biological entities such as plants and brain, to adapt to external constraints so as to preserve continuous usage. Applied to HCI, UI's plasticity is the capacity of UIs to adapt to the context of use while preserving usability (Thevenin, 1999). By context of use, we mean a triplet <User, Platform, Environment> where:

- The User denotes the archetypal person who is intended to use, or is actually using, the interactive system. This includes profile, idiosyncrasies, tasks, and activities.

- The Platform describes the computing, sensing, networking, and interaction resources that bind together the physical environment with the digital world.
- The Environment makes reference to the physical space where the interaction will take place, or is actually taking place. This includes numeric and/or symbolic locations (e.g., at home, in a public space, on the move in the street, in the train or car), social rules and activities, light, heat, and sound conditions.

As the platform is no more limited to a unique computer but becomes a cluster of maybe heterogeneous and dynamic elementary platforms (e.g., a PC and a PDA), adaptation is much more complex than selecting the most appropriate modality when the context of use changes. Now, UIs can be distributed among a set of elementary platforms and can migrate according to the arrival and departure of resources. As a result, there are two means for adapting a UI to its context of use: remolding and redistribution.

- Remolding consists in reshuffling the UI without changing its distribution state among the available resources (e.g., compacting radio buttons in a combo-box without migrating part or all of the UI; switching from vocal to graphics when entering into a public space). Clearly, modality and multimodality provide means for remolding.
- In contrast, redistribution changes the allocation of the UI's elements among the available resources (e.g., migrating all of the input tasks from a PC to a PDA in order to get a remote controller; migrating all of the UI from a PDA to a PC when the PDA's battery is low). In case of heterogeneous resources, redistribution may require a remolding.

8.2.1 Case Study

The case study is about controlling comfort at home using different devices ranging from dedicated wall-mounted displays to Web browsers. Figure 8.1 presents four Web UIs depending on the screen size, the number of rooms, as well as the usability properties that the HCI designer has elicited as key:

- In Figure 8.1a–c, the rooms are browsable wheras they are directly observable in Figure 8.1d. Browsability has a human cost: it is physically and cognitively demanding to select a room (one physical action per room) and compare temperatures. If human workload has been elicited as key, then browsability is not a good option — except if the number of rooms is not limited (e.g., twenty rooms) and the display surface is not extendable. In that case, the designer has to prioritize the different facets of workload (Card et al., 1983): motor (for navigating between rooms), cognitive (for memorizing temperatures), but also perceptual as the information density will increase with the number of rooms. Human Workload is one ergonomic criterion in Bastien and Scapin's framework (Bastien and Scapin, 1991). In this framework, another criterion is Guidance. Guidance is refined into four subcriteria among wich is the Grouping/Distinction among items. With regard to this subcriterion, Figure 8.1a–c are

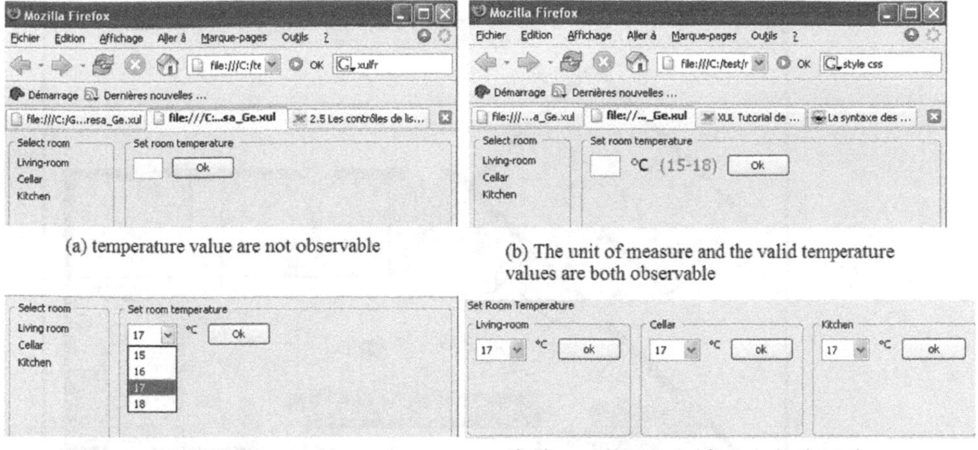

(a) temperature value are not observable

(b) The unit of measure and the valid temperature values are both observable

(c) The user is prevented from making errors

(d) The user is prevented from navigation tasks

Figure 8.1 Four functionally equivalent UIs that differ from the set of usability criteria

valuable as one workspace is associated per task: the left one for selecting the room, the right one for specifying the desired temperature of the selected room

- Figure 8.1-b enhances Figure 8.1-a with the observability of both the temperature unit (°C) and the range of possible values (from 15 to 18). With regard to Bastien-Scapin's Guidance ergonomic criterion, this enhancement is a good point for improving Prompting (one of the four Guidance subcriteria). Prompting might reduce the risk of error

- Figure 8.1-c goes one step further in shielding the user against error thanks to combo-boxes. Error management is one ergonomic criterion in Bastien-Scapin's framework. It is decomposed into three subcriteria among which is Prevention against error.

- In contrast to Figure 8.1a-b-c that are clearly task-driven, Figure 8.1d is more concept-driven. User's tasks are considered as operations that are applicable to the concepts. The Grouping/Distinction among items is led by concepts: one workspace is associated per room, and it is in charge of supporting all the tasks that are applicable to the concept. Figure 8.2 is an alternative of Figure 8.1d. It improves Bastien and Scapin's Compatibility criterion thanks to a clickable map of the house. Whilst all of the UIs in Figure 8.1 are coded, Figure 8.2 is only a hand-made mock-up.

Clearly, the task driven UIs presented in Figure 8.1a–c are more distributable than the ones depicted in Figure 8.1d and 8.2. Figure 8.3 shows an example where the task Select a room has migrated to the PDA. The redistribution has triggered a remolding: hyperlinks have been replaced with radio-buttons.

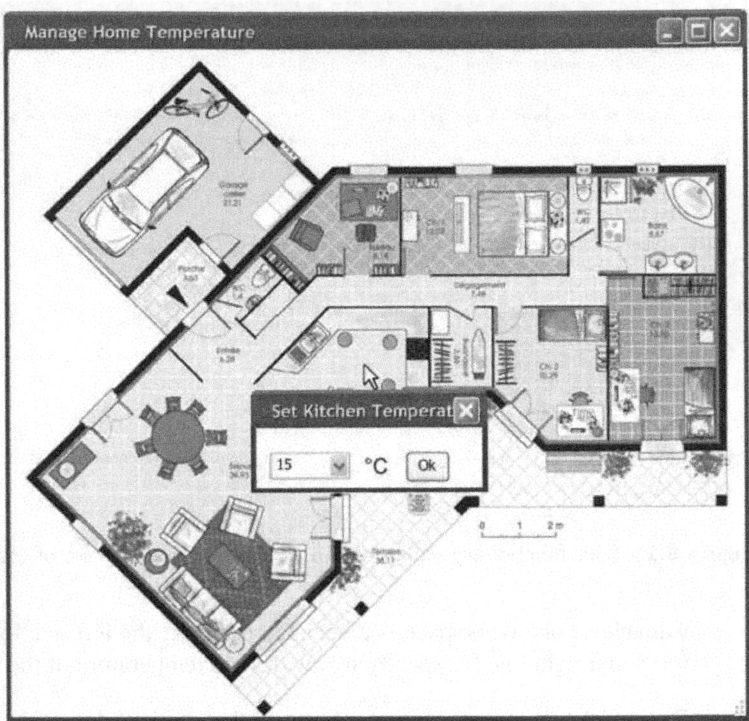

Figure 8.2 A hand made mock-up similar to Figure 8.1d, but that improves the Compatibility criterion thanks to a clickable map of the house

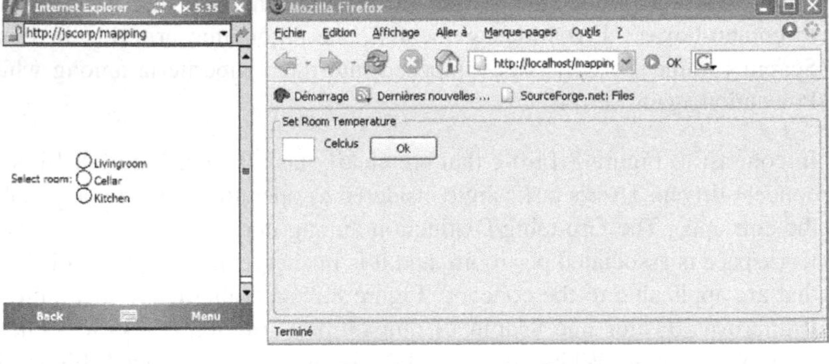

(a) "Select a room" has migrated to the PDA

(b) "Select a room" has disappeared from the PC

Figure 8.3 A distributed version of HHCS: selecting a room is done on the PDA the temperature is specified on the PC

The distributable feature of a UI is not an ergonomic criterion yet. It can be hosted under the umbrella of Grouping/Distinction among items, the means being an allocation on different platforms. But clearly, usability frameworks remain mostly general, implicitly focusing centralized UIs (e.g., Bastien and Scapin, 1991; Shackel, 1991; Abowd et al., 1992; Dix et al., 1993; Nielsen, 1994; Preece et al., 1994; IFIP, 1996; Shneiderman, 1997; Constantine and Lockwood, 1999; Van Welie et al., 1999; as well as Seffah et al., 2006, who propose QUIM, a unifying structure to reconcile existing frameworks). Thus, new properties such as Continuity (Trevisan et al., 2003), Detachability (Grolaux et al., 2005), Migratability (Grolaux et al., 2004) or Plasticity have still not been integrated into usability frameworks either from a system-centered perspective or from a user-centered perspective. As a result, when reasoning on usability, we promote an open approach that lets the framework open so that designers can take benefit from new ones or use their favorite one.

The next section considers SE issues when engineering plastic UIs. Issues are illustrated on the case study.

8.2.2 Software Engineering Issues

Engineering UIs is a series of trade-offs conciliating functional and non-functional requirements. Whatever the approach is (forward engineering, sketching, reverse engineering, etc. Calvary et al., 2003), the design process takes, at least implicitly, into account a specification of both the targeted context of use and the expected quality among which is the quality in use (Calvary et al., 2004). The problems in ubiquitous computing are that:

- The context of use is no more fixed, set at design time, but may be variable and unforeseeable, typically depending on the arrival and departure of platforms that have not necessarily been envisioned at design time.
- The quality in use is no more intrinsic to the UI but may depend on the user's experience, typically taking into account inter-usability issues (Denis and Karsenty, 2004).

The quality in use is no more intrinsic to the UI but may depend on the user's experience, typically taking into account inter-usability issues (Denis and Karsenty, 2004).

- Interactive systems: the one under study and all other ones.
- The underlying infrastructure: the middleware and the reusable components (models and/or pieces of code of both UIs and UIs transformers).
- Human actors: end-users but perhaps also designers.

Thus, based on an understanding of the user's needs, all of the stakeholders collaborate in order to produce the best UI given internal capabilities and external constraints (the current context of use, the expected quality in use, the past user's experience and perhaps his/her future envisioned needs).

In a similar approach, the interactive system handles the adaptation alone. This means perceiving the context of use, detecting situations that require adaptation, computing a reaction, and generating the appropriate UI (Balme et al., 2004). In an open approach, the tiers take over all of the process. In a mixed approach, there is a collaboration between the interactive system and another software stakeholder at least for either complementing each other (see the CARE Complementarity property (Coutaz et al., 1995)) or improving the quality of the decision process (CARE Redundancy).

Open adaptation requires that the UI provides the world with management mechanisms. Management mechanisms include self-descriptive meta-data (such as the current state, the services it supports and requires), and the methods to control its behavior such as start/stop and get/set-state. As plasticity may occur at any level of abstraction ranging from domain-dependent Concepts and Tasks to rendering concerns, there is a need for:

- Describing the UI at any level of abstraction including its deployment on both the functional core and the context of use;
- And keeping trace of how the UI meets the initial requirements.

From a conceptual point of view, there is a consensus today that the UI's design process be structured around three levels of abstraction:

- A domain-dependent specification in terms of Concepts and Tasks. A domain concept is a concept that is relevant to users to accomplish tasks in a particular domain (e.g., home, room, temperature). Concepts are classically modeled as UML classes that are linked together by way of associations (e.g., home is made of a set of rooms) (Figure 8.4). A task is a couple <Goal, Procedure> where the Goal is the user's objective and the procedure in the way to achieve the goal. The procedure is a recursive decomposition of the task into subtasks that are related by operators (e.g., enabling). A task may be decorated with unary operators (e.g., optional, iterative). For instance, Managing temperature at home is a goal that can iteratively be achieved by first selecting a room and then specifying the desired temperature for this room. CTT (Paterno et al., 1997) is a widespread notation for task modeling (Figure 8.4).
- A structural specification organizing the UI into workspaces. A workspace is an abstract structuring unit that supports a set of logically connected tasks. Clearly, the rationale of the notion of Workspace comes from the Guidance/Grouping-Distinction among items criterion: the idea is to group together (respectively isolate) tasks and concepts that are logically connected (respectively not connected). As pointed out in Bastien and Scapin's framework, there are two means for grouping/distinguishing items: position and format. At this level of abstraction, the leverage is the position. The format is about rendering. It comes into play at the interactors level. A workspace may recursively be decomposed into workspaces whose relations should express the semantics of tasks operators (e.g., gives access to for the enabling operator) so as to be task compliant. Compatibility is one ergonomic criterion. In Figure 8.1a–c, there is one workspace per task, thus supplying both of the criteria.
- An interactor is the basic construct for concretizing UIs (e.g., window, panel, group box, link, text field, button). In Figure 8.1a, four interactors are associated with the task "Specify temperature": the right panel for satisfying the

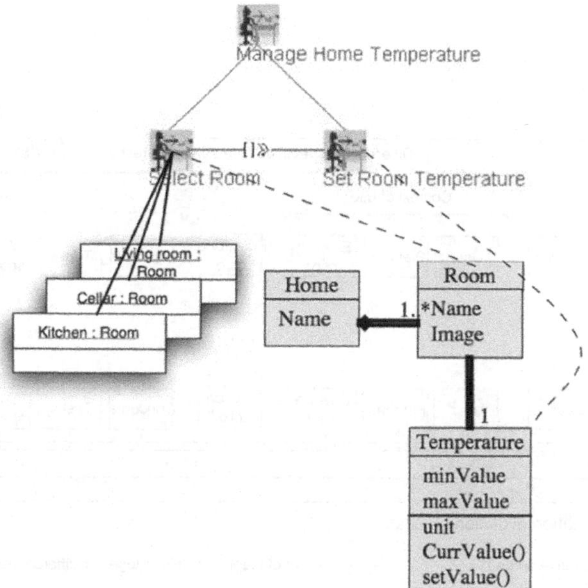

Figure 8.4 A CTT task model and an UML domain model of the case study

Guidance-Grouping/Distinction among items by the position" criterion, the label "Set room temperature" for supporting the Guidance-Prompting, the input field for the task per se, and the "Ok" button for explicitly validating the task. This prevention satisfies the Explicit control criterion.

In the same way, from an implementational perspective, the code should be able to tell the architecture style it is compliant with, as well as the implementation language it is coded in. As this level of abstraction is not specific to HCI, we did not explore this issue in depth.

Figure 8.5 makes explicit the three dimensions of self-description:

- The vertical design process transforms requirements into an interactive system;
- The horizontal mappings link together the different perspectives on the same interactive system in a consistent way;
- The transversal transformations support the switch to another interactive system. This is typically the case when the current context of use is moving outside the plasticity domain of the current interactive system, i.e., the current interactive system is unable to cover this new context of use.

Behind Figure 8.5 is exactly the notion of megamodel as defined in MDE. Section 8.3 proposes an overview of the MDE core concepts that we have successfully transposed to HCI and experienced in the HHCS case study.

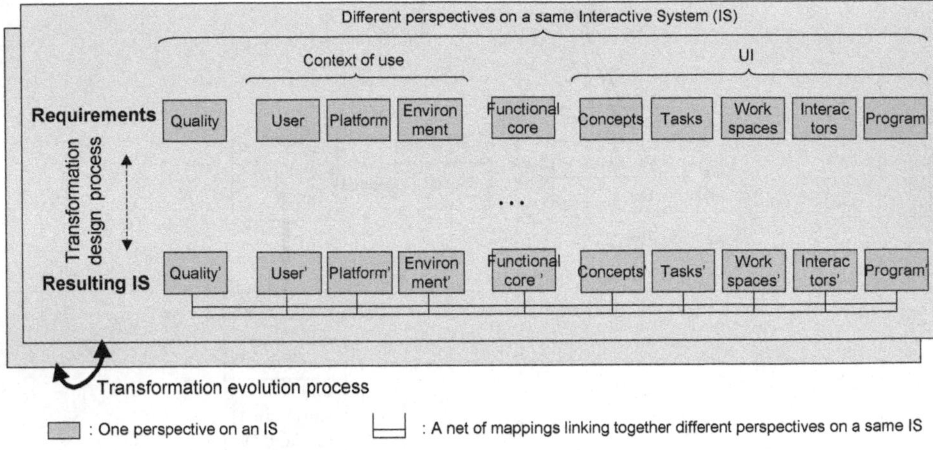

Figure 8.5 Self-description is three-fold. It covers the design rationale (i.e., the design process transforming requirements into a resulting interactive system (IS)), the resulting IS itself (i.e., a net of mappings linking together different perspectives in a consistent way), and the evolution process for supporting the switch to another interactive system.

8.3 MODELING, METAMODELING, AND MEGAMODELING

MDE took its root in the OMG MDA. This set of standard is comprised of quite complex technologies and acronyms (e.g., CWM, XMI, SPEM, PIM, CIM, HUTN, etc.). Specification documents exist in many different versions and thousands of pages. This complexity leads to specifications that are never fully implemented, and that sometimes do not have any tool implementation. As a result, major software editors such as Microsoft, IBM or Borland are now developing their own MDE technologies. More than eighty tools or prototypes are today referenced on planetmde.org. As a result, entering this technological world is far from easy, especially since the various approaches are based on several assumptions that very often remain implicit and sometimes contradictory.

Fortunately, all MDE approaches share the core concepts of models, metamodels, and transformations. But unfortunately, even the single word "model" can lead to confusion and misunderstanding as at least four senses can be associated with this word today (Favre, 2005). Adding "meta" levels and dealing with a mixture of abstraction, jargon and technology issues lead to what is sometimes called the "meta-muddle".

Clarifying the fundamental concepts of MDE is necessary, especially since the approach is no more limited to MDA, but covers other technical spaces (Kurtev et al., 2002) such as Grammarware, XMLware, etc. This section introduces the key concepts of Systems, Models, Metamodels, Actors, Transformations and Megamodel that will all be transposed to HCI in Section 8.4.

8.3.1 Systems (δ)

Systems denote elements of our universe of discourse. The term *system* conveys the idea of some complexity: systems can be decomposed into subsystems (relation noted (δ)).

Systems can be classified according to various properties. For instance, we can make the distinction between static systems and dynamic systems. HHCS is obviously a dynamic system. Physicality is another example of property. We can make the distinction between physical systems, digital systems (those that are manipulated by computers), and mental systems (those that are manipulated by brains). Hybrid systems are obtained when combining this physicality with the notion of subsystem (those systems that combine subsystems from different categories).

Decomposition can be powerful in pointing out subtle issues when required. For instance, a UI can be seen as a hybrid system if we consider it as a composition of a software (a digital system), and some hardware (a physical system). The mental representation a user may have of it is a mental system. As shown below, this kind of combination is common when considering models as specific kinds of systems.

8.3.2 Models (μ)

The notion of "model" is not new in computer science. Recall for instance the use of flowcharts in the early days of computer science. Nevertheless, the word still leads to lively debates across communities, as well as inside the MDE community. This is not surprising as the term "model" is polysemous and people forget to define it before using it. The meanings of the word "model" can be gathered in four main groups, each group corresponding to a different synonym of the word (Favre, 2005). For instance, in the expression "relational model", "model" stands for "language", as one could also say "relational language". In the context of MDE, the current trend is to use the term *model* as a synonym of "representation". In that sense, a map of France may be a model of this country: it is a representation of it. In the context of this chapter, we adhere to the following definition (Bézivin, 2004):

> "A model is a simplification of a system built with an intended goal in mind. The model should be able to answer questions in place of the actual system".

In other words, a model is a simplified representation of a given system, sometimes called the "system under study." It is of paramount importance to understand that nothing is a model per se. A model is a role that a system may play with respect to a given system (playing therefore the role of "system under study"). For instance, both the map and the French territory are physical systems. But the map can serve as a model to answer questions about the French territory. Models and systems under study are linked by the relation "represented by" (relation noted μ).

In contrast to a quite popular idea, it is very important to note that a model of a model is not a metamodel. The concept of metamodel will be introduced in the next section and is related to the notion of language. Models of models of models, etc., that is μ chains are very common in practice. Let's consider for instance a satellite image (a digital system) of the French territory displayed on a computer screen (a physical system) and helping the user in creating a mental model of the territory (mental system). Here, all the systems play the role of model, except the territory which is at the beginning of the μ chain. Models can be combined together (e.g., adding a model about demography), leading to μ graphs. In fact, in contrast to metamodel graphs presented in the next section, dealing with μ graphs is not really difficult, even if these graphs cross the boundaries of mental, physical, and digital worlds.

Note that HCI aims at synchronizing the digital world and the mental world through the physical world, and that MDE concentrates on digital models, those that live in computers. A sketchy concept diagram on a napkin will not be considered a "model" in the MDE community, though its use could perfectly make sense in communication processes among designers.

Here, there is a strong departure between MDE and the many traditional modeling methods developed during the 1980's and 1990's in the context of SE. MDE aficionados love to distinguish contemplative models (those that are interpreted by humans), from productive models (those that are interpreted by computers). Obviously, with the strong focus on automation that characterized the first years of MDE, the emphasis has so far been almost exclusively productive, with a strong emphasis on internal representation and abstract syntax (leading for instance to XMI and other XML dialects for model interchange between MDE tools).

However, there is no doubt that as long as human intervention is required in MDE processes, models should as long as possible be understandable by both machine and humans. We believe that Model Understandability could appear as the key for the adoption of MDE techniques. In particular, given an abstract model, it should be possible to derive many (sub)models with maybe different concrete syntaxes, depending on the skill of the human who is intended to understand or use the model. This point is key, as we propose to give access to HCI models to both designers and end-users. In other terms, the challenge is to provide designers and end-users tools to understand μt links, and possibly to act on them to transform the system.

8.3.3 Metamodels(χ)

Whereas the notion of model has existed for ages, the notion of metamodel is new, and the need of a systematic use no more discussed. Clearly, MDE should stand for Metamodel Driven Engineering that would more accurately point out the novelty and strength of the approach. There is quite an agreement today in the MDE community around the following definition (Favre, 2004):

> A metamodel is a model of a modeling language.

Basically, all models expressed in a given language must conform to the metamodel of this language. There is a "conforms to" relationship (relation noted χ) between a model and a metamodel. This χ relation should not be confused with the representation relation (μ), though it is based on it. A metamodel does not represent a particular model. It represents the syntactic and semantic conventions that are shared by all models in the language. In practice, a metamodel is therefore used to describe the language on a whole, and to avoid misinterpretation of particular models at hand.

By definition, metamodels are particular kinds of models (as they represent languages).

Metamodels are therefore systems, and as a result can be classified according to their physicality (physical, digital and mental). For instance, an English dictionary or a grammar book are physical models of the English language: they represent different facets of it. While in theory all well-formed English sentences must conform to English metamodels, in practice explicit metamodels are scarcely used in human communication. Moreover, most of the available languages today (either natural or artificial) have never been explicitly represented. Participants build their own mental metamodel in a language acquisition process.

Many SE and HCI methods developed in recent decades were based on the assumption that designers shared somehow a "reasonable understanding" of the language they used. MDE breaks with this situation. All "(productive) models" should be linked with an explicit metamodel in order to be interpretable by the machine.

8.3.4 The Pyramid of Models and the Pyramid of Actors

While combining μ links is conceptually not very difficult, this is not the case with χ links (Favre, 2004). Fortunately, in most common situations, MDE artifacts can be arranged in a pyramid-like structure driven by the conformance relation (χ) (left part of Figure 8.6). This means that, whatever the level Ln is, each model at the Ln level should conform to a model of the upper level Ln+1. In other words, metamodels (e.g., the UML metamodel or the metamodel of a task language) should themselves be written in a well-defined (meta)language represented by a meta-metamodel. According to OMG, the MOF standard should be used at the highest level to stop the ?-chain, the MOF metamodel being described using itself. In fact, there is no agreement on the number of levels, and the exact status of the bottom level of the pyramid (named M0 in the MDE jargon) is subject to various interpretations. This is particularly due to the fact that the MDE standard fails to recognize that the notions of model and metamodel are not absolute but relative.

In this chapter, we assume that the bottom level (named L+0) is the "execution level" where the state of the application represents (μ) the situation the end-user is dealing with in the real world.

This interpretation is favored by its high consistency with what we call the pyramid of actors, a human centered view of MDE (see the right part of Figure 8.6). Whilst the models pyramid is made of digital models, the outside of the pyramid is the real world where humans live. We restrict the scope to computer-related activities: all the actors are either computer end-users (L+0) or computer professionals.

The main benefit of the pyramid of actors is that it gives a global view of processes that too often remain implicit. For instance, SE (L+2) is often confused with application development (L+1), while Human Computer Interaction is often restricted to the use of applications by end-users (L+0).

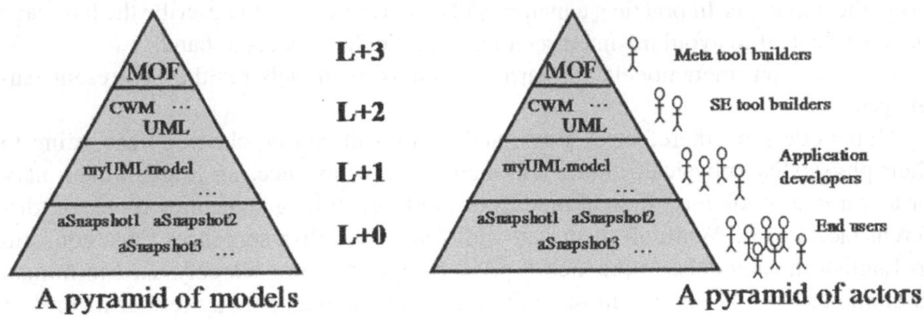

Figure 8.6 The pyramid of models and the pyramid of actors

The pyramid of models and the pyramid of actors are obviously connected. At a given level Ln+1, actors are dealing with the corresponding kind of models. These models are intended to fashion tools to the user of the level below. On the other hand, each actor is constrained by the (meta)models designed by the actors of the level above, leading to the conformance relation (χ). At each level, actors interact with computers to do their job. As suggested by the pyramid morphology, the more the level is high, the less the users are numerous, but the more skills in computer science are required.

To better understand the pyramid, let us review the levels starting from the bottom.

- L+0. End-user's level. At this level (often called "execution level"), the end-user is controlling a software application through a "regular" UI. For instance, the owner of a house uses HHCS to control his/her comfort at home. The state of HHCS plays the role of model with regard to the house. In an either proactive or reactive manner, the application controls that the end-user's behavior is compliant with the interaction language defined at the level above, same thing stands for the system state. With respect to the shape of the actor pyramid, let us point out that the number of users could there range from thousands to millions, and that no special skill in computer science is there required.

- L+1. Application developer's level. This level corresponds to the application development level. Here, the number of actors is typically one order of magnitude lower than at the level below, the size of medium to large teams ranging from ten to hundred of developers. In fact, what is even more important is the diversity of skills that are necessary to develop interactive systems. MDE is all about separation of concerns and many different languages are involved in the development of modern software applications. For instance, in an MDE based approach, UI designers produce task models, workspace models, interactor models, etc. Software engineers may use other kinds of models to describe database structures, component behaviors, etc. Because of the "productive" feature of models, tooling is of great importance. For each kind of model, a corresponding toolset including model editors, conformance checkers, transformers, etc., is needed. Model editors may have complex UIs, and are software too. This leads to the upper level, which usually remains implicit in HCI, modeling tools being developed in a quite ad-hoc way so far.

- L+2. Tool builder's level. Tooling has probably been the worst enemy of model-based approaches in HCI. Without tools of good quality, it is difficult to transfer concepts to industry, and as a result apply them in real case studies. While in SE there is some agreement around UML as standard, we are quite far from a unified (set of) modeling language(s) for HCI. But, would general purpose languages fit the real needs? Domain Specific Languages (DSL) would probably be the best suited for tackling specific problems. For instance, a company specialized in games on cell-phones would undoubtedly appreciate modeling languages and tools specifically suited to its business. Today some DSL exist (e.g., for Web applications). In fact, building an SE environment for HCI is much more a SE than HCI issue. The specificity of MDE approach is to address this problem explicitly thanks to the notion of productive metamodels at the L+2 level. Whereas tools like TERESA (Mori et al., 2004) were built in an ad-hoc manner, the promise of MDE is to derive tools such as editors and conformance checkers from metamodels, providing standard means for tools interoperability as well. Tool building and interoperability have not been addressed by previous model-based approach in HCI, and this is why we believe "metamodel-driven engineering" would be a better name for this novel approach. Note that, in a large company, there may be ten to hundred application developers (actors at L+1), but only a few of them in charge of building modeling tools for them (actors at L+2). In any case this should be interpreted as being of a less importance for the company. It is the otehr way around: metamodels capitalize the know-how of the company. In the long term, this knowledge might be far more important than the one put in individual applications. Dealing with metamodels and building tools require special skills in so-called "language engineering." If a particular DSL is to be instrumented, then high skills in this specific domain are highly required. At this L+2 level, actors produce modeling tools for the level below, and in order to do so they use meta tools or frameworks provided by the level above (L+3). For instance, they could use the EMF or GMF interfaces to generate model editors.

- L+3. Meta tool builder's level. This is the highest level as defined in MDA. It is the level of meta-metamodels. Only a few teams over the world tackle this level, since for interoperability purposes this level is assumed to be quite stable and under the control of standardization bodies. OMG advocates for the MOF standard, but revisiting this level is a matter of research. In practice, Microsoft and IBM propose their own meta-metamodels and corresponding toolsets EMF and GMF.

The core benefit of the actors pyramid is to make explicit levels that classically remain implicit though existing in the real world. Understanding these levels and instrumenting them as proposed by the MDE approach could lead to significant improvements. Conceptually, the regularity of the structure is quite striking, and some phenomenon apparently disconnected could be better explained with this framework.

For instance, while the L+0 level is often called the "execution" level, in reality some software is executed at each level. In some cases, actors want to cross the level boundaries leading to co-executions. For instance, an actor at the level Ln may want to validate his model by executing a prototype at the level Ln-1. In this case, he plays the role of user with regard to the tool he is building. When transposing to HCI at the L+1 level for instance, this corresponds to the "test mode" of GUI builder tools where the designers play the role of end-users (L-1 level). Note that in this case, there is logically no problem as actors have enough skills to deal with the lowest levels. But this is not true on the other side.

An actor at the Ln level may want to adapt the software he/she is using to better fit to a particular context. To that end, he/she may need to get access to the models of the higher level (Ln+1) and change some design choices. For instance, if we consider the L+0 level, an end-user may want to tune the workspace model and for that execute a workspace model editor. Obviously depending on the model, this raises a challenge in model understanding because the skills required are increasing when going to higher levels. In such a scenario, one could imagine providing simplified models to actors that want to get to higher levels without the burden of dealing with separated tools and skills.

Note that such scenarios may occur at any level of the pyramid, not only at the bottom level. For instance, at the L+1 level, many UML editors allow application developers to define their own stereotypes such as <<Concept>> or <<Task>>. By doing so, they give them access to the upper level. It is an ad-hoc "end-user" way to define a new language as UML extension. A much better approach is to let actors at higher level define the languages that should be used in the company and configure the UML environment through a tool usually called "profile builder" tool.

8.3.5 *Transformations* (τ)

Roughly speaking, a transformation is the production of a set of target models from a set of source models, according to a transformation definition. A transformation definition is modeled as a set of transformation rules that together describe how source models are transformed into target models (Mens et al., 2004). Source and target models are related by the τ relation "is transformed into." Note that a set of transformation rules is a model (a transformation model) that complies with a transformation metamodel. This metamodel represents a transformation language such as QVT, the standard from OMG. Obviously, transformation engines are required to execute model transformation.

τ expresses an overall dependency between source and target models. However, experience shows that a finer grain of correspondence needs to be expressed. Typically, the incremental modification of one source element should be easily propagated into the corresponding target element(s) and vice versa. While τ links relate two models considered as a whole, mappings give the details on how elements of the source and target models relate to each other. For example, in HCI, rendering is a transformation where tasks are mapped into workspaces which, in turn, are mapped into windows populated with widgets in case of graphical UIs. Section 8.4 claims for maintaining as mappings the correspondence between the source task (decorated with domain concepts) and its target workspace(s) and widgets.

Transformations can be characterized within a four-dimension space: The transformation may be automated (it can be performed by a computer autonomously), it may be semi-automated (requiring some human intervention), or it may be manually performed by a human. For example, given our current level of knowledge, the transformation of a "value-centered model" (Cockton, 2005) into a "usability model" can only be performed manually. On the other hand, UI generators such as CTTE (Mori et al., 2002) produce UIs automatically from a task model. A transformation is vertical when the source and target models reside at different levels of abstraction (e.g., tasks and workspaces). Traditional UI generation is a vertical top-down transformation from high-level descriptions (such as a task model) to code generation. Reverse engineering is also a vertical transformation but it proceeds bottom up, typically from executable code to some high-level representation by the way of abstraction. A transformation is horizontal when the source and target models reside at the same level of abstraction. For example, translating a Java source code into C code preserves the original level of abstraction (i.e., Program).

8.3.6 Megamodels

Megamodels aim at providing structures to avoid the meta-muddle. A megamodel is "a model which elements represent models, metamodels and other global entities" (Bézivin, 2004). While Modeling-in-the-small is the activity that considers the details of models (i.e., model elements),

Modeling-in-the-large, so-called Megamodeling, considers the global relationships between the MDE artifacts, without considering their content. As discussed above, MDE processes involve complex structures of models, metamodels, transformations but also artifacts such as interpreters, transformation models, transformation engines, models editors, and so on. Thus, to be useful, a model needs a metamodel of course, but also transformations that operate on it, plus tooling including transformation engines to interpret the transformation models, interpreters to interpret the language in which the transformation engines are written, and so on. A megamodel is a model that represents this kind of complex structure. It is a graph whose nodes are systems (as defined in Section 8.3.1), and edges are for instance μ χ or τ links (note that only the most fundamental relations have been introduced in this chapter for the sake of simplicity). An example of megamodel is provided in Figure 8.7. It links together the core concepts of MDE using the basic relations ϵ, μ, and χ.

In practice, it is quite temping to confuse the notion of metamodel and megamodel. But, really, these two concepts have different purposes. Metamodels aim at describing modeling languages (the prefix meta means "beyond" or "after" just like in metalanguage). In contrast, a megamodel aims at modeling how large sets of MDE artifacts (in particular including metamodels) are connected together (the mega prefix means big or large). Note that since a megamodel is still a model, all the Section 8.3 applies to the notion of megamodel, but let's keep it simple! A few basic observations are, however, of particular relevance here.

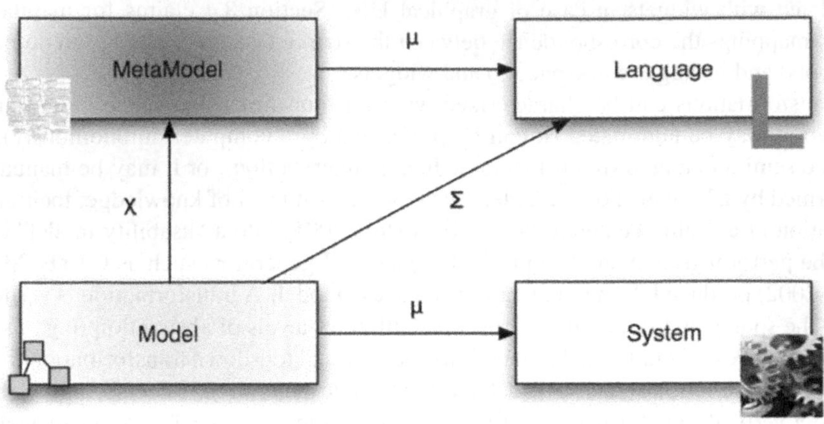

Figure 8.7 An example of megamodel charting the basic concepts and relations in MDE

First, it is important to distinguish contemplative megamodels from productive megamodels, even if both of them present some interests on their own. Contemplative megamodels are powerful communication aids when explaining and reasoning about complex MDE situations. In such a megamodel, μ can safely point to systems that are not in the digital world expressing for instance that a digital model represents the earth. Connections with real-world and non digital entities are impossible in productive megamodels since they are interpreted by the machine and live in the digital world only. Productive megamodels are digital structures that relate together digital artifacts that otherwise would be disconnected.

Second, megamodels can be used to manage MDE structures at various levels. For instance, at the global level, contemplative megamodels could be used to describe how MDE standards relate to each other. At the level of a company, productive megamodels can be used to describe the structure of the MDE repository where all artifacts produced by the company are stored. In this case, all metamodels, transformations, model editors are registered for further reuse. There the purpose of megamodeling is to define the structure of such repository. At the level of a software application, only the MDE artifacts required by this application will be present in the megamodel of this application, unless we want to keep the link between the application and the repository, for instance in order to support adaptation.

The next section transposes these MDE core concepts and relations to HCI for the engineering of plastic UIs.

8.4 MDE FOR PLASTICITY

This section bridges the gap between MDE and HCI for the engineering of plastic UIs. It first transposes the notion of megamodel to HCI, thus providing the global picture of the approach. Then, it focuses on the cornerstone, the notion of mapping, that in

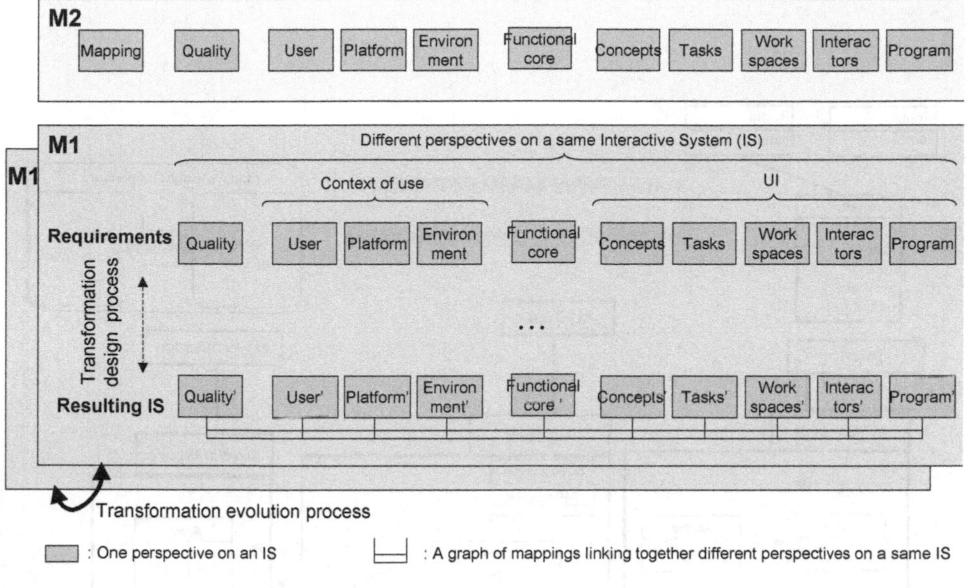

Figure 8.8 The megamodel coverage

HCI supports the key challenge of usability. It proposes a mapping metamodel that covers both design and adaptation transformations. Finally, it raises the issue of the understandability of the megamodel via the novel notion of Mega-UI.

8.4.1 Megamodel in HCI

When integrating the MDE core notions of Metamodel and Mapping in Figure 8.5, we obtain Figure 8.8. So far, we have put our effort in the UI's (Concept, Task, Workspace and Interactor) modeling (M1) and metamodeling (M2) for the resulting interactive system.

Our purpose is not to define new meta-models, but to show how a systematic compliance with metamodels (even for mappings) is key for plasticity. What ever the perspective on a UI is (e.g., task, concept, workspace, interactor), it has to be compliant with an explicit metamodel so that any actor (machine and/or human) can reason about it. Figure 8.9 shows a subset of the HHCS graph of models corresponding to Figure 8.1a. The deployment on the functional core and the context of use is not depicted. Only a few mappings are mentioned: those that link together tasks and concepts, tasks and workspaces, and so on. Here, we use UML as meta-metamodel (M3-level model).

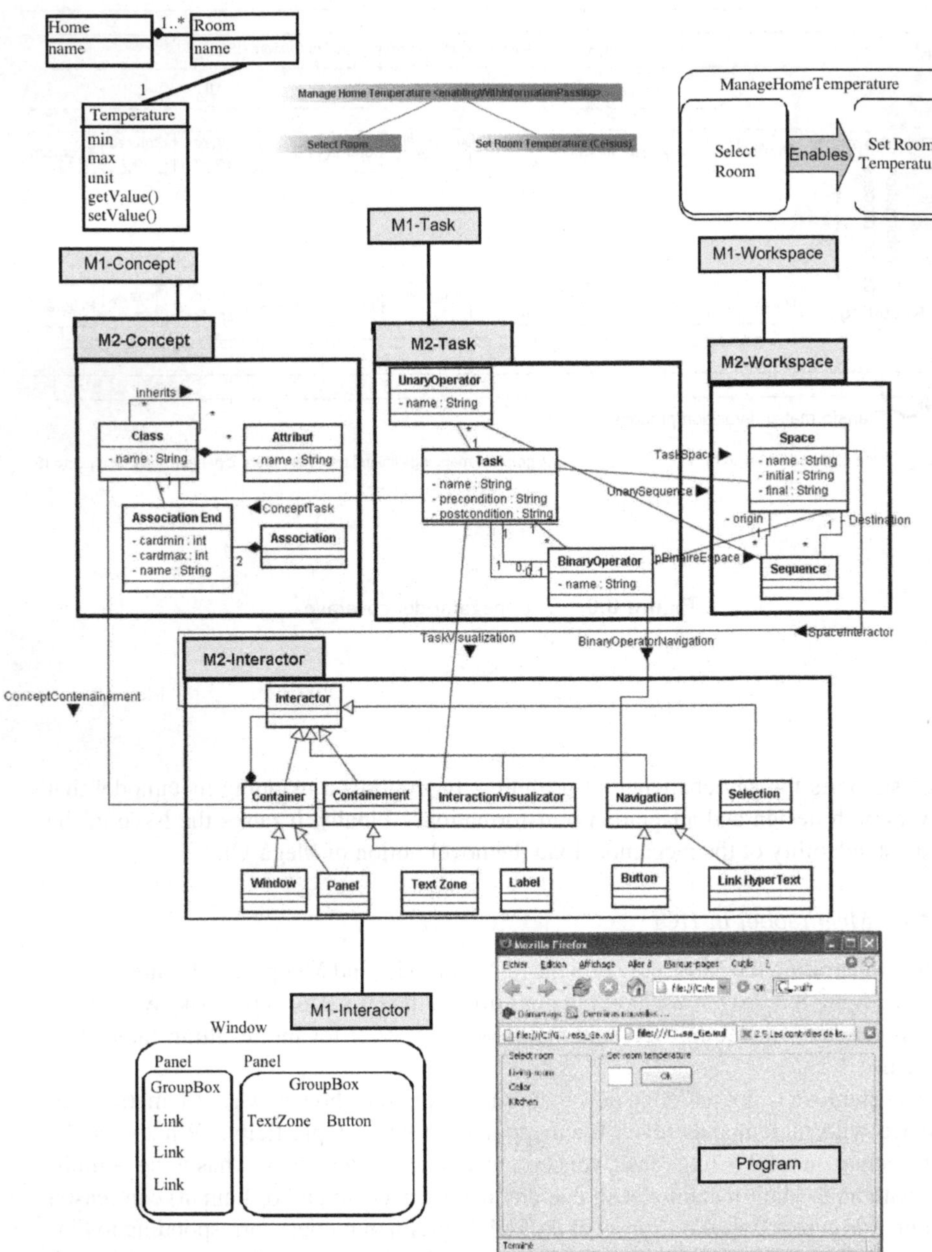

Figure 8.9 An excerpt of the megamodel for HCI. The coverage is limited to UI. Neither the functional core nor the context of use are considered

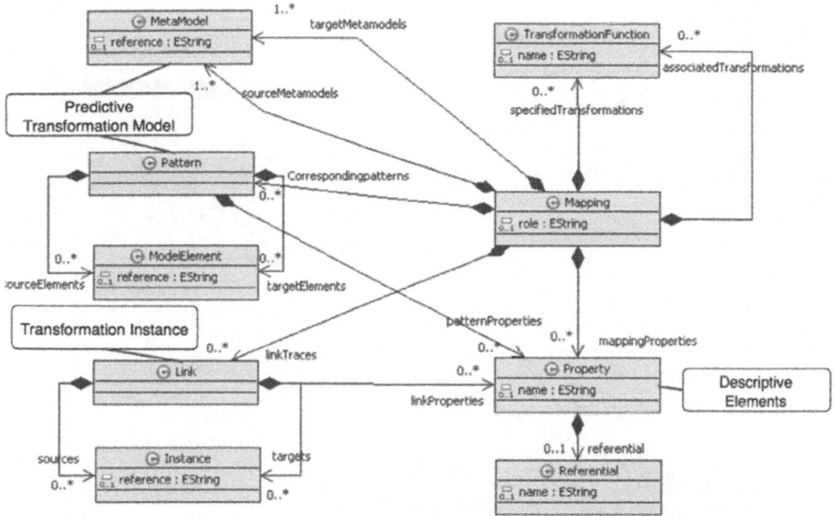

Figure 8.10 A mapping metamodel for general purpose. The composition between Mapping and Metamodel is due to EMF (Eclipse Modeling Framework)

Keeping such a graph alive at runtime is a means for sustaining plasticity as mappings convey the design rationale of the UI in terms of the usability properties they have been driven by. The next section is about mappings.

8.4.2 Mapping Metamodel for Plasticity

The mapping metamodel provided in Figure 8.10 is a general purpose mapping metamodel. The core entity is the Mapping class. A mapping links together entities that are compliant to Metamodels (e.g., Task and Interactor). A mapping makes explicit the corresponding Transformation functions. The transformation model can be done by patterns (e.g., to the task pattern Select a room, apply the pattern: one hypertext link per room, the name of the link being the name of the room). A Pattern is a transformation model that links together source and target elements (ModelElement) to provide a predictive description of the transformation function. Patterns are powerful for ensuring UI's homogeneity-consistency, which is one ergonomic criterion (Bastien and Scapin, 1991). In addition, a mapping may describe the execution trace of the transformation function. The trace is a set of Links between Instances of ModelElements (e.g., the hypertext link Kitchen and the task Select a room when applied to the concept of kitchen).

A mapping conveys a set of Properties (e.g., "Guidance-Prompting"). A property is described according to a given reference framework (Referential) (e.g., Bastien and Scapin, 1991). Whatever the framework is, the properties are descriptive. They qualify either the global set of mappings or one specific element: a mapping, a pattern or a link.

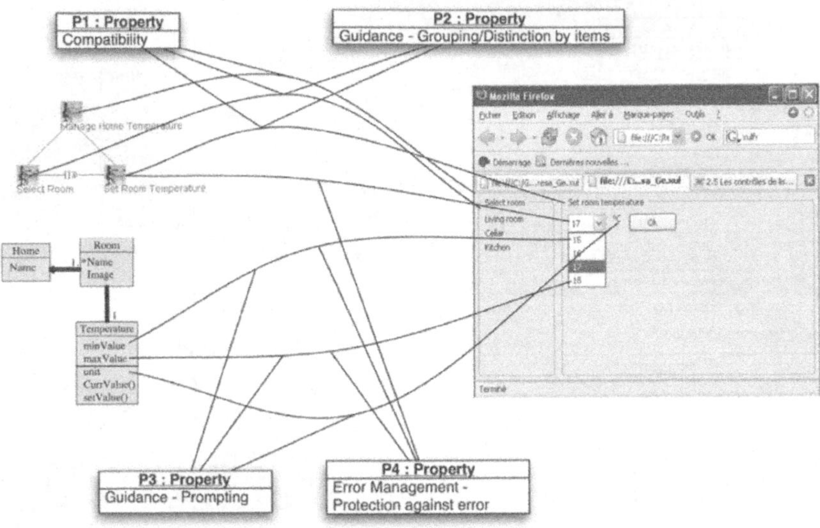

Figure 8.11 Examples of mappings in HHCS. Mappings tell the usability properties they satisfy. Here properties are expressed in Bastien-Scapin's framework

Associated transformations (see the UML and associated transformations association between the classes Mapping and TransformationFunction in Figure 8.10) are in charge of maintaining the consistency of the graph of models by propagating modifications that have an impact on other elements. For instance, if replacing an interactor with another one decreases the UI's homogeneity-consistency, then the same substitution should be applied to the other interactors of the same type. This is the job of the associated functions, which perform this adaptation locally.

Figure 8.10 exemplifies mappings on the specific case of Figure 8.1c. Further examples can be found in Scottet et al. (2007)(Sottet et al., 2007).

Note that the mapping metamodel is general. The HCI specificity comes from the nature of both the metamodels (Metamodel) and the framework (Referential). Currently in HCI, effort is placed on metamodeling (see `www.usixml.org` for instance) but the mapping metamodel is still under explored. Beyond the definition of usability criteria, we need metrics. Metrics make it possible for the system to self-evaluate when the context of use changes, and trigger the most appropriate adaptation rule (Sottet et al., 2007). The fitness of the rule depends on the context of use of course, but also of the quality the rule is able to guarantee. Adaptation may be performed under the control of the end-user. The next section is about the UI of the megamodel.

8.4.3 Mega-UI

The scope of a UI is defined by the user's task it is intended to support. The other tasks (i.e., the tasks that do not belong to the task model) are not part of the UI: we call them Extra-tasks. It is typically the case of tasks that support the observation

(a) A running Extra-Ui for users familiar with

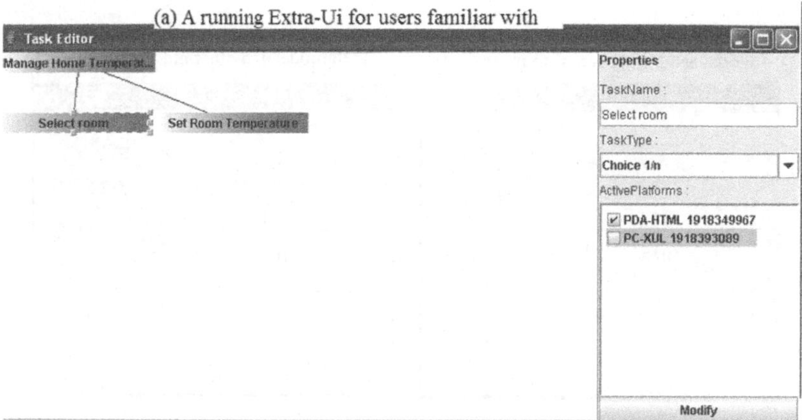

(b) A hand-made mock-up for other users

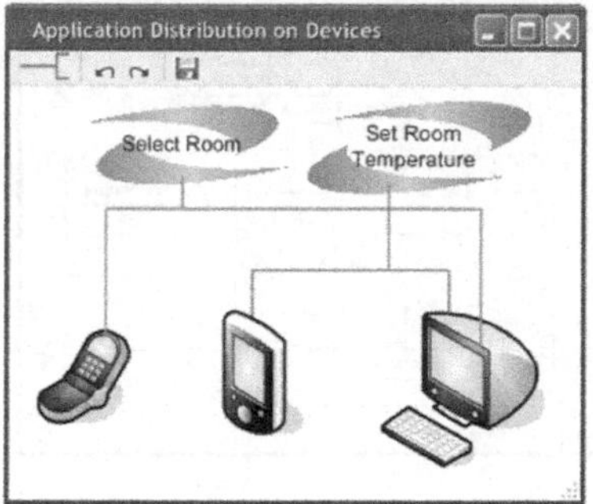

Figure 8.12 Extra-UIs for observing and controlling the tasks distribution on platforms

and redistribution of UIs when these have not been incorporated in the task model. We call Extra-UIs UIs in charge of Extra-tasks. A running example is provided in Figure 8.12a. By simply selecting a task in the task model (right part of the window), the user (yet the designer) controls the platforms on which he/she would like to get the task (only on the HTML PDA in Figure 8.12a). Such UIs were previously called Meta-UI (Sottet et al., 2007) based on Coutaz (2006). But, as Meta has there no ? semantics (but a ? one!), we prefer the prefix Extra to point out it is outside the pure (Intra)-UI even if Extra- and Intra-UIs might be merged together (Coutaz, 2006). Depending on the user's skills, different Extra-UIs have to be explored. A hand-made mock-up has been sketched in Figure 8.12b for users not familiar with task models.

Unlike Extra-UIs that lie on μ links, Meta-UIs browse χ links. Figure 8.13 combines Extra- and Meta-UIs to force the distinction: the Meta-UI (Figure 8.13c) comes into play for giving access to the task metamodel. In summary, when the purpose is just to represent (mu) models (e.g., the task model in Figure 8.13a), then the UI is an Extra-UI. When links are crossed over, the UI is a Meta-UI.

In reality, Intra-, Extra- and Meta-UIs are parts of the Mega-UI, i.e., the UI of the Megamodel.

(a) Extra-UI for observing the task model and having access to more extra

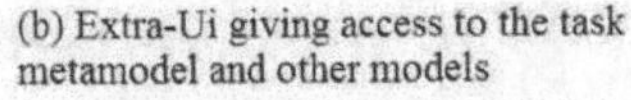
(b) Extra-Ui giving access to the task metamodel and other models

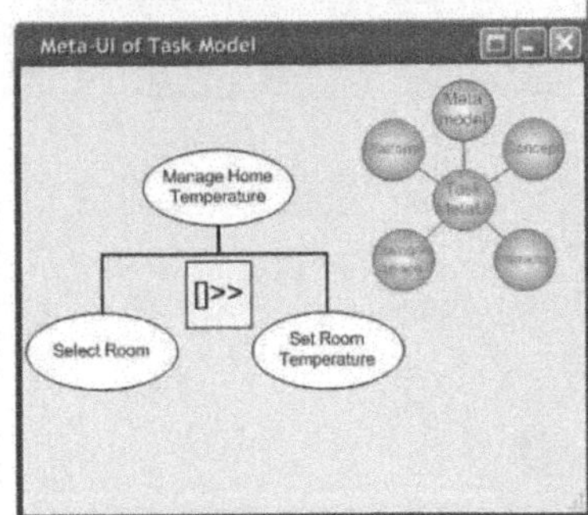

(c) Meta-UI for defining the task metamodel and having access to more meta

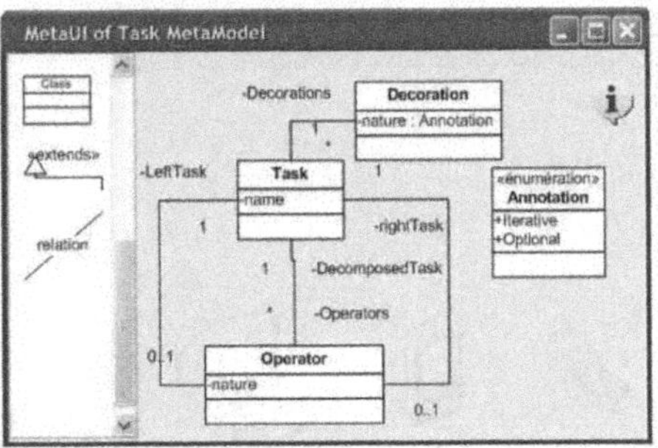

Figure 8.13 Extra- and Meta-UIs

Intra- and Extra-UIs are in charge of μ links, Meta-UIs of χ links. Figure 8.14 sketches a Mega-UI centered around the notion of ecosystem, i.e., the interactive system when deployed in its context of use. In (a), the user has access to an Extra-UI. This Extra-UI (b) makes the ecosystem observable (left part of the window). The current UI (right part) is the Interactors perspective on the ecosystem. By clicking on an interactor, the user triggers the display of a menu giving him/her access to the corresponding metamodel (Interactor) but also to the other perspectives (Concept, Task, etc.)

8.5 CONCLUSION AND PERSPECTIVES

Initially tackling the problem of plasticity, we finally have the feeling of having contributed to HCI in general. It seems to us that, pushed by plasticity that called for making explicit things (the context of use, the quality, the rationale of transformations, and languages), we have dug deeper and deeper, until understanding the way UIs were really engineered. Now, we are at the point where there are Many Faces of UIs (have in mind the CHI'06 workshop on The Many Faces of Consistency (Sottet et al., 2006)). Traditional UIs are in fact a curtailed view of the Mega-UI: the one that

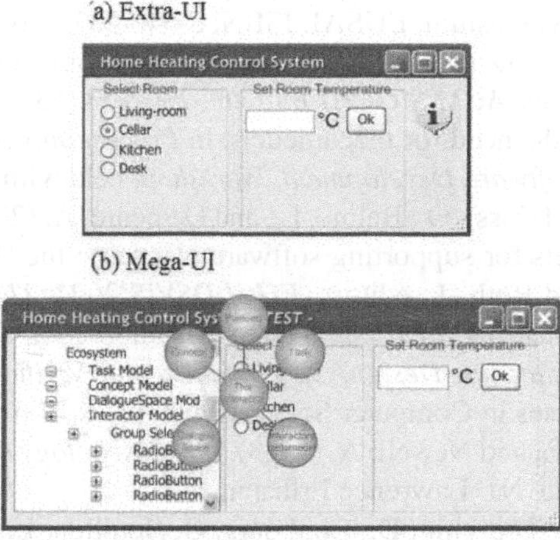

Figure 8.14 Beyond UIs: Mega-UIs

corresponds to the Interactors of the Intra-UI. We now have to explore the added value of UIs for the other perspectives, levels, and actors. It is as if we had opened the door and discovered new horizons.

The trouble could come from the complexity of the Mega-stuff. We already anticipate funny challenges such as: What about Mega-UIs for Mini-devices? It is clear that we need to cope with real applications. Nevertheless, whatever the conclusions will be, the better understanding and formalization we earn is a key result both for research and for teaching. Note that teaching MDE using HCI as field study seems to be pedagogically promising.

Finally, let us go back to Weiser's vision (Weiser, 1991) of calm technology. We are very far from it when considering the HCI researcher in charge of Mega-UIs.

Acknowledgements

This work has been supported by the network of excellence SIMILAR and the ITEA EMODE project. The authors warmly thank Xavier Alvaro for the implementation of the HHCS prototype.

References

Abowd, G., Coutaz, J., and Nigay, L. (1992). Structuring the space of interactive system properties. In Larson, J. and Unger, C., editors, *Engineering for Human-Computer Interaction*. Amsterdam: North-Holland. IFIP.

Balme, L., Demeure, A., Barralon, N., Coutaz, J., and Calvary, G. (2004). CAMELEON-RT: A software architecture reference model for distributed, migratable, and plastic user interfaces. In Markopoulos, P., et al. editors, *Lecture Notes in*

Computer Science, pages 291–302. Berlin: Springer-Verlag, Ambient Intelligence: Second European Symposium, EUSAI. ISBN: 3-540-23721-6.

Bastien, C. and Scapin, L.D. (1991). A validation of ergonomic criteria for the evaluation of user interfaces. *ACM SIGCHI Bulletin*, 23(4):54–55.

Bézivin, J. (2004). On the need for megamodels. In *Proceedings of the Best Practices for Model-Driven Software Development, Workshop*, held with OOPSLA.

Calvary, G., Coutaz, J., Dâassi, O., Balme, L., and Demeure, A. (2004). Towards a new generation of widgets for supporting software plasticity: the "comet". In Bastide, R., Palanque, P., and Roth, J., editors, *EHCI-DSVIS'2004, The 9th IFIP Working Conference on Engineering for Human-Computer Interaction Jointly with The 11th International Workshop on Design, Specification and Verification of Interactive Systems*, Lecture Notes in Computer Science 3425, pages 306–323. Springer.

Card, S. K., Moran, T. P., and Newell, A. (1983). *The Psychology of Human-Computer Interaction*. Hillsdale, NJ: Lawrence Erlbaum.

Calvary, G., Coutaz, J., Thevenin, D., Limbourg, Q. Bouillon, L., and Vanderdonckt, J. (2003). A Unifying Reference Framework for multi-target user interfaces, *Interacting with Computers*, 15(3), pages 289–308.

Cockton, G. (2005). A development framework for value-centered design. In *Proceedings of ACM CHI'05: CHI'05 on Human Factors in Computing Systems (Extended Abstracts)*, pages 1292–1295, ACM Press.

Constantine, L. L. and Lockwood, L. A. D. (1999). *Software for Use: A Practical Guide to the Models and Methods of Usage-Centered Design*. Reading, MA: Addison-Wesley.

Coutaz, J. (2006). Meta-user interfaces for ambient spaces. In *Interational Workshop on Task Model and Diagram (TAMODIA'06)*.

Coutaz, J., Nigay, L., Salber, D., Blandford, A., May, J., and Young, R. M. (1995). Four easy pieces for assessing the usability of multimodal interaction: the CARE properties. In Nordby, K., Helmersen, P. H., Gilmore, D. J., and Arnesen, S. A., editors, *Human-Computer Interaction, INTERACT '95, IFIP TC13 International Conference on Human-Computer Interaction, 27-29 June 1995, Lillehammer, Norway*, IFIP Conference Proceedings, pages 115–120. Chapman & Hall.

Denis, C. and Karsenty, L. (2004). Inter-usability of multidevice systems—a conceptual framework. In Seffah, A. and Javahery, H., editors, *Multiple User Interfaces: Cross-platform Applications and Context-Aware Interfaces*, pages 373–385. New York: Wiley.

Dix, A., Findlay, J., Abowd, G., and Beale, R. (1993). *Human Computer Interaction*. New York: Prentice Hall.

Elwert, T. and Schlungbaum, E. (1995). Modeling and generation of graphical user interfaces in the TADEUS approach. In Palanque, P. A. and Bastide, R., editors, *Design, Specification and Verification of Interactive Systems '95, Proceedings of the Eurographics Workshop in Toulouse, France June 7-9, 1995*, pages 193–208. Springer.

Favre, J. (2004). Towards a basic theory to model model driven engineering. In *Workshop on Software Model Engineering, WISME 2004, joint event with UML2004*.

Favre, J. (2005). Megamodeling and etymology—a story of words: From MED to MDE via MODEL in five milleniums. Technical report, appeared in DROPS 05161, ISSN 1862-4405, published by IBFI, Dagstuhl Seminar 05161 on Transformation Techniques in Software Engineering, Dagstuhl, Germany. 22 pages.

Grolaux, D., Van Roy, P., and Vanderdonckt, J. (2004). Migratable user interfaces: Beyond migratory interfaces. In *Proc. of Mobiquitous 2004 The First Annual International Conference on Mobile and Ubiquitous Systems Networking and Services.*

Grolaux, D., Vanderdonckt, J., and Roy, P. V. (2005). Attach me, detach me, assemble me like you work. In Costabile, M. F. and Paternò, F., editors, *Human-Computer Interaction—INTERACT 2005, IFIP TC13 International Conference, Rome, Italy, September 12-16, 2005, Proceedings*, volume 3585 of *Lecture Notes in Computer Science*, pages 198–212. Springer.

IFIP (1996). Design Principles for Interactive Systems. London: Chapman and Hall.

Johnson, P., Wilson, S., Markopoulos, P., and Pycock, J. (1993). ADEPT—advanced design environment for prototyping with task models. In *ACM Annual Conference on Human Factors in Computing Systems*, pages 56–57.

Kurtev, I., Bézivin, J., and Aksit, M. (2002). Technological spaces: An initial appraisal. In *Proceedings of the Confederated International CoopIS, DOA, and ODBASE 2002, Industrial track.*

Lonczewski, F. and Schreiber, S. (1996). The FUSE-system: an integrated user interface design environment. In Vanderdonckt, J., editor, *Computer-Aided Design of User Interfaces I (CADUI), Proceedings of the Second International Workshop on Computer-Aided Design of User Interfaces, June 5-7, 1996, Namur, Belgium*, pages 37–56. Presses Universitaires de Namur.

Luo, P., Szekely, P., and Neches, R. (1993). Management of interface design in HUMANOID. In *INTERCHI'93, Amsterdam.*

M`artin, C. (1996). Software lifecycle automation for interactive applications: The AME design environment. In Vanderdonckt, J., editor, *CADUI*, pages 57–76. Presses Universitaires de Namur.

Mens, T., Czarnecki, K., and Gorp, P. V. (2004). 04101 discussion—A taxonomy of model transformations. In Bézivin, J. and Heckel, R., editors, *Language Engineering for Model-Driven Software Development*, volume 04101 of *Dagstuhl Seminar Proceedings*. Internationales Begegnungs- und Forschungszentrum f`ur Informatik (IBFI), Schloss Dagstuhl, Germany.

Mori, G., Paternò, F., and Santoro, C. (2002). CTTE: support for developing and analyzing task models for interactive system design. *IEEE Trans. Softw. Eng.*, 28(8):797–813.

Mori, G., Paternò, F., and Santoro, C. (2004). Design and development of multidevice user interfaces through multiple logical descriptions. *IEEE Trans. Software Eng*, 30(8):507–520.

Myers, B. A., Hudson, S. E., and Pausch, R. F. (2000). Past, present, and future of user interface software tools. *ACM Trans. Comput.-Hum. Interact*, 7(1):3–28.

Nielsen, J. (1994). Heuristic evaluation. In Nielsen, J. and Mack, R. L., editors, *Usability Inspection Methods*. New York: Wiley.

Paterno, F., Mancini, C., and Meniconi, S. (1997). Concurtasktrees: a diagrammatic notation for specifying task models. In *Proceedings of IFIP INTERACT'97: Human-Computer Interaction*, pages 362–369.

Preece, J., Rogers, Y., Sharp, H., Benyon, D., Holland, S., and Carey, T. (1994). *Human-Computer Interaction*. Reading, MA: Addison-Wesley.

Seffah, A., Donyaee, M., and Kline, R. B. (2006). Usability measurements and metrics: A consolidated model. *Software Quality Journal*, 14(2): 159–178.

Shackel, B. (1991). Usability-context, framework, design and evaluation. In *Human Factors for Informatics Usability*, pages 21–38. Cambridge University Press.

Shneiderman, B. (1997). *Designing the User Interface: Strategies for Effective Human-Computer Interaction (3rd. ed.)*. Addison-Wesley, Reading: MA.

Sottet, J., Calvary, G., Coutaz, J., and Favre, J. (2007). A model-driven engineering approach for the usability of plastic user interfaces. In *Engineering Interactive Systems 2007 joining Three Working Conferences : IFIP WG2.7/13.4 10th Conference on Engineering Human Computer Interaction, IFIP WG 13.2 1st Conference on Human Centered Software Engineering, DSVIS - 14th Conference on Design Specification and Verification of Interactive Systems, University of Salamanca.*

Sottet, J., Calvary, G., Favre, J., Coutaz, J., and Demeure, A. (2006). Towards mappings and model transformations for consistency of plastic user interfaces. In Richter, K., Nichols, J., Gajos, K., and Seffah, A., editors, *The Many Faces of Consistency 2006. Proc. Workshop held at ACM Conference on Human Factors in Computing Systems (CHI2006)*.

Thevenin, D. (1999). Plasticity of user interfaces: Framework and research agenda. In Sasse, A. and Johnson, C., editors, *Interact'99*, pages 110–117. IFIP IOS Press.

Trevisan, D., Vanderdonckt, J., and Macq, B. (2003). Continuity as a usability property. In *Proceedings of the Tenth International Conference on Human-Computer Interaction*, volume 1 of *Human Factors and Ergonomics*, pages 1268–1272.

Van Welie, M., van der Veer, G., and Eliëns, A. (1999). Usability properties in dialog models. In *6th International Eurographics Workshop on Design Specification and Verification of Interactive Systems DSV-IS'99*, pages 238–253.

Weiser, M. (1991). The computer for the 21st century. *Scientific American*, 265(3):1613–1619.

9 CAUSE AND EFFECT IN USER INTERFACE DEVELOPMENT

Ebba Thora Hvannberg

University of Iceland, Hjardarhaga 2-6, Reykjavík, 107 Iceland

Abstract. There is a lack of means of translating work products of elicitation to design and using results of evaluation as feedback to design. This paper lays the foundation of a model of evaluation to be built concurrently with the design activity. The evaluation model describes the implications which work models have on design and records the cause/effect relationship between design and the problem domain. The paper presents two case studies from air traffic control that are meant to motivate the need for such an evaluation model and serve as input to its design.

9.1 INTRODUCTION

A prerequisite to design is the wish to change the problem domain by using new technology for improvement. In other words, we foresee an intervention that will change the problem domain. The difficult challenge in design is hence not merely on characterising the current domain, but to try to predict how the domain will change with new interventions and to foresee the altered behavior under varying conditions. This is what makes the science of the artificial different from the sciences of the natural. Whereas, in the former case, the emphasis is on how to make artifacts with desired properties and how to design artifacts that adapt well to its environment or vice versa, in the latter case, the task is to learn about how natural things are and how they work (Simon, 1996). Much effort is still beinn spent on learning how to understand characteristics of contexts (Beyer and Holtzblatt, 1998) and domains. Domain engineering is characterised as the study of domains for the purpose of reuse and is distinguishable from the machine being built or the application engineering (Björner, 2006).

Design has many facades, and designers employ numerous strategies, both implicitly and explicitly. Much of design comes from experience and if a designer has successfully designed a solution to a problem and it has worked well, it can be used on the next similar problem. Designers reuse or adapt previous designs, not necessarily whole designs but frameworks or patterns of designs. Empirical research has been conducted on designs in order to show that they work, with the aim of extracting new strategies. An obstacle in the development of user interfaces has been the lack of means of translating desired properties, coming either from elicitation or evaluation, to design ideas. These ideas are generated from insight or inspiration of the authors and alternatives are searched for the most desirable solution (Simon, 1996). In past years, creativity has been a growing field that includes techniques such as brainstorming, mind mapping and lateral thinking. In some of these methods, emphasis is on learning about associations between phenomena, collaborating with others in the team and disseminating the design for peer review (Shneiderman, 2002). Instead of focusing on the design solution, another strategy is to relax assumptions and trade-off conflicting constraints that cannot be resolved, and thereby refine the design problem (Hoffman, Roesler, and Moon, 2004).

During evaluation, we need to predict how an intervening design changes the problem domain. We can try several alternatives, accept some, develop others further, or reject them. If a design for a feature needs further development, it can be difficult to decide how it should be changed. We need to go back to the drawing board to create still new design ideas. Revisions need to take place that modify the implementation, the solution, or one's comprehension (Gray and Anderson, 1987) as referred to in Hoffman et al. (2004).

The three activities which have been discussed above, learning about the domain, design and evaluation, are main components in user interface development, but are divided into four activities in a lifecycle of user centered user interface development. More specifically they are eliciting user needs and their environment, specifying the user and organizational requirements, producing design solutions followed by evaluation, usually in several iterative cycles in an interdisciplinary team (ISO/IEC, 1999). These four activities have input and output work products. The input is the basis for the activity and the output is its deliverable and usually input into a successor activity in the lifecycle. The output of elicitation can be user, task or work models of various types, and description of actors and their environment, i.e., a context. The output of the design activity is one or several design ideas for a feature, realized in low- to high-fidelity prototypes, a model, or a final system. The output of the evaluation activity can be failures detected, observed constraints, facilitators, new or modified goals, positive or negative consequences of a designed feature. How information flows between these four activities is not as well known and we conjecture that this may contribute to the lack of interplay between evaluation and design. We propose that an evaluation model, which captures better the relationship between cause and effects, can mitigate this deficiency. In the evaluation model we recognise the interplay between all three activities, problem domain analysis, design and evaluation, but as pointed out by

Cockton (2006) the interplay between contextual research and design is critical, and an evaluation of problem domain analysis is as important as evaluation of end products (Hoegh, et al., 2006). Before proceeding further, we cover more deeply causes, effects, and current evaluation models.

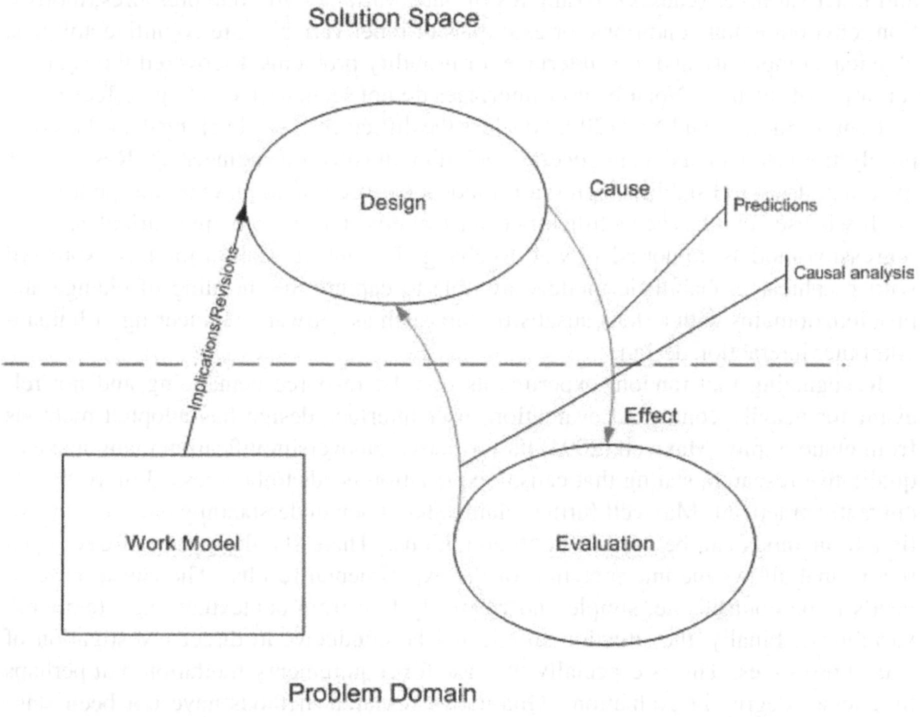

Figure 9.1 Cause in Design and Effect in Problem Domain

9.1.1 Causes and Effects

Two activities are prevalent in design and its revisions. When the designer is evaluating designs, he or she is continuously trying to (i) predict *effects of designs* in future changing environments, even several years ahead, and (ii) finding *causes of problems* of implemented designs when they have been incorporated into their environment (see Figure 9.1). The former concerns the actual design activity, and naturally, we want to be able to make accurate predictions to minimize problems in the implemented designs.

The discussion on the relationship between cause and effect is an ancient subject of philosophy (Hume, 1978–1982), but recent examples can be related to information technology. Pearl (Pearl, 2000) has investigated the importance of researching causes of effects and has presented a diagrammatical notation to enable researchers to exchange descriptions about causality. He has argued that statisticians have been too reluctant in investigating causality because of hesitation of relating causality with correlation.

In the field of human computer interaction Galliers, Sutcliffe, and Minocha (1999) have suggested that Bayesian modeling can be used to describe the relationship of users' mistakes and slips (the effects) that can be attributed to miscellaneous outer and inner variables (causes). Examples of outer variables are time pressures, motivation, environmental conditions, or examples of inner variables are cognitive abilities, physical complexity and user interface, or usability problems discovered through observation of the user. Notably, user interfaces do not seem to play a large effect.

Fenton, Krause, and Neil (2002) discuss the difficulty of establishing causal models purely from statistical data in general, including in software engineering. Researchers have e.g., tried to establish regression models between internal, external quality and quality in use but it has been difficult because of possible confounding variables. Also, regression models do not adapt well to change in context. Causal models expressed with graphical probabilistic models are able to capture the meaning of change and problem domains with a rich causal structure such as software engineering or human-computer interaction design.

Recognizing that random experiments may be resource demanding and not relevant for heavily contextual evaluation, user interface design has adopted methods from ethnography. Maxwell (2004) has criticised an oversimplification many make of qualitative research, stating that causal explanation needs to be stressed more than is currently practiced. Maxwell further claims that when understanding causality, quantitative methods can be used in three conditions. There should be a well-developed theory that allows the interpretation of the experimental results. The causal process needs to be controllable, simple and relatively free from contextual, e.g., temporal, variability. Finally, the situation should not be conducive to direct investigation of causal processes. This is especially the case for requirements elicitation, but perhaps to a lesser degree in evaluation. Qualitative research methods have not been standardized or refined, perhaps because researchers are encouraged to go their own way (Taylor and Bogdan, 1998). This may explain why they are less easily adoptable and require more expertise. User interface designers and evaluators can still learn from qualitative research methods.

There are several tools to derive propositions about causality and implications in qualitative methods. The aim is to look at variables that emerge from codification of the qualitative data and understand the association between them. We seek to understand whether one predicts or precedes another, how one variable impacts another, whether two comprise one, whether one generalizes another, etc. We look for contrasts and contradictions. Causal networks (Miles and Huberman, 1994, p. 222) are examples of a tool that describe relationship between phenomena,.

To find causes of problems (e.g., undesirable effects) at the time of evaluation, it is necessary to try to understand and describe the design features and their intended effect at design time. A prerequisite is to investigate thoroughly the implications a work model is meant to have on design (see Figure 9.1). The causes may be miscellaneous and even multiple; they can be within design features or the underlying work model. In software development, finding root causes has been widely used and various successful efforts have been reported on how to analyze defects, including an Ishikawa or fishbone diagram (Grady, 1992). The CUP (Classification of Usability Problems) (Hvannberg and Law, 2003) method has been suggested to further classify attributes of failures in user interaction and to find their roots in processes of the lifecycle of user interface development.

9.1.2 Evaluation Models

Various frameworks have been proposed for creating measurement models. These models quantify some parameters of the software system and set forward a hypothesis on the relationship between them. The Goal Question Metric was proposed to find the metrics, by stating the goals of the measure, asking questions that could meet the goals, and proposing metrics that could answer the questions. In the work on GQM/MEDEA (Briand, Morasca, and Basili, 2002), the aim is to make a prediction system, i.e., one that sets forth hypothesis on relationships between the metrics, that aims to make them quantitatively verifiable. The first step is to create the setting of the empirical study by identifying measurement goals. These motivate an empirical hypothesis that relates independent attributes to other dependent attributes. After careful definitions of measures for the independent and the dependent measures, the hypotheses are refined and verified. GQM/MEDEA takes also the experience factory as a factor into the experimental setting, as we have seen useful. Another measurement framework, SQUID (Software Quality in Development Projects) (Bøegh, et al., 1999) involves determining internal and external measures from a quality framework and subsequently attempts to find the relationships between them. The SQUID Data Model and Quality Process provide a method for this work. An important factor of SQUID is to store the inferred relationships in the software development's experience base. In GQM/MEDEA, the input to the setting of the empirical study is the current literature and the experience factory. Of course, those models can be used for user interface evaluation, but case studies with that focus are lacking to the best of our knowledge. Research on user interface evaluation has focused on problem detection and correction, e.g., comparison between methods for uncovering usability problems and characteristics of such problems with the aim of understanding them, prioritizing their removal and ideas for redesign. In a review of articles appearing in a special issue on interplay between evaluation and user interface design (Hornbaek and Stage, 2006), Cockton (2006) calls for further research on richer evaluation planning, including answering questions on why we are evaluating, which instruments will be used, which levels of performance will designate success, and what information and artifacts are given to evaluators?

9.2 RESEARCH STUDY

In this paper, we set forth research questions that have emerged from our work in prototyping and evaluation of two case studies in the domain of air traffic control. The aim of presenting the case studies is to learn how an evaluation model can help us better understand the relationship between cause and effect in user interface development, hoping to thereby elevate our comprehension of the interaction between design and evaluation. The next section gives an overview of two design experiments where low-fidelity prototypes have been used and a third one that was evaluated with a high-fidelity prototype. Examples in the remainder of the paper are taken from the case studies.

9.2.1 *Case Studies*

The two case studies reported here are taken from the domain of air traffic control. The duty of the air traffic controllers in the studies is to service aircraft en route in oceanic environments, i.e., cross the North-Atlantic. They monitor aircraft against predetermined routes, but issue clearances for requests for different routes provided it is safe, i.e., if aircraft adhere to separation rules. Source and means of data communication varies, ranging from automatic data transfer from radar to interactive communication via voice through radio. In the following two subsections, we describe how elicitation, design and evaluation were carried out in these projects. Each of the subsections is divided into short description of goals, elicitation of needs, design of the user interfaces and an informal self-assessment on the success of the methods. Table 9.1 provides an overview of the methods used.

Table 9.1 Methods used in case studies

Activity/Case	Speech Agent	Integrated workstation	
		1st iteration	2nd iteration
Elicitation	Literature review Observation Interview	Observation Interview Existing systems and requirements studies Class and Collaboration diagrams COGNITIVE MODELS OF USER'S WORK Heuristics evaluation using cognitive principles	
Design	Architecture Sequence diagrams Prototype	Paper sketches Three alternative approaches suggested	High-fidelity prototype of three features.
Evaluation	Wizard of Oz with air traffic controllers Post-experiment questionnaire Qualitative and Quantitative data gathered	Claims analysis Walk-through of drawings of user interface with participation of air traffic controllers post-task questionnaire Qualitative data gathered	Hypothesis formed Think-aloud usability test with users post-task questionnaire post-experiment questionnaire

9.2.2 *Using Language Technology to Improve Communication in ATC*

Short Description of Goals . Voice communication in Air Traffic Control is the most volatile part of the Air Traffic Control System. The aim of the project of the first case study was to use language technology to make communication more reliable and efficient, thus improving safety in aviation (Ragnarsdottir, Waage, and Hvannberg, 2003).

Elicitation. During the elicitation phase, previous literature on voice communication in Air Traffic Control was analyzed. Oceanic Air Traffic Controllers were observed while at work at a center of air traffic control and so were operators at a Center of Radio Communication. The researcher interviewed expert controllers to learn about the domain of Air Traffic Control and to understand the role of voice communication. The challenge in this domain is that fortunately errors in voice communication are relatively infrequent so they are not easily observed.

Design. A prototype of a speech agent was developed with the goal of recognizing errors in the communication between pilot and controller. Several options to replace or add a speech agent to existing voice communications were explored and their architecture designed, but a prototype of one was implemented. Sequence diagrams in UML describing realistic scenarios, edited by expert users, of dialogues were created for three characteristic scenarios of the problem domain.

Evaluation. A Wizard of Oz evaluation was conducted with five air traffic controllers of varying expertise. The evaluation was scripted, using the dialogues described in the previous section, with the tester playing the role of the pilot against each of the controllers. Quantitative data was gathered on errors made by a speech server during evaluation. Quantitative and qualitative data on controllers' attitude towards trust and performance was gathered in a post-test questionnaire. The evaluator asked questions about the type of feedback a speech agent should give in case of error in the voice communication between controller and pilot.

Since the prototype was of low fidelity, it was not feasible to evaluate it in context, other than to create real life scenarios and to have actual users. Evaluators were not conducted in Air Traffic Controllers' room or in a group with collaborators of the work, such as controllers of the same center, supervisors, or controllers of adjacent centers. Although this is considered important, and perhaps especially so when researching voice communication, it would have been impossible to get permission for evaluation on site and hence had to be staged.

Assessment of Methods. Since the tests had to be scheduled in advanced, and resources were scarce, there was no time to pilot test the evaluation on site. Hence, some of the evaluation instances were flawed because of failures in the supporting technology. The script worked very well, the performance of the speech agent was measured and the controllers were able to understand and reflect on the concepts. Controllers' attitude towards expected efficiency, safety and their trust on the speech agent has to be viewed in context of the artifact evaluated, but were good enough to proceed to the next phase. Performance of the speech agent gave the designer good ideas on how to improve its design and implementation.

9.2.3 Integrating Different User Interfaces in a Controller's Workstation

Short Description of Goals. The controller workstation under examination consists of three main systems with graphical user interfaces. The Flight Data Processing System (FDPS) system, which manages electronic flight strips, the Radar Display, which displays radar data and Situation Display, which is a backup system for the FDPS system and displays the data from on a geographical background. The fourth system is the communication system. The project investigated the integration of the above systems and proposed a spatial display, taking into account emerging technological and organizational contexts (Johannsson, 2004).

Elicitation. As in the previous case study, observations were made during elicitation of the problem, but a wider range of controllers was interviewed (Johannsson and Hvannberg, 2004). The architecture of different subsystems of a workstation was analyzed including their relationships.

An abstract model of the problem domain was created based on manuals of operations, previous requirements studies, observation of work and current systems. The model was expressed with text and UML diagrams.

A user interface model was reengineered from two current systems in order to find possible anomalies and basis for integration of two user interfaces. Cognitive models of user's work were examined (Major, Johannsson, Davison, Hvannberg, and Hansman, 2004). Heuristic evaluation, using cognitive principles, was carried out on current ATC's workstation to find deficiencies.

Design. Three alternative approaches to integration were described but one of them was designed in detail as drawings of user interfaces. Snapshots of user interfaces of design ideas for several features were created in a drawing tool. Sketches were ordered into a short storyboard explaining a scenario of work. Except for the description of the integration of the three alternatives, no models of designs were made, neither as scenarios, interactions, navigations, dialogues nor structure of user interfaces. The second iteration of the workstation was implemented in a high fidelity prototype.

Evaluation. Evaluation did not take place in context, except that participants were air traffic controllers. Controllers were asked to give a preference to one of three alternative approaches to integration of the two user interfaces. In a first part of the evaluation, a researcher conducted claims analysis (Rosson and Carroll, 2002) of three alternative approaches to integration.

In a second part, evaluations of snapshots were made with controllers of varying expertise. No interaction took place in the evaluation of the first version, but instead the researcher described situations to users. For some features, several alternatives were presented and users were asked to rate them and discuss, but for others only one design was presented. The method of evaluation was an interview with predetermined questions about safety, performance, and invited design suggestions from the controllers.

Two iterations of the storyboard evaluations took place with feedback from the former affecting the latter.

After an implementation of the proposed user interface of the workstation in a high-fidelity prototype, air traffic controllers evaluated it in a think-aloud test with five scenarios and answered post-scenario and post-experiment questionnaires.

Assessment of Methods. The snapshots of designs of user interfaces provided valuable means for interviewing users about the new ideas. Researchers received good ideas from users and the two iterations showed that improvements were achieved. The triangulation of evaluation methods, i.e., claims analysis and users' preference gave researchers additional confidence in the results.

The abstract models drawn and the cognitive models examined during elicitation were both useful to understand the complex problem domain and to explore new design ideas for specific aspects. The diagrammatical models were particularly helpful in moving away from the current context to try to predict the technological and organizational contexts. For the high-fidelity prototype, it proved challenging to design evaluation task scenarios and data that was convincing and close to the context.

9.3 ELICITING NEEDS AND CONTEXT

In this and the following two sections, we describe the activities of the lifecycle of user interface development, with the aim of linking them together. We end each section with questions or challenges as means towards this goal and we cite examples from the two case studies to support the questions. The first activity in a human-centered design is to understand and specify the context of use. Contextual inquiries (Beyer and Holtzblatt, 1998) and ethnographic approaches have been gaining popularity in recent years. Less is known about how to create work products that are useful for software engineers or user interface designers. Context, partnership, interpretation, and focus are four principles that guide contextual inquiry. The first and most basic requirement of Contextual Inquiry is to go to the customer's workplace and observe the work. The second is that the analysts and the customer together in a partnership understand this work. The third requirement is to interpret work by deriving facts, or make hypothesis that can have implication for design. The fourth principle is that the interviewer defines a point of view while studying work. The output of this activity can be e.g., a work model and Beyer and Holtzblatt (1998) suggest several models that comprise the work model, i.e., a model of communication, a sequence model, an artifact, or cultural and physical models. The lack of formalism in these models makes them difficult for practitioners like engineers to adopt. Semi-formal models in UML could replace or complement these informal models. Both task models and cognitive models, describing the problem domain, have been widely discussed, but, apart from a few exceptions, models that analyze (e.g., Jackson, 1995, p. 31; Bergh and Coninx, 2005) and predict behavior of designs in the problem domain are absent.

Vicente (1999) argues that work analysis for systems should identify and model intrinsic work constraints, and that the models should have formative implications for design. The motivation is that there is no systematic way to go from results of testing to prototype attributes, therefore we are dependent on the creativity of the designer to revise the prototype to remove the problematic effect. Cognitive Work Analysis (CWA) is an example of such a formative approach to work analysis and so is the Contextual Design proposed by Beyer and Holtzblatt (Vicente, 1999). Above we listed the models of Contextual designs that are created, but CWA presents other conceptual distinctions (Vicente, 1999): *Work Domain, Control Tasks, Strategies, Social-Organizational* and *Worker Competencies*. Through analysis of these distinctions, models of intrinsic work constraints are created that again lead to system design interventions. In the following, we give examples of interventions for Strategies, Social-Organization, and Worker Competencies. Dialogue modes and process flow are based on constraints derived from *strategies*. Role allocation and organizational structure are based on *social-organizational* constraints. Training and interface form are based on constraints derived from *worker competencies*. Neither Vicente nor Beyer and Holtzblatt express explicitly or maintain in a formal way the design implications of work analysis. Vicente gives informal relationships between the two activities by taking examples, but work analysis is the subject of Vicente (1999) and not design.

Usually, motivations for system implementation are changes. Those changes are e.g., due to changing technological contexts of the problem domain, increased scale, increased demand for quality or changing technological changes in the solution space. Below, is an example that shows how proposed changes in social-organizational conceptual distinction have an implication on a design.

A simplified example from the speech agent
Social-Organizational: A speech agent replaces a radio operator.
How can implications of work models on design intervention be modelled and maintained?

9.4 DESIGN

The data collected during elicitation and evaluation of the modified problem context will guide new design ideas. Design can be abstract such as redesign of work or structure of information, to detailed interactions between a product and the context.

9.4.1 Different Models of Design

Before a user interface is programmed, we can create a model of the design that we use to evaluate against our requirement and assumptions. The model may range from being abstract, like diagrams or wire frame, or detailed, such as sketches. Prototypes of various types, i.e., low vs. high fidelity, experience prototypes (Buchenau and Suri, 2000), vertical and horizontal, throwaway and incremental prototypes, are popular since they give the user an idea about the look and the feel of the interface. Modeling languages can describe certain aspects of a user interface such as navigation, dialogue or architecture such as diagrammatic models e.g., in UML or extensions thereof. As we saw in our case study, storyboards and textual scenarios are often useful to present design ideas or concepts respectively early on.

Designers should select the type of model that is most appropriate for the design feature at hand. For example, when designing complex navigations, a navigational diagram that gives an overview of the traversals between contexts will be more useful than many detailed sketches of designs. On the other hand, when designing presentations for entities that contain a rich collection of information, sketches are more useful. A complex dialogue implementing a scenario may be best presented with both sketches and diagrammatic models.

Integrated workstation: Class diagrams were used to analyze consistency between designs

How can we guide designers to select appropriate models to achieve design goals?

Speech agent: Sequence diagram that described the evaluated scenarios supported the Wizard of oz evaluation.

How can we guide designers to use a combination of different modeling tools, such as different fidelities of prototypes, diagrammatic models, text scenarios, or text use cases?

9.4.2 Multiple Design Ideas

One of the fundamental principles of design is to create multiple design ideas. This can be a result of a brainstorming session within an interdisciplinary team including users. When the design team has been a participant in the whole lifecycle, design ideas are implicitly linked to user needs and context of work.

The rationale for the design idea needs to be made explicit. Otherwise, it will be difficult during evaluation to validate whether the design feature is coherent in the problem domain. Several methods have been designed to capture design rationale. QOC (MacLean, Bellotti, Youngl, and Moranz, 1991) consists of a tree where the root is the Question or the problems, its children are Options that designers propose to meet the goals, and the third level is the Criteria according to which we should evaluate the options. In a study (Shum, 1996) where designers were observed while using QOC, it was noted that they spent a fair amount of time on renaming and restructuring the trees. It was also noted that designers had the need to pose questions in the form of constraints, and to describe trade-offs between options (see the next section). The tree formalism can grow quite complex, since normally we want to evaluate several disjoint options together that each represent a solution to a problem, or set forward an option as a hierarchy of other options. An empirical study showed that while QOC's focus is on arguing about multiple Options, it is poorly suited to work with evolution of a single option, where a single idea is revised iteratively after evaluation.

One of the concerns expressed by the designers was the lack of knowing how to *evaluate* the options. A suggestion by Bastide et al. (2005) is to connect a task model or a scenario to the option that would then provide a basis for evaluation. Additionally, we suggest that in order to support the whole lifecycle, there should be a link from the evaluation context to the result of the evaluation, so that it can be assessed whether the result meets the posed criteria.

Evaluation of the design should be prepared during the design phase. In our experience, it is not adequate to ask whether a design meets requirements of efficiency, effectiveness, and satisfaction. This is especially true for design ideas produced early in the lifecycle, often in low-fidelity prototypes. Designers should associate evaluation questions with the design ideas during design but not after it and describe the expected effect of the design once joined in the problem domain. To accomplish this, usability specialists should either work on the design team, or, in small organizations, designers should take on the role of usability test designers.

Integration of ATC: Three alternative design ideas for integration were presented. Claims analysis was applied to elicit positive and negative consequences. Questionnaires were posted to elicit views on usability of the alternatives.
Integration of ATC: Controls for selecting altitude levels will have the effect on the controller to focus on specific critical air traffic and reduce the cognitive load, thereby making decisions easier.

How can we design and describe evaluations of user interfaces that can answer specific questions about the expected effect of the design?

9.4.3 Trade-offs

Design ideas are created to change a problem domain. There may be different motivation for the change, i.e., technical, social, organizational, or economical. Common effect of the changes that we are aiming for are increased effectiveness, efficiency, or satisfaction during operation. Other changes may result in increased safety or less time for training. A design idea that may cause a positive effect of one aspect of the problem domain may at the same time cause a negative effect of another. Altshuller (1996) describes inventions as removing a technical contradiction that comes about when improving one characteristic, it impairs another. We take an example from combining two user interfaces, Flight Data Processing (Flight strips) and Radar Data into one. The merging of the two interfaces will eliminate the need to integrate information in the user's head but can increase clutter on the display. More automation in the Flight Controller workstation can lead to less workload in easy low-traffic situations but may blur the controllers' mental picture (leading to less efficient or safe operations) during difficult high-traffic or critical situations. In Altshuller's (1996) opinion, if we manage to remove the need to make the choice, but instead propose a solution to remove the technical constraints, we have an invention. These technical contradictions can be discovered, e.g., with claims analysis (Rosson and Carroll, 2002) where positive and negative consequences of a single design feature are gathered. In Rosson and Carroll's proposed claims analysis, consequences to the user are analyzed, but a more detailed analysis should discover what quality characteristic or parameters of a computer or a human system are affected. In his Theory of Inventive Problem Solving (TRIZ), Altshuller (1996) has put forward a way of matching technical constraints between two parameters with a known inventive solution. In this, Altshuller reuses or adapts a previous design, not unlike it is done with design patterns. Reuse is the idea here, just as in design patterns where problems are solved with known patterns that have proved to be useful in practice.

A different approach is to live with the trade-offs but make them explicitly visible and traceable. Architecture Trade-off Analysis Method (ATAM) (Clements, Kazman, and Klein, 2002) describes how we can analyze trade-offs between parameters that appear in architectural decisions. The method also encourages the designer to identify risks, sensitivity points, and non-risk, but these are all tools to make the design process more transparent. These items can help the designer to devise evaluations to determine whether the risks materialise or the trade-offs are acceptable. ATAM is a general tool for architectural analysis but has been used specifically to analyze the effect of certain design patterns on usability (Bass and John, 2003). The more we know about the parameters of a design, the more targeted evaluations we can make, and hopefully make a decision on how to revise or abandon the design features.

Integration of ATC: Controls for selecting altitude levels cause the controller to miss information in deselected altitudes and therefore deteriorating the mental model of the current state of the system.

As we see above, when creating different design ideas, there can also be trade-offs between them. Again, an example is taken from ATC. Either adaptable (i.e., adapted by the user) or adaptive (i.e., adapted by the computer) user interfaces are meant to solve the problem of display clutter that can occur during high traffic situations.

Integration of ATC: An adaptive interface can be more efficient than adaptable interface to the controller but less satisfying.
How can we express predicted trade-offs of effects between design ideas?
How can we express conflicting constraining parameters so that we are aware of them and can even remove them?

9.4.4 Scientific Knowledge

Not only is the domain knowledge input to the design process but also the scientific domain consisting of the relevant scientific knowledge we have gained. In the scientific domain of air traffic control, a model of air traffic controller's cognitive abilities, Modell des Fluglotsenleistungen (MOF1), has been developed (Niessen and Eyferth, 2001). It consists of five modules: *data selection, anticipation, conflict resolution, update* and *control.* These modules exist in a lifecycle of the monitoring cycle, anticipation cycle, conflict resolution, and control, but in the last one, the controller attempts to sequence his actions because he usually needs to fulfill many simultaneous goals at the same time. The features that were selected for implementation in the prototype of the Integrated Workstation, were in the module *data selection* and *anticipation.* For example, the following quote from Niessen and Eyferth (2001), motivated us to experiment with two different ways of showing extended data blocks with additional information, either with a tool-tip or with a full selection of a data block.

Integrated workstation: "... aircraft become highly activated, meaning that they are objects that need attention. Aircraft without these features [vertical movements, proximity to other aircraft or points in airspace where conflicts frequently occur], are less activated, and are vaguely represented with a few data that only indicate their existence." (Niessen and Eyferth, 2001)

This raised a question, whether controllers foresaw the need to receive assistance from the system to filter out the relevant flights.

How can we link design decisions to scientific knowledge and experience base?

9.5 EVALUATION IN CONTEXT

By introducing the new design to the problem domain, we thereby modify it. The goal of the evaluation is to see how the proposed changes interact with the problem domain. Many methods of evaluation have been proposed, both analytical and empirical, and most are manual but some are also automatic. The evaluation results are either qualitative or quantitative and sometimes both. Evaluations are done at different phases in the development life cycle, but close interaction with users from an early stage has been advocated. Evaluating finished products may be easier but failures detected at such a late stage may be costly to correct. Hence, designers have focused on early evaluation with low-fidelity prototypes. The downside is that these evaluations without completed systems or high-fidelity prototypes may not be as reliable e.g., in safety critical situations.

Although contextual inquiries have been promoted, there has been less emphasis on evaluations of design in real contexts and, in the case of early evaluation, this may prove to be infeasible. Experience prototyping (Buchenau and Suri, 2000) has been proposed as a tool to use for this purpose. Every effort should be made to place the design in real contexts. One way is to provide training facilities that can accomplish this and simulators may be another. Designing test scenarios comprises at least two main factors, the goals, or the task scenario, and the data. A domain expert needs to be involved in the design of an evaluation. The goal needs to be realistic and not give away too much information, as occurred in the case of the following example, where the controller did not look at the screen but saw the answer in the task scenario.

Integrated workstation: Task Scenario: Identify flight NWA67. Assess its surrounding traffic by filtering the display so that you are only viewing traffic on flight levels **340**, **350**, and **360**.

Instead of letting the controller find which flight levels to view by looking at surrounding traffic of flight NWA67, the task gives away those flight levels. Hence, the user does not need to view the display, but consults the task scenario for the information.

The task scenario needs to be able to test some specific hypothesis. As we discussed in the previous section, a designer needs to have a goal. He or she proposes a feature, a solution to a problem, a resolution of a technical constraint, and he/she wants to learn whether the solution is working. For example, the following hypothesis was put forward for a feature called flight level filter. Such a filter displays all flights of one or more flight levels that are selected.

Integrated workstation: The flight level filter poses a risk if it is left in such a state that some flight levels were deselected, especially by another person than the current controller.

By describing the hypothesis, it will be easier to design the task scenario. For example, in the case above, we need to simulate the situation that the controller is coming to the workstation after a break and design a situation where critical traffic becomes invisible because of the deselected flight levels. The hypothesis is confirmed or rejected after having observed participants while they perform the task. If the test had shown that the hypothesis is confirmed, further restrictions may be needed on flight level filters such that flight levels are deselected when a controller resumes his working position, or the controller needs to be warned when critical traffic is not in view. In addition to the task scenarios, participants and other contextual parameters, e.g., from the surroundings, need to be selected. An evaluator needs to be careful to control for confounding parameters, or otherwise it may be difficult to draw the implications.

Speech agent: Controllers were recruited to participate in the evaluation; scenarios were carefully designed and verified by domain experts to emulate real contexts.

How can we build a context for evaluation of designs during early phases?

Another decision for evaluation is the extent of scope. If the scope is narrow, i.e., evaluation is done at one site and the sites are heterogeneous, results may not be generalizable to another site where contexts are different. Discovering problems encountered during task observations is not the only goal, but the problems need to be linked to specific design features; if not it may prove difficult to remove the defect. The results of an evaluation can be twofold; either the design ideas were not able to correctly fulfill the assumptions or the underlying model of the problem domain proved incorrect. This calls for changing the model or changing the design. In the former case we might have assumed something about the work or its context, but found out during subsequent evaluation that the assumption was not correct. An example from the speech agent is that we assumed that controllers spoke at a specific speed with no delays, which lead to a certain configuration in the agent. This is an example of a relationship between how some knowledge about the problem domain leads to a design decision. During evaluation, it became evident that the assumption was not correct. If we have a model of the relationship between the problem domain and the new design ideas, it will be easier to trace back the causes of failures, correct the underlying model, and adapt the design. Not all such relationships may be evident beforehand and some are only realized during evaluation.

Although we have specified the expected effect of a design idea, it may be that it will lead to some unforeseen effect. The evaluation in context is about finding out how the new design ideas interact in the changed problem domain. Hence we try to observe what changes the ideas bring about to the entire problem domain, not only the immediate user, but other systems and stakeholders.

How can we express the actual effect in the problem domain, resulting from changes brought on by design ideas?

If we fail to reach the desired effect, we may either trace backward to the documented causes of the desired effect or else we need to trace it to failed designs or wrong assumptions in the problem domain.

How can failures (in reaching the desired effect) lead us to failed designs (causes) or wrong assumptions in the work model?

9.6 FOUNDATION AND CONTEXT OF AN EVALUATION MODEL

Much of what we have discussed above, concerns ways in which to describe more accurately implications work model changes have on design, predictions of interventions' effects, or causes of (unwanted) effects. Thereby, we have attempted to fill

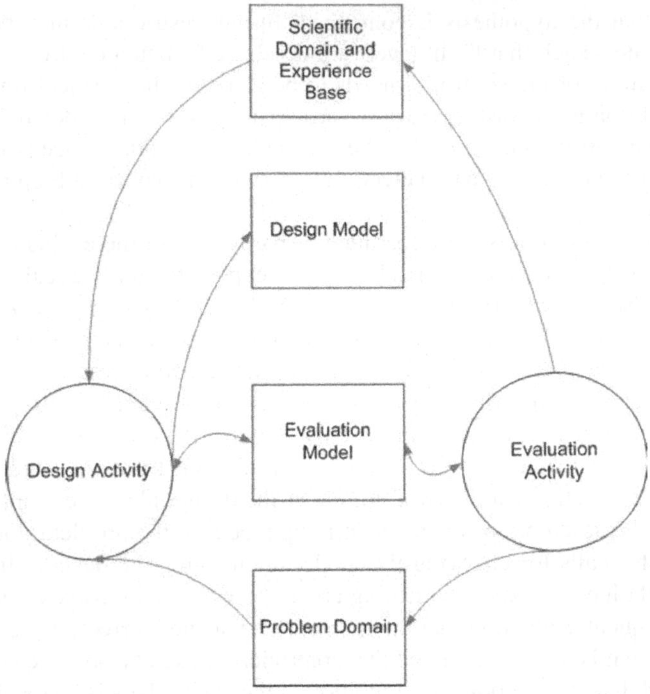

Figure 9.2 Development model

the gap identified in the beginning of this paper, namely, that there is a lack of flow of work products between individual activities of a user centered lifecycle. With the case studies described in the paper, we have argued that relating the evaluation model strongly with design will aid design, either initial proposals or revised designs.

Although it is easier for developers to understand the lifecycle consisting of separate activities and we understand that it is important to have several iterations of the activities, the gap between them may be unnecessary. We propose (Figure 9.2) to have two activities, design and evaluation, which are run concurrently. In addition to traditional models of problem domain and design, we suggest a further evaluation model as a central repository. The fourth component, the experience base, will provide us a knowledge repository to draw upon. These will make up the link between the two activities of design and evaluation. You will notice that there is no separate elicitation activity and this is intentional. The distinction between elicitation and evaluation may not always be clear since evaluation elicits new information and gives us further data about user needs and their environment. The only difference between them is that at elicitation usually (but not always) no new design of features is presented. This constitutes the first iteration, but in subsequent iterations, we use the term *evaluation* because some product of the design has entered the domain. The evaluation activity should not be conducted as a separate activity after the design, but instead planned for during design and then carried out. We have a practice in software development where it is recommended to design the test before the implementation. Extreme Programming (Beck, 2002), which is a type of an agile development methodology, has this practice as one of its main guidelines.

This paper does not suggest instruments to use in the proposed evaluation model, but rather suggests what questions it should address in Table 9.2.

Table 9.2 Requirements for the design of an evaluation model

Requirements
How can implications of work models on design intervention be modelled and maintained?
How can we build a context for evaluation of designs during early phases?
How can we design and describe evaluations of user interfaces where specific questions about the expected effect of the design are answered?
How can we express predicted trade-offs of effects between design ideas?
How can we express the actual effect in the problem domain, resulting from changes brought on by design ideas?
How can failures (in reaching the desired effect) lead us to failed designs (causes) or wrong assumptions in the work model?

It may not be clear which questions should be answered in the evaluation model and which should be answered in the design model, but we suggest that the questions of Table 9.3 should be answered in the design model.

Table 9.3 Requirements for a design model

Requirements
How can we link design decisions to scientific knowledge and experience base?
How can we express conflicting constraining parameters so that we are aware of them and can even remove them?

Finally, we restate a requirement to a design activity: *How can we guide designers to use a combination of different modeling tools, such as different fidelities of prototypes, diagrammatic models, text scenarios, or text use cases, appropriately to achieve a design goal?*

Although it is stated that the metrics in a GQM/MEDEA measurement model do not need to be quantitative, the difficulty with a quantitative measure is the requirements of randomised assignment in experiment and the need for a large number of subjects. However, one of the benefits of the approach is that the measurement model takes into account the tactical goals, e.g., the available resources for the study. In studies that collect qualitative data, hypotheses are not set forward beforehand. Observations are made and qualitative data, e.g., text or pictures, are coded, either using predefined codes or creating categories during the coding process. In the context of HCI, an example of the former is severity of the usability problem, but an example of the latter is a particular context of the problem.

Even if qualitative data are collected in usability studies, by describing in text the problems, the analysis often stops after the data have been coded into usability problems, number of usability problems, identification of unique problems, classification of severity etc. When the coding has been completed, there are several ways to derive a theory (Seaman, 1999). First, a set of statements or propositions is derived from the codes and the associated patterns of text. In the constant comparison method, codes are associated with a common theme of interest to the study and thereafter, segments are grouped into patterns according to the codes they have been assigned. Once a proposition is developed into a hypothesis, it needs to be confirmed. Again, ways to carry out the confirmation, apart from careful validation, include triangulation, thus looking for other ways of deriving the proposition, anomalies in the data, or outliers, negative case analysis that may contradict the proposition, or replication where only portions of the study relevant to the hypothesis are repeated. Current practices in qualitative usability evaluation have not focused heavily on deriving a theory in such a way.

9.7 CONCLUSION

In a fast-paced world, yet another model may not seem necessary in the process of development. In recent years, there has been a strong trend to advocate various methods that give the developer the opportunity to show results soon, e.g., with rapid prototyping methods or agile methods with close cooperation with the customer and frequent releases in iterative or incremental versions. Grudin's (1996) criticism of the design rationale methods was that if methods appear too scientific, which is the danger when invented by scientists and not practitioners, they may be inefficient and not adopted in practice. Engineering methods, where there is an understanding when to stop analyzing constraints, trade-offs etc. and plunge ahead and deliver a solution, may be more likely to return a profit. In engineering, producing cost-effective solutions is high priority. We should not forget that the characteristics of engineering are to use known methods and designs, evaluate alternatives, including trade-offs, based on best practice and scientific knowledge, so that it is possible to make decisions, and for that we need expertise.

Standards and models have in common that they make development less reliant on experts. For someone with years of experience in design and evaluation, a large database of expertise has been built, not only personally, but within his/her surroundings in a company, or institution. For someone starting in the area, tools and models are a necessity. It has been suggested that agile methods for example are not good for beginners. They make tasks explicit, whereas experts need not rely on strict methods or models, since they follow or build them mentally. With improved possibilities to gather experiences, patterns and cooperate more widely digitally, we will be able to see the benefit of building or reusing evaluation models.

This paper has presented challenges that need to be addressed to better integrate evaluation and design. The approach proposed involves specifying different work products and asking questions about implications of work to design, and cause and effect. We have used two case studies to illustrate our challenges with simple examples, expressed above in boxes. They are not meant to be examples of how to address these challenges, but rather give some initial illustration of the concepts. The case studies presented in this paper have motivated us to set forward requirements for more formal description of the processes in human computer interaction development. Many of the suggestions are rooted in software design and mathematics that can be transferred to user interface development. While researching the current literature on design, evidently considerable accomplishments have been achieved in each of design and evaluation. Very little has been done to research models that give practitioners tools to relate implication of work practices to design, to relate predictions of design to future work practices (problem domains) or determine causes of undesired behaviors although some signs of the latter have been noticed. We conclude that the questions raised, when determining what type of evaluation should be conducted and how the results of evaluation can be best used, call for a more formal description that is envisioned in a semi-formal or formal model. We have motivated the requirements for such a model and pointed to several areas that we hope will inspire researchers to propose a modeling language for an evaluation model, but we have not gone so far as to suggest a specific instrument.

Acknowledgments

Margrét Dóra Ragnarsdóttir, Hlynur Jóhannsson and Jóhann Möller have designed and evaluated the prototypes of the speech agent and integration of user interfaces (1st and 2nd versions) respectively.

References

Altshuller, G. and Altov, H. (1996). *And Suddenly the Inventor Appeared: TRIZ, the Theory of Inventive Problem Solving*. Technical Innovation Center, Worcester, Massachusetts, USA, 2nd edition.

Bass, L. and John, B. E. (2003). Linking usability to software architecture patterns through general scenarios. *Journal of Systems and Software*, 66(3):187–197.

Bastide, R., Lacaze, X., Navarre, D., Palanque, P. A., and Galindo, M. (2005). Can we rationalise the design and construction of air traffic management systems. In *HCI International 2005, Las Vegas, Nevada, USA, July 22-27*, volume 7, pages CD–ROM. TBD.

Beck, K. (2002). *Test-Driven Development*. Reading, MA.: Addison-Wesley

Bergh, J. V. and Coninx, K. (2005). Towards modeling context-sensitive interactive applications: the context-sensitive user interface profile (CUP). In Naps, T. L. and Pauw, W. D., editors, *Proceedings of the ACM 2005 Symposium on Software Vi-*

sualization SOFTVIS, St. Louis, Missouri, USA, May 14-15, 2005, pages 87–94. ACM.

Beyer, H. and Holtzblatt, K. (1998). *Contextual Design: Defining Customer-Centered Systems*. San Francisco, CA: Morgan Kaufmann.

Björner, D. (2006). *Software Engineerng 3*. Berlin: Springer-Verlag.

Bøegh, J., Depanfilis, S., Kitchenham, B., and Pasquini, A. (1999). A method for software quality planning, control, and evaluation. *IEEE Software*, 16(2):69–77.

Briand, L. C., Morasca, S., and Basili, V. R. (2002). An operational process for goal-driven definition of measures. *IEEE Trans. Software Eng.*, 28(12):1106–1125.

Buchenau, M. and Suri, J. F. (2000). Experience prototyping. In *Proceedings of DIS'00: Designing Interactive Systems: Processes, Practices, Methods, and Techniques*, User Experience, pages 424–433, New York.

Clements, P., Kazman, R., and Klein, M. (2002). *Evaluating Software Architectures: Methods and Case Studies*. Reading, MA: Addison-Wesley

Cockton, G. (2006). Focus, fit, and fervor: Future factors beyond play with the interplay. *International Journal of Human-Computer Interaction*, 21:239–250.

Fenton, N., Krause, P., and Neil, M. (2002). Software measurement: Uncertainty and causal modeling. *IEEE Software*, 19(4):116–122.

Galliers, J., Sutcliffe, A., and Minocha, S. (1999). An impact analysis method for safety-critical user interface design. *ACM Transactions on Computer-Human Interaction*, 6(4):341–369.

Grady, R. B. (1992). *Practical Software Metrics for Project Management and Process Improvement*. Englewood Cliffs, NJ: Prentice-Hall.

Gray, W. D. and Anderson, J. R. (1987). Change-episodes in coding: When and how do programmers change their code? In Olson, G. M., Sheppard, S., and Soloway, E., editors, *Empirical Studies of Programmers: Second Workshop*, Human/Computer Interaction: A Series of Monographs, Edited Volumes, and Texts, pages 185–197. New York: Ablex Publishing.

Grudin, J. (1996). Evaluating opportunities for design capture. In Moran, T. and Carrol, J., editors, *Design Rationale: Concepts, Techniques, and Use*, pages 453–470. Hillsdale, NJ: Erlbaum.

Hoegh, R. T., Nielsen, C. M., Overgaard, M., Pedersen, M. B., and Stage, J. (2006). The impact of usability reports and user test observations on developers' understanding of usability data: An exploratory study. *International Journal of Human-Computer Interaction*, 21:173–196.

Hoffman, R. R., Roesler, A., and Moon, B. M. (2004). What is design in the context of human-centered computing? *IEEE Intelligent Systems*, 19(4):89–95.

Hornbaek, K. and Stage, J. (2006). The interplay between usability evaluation and user interaction design. *International Journal of Human-Computer Interaction*, 21:117–123.

Hume, D. (1978–1982). *1711-1776: A treatise of human nature: being an attempt to introduce the experimental method of reasoning into moral subjects*. Glasgow: Fontana/Collins.

Hvannberg, E. T. and Law, L. (2003). Classification of usability problems (CUP) scheme. In *Proceedings of IFIP INTERACT'03: Human-Computer Interaction*, 2: Usability testing, page 655.

ISO/IEC (1999). *ISO/IEC 13407: Human-Centered Design Processes for Interactive Systems*. ISO/IEC 13407: 1999 (E).

Jackson, M. (1995). *Software Requirements and Specification*. Reading, MA: Addison Wesley.

Johannsson, H. (2004). Integration of air traffic control user interfaces. Technical report, University of Iceland, Reykjavik.

Johannsson, H. and Hvannberg, E. T. (2004). Integration of air traffic control user interfaces. In *The 23rd DASC, Digital Avionics Systems Conference, Salt Lake City, USA*. IEEE Computer Society.

MacLean, A., Bellotti, V., Young, R. M., and Moran, T. P. (1991). Reaching through analogy: A design rationale perspective on roles of analogy. In *Proceedings of ACM CHI'91 Conference on Human Factors in Computing Systems*, Use of Familiar Things in the Design of Interfaces, pages 167–172.

Major, L., Johannsson, H., Davison, H. J., Hvannberg, E. T., and Hansman, R. J. (2004). Key human-centered transition issues for future oceanic air traffic control systems. In *HCI-Aero*, Toulouse.

Maxwell, J. A. (2004). Causal explanation, qualitative research, and scientific inquiry in education. *Educational Researcher*, 33(2):3–11.

Miles, M. B. and Huberman, M. (1994). *Qualitative Data Analysis: An Expanded Sourcebook, 2nd ed*. Thousand Oaks, CA: Sage Publications.

Niessen, C. and Eyferth, K. (2001). A model of the air traffic controller's picture. *Safety Science*, 37:187–202.

Pearl, J. (2000). *Causality: Models, Reasoning and Inference*. London: Cambridge University Press.

Ragnarsdottir, M. D., Waage, H., and Hvannberg, E. T. (2003). Language technology in air traffic control. In *the 2nd DASC, Digital Avionics Systems Conference*, Indianapolis, IN.

Rosson, M. B. and Carroll, J. M. (2002). *Usability Engineering: Scenario-Based Development of Human-Computer Interactions*. San Francisco, CA: Morgan Kauffmann.

Seaman, C. B. (1999). Qualitative methods in empirical studies of software engineering. *IEEE Transactions on Software Engineering*, 25(4):557–572. Special Section: Empirical Software Engineering.

Shneiderman, B. (2002). Creativity support tools. *Communications of the ACM*, 45(10):116–120.

Shum, S. B. (1996). Analyzing the usability of a design rationale notation. In Moran, T. P. and Carroll, J. M., editors, *Design Rationale: Concepts, Techniques, and Use*, pages 185–215. Hillsdale, NJ: Erlbaum.

Simon, H. A. (1996). *The Sciences of the Artificial*. MIT Press.

Taylor, S. J. and Bogdan, R. (1998). *Introduction to Qualitative Research Methods, 3rd ed*. New York: Wiley.

Vicente, K. J. (1999). *Cognitive Work Analysis: Toward Safe, Productive, and Healthy Computer-Based Work*. Lawrence Erlbaum Associates, New Jersey.

III Interactive Systems Architectures

10 FROM USER INTERFACE USABILITY TO THE OVERALL USABILITY OF INTERACTIVE SYSTEMS: ADDING USABILITY IN SYSTEM ARCHITECTURE

Mohamed Taleb, Ahmed Seffah, and Daniel Engleberg

Human-Centered Software Engineering Group
Department of Computer Science and Software Engineering,
Concordia University, Montreal, Canada
mtaleb@encs.concordia.ca, seffah@cs.concordia.ca,
dan.engleberg@sympatico.ca

Abstract. Traditional interactive system architectures such as MVC and PAC decompose the system into subsystems that are relatively independent, thereby allowing the design work to be partitioned between the user interfaces and underlying functionalities. Such architectures extend the independence assumption to usability, approaching the design of the user interface as a subsystem that can be designed and tested independently from the underlying functionality. This Cartesian dichotomy can be fallacious, as functionalities buried in the application's logic can sometimes affect the usability of the system. Our investigations model the relationships between internal software attributes and externally visible usability factors. We propose a pattern-based approach for dealing with these relationships. We conclude by discussing how these patterns can lead to a methodological framework for improving interactive system architectures, and how these patterns can support the integration of usability in the software design process.

10.1 INTRODUCTION

Software architecture is defined as the fundamental design organization of a system, embodied in its components, their relationships to each other and the environment, and the principles governing its design, development and evolution [ANSI/IEEE Std 1471-2000, Recommended Practice for Architectural Description of Software-Intensive Systems]. In addition, it encapsulates the fundamental entities and properties of the application that generally insure the quality of application (Kazman et al., 2000).

In the field of interactive systems engineering, architectures of the 1980s and 1990s such as MVC and PAC are based on the principle of separating the functionality from the user interface. The functionality is what the software actually does and what information it processes. The user interface defines how this functionality is presented to end-users and how the users interact with it. The underlying assumption is that usability, the ultimate quality factor, is primarily a property of the user interface. Therefore separating the user interface from the application's logic makes it easy to modify, adapt, or customize the interface after user testing. Unfortunately, this assumption does not ensure the usability of the system as a whole.

We now realize that system features can have an impact on the usability of the system, even if they are logically independent from the user interface and not necessarily visible to the user. Bass and John observed that even if the presentation of a system is well designed, the usability of a system could be greatly compromised if the underlying architecture and designs do not have the proper provisions for user concerns (Bass and John, 2001; Raskin, 2000). We propose that software architecture should define not only the technical interactions needed to develop and implement a product, but also interactions with the users.

At the core of this vision is that invisible components can affect usability. By invisible components, we mean any software entity or architectural attribute that does not have visible cues on the presentation layer. They can be an operation, data, or a structural attribute of the software. Examples of such phenomena are commonplace in database modeling. Queries that were not anticipated by the modeler, or that turn out to be more frequent than expected, can take forever to complete because the logical data model (or even the physical data model) is inappropriate. Client-server and distributed computer architectures are also particularly prone to usability problems stemming from their "invisible" components.

Designers of distributed applications with Web interfaces are often faced with these concerns: They must carefully weigh what part of the application logic will reside on the client side and what part will be on the server side in order to achieve an appropriate level of usability. User feedback information, such as application status and error messages, must be carefully designed and exchanged between the client and server part of the application, anticipating response time of each component, error conditions and exception handling, and the variability of the computing environment. Sometimes, the Web user interface becomes crippled by the constraints imposed by these invisible components because the appropriate style of interactions is too difficult to implement.

Like other authors (Bass and John, 2001; Folmer and Bosch, 2004), we argue that both software developers implementing the systems features and usability engineers in charge of designing the user interfaces should be aware of the importance of this intimate relationship between features and the user interfaces. This relationship can inform architecture design for usability. With the help of patterns, this relationship can help integrate usability concerns in software engineering. Beyond proposing a list of patterns to solve specific problems, our long-term goal is to define a framework for studying and integrating usability concerns in interactive software architecture via patterns.

10.2 BACKGROUND AND RELATED WORK

A large number of architectures for interactive software have been proposed, e.g., Seeheim model, Model-View-Controller (MVC), Arch/Slinky, Presentation Abstraction Control (PAC), PAC-Amadeus and Model-View-Presenter (MVP) (Bass et al., 1998). Most of these architectures distinguish three main components: (1) abstraction or model, (2) control or dialog, and (3) presentation. The model contains the functionality of the software. The view provides graphical user interface (GUI) components for a model. It gets the values that it displays by querying the model of which it is a view. A model can have several views. When a user manipulates a view of a model, the view informs a controller of the desired change. Figure 10.1 summarizes the role of each these three components for an MVC-based application.

The motivation behind these architecture models is to improve, among others, the adaptability, portability, complexity handling, and separation of concerns of interactive software. However, even if the principle of separating interactive software in components has its design merits, it can be the source of serious adaptability and usability problems in software that provides fast, frequent, and intensive semantic feedback. The communication between the view and the model makes the software system highly coupled and complex.

The major weakness of this architecture is the lack of provisions for integrating usability in the design of the model or abstraction components. For example, Bass and his colleagues (Bass et al., 2001) identified specific connections between aspects of usability (such as the ability to "undo") and the model response (processed by an event-handler routine).

To study these intimate relationships between the model and the interface, we proposed the following methodological framework to:

1. Identify and categorize typical design scenarios that illustrate how invisible components and their intrinsic quality properties might affect the usability
    (a) Model each scenario in terms of a cause/effect relationship between (a) the attributes that quantify the quality of an invisible software entity and (b) well-known usability factors such as efficiency, satisfaction, etc.
    (b) Suggest new design patterns or improve existing ones that can solve the problem described in similar scenarios
    (c) Illustrate, as part of the pattern documentation, how these patterns can be applied within existing architectural models such as MVC.

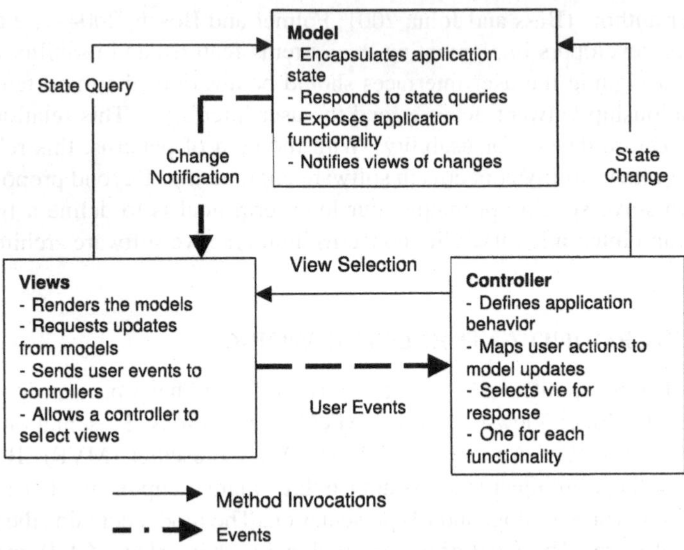

Figure 10.1 The roles of the MVC architecture components

10.3 IDENTIFYING AND CATEGORIZING TYPICAL SCENARIOS

The first step in our approach for achieving usability via software architecture and patterns is to identify typical situations that illustrate how invisible components of the model might affect usability. Each typical situation is documented using a scenario. Scenarios are widely used in HCI and software engineering (Carroll, 2000). Scenarios can improve communication between user interface specialists and software engineers who design invisible components—this communication is essential in our approach. Within our approach, we define a scenario as a narrative story written in natural language that describes a usability problem (effect) and that relates the source of this problem to an invisible software entity (cause). The scenario establishes the relationship between internal software attributes that are used to measure the quality of the invisible software entity and the external usability factors that we use for assessing the ease of use of the software systems.

The following are some typical scenarios we extracted from our day-to-day experiences and from a literature review. Other researchers also proposed other scenarios (see Kazman and Bass, 2002). The goal of our research was not to build an exhaustive list of scenarios, but rather to propose a methodological framework for identifying such scenarios and to define patterns that be used by developers to solve such problems. The scenarios are therefore intended as illustrative examples.

Scenario 1: Time-Consuming Functionalities

It is common for some the underlying functionalities of an interactive system to be time consuming. Several quality attributes can increase the time for executing these functionalities. A typical situation is the case where a professional movie designer expects high-speed Internet access when downloading large video files, but the technology of Internet connection makes configuration overly difficult.

The user needs feedback information to know whether or not an operation is still being performed and how much longer he will need to wait, but sometimes this information is not provided. Feedback tends to be overlooked, in particular, when the designers of the user interface and those developing the features are not the same and there is a lack of communication between them.

Scenario 2: Updating the Interface When the Model Changes Its State

Usability guidelines recommend helping users understand a set of related data by allowing them to visualize the data from different points of view. A typical method is to provide graphical and textual representations of the same underlying data model.

Whenever the data model changes, the underlying model should update the graphical and textual representations. In certain cases, the system might not be designed to automatically update all views when one view changes. This can result in inconsistent views that can in turn increase the user's memory load, frustration, and errors.

Scenario 3: Performing Multiple Functionalities Using a Single Control

It is recommended to use a dedicated control for each functionality and in particular for critical functions, even at the expense of more buttons and menus. When a single control performs multiple operations, it requires a complex menu structure and choice of modes, which increases the likelihood of mode errors and other usability problems.

Unfortunately, there is a design trade-off between simplicity in appearance and simplicity in use. This is a dangerous design trap. Alas, consumers (and organizations) make purchase decisions based on appearance first, so this is a fundamental conflict (Norman, 2002).

Scenario 4: Invisible Entities Keep the User Informed

We know that providing the user with an unclear, ambiguous, or inconsistent representation of the system's modes and states can compromise the user's ability to diagnose and correct failures, errors, and hazards. This can happen when a system functionality allows the user to visualize information that competes or conflicts with previously displayed information in other views.

To avoid such situations, it is important for the functionality developers to communicate the system's modes and states to the user interface designer. User interfaces designers should inform the developers about all of the visible consequences related to the states and modes of the systems.

Scenario 5: Providing Error Diagnostics When Features Crash

When a feature failure occurs due for example to exception handling, the interface sometimes provides unhelpful error diagnostics to the user.

The user should be notified of the state that the system is currently in and the level of urgency with which the user must act. The system feature should help the user to recognize potential hazards and return the system from a potentially hazardous state to a safe state. Messages should be provided in a constructive and correct manner that helps restore the system to a safe state.

Scenario 6: Technical Constraints on Dynamic Interface Behavior

Particularly in Web-based transactional systems, technical and logistic constraints can severely limit dynamic behavior of the interface within a given page. It can therefore be difficult or impossible to design elements that automatically update as a result of an action elsewhere on the same page. For example, in a series of dependent drop-down lists "Country", "Province" and "City", it may be impossible to automatically update "Province" as a function of the "Country" selection.

These technical constraints against dynamism are often imposed in Web-based client-server contexts due to the dictum that the business rules must be separate from the user interface. Dynamic interface behavior can require the user interface to have a degree of intelligence that incorporates certain business rules, which conflicts with the "separate layers" dictum. The alternative is for the client to call the server more frequently to refresh the page dynamically, but architects tend to avoid this approach because of the presumed extra demand on bandwidth.

There is no easy solution to this problem. The most important principle in this situation is to analyze user needs relating to dynamism before making technology decisions that could have an impact on dynamism. Transactional systems often require considerable dynamism, whereas purely informational systems can often get by without dynamism in the user interface. If it is unacceptable for business rules to be incorporated into the client, then it might be possible to make a business case for increasing the network bandwidth so as to better support pseudo-dynamic behavior, involving more frequent page refreshes through calls to the server.

The preceding scenarios are used as an illustrative sample. In total, we have identified more than 24 scenarios. Len Bass also described a list of 26 scenarios, some of which were a source of inspiration for our work. Providing an exhaustive list of scenarios is certainly useful from the industry perspective. However, our goal for this research is to better understand and validate how software features affect usability in general, and as such our focus is to model the scenarios in terms of a cause/effect relationship. This relationship connects the quality attributes of invisible components with recognized usability factors. Section 10.5 details this perspective.

10.4 PATTERNS AS SOLUTIONS TO THE PROBLEMS DOCUMENTED AS SCENARIOS

There are different ways to document solutions for the problems described in the preceding scenarios. In our framework, we have been using design patterns (Alexander et al., 1997; Gamma et al., 1995). Since the relationship between usability and internal software properties defines the problem, it has been added into the pattern descriptions that follow. This measurement relationship is what makes a pattern a cost-effective solution. In short, if a pattern does not improve at least one of the factors described in the measurement relationship, then it is not a good pattern for the problem described in the scenario. This aspect is detailed in the next section.

In this section, we present two different types of architecture-sensitive patterns:

- Software design patterns. The aim of these design patterns is to propose software designs and architectures for building portable, modifiable, and extensible interactive systems. A classical pattern of this category is the Observer that acts as a broker between the user interface (views) and the model (Gamma et al., 1995). When the observers receive notification that the model has changed, they can update themselves. This pattern provides a basic solution to the problem described in scenario 3.

- Interaction design patterns, defined at the level of the graphical user interface. These are proven user experience patterns and solutions to common usability problems. A number of pattern languages have been developed over the last few years. Among them, the Common Ground and Amsterdam catalogues play a major role (Tidwell, 1998; Welie, 1999).

Software design patterns, widely used by software engineers, are a top-down design approach that organizes the internal structure of the software systems. Interaction design patterns, promoted by human computer interaction practitioners, are used as a bottom-up design approach for structuring the user interface. Our position is that these two categories of patterns need to be combined in order to provide an integrated design framework to problems described in our scenarios. To illustrate how these diverse patterns can be combined to provide comprehensive solutions, in the following sections we describe our five scenarios using interaction and design patterns.

Although a number of de facto standards have emerged to document patterns, we use a simple description with the following format:

- "Name" is a unique identifier.
- "Context" refers to a recurring set of situations in which the pattern applies.
- "Force": The notion of force generalizes the kinds of criteria that we use to justify designs and implementations. For example, in the study of functionality, the main force to be resolved is *efficiency* (time complexity). However, patterns deal with the larger, harder-to-measure, and conflicting sets of goals and constraints encountered in the design of every component of the interactive system.
- "Problem" refers to a set of constraints and limitations to be overcome by the pattern solution.
- "Solution" refers to a canonical design form or design rule that someone can apply to resolve these problems.
- "Resulting context" is the resulting environment, situation, or interrelated conditions.
- "Effects of invisible components on usability" which defines the relationship between the software quality attributes and usability factors.

10.4.1 Software Design Patterns

The first pattern that we have considered is the Abstract Factory pattern, which provides an interface for creating families of related or dependent objects without specifying their concrete implementations (e.g., The Toolkit class). In other words, this pattern provides the basic infrastructure for decoupling the views and the models. Given a set of related abstract classes, the Abstract Factory pattern provides a way to create instances of those abstract classes from a matched set of concrete subclasses. The Abstract Factory pattern is useful for allowing a program to work with a variety of complex external entities such as different windowing systems with similar functionality. The second pattern we implemented within our framework is the Command pattern, which complements the abstract factory by reducing the view/controller coupling.

Another pattern that complements the patterns mentioned in the last paragraph is the Working Data Visualization pattern.

Name: Working Data Visualization

(Scenario addressed: 2. Updating the Interface When the Model Changes its State)

Problems

If the user cannot see working data in different view modes so as to get a better understanding of it, and if switching between views does not change the related manipulation command, then usability will be compromised.

Context

Sometimes users want to visualize a large set of data using a different point of view, so as to better understand what they are doing and what they need to edit to improve their documents.

Forces

- Users like to gain additional insight about working data while solving problems.
- Users like to see what they are doing from different viewpoints depending on the task and solution state.
- Different users prefer different viewpoints (modes).
- Each viewpoint (mode) should have related commands to manipulate data.

Solution

Data that is being viewed should be separate from the data view description, so that the same data can be viewed in different ways according to the different view descriptions. The user gets the data and commands according to the user-selected view description.

Effects of invisible components on usability

Effect 1

- Quality attributes of invisible components: Integrity
- Usability factors affected: Visual consistency

Other relevant patterns we used include Event Handler, Complete Update, and Multiple Update (Sandu, 2001). We use them to notify and update views (scenario 1) using traditional design patterns such as Observer and Abstract Factory. We incorporated these patterns into the Subform pattern that groups the different views in the same container, called the Form (Table 10.1). The Event Handler, Complete Update, and Multiple Update patterns can be applied in two phases. The first phase changes the states of the user interface models in response to end-user events generated by the visual components, and the second phase updates the visual components to reflect the changes in the user interface model. Since the update phase immediately follows the handling phase, the user interface always reflects the latest changes.

Table 10.1 Example of design patterns

Pattern	Problem	Solution
Event Handler	How should an invisible component handle an event notification message from its observable visual components?	Create and register a handler method for each event from observable visual components.
Complete Update	How to implement behavior in the user interface to update the (observer) visual component from the model	Assume all (observer) visual components are out-of-date and update everything.
Multiple Update	How to implement changes in the model of subform to reflect parent of subform, child of subform, siblings of subform	Each subform should notify its parent when it changes the model. The parent should react to changes in the subform via the Event Handler and update its children components via Complete Update.
Subform	How to design parts of user interfaces to operate on the model in a consistent manner	Groups the components that operate on the same model aspect into subforms

The next example of software design patterns we propose is the Reduce Risk of Errors pattern.

Name: Reduce Risk of Errors

(Scenarios addressed: 2. Updating the Interface When the Model Changes Its State; 4. Invisible Entities Keep the User Informed)

Problem

How can we reduce the likelihood of accidents arising from hazardous states?

Forces

- Hazardous states exist for all safety-critical systems; it is often too complex and costly to find every hazardous state by modeling all system states and user tasks;
- Risk can be effectively reduced by reducing the consequence of error rather than its likelihood;
- When a hazardous state follows a non-hazardous state, it may be possible to return to a non-hazardous state by applying some kind of recovery operation.

Solution

Enable users to recover from hazardous actions they have performed. Recovering a task is similar to undoing it, but promises to return the system to a state that is essentially identical to the one prior to the incorrect action. This pattern may be useful for providing a Recover operation giving a fast, reliable mechanism to return to the initial state. Recovering a task undoes as much of the task as is necessary (and possible) to return the system to a safe state.

Resulting Context

After applying this pattern, it should be possible for users to recover from some of their hazardous actions. Other patterns can be used to facilitate recovery by breaking tasks into substeps, each of which may be more easily recovered than the original task. The user should be informed of what the previous state is that the system will revert to.

Effects of invisible components on usability

Effect 1:

- Quality attributes of invisible components: Integrity
- Usability factors affected: Visual consistency

Effect 2:

- Quality attributes of invisible components: Suitability
- Usability factors affected: Operability

The last example of software design patterns is the Address Dynamic Presentation pattern.

Name: Dynamic presentation in user interface

(Scenarios addressed: 6. Technical constraints on dynamic interface behavior)

Problem: How can we avoid technical constraints on dynamic behavior of the user interface?

Forces

- Users benefit from immediate feedback on their actions.
- Dynamically updating fields can reduce the time required to accomplish a task.

Solutions

- Analyze user needs relating to dynamism before making technology decisions that could have an impact on dynamism. Transactional systems often require considerable dynamism.
- If it is unacceptable for business rules to be incorporated into the client, then it might be possible to make a business case for increasing the network bandwidth so as to better support pseudo-dynamic behavior, involving more frequent page refreshes through calls to the server.

Resulting Context

After applying this pattern, users will have more immediate feedback on the consequences of their actions, increasing the understandability of the user interface and reducing errors; in addition, time and effort to accomplish a task will be reduced in certain cases.

Effects of invisible components on usability

Effect 1:

- Quality attributes of invisible components: Functionality
- Usability factors affected: Understandability

Effect 2:

- Quality attributes of invisible components: Suitability
- Usability factors affected: Operability

10.4.2 Interaction Design (HCI) Patterns

Many groups have devoted themselves to the development of pattern languages. Among the heterogeneous collections of patterns, "Common Ground" and "Amsterdam" play a major role in this field and wield significant influence (Tidwell, 1998; Welie, 2000). We also adapated and use some these patterns.

The first basic HCI pattern that we used is the Progress Indicator pattern (Tidwell, 1997). It provides a solution for the time-consuming features scenario (scenario 1).

Name: Progress Indicator

(Scenario addressed: 1. Time-Consuming Functionalities)

Problem

A time-consuming functionality is in progress, the results of which are of interest to the user. How can the artifact show its current state to the user, so that the user can best understand what is happening and act on that knowledge?

Forces

- The user wants to know how long they have to wait for the process to end.
- The user wants to know that progress is actually being made, and that the process has not just "hung."
- The user wants to know how quickly progress is being made, especially if the speed varies.
- Sometimes it is impossible for the artifact to know how long the process is going to take.

Solution

Show the user a status display of some kind, indicating how far along the process is in real time. If the expected end time is known, or some other relevant quantity (such as the size of a file being downloaded), then always show what proportion of the process has been finished so far, so the user can estimate how much time is left. If no quantities are known—just that the process may take a while—then simply show some indicator that the process is ongoing.

Resulting Context

A user may expect to find a way to stop the process somewhere close to the progress indicator. It's almost as though, in the user's mind, the progress indicator acts as a proxy for the process itself.If so, put a "stop" command near the Progress Indicator if possible.

Effects of invisible components on usability

Effect 1:

- Quality attributes of invisible components: Performance
- Usability factors affected: User satisfaction

The second pattern that we integrated in our framework is the Keep the User Focused pattern, which brings an integrated solution to the problems described in scenarios 2, 3, and 4.

Name: Keep the User Focused

(Scenario addressed: 2. Updating the Interface When the Model Changes Its State; 3. Performing Multiple Functionalities Using a Single Control; 4. Invisible Entities Keep the User Informed)

Context

An application where several visual objects are manipulated, typically in drawing packages or browsing tools

Problem

How can the user quickly learn information about a specific object they see and possibly modify the object?

Forces

- Many objects/views can be visible but the user usually works on one object/view at a time.
- The user wants both an overview of the set of objects and details on attributes and available functions related to the object he or she is working on.
- The user may also want to apply a function to several objects/views.

Solution

Introduce a focus in the application. The focus always belongs to an object present in the interface. The object of focus on which the user is working determines the context of the available functionality. The focus must be visually shown to the user, for example, by changing its color or by drawing a rectangle around it. The user can change the focus by selecting another object. When an object has the focus, it becomes the target for all the functionality that is relevant for the object. Additionally, windows containing relevant functionality are activated when the focus changes. This reduces the number of actions needed to select the function and execute it for a specified object. The solution improves the performance and ease of recall.

Resulting Context

The Keep the User Focused pattern complements the software design patterns in the following situations:

- Helping users anticipate the effects of their actions, so that errors are avoided before calling the underlying features.
- Helping users notice when they have made an error (provide feedback about actions and the state of the system).
- Providing time to recover from errors.
- Providing feedback once the recovery has taken place.

Effects of invisible components on usability
Effect 1:

- Quality attributes of invisible components: Integrity.
- Usability factors affected: Visual consistency.

Effect 2:

- Quality attributes of invisible components: Functionality.
- Usability factors affected: Understandability.

Effect 3:

- Usability factors affected: Operability.
- Quality attributes of invisible components: Suitability.

There is not a one-to-one mapping between software design patterns and HCI patterns. The problems described in a specific scenario can require any number of HCI and software design patterns, and each pattern may be affected by a number of problems described in different scenarios. In our approach, we argue that using even a few patterns can be very valuable, even without an entire pattern language.

Our list of patterns is not intended to be exhaustive. We still are considering some of the existing patterns (Newman et al., 1995; Buschmann et al., 1996). However, most of the existing patterns have not originally been proposed to cope with the problem we are addressing. We are therefore adapting them as we did with the ones we introduced in this section.

10.5 MODELING CAUSE-EFFECT RELATIONSHIPS BETWEEN SOFTWARE ELEMENTS AND USABILITY

In Sections 10.3 and 10.4, we focused on specific ways in which internal software properties can have an impact on usability criteria. In this section, we attempt to provide a more general, theoretical framework for the relationships between usability and invisible software attributes. In particular, among the huge or potentially infinite number of ways that invisible components can affect usability, we wish to understand whether there are specific places where we are more likely to find these relationships or effects. We also wish to know whether there is any structure underlying these relationships, which would allow us to define a taxonomy of how usability issues arise from invisible components.

10.5.1 Traditional Model of Relationship Between Invisible Software Elements and Usability

Usability is often thought of as a modular tree-shaped hierarchy of usability concepts, rooted in the level of GUI objects, and abstracting progressively up to low-level usability criteria or measures and then high-level usability factors. Figure 10.2 illustrates this definition of usability and its relationship to parallel "towers" of other software attributes.

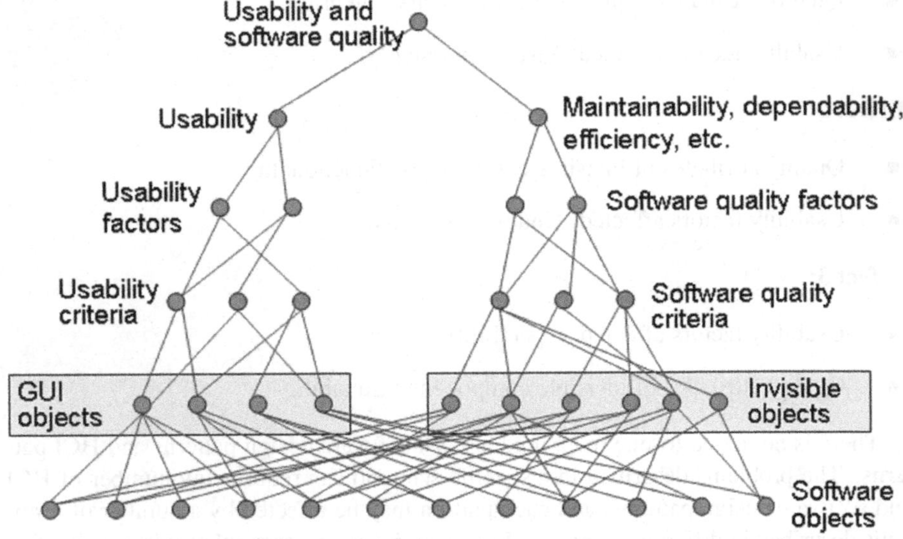

Figure 10.2 Traditional "twin towers" model of usability and other software quality factors

Table 10.2 provides more detailed information on the software quality factors and criteria referred to schematically in the right-hand branch of Figure 10.2. (In principle, each quality factor would form a separate branch.) In our work, we have adopted the software quality model proposed by ISO 9126. Table 10.2 is an overview of the consolidated framework we have been using (Abran, 2003, 2003). The details of this framework are outside the scope of this paper. The table shows the criteria for measuring usability as well as five other software quality factors including functionality, reliability, efficiency, maintainability, and portability. This measurement framework automatically inherits all the metrics and data that are normally used for quantifying a given factor. The framework helps us to determine the required metrics for (1) quantifying the quality factors of an invisible software entity, (2) quantifying the usability attributes, and (3) defining the relationships between them.

Table 10.2 A partial vision of the consolidated ISO 9126 measurement framework

Software quality factor	Measurement criteria
Functionality	Suitability Accuracy Interoperability Security
Reliability	Maturity Fault tolerance Recoverability
Usability	Understandability Learnability Operability Attractiveness
Efficiency	Time behavior Resource Utilization
Maintainability	Analyzability Changeability Stability Testability
Portability	Adaptability Instability Coexistence Replaceability

10.5.2 Taxonomy of Usability Issues Arising from Invisible Components

Relationships between software attributes of invisible components and usability factors have two properties:

1. They are lateral relationships between the modules of usability and architecture.
2. They are hierarchical relationships between two or more levels of description, since usability properties are a higher-level abstraction based on architectural elements.

Thus, to understand the relationship, we need an approach that takes into account both modularity and hierarchy. In "The Architecture of Complexity" (1962), Herbert Simon discusses "nearly decomposable systems." In hierarchic systems, interactions can be divided into two general categories: those among subsystems, and those within subsystems. We can describe a system as being decomposable into its subsystems. However, as a more refined approximation, it is possible to speak of a system being "nearly decomposable", meaning that there are in fact interactions between the subsystems, and that these interactions are weak but non-negligible.

Nearly decomposable systems have two properties:

1. Modularity: In the short-run, the behavior of each subsystem is approximately independent of the other subsystems;

2. Hierarchy (or aggregation): In the long run, the behavior of any one subsystem depends in only an aggregate way on the other subsystems.

These properties indicate that in reality, the traditional model of usability is an over-simplification. Although the usability subsystem is fundamentally modular from the architecture, Simon's principle of nearly decomposable systems predicts that it is possible for usability properties to be affected to some degree by architectural properties. Figure 10.3 illustrates an interpretation of this alternative model of usability.

In Figure 10.3, a node (usability property) at any level of usability can potentially be influenced by nodes at any lower level of architecture, or conceivably even by combinations of several different levels of architecture. Figure 10.3 is a first approximation. Simon's second principle of near-decomposability states that subsystems depend in only an aggregate way on other subsystems.

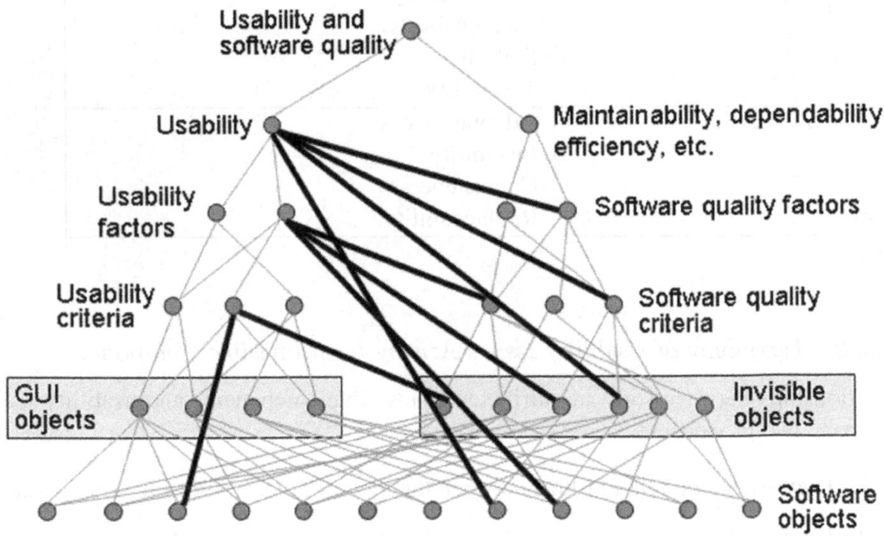

Figure 10.3 Revised model of usability, including possible types of cross-relationships with architecture (bold links)

This principle implies that if architecture has an effect on usability, it will tend to be in an aggregate way and therefore at a higher level of architecture, rather than through the effect of an individual low-level architectural component. We interpret this principle to mean that the effects of architecture on usability will tend to propagate from levels of architecture that are closer to the level of usability, rather than farther away.

Therefore to refine the model, we will assume that the most likely relationships occur between usability properties and the immediately closest lower architectural level, and that more distant architectural levels have an exponentially decreasing probability of having an effect on usability. The revised model, based on this assumption, is illustrated in Figure 10.4. This model reflects a more clearly recursive definition of usability.

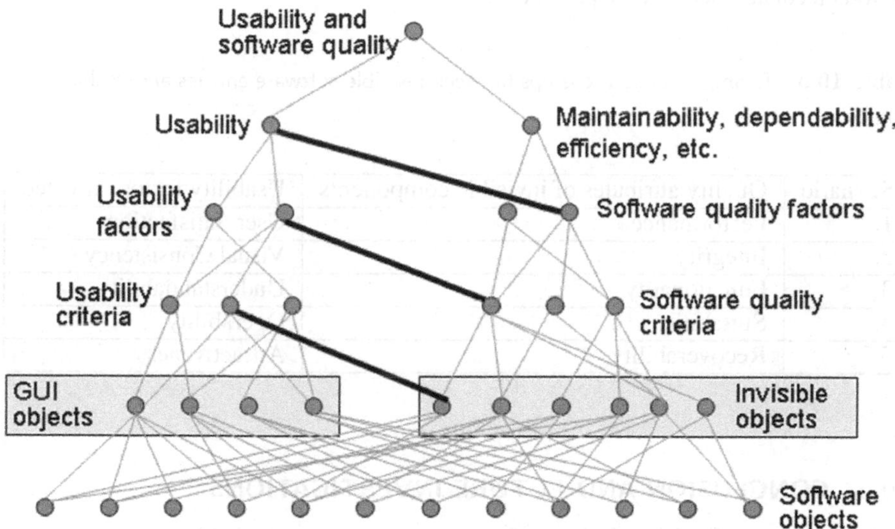

Figure 10.4 Most probable types of cross-relationships between usability and architecture (bold links)

Based on Simon's principles of nearly decomposable systems, we can conclude that these types of relationships between architecture and usability are the exception to the rule, but frequent enough that they should not be neglected.

10.5.3 Application

This measurement model provides a framework within which to explore these exceptional ways that architecture can affect usability, so as to work toward a more complete model of usability. The model is useful because it helps us know where to look for relationships between architecture and usability. Further progress will require detailing the hierarchies on both sides of the tree, and considering each possible relationship between nodes at proximate levels. Another goal will be to provide other heuristic principles to further narrow down the likely interrelationships between these two branches.

Table 10.3 provides examples of the specific types of relationships that occur in the scenarios described in section 10.2. The second column refers to the invisible object's properties and software qualities identified in the right-hand branch of figures 10.2 through 10.4, and the third column represents the usability properties identified in the left-hand branch of those figures.

For example, scenario 1 can be modeled as a relationship that connects the performance of the software feature with certain usability attributes such as user satisfaction. It can lead to the following requirement related to scenario 1: "To ensure an 80% level of satisfaction, the maximum acceptable response time of all the underlying related features should not exceed 10 seconds; if not the user should be informed and a continuous feedback needs to be provided".

Table 10.3 Examples of relationships between invisible software entities and usability factors

Scenario	Quality attributes of invisible components	Usability factors affected
1.	Performance	User Satisfaction
2.	Integrity	Visual Consistency
3.	Functionality	Understandability
4.	Suitability	Operability
5.	Recoverability	Attractiveness

10.6 CONCLUSION AND FUTURE INVESTIGATIONS

In this paper, we first identified specific scenarios as to how invisible software components can have an effect on the usability of the interactive system. Then, we provided a list of patterns that solved the problems described in the scenarios. This research effort can benefit software architecture designers and developers, who can use our approach in two different ways. First, the scenarios can serve as a checklist to determine whether important usability features (external attributes) have been considered in the design of the features and the related UI components. Second, the patterns can help the designer incorporate some of the usability concerns in the design.

More than defining a list of scenarios and patterns that describe the effects of invisible software attributes on software usability, our long-term objective is to build and validate a comprehensive framework for identifying scenarios. The goal of the framework is to define these patterns as a relationship between software quality factors and usability factors. In this paper, we have suggested different HCI and software design patterns as solutions to the problems described in these scenarios and in similar ones. Every pattern has a set of problems to be solved and a set of goals to be achieved.

We expect that as we gain a better understanding of the relationship between interaction design patterns and software architecture patterns, this knowledge will affect the evolution of standards in architecture design and GUI software libraries. In fact, this has already started. Increasingly, developers are making proper use of standard

GUI libraries and respecting interface design guidelines in a way that considerably increases the usability of interactive applications. However, more can be done in this direction, and the approach we have outlined in this paper is an attempt to build a better and more systematic understanding of how usability and software architecture can be integrated.

References

Abran, A., Khelifi, A., Suryn, W., and Seffah, A. (2003). Usability meanings and interpretations in ISO standards. *Software Quality Journal*, 11(4):325–338.

Alexander, C., Ishikawa, S., Silverstein, M., Jacobson, M., Fiskdahl-King, I., and Angel, S. (1997). *A Pattern Language*. London: Oxford University Press.

Bass, L., Clements, P., and Kazman, R. (1998). *Software Architecture in Practice*. Reading: MA: Addison-Wesley.

Bass, L. and John, B. E. (2001). Supporting usability through software architecture. *Computer*, 34(10):113–115.

Buschmann, F., Meunier, R., Rohnert, H., Sommerlad, P., and Stal, M. (1996). *Pattern-Oriented Software Architecture: A System of Patterns.*, Volume 1. New York: Wiley.

Carroll, J. (2000). *Scenario-Based Design of Human-Computer Interactions*. MIT Press.

Folmer, E. and Bosch, J. (2004). Architecting for usability. *Journal of Systems and Software*, 70(1):61–78.

Gamma, E., Helm, R., Johnson, R., and Vlissides, J. (1995). *Design Patterns: Elements of Reusable Object-Oriented Software*. Addison-Wesley Professional Computing Series. Reading, MA: Addison-Wesley. http://www.aw.com.

Kazman, R. and Bass, L. (2002). Making architecture reviews work in the real world. *IEEE Software*, 19(1):67–73.

Kazman, R., Carrière, S. J, and Woods, S. G. (2000). Toward a discipline of scenario-based architectural engineering *Annals of Software Engineering*, 9(1):5–33.

Newman, W. and Lamming, M. (1995). *Interactive System Design*. Addison-Wesley, Reading: MA.

Norman, D. (2002). Beyond the computer industry. *Commun. ACM*, 45(7):120.

Raskin, J. (2000). *Human Interface: New Directions for Designing Interactive Systems*. Addison-Wesley, Reading: MA.

Sandu, D. (2001). User interface patterns. In 8th *Conference on Pattern Languages of Programs*, Park Monticello, IL, USA.

Simon, H. (1962). The architecture of complexity. *Proceedings of the American Philosophical Society*, 106:467–482.

Tidwell, J. (1998). Common ground: A pattern language for human-computer interface design [online]. Technical report, `http://www.mit.edu/~jtidwell/common_ground.html`.

Welie, M. (1999). Patterns in Interaction Design: The Amsterdam Collection. http://www.welie.com/index.html.

11 TOWARD A REFINED PARADIGM FOR ARCHITECTING USABLE SYSTEMS

Tamer Rafla, Michel C. Desmarais, and Pierre N. Robillard

École Polytechnique de Montréal,
P.O. Box 6079, Station Center-Ville, Montreal, QC, H3C 3A7, Canada

Abstract. Recent investigation reveals that few usability enhancements can be easily incorporated into the existing design as they are only related to the design of UI; but many of which may be prohibively expensive. A more recent perspective on the usability of software systems is that making software more usable is a lot easier to do if the high-level architecture was designed with usability in mind. Hence, software architects should ponder usability before usability professionals are brought into the project, more specifically during the elicitation of functional requirements. Unfortunately, there is a scarcity of methods and guidelines with the scope to ensure that software developing corporations consider usability requirements in their architectural design activities. This chapter addresses this need and provides a more developed approach for architecting usable systems. A non-formal exercise reveals that this proposed methodology was well-received by participants with different knowledge of usability. They found the process not too onerous as it guided them in discerning the concerns that could have a real impact on the architecture.

11.1 INTRODUCTION

Usability is perceived by many to be a concept associated with the design of the user interface (UI) and has received little attention from software architects. In fact, the history of UI and software architecture has been marked by the decoupling of the two disciplines, on the basis that the UI can be changed in any way and at any time without affecting the software architecture. Classic concepts such as MVC (model-view-controller) (Goldberg and Robson, 1983) and UIMS (User Interface Management Systems) (Pfaff, 1985), as well as the more recent trend toward user interface markup languages (UIML) (Phanouriou , 2000) all accept the implicit assumption that the UI and the software architecture can evolve independently during the software development lifecycle.

However, this is not always the reality as some usability requirements may arise later in the development cycle, necessitating costly architectural changes. We recently presented a case study that involved quantifying and analyzing the impact of the late implementation of usability requirement changes on the architecture (Rafla et al., 2004, 2006). The impact of such changes could have been reduced, or even avoided, if those usability requirements had been defined and considered prior to the architectural design phase. The most cost-effective way of ensuring the usability of software systems is to consider the integration of usability into the initial discussion of quality requirements.

Bass and John (2003) and Folmer and Bosch (2004) proposed a relatively different approach to identify the connection between usability and software architecture. Unfortunately, their work is theoretical and high-level, and no significant investigation of their application has been presented. Little is known yet as to how to capture and organize the usability requirements that are architecturally significant. Information technology (IT) organizations will face numerous obstacles when trying to implement these frameworks in their existing software processes. The questions that need to be addressed are: (i) Which of these approaches should be used in practice? (ii) Can they be combined to facilitate the integration of usability practices into software development? (iii) What are the necessary tools and guidelines to ensure a seamless integration of these usability engineering best practices into the current software development activities?

This chapter is structured as follows. We begin by presenting an overview of Bass and John's and Folmer's models to then discuss the need and the motivation behind combining their work. We present a non-formal exercise to discuss the utility of the proposed paradigm and then show how software process practices can be adapted to include the newly presented usability method.

11.2 AN OVERVIEW OF PREVIOUS WORK

11.2.1 Usability-Driven Software Architecture Patterns

Bass and his colleagues (2003) at the Software Engineering Institute (SEI) initiated the idea of linking usability to software architecture. Using fieldwork observations of software development projects, they generated scenarios that expressed a set of general usability issues that have potential architectural implications. They also provided corresponding architectural patterns for implementing every scenario.

For example, Table 1, illustrating the *canceling commands* scenario, describes the circumstances under which a user might need to cancel an operation. Being independent from the design of the UI, if this requirement is not devised when the software architecture is established, it may be costly to incorporate afterwards.

Table 11.1 Canceling commands (Bass and John, 2003)

Canceling commands
A user invokes an operation, and then no longer wished the operation to be performed. Systems should allow users to cancel operations.

11.2.2 Architecturally-oriented Usability Patterns

In their investigation of the relationship between usability and software architecture, Folmer et al. (2004) defined a three-layer model that links general usability requirements to more specific usability patterns. They started with attributes that typically define usability, gradually refining this definition until they arrived at usability properties (similar to usability requirements) and finally linking those properties to architecturally sensitive usability patterns. The three layers defined, shown in Figure 11.1, are detailed below:

- **Usability Attributes:** This first layer incorporates a number of high-level standard usability metrics. Such attributes (ISO/IEC, 1998) are: (i) learnability—how quickly and easily users can be productive with a system that is new to them; (ii) efficiency—the number of tasks per unit time that the user can perform; (iii) reliability—the error rate in using the system and the time it takes to recover from errors; and, finally, (iv) satisfaction—the user's comfort level, a measure of his positive attitude toward the use of the system.

- **Usability Properties:** The usability properties are the design principles that have a direct bearing on system usability. These properties can guide the requirements gathering and analysis stage of a software development process (for example, providing feedback to the user, providing explicit user control, providing guidance, etc.).

- **Usability Patterns:** The architecturally sensitive usability patterns present a high-level response to a need specified by a usability property (Ferre et al., 2003; Folmer and Bosch, 2004). They do not provide any specific software solution to be incorporated into software architecture; they only suggest some abstract mechanism that could be used to improve usability.

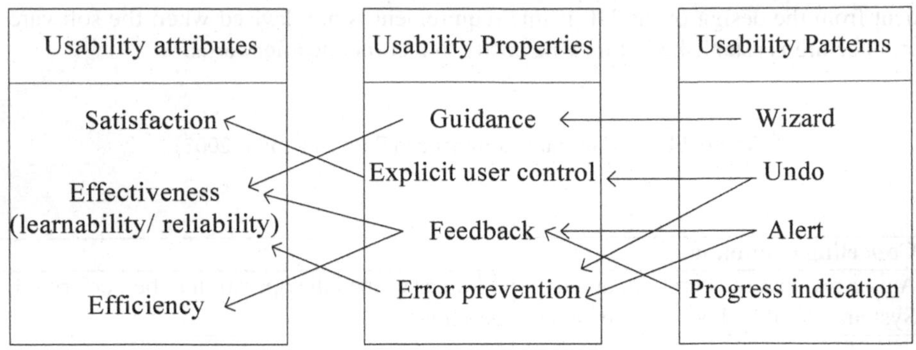

Figure 11.1 Three usability layers of Folmer's framework

11.3 USABILITY AT THE REQUIREMENTS DEFINITION STAGE

11.3.1 Motivation

We recently presented work that consisted of quantifying the impact of the late implementation of some of Bass's usability scenarios into an existing architecture (Rafla et al., 2006). The architecture of a working Web system was analyzed to note the usability concerns that need to be addressed in order to make the application more usable. The ones that will inevitably increase the usability of our system were extracted.

This study suggested that these architecturally significant usability scenarios are very high-level and are common to many interactive systems. It proved hard to find the applicable ones as they are not related to the domain functionality of any system. The next section discusses how Bass's usability scenarios can be used in conjunction with Folmer's usability properties to facilitate the elicitation of the usability requirements process.

11.3.2 Capturing Architecturally-relevant Usability Requirements

A Three-Step Brainstorming Session. The purpose of this usability requirements brainstorming session is to identify the high-level tasks that the users are expected to accomplish with the system. End-users may have no clear idea of their usability requirements and therefore ought to be involved to a small extent in the usability requirements gathering process. It is our conjecture that usability analysts should be at the heart of that process and should ensure that the usability concerns identified by the end-users are realistic and feasible.

In the first step, usability analysts detail Folmer's usability properties to the users and provide them with general examples that reflect every usability property. Since those properties are very high-level, stakeholders are asked to sketch their own usability requirements in light of these more general ones. The process is the following: Users read the entire description of the property (which consists of a brief explanation of the feature and a general example), and provide a user task related to the system being developed. Once the usability analysts confirm that this example is valid and applicable to the system being developed, users are then asked to document this example in detail, or provide other examples that they see as more relevant. This process is conducted for all of the properties, which ensures that they are completely understood by the users and that clear usability requirements are captured.

In the second step of the requirements generation phase, users are familiarized with Bass's usability scenarios. As the description of each scenario is fairly short (two to four lines), usability analysts read every scenario out loud and provide a general example that would fulfill each one. Providing examples to users is fundamental, as some of the scenarios are not self-explanatory and not related to the domain functionality of any system. While usability analysts go through the list of scenarios, users identify the ones they feel are relevant to their system and write down a concrete example to ensure that the scenarios are correctly grasped. The scenarios they have trouble understanding are also recorded. This small exercise is conducted until all of the scenarios are understood and the ones that are likely to increase the usability of the system are extracted.

Once the scenarios from the previous steps are consolidated and prioritized, usability analysts examine the list of usability requirements and go into greater detail about the requirement by defining use cases that include the interaction required between the actor(s) and the system (Artim, 1997; Seffah and Hayne, 1999; Seffah et al., 2005). The defined use cases are used to understand and reason about usability requirements, and they represent a high-level understanding of the user interface. The process of writing use cases that correspond to existing high-level tasks can prove useful in forcing consideration of error conditions and failure modes. Having to supply pre- and post-conditions for each use case forces usability analysts to think more logically about the usability requirements and goals of the user.

Reflection. As users may have a fuzzy understanding of usability in general, and also of the system being developed, this two-step usability brainstorming session can provide them with a basis for documenting their usability requirements. First, it would help them focus on building the required understanding of a system they will use (Folmer's usability properties), and second, it will develop their tacit knowledge, which they cannot verbalize or describe due to their lack of experience (Bass's usability scenarios). Presenting the usability properties at the initial stages of the requirements generation phase helps users expand their comprehension of the system and guides them in uncovering the usability issues that could impact their performance and productivity. This practice serves two purposes: it helps users get a clearer image of the system, and it presents high-level usability features. The latter could help users lacking an understanding of usability to widen their usability perspective.

Some usability properties provide an overview of the important usability issues that need to be considered before the software architecture is devised. However, sometimes users may not be able to capture usability requirements due to their lack of familiarity with software usability. The purpose of the scenarios is to present them with specific usability concerns that have architectural implications. This helps develop users' tacit knowledge of usability and allows them to define requirements that might have been disregarded in the first step of the brainstorming session. It is a step that would also be helpful for users who have an above-average understanding of usability and wish to further develop their tacit knowledge and define more detailed requirements. Hence, considering the usability properties along with the usability scenarios allows the complete coverage of major usability requirements and ensures that architecturally relevant usability specifications are identified, documented, and organized prior to architectural design.

Informal Empirical Investigation. An empirical study is conducted to evaluate the benefits and utility of providing usability scenarios once the usability properties have been considered. This study required the participants to capture and define the usability requirements for an existing Web system implemented by a team of software engineering students at Ecole Polytechnique de Montreal.

Six graduate computer engineering students participated in this exercise. Three of those participants had successfully taken a 45 hour course on human-computer interaction and a 39 hour course on Web usability. Also, one of them had working experience with the system in one of his software engineering classes. These participants are referred to here as the *Experienced* (EXP) team. The other three participants, who had never been exposed to usability or interface development, are referred to as the *InExperienced* (InEXP) team. The reason we grouped the participants into different teams according to their understanding of usability was to determine whether or not the users' understanding of usability and experience has an impact on our proposed usability requirements brainstorming workshop. At the start, the participants were given the functional requirements of the system and were asked to study them to acquire a comprehensive knowledge of the system. The participants were then given a list of all nine usability properties identified by Folmer and his team, with the following aspects provided for each property. Table 2 illustrates the *error management* property as an example.

After having thoroughly examined the list of usability properties, participants formulate usability requirements and associate them with usability properties. More specifically, they were asked to instantiate the properties in the Web system. For example, one of the participants identified the need to provide a mechanism for end-users to retrieve forgotten passwords without external assistance. This usability requirement can be associated with the *explicit user control* property. After having identified their requirements, Bass's list of usability scenarios was provided to them. They were then asked to select the ones that would apply to the system.

Four of the six participants, three from InEXP and one from EXP, found that the usability properties provided a solid basis for the identification of their usability needs and guided them in formulating complete requirements. The other two participants, both from the EXP team, found the properties too high-level, and that more explanations and/or examples should have been provided. However, all six participants found that the usability scenarios concretely covered a large number of important usability requirements. They found them to be rather precise and that it was not difficult to see their relevance to the Web system. Overall, all the participants found the idea of providing the usability properties before the scenarios are created very helpful, as it allows them to acquire a general high-level idea of user needs before setting out their

Table 11.2 Providing feedback property (Folmer et al., 2003)

Error management	
Intent:	The system should prove a way to manage user errors. This can be done in two ways: ▪ By preventing errors from happening, so users can make no or less mistakes. ▪ By providing an error mechanism, so that errors made by users can be corrected.
Usability attributes affected:	*Reliability* (+): error management increases reliability because users make fewer mistakes. *Efficiency* (+): efficiency is increased because it takes less time to recover from errors.
Example:	Red underline for a syntax error in Eclipse (a popular Java development environment)

own requirements. It helped the InEXP team gain additional knowledge of the usability aspects that might impact the system. The scenarios helped in the refinement of some of the requirements already formulated, as well as in the discovery of new ones that might have been neglected when working with the usability properties. The participants were also asked if they had selected usability scenarios that were not explicitly captured in the usability properties. Our observations are summarized in Table 3 but the complete analysis of the results can be found in Rafla et al. (2007).

Limitations of this Work. Several of the usability properties, those extracted from Folmer's work, are somewhat high-level and the list is in no way exhaustive. Also, some of those usability features need a good deal of interpretation that end-users might not be capable of providing. They would, for example, require expertise to understand and apply to the design, and this might be too much to ask of those users. This point can be taken care of by ensuring that technically strong usability analysts, preferably experienced software architects with sound knowledge of usability, drive the usability requirements brainstorming session. Unfortunately, as the link between usability and software architecture has only recently been discovered, few software professionals have the required knowledge and proficiency to lead such a usability requirements generation session.

11.4 USABILITY-CENTERED SOFTWARE DEVELOPMENT PROCESS

This section discusses how usability concerns can be considered in a software process and how architecturally sensitive usability requirements can be taken into account in

Table 11.3 Summary of observations

	Usability Properties (9)	Usability Scenarios (27)	Properties vs. Scenarios
EXP-erienced	6 The only participant who had already worked with the system covered explicit user control.	21	
InEXP-erienced	3 The following five properties were not covered by these participants: + Consistency + Guidance + Minimize cognitive load + Explicit user control + Natural mapping ▪ Examples provided with the properties were very helpful. ▪ More examples should be presented and categorized by the type of application to which they belong.	14 The following properties were confusing: + Supporting comprehensive searching + Operating consistently across views The following properties depicted the same usability feature: 1. Supporting visualization 2. Making views accessible	Did the scenarios cover usability aspects that were neglected by the usability properties? Error management Checking for correctness √ Guidance Proving good help √ Accessibility Supporting Internationalization √

the construction of the initial draft of the architecture. More specifically, the previously defined usability requirements brainstorming session will be introduced as an activity in the requirements phase of a development process.

The requirements discipline, an integral part of a software development process, is concerned with understanding the proposed solution to facilitate the design and implementation of appropriate software systems. It consists of three activities: Understanding the users' needs by finding actors and writing use cases, defining the system by structuring and documenting the use cases and finally reviewing the requirements

(Figure 11.2). The gathering of usability requirements is conducted concurrently with eliciting the stakeholder requests, and is part of the *understand the users' needs* workflow.

The introduction of the brainstorming session to this workflow adds a new role, which is that of the usability analyst who is responsible for incorporating the user-centered methodology and guiding stakeholders in eliciting their usability requirements. The usability requirements are recorded into the supplementary specifications artifacts of this generic software process model. The improved supplementary specifications and the use case model in combination capture a complete set of the system's functional and quality requirements.

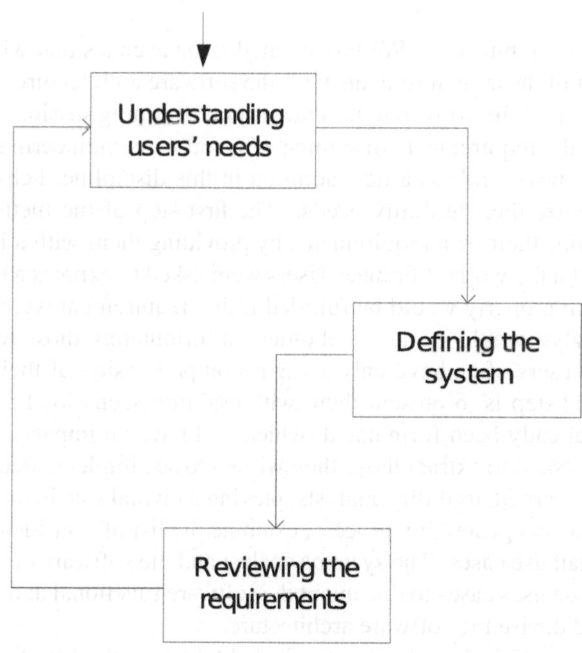

Figure 11.2 The requirements elicitation workflow

The new role of usability analyst is depicted in Figure 11.3. The usability analyst works in close collaboration with stakeholders and users to identify the usability components that are relevant in the system. The result of the elicitation process is a list of usability specifications with assigned priority levels. This information is recorded as architecturally relevant usability requirements, which can be a part of the supplementary specifications artifact.

11.5 CONCLUSION

The later the changes are made to the system, the more expensive they are to implement, as certain architectural solutions may hamper usability requirements. Therefore, usability should be qualified early in the development of a system to support the de-

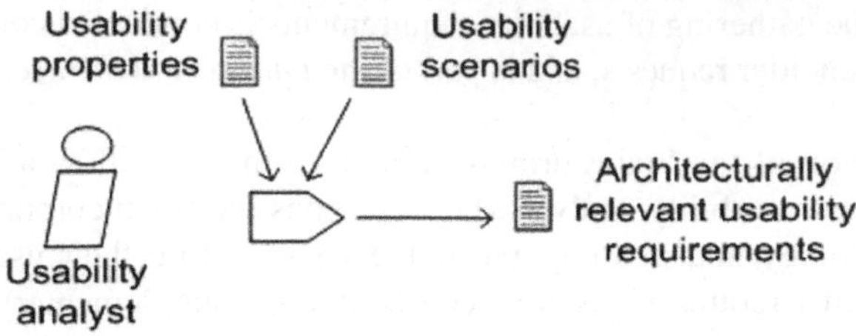

Figure 11.3 Extra activity in "understanding users' needs" workflow detail

sign of a satisfying architecture. We investigated some avenues that will facilitate the proper alignment of those requirements with the software architecture.

We proposed a usability-driven requirements brainstorming session that is modeled as an activity in the requirements discipline of a software engineering process. The usability analyst, whose role is a new addition in this discipline, helps stakeholders define and formalize their usability needs. The first step of the method consists in helping users define their own requirements by providing them with a list of usability properties based on the work of Folmer. Users were asked to express a requirement by underlining which property would be fulfilled if that requirement were implemented. The usability analyst would guide stakeholders in formulating those requirements as scenarios. Since users often have only a vague comprehension of their own requirements, the second step is to present them with usability scenarios from the work of Bass, that have already been formulated, which will have an impact on the architecture. Users were asked to extract those they wished to see implemented. Once similar requirements are merged, usability analysts, playing a pivotal role in the success of the usability requirements generation process, examine the list of user identified usability concerns and detail use cases. The systems analyst and the software designer will subsequently use those uses cases to document the software functional and non-functional requirements and devise the software architecture.

A preliminary empirical study was conducted to assess the benefits and utility of this workshop. Participants found the usability properties useful, as they provided them with a guide in articulating their usability requirements. Also, they found the usability scenarios offered an adequate level of detail, as they provided them with concrete examples of usability requirements.

References

Artim, J. M. (1997). Integrating user interface design and object-oriented development through task analysis and use cases. *ACM SIG CHI Bulletin*, 30(4).

Bass, L. and John, B. E. (2003). Linking usability to software architecture patterns through general scenarios. *Journal of Systems and Software*, 66(3):187–197.

Ferre, X., Jursito, N., Moreno, A. M., and Sanchez, M. I. (2003). A software architectural view of usability patterns. In 2nd *Workshop on Software and Usability Cross-Pollination: The Role of Usability Patterns (Interact)*, Zurich, Switzerland.

Folmer, E. and Bosch, J. (2004). Architecting for usability. *Journal of Systems and Software*, 70(1):61–78.

Folmer, E., van Gurp, J., and Bosch, J. (2003). Investigating the relationship between software architecture and usability. In *Software Process - Improvement & Practice: Special Issue on Bridging the Process and Practice Gaps between Software Engineering and Human Computer Interaction.*

Goldberg, A. and Robson, D. (1983). *Smalltalk-80: The Language and its Implementation.* Reading, MA: Addison-Wesley.

ISO/IEC (1998). *ISO/IEC 9241-11: Ergonomic requirements for office work with visual display terminals (VDT)s—Part 11 Guidance on usability.* ISO/IEC 9241-11: 1998 (E).

Pfaff, G., editor (1985). *User Interface Management Systems.* Springer-Verlag, New York. Proceedings of the IFIP/EG Workshop on User Interface Management Systems, Seeheim, FRG, Oct. 1983.

Phanouriou, C. (2000). *UIML: A Device-Independent User Interface Markup Language.* Ph.D. thesis, Vermont University.

Rafla, T., Oketokoun, R., Wiklik, A., Desmarais, M. C., and Robillard, P. N. (2004). Accommodating usability-driven changes in existing software architecture. In *IASTED 8th International Conference on Software Engineering and Applications (SEA)*, pages 150–154, Cambridge, MA.

Rafla, T., Robillard, P. N., and Desmarais, M. C. (2006). Investigating the impact of usability on software architecture through scenarios: A case study on Web systems. *Journal of Systems and Software*, 79(3):415–426.

Rafla, T., Robillard, P. N., and Desmarais, M. C. (2007). A method to elicit architecturally sensitive usability requirements: its integration into a software development process. *Software Quality Journal.*

Seffah, A., Gulliksen, J., and Desmarais, M. C., editors (2005). *Human-Centered Software Engineering: Integrating Usability in the Development Process.* New York: Springer.

Seffah, A. and Hayne, C. (1999). Integrating human factors into use cases and object-oriented methods. *Lecture Notes in Computer Science*, 1743:240–250.

12 TRACE-BASED USABILITY EVALUATION USING ASPECT-ORIENTED PROGRAMMING AND AGENT-BASED SOFTWARE ARCHITECTURE

Jean-Claude Tarby*, Houcine Ezzedine**, and Christophe Kolski**

*Laboratoire LIFL-Trigone, University of Lille 1,
F-59655 Villeneuve d'Ascq Cedex, France
**2 LAMIH – UMR8530, University of Valenciennes and Hainaut-Cambrésis,
Le Mont Houy, F-59313 Valenciennes Cedex 9, France
{houcine.ezzedine, christophe.kolski}@univ-valenciennes.fr

Abstract. To evaluate how people use interactive applications, many techniques and methods are proposed. In this chapter, we describe two innovative evaluation approaches that exploit the concept of traces as a way of capturing the usage of the system. The first approach uses Aspect-Oriented Programming; the second proposes an explicit coupling between agent-based architecture and evaluation agents. These two approaches are compared.

12.1 INTRODUCTION

Interactive system evaluation has been a very rich research and application domain since the 1970s. To evaluate how people use interactive applications, many techniques and methods can be applied; they have been the subject of numerous studies and classifications (Jacko and Sears, 2002; Jordan et al, 1996; Nielsen, 1993; Sweeney, M.,

Maguire, M., and Shackel, 1993; Whitefield et al., 1991; Wilson and Corlett, 1996) . Most of them are widely used in companies and research laboratories. New methods or variants of methods appear and are tested progressively, according to new needs and specificities coming from the emergence of information and communication sciences and technologies. Among them, automatic and semi-automatic methods and tools are considered as promising (see for instance Hilbert and Redmiles, 2000, and Ivory and Hearst, 2001), both generally and in specific application domains, such as website evaluation (Beirekdar, 2004; Ivory, 2004; Mariage et al., 2005).

In this chapter, expanding on Tarby et al. (2007), we present two complementary approaches that help to prepare the evaluation as from the early stages of a project: the objective is to couple design and evaluation by using innovative technologies and paradigms. The aim of this coupling is to produce usage-oriented traces to evaluate the utility and usability of interactive applications. The first approach uses the paradigm of aspect-oriented programming in order to integrate the mechanisms of traces into interactive applications. The notion of trace has been the subject of various studies in the HCI field (Hilbert and Redmiles, 2000). The second approach proposes an explicit coupling between the agents of an architecture based on software agents on the one hand, and evaluation agents on the other hand. In this chapter, these two approaches are first described; then they are compared using methodological criteria as well as technical ones.

12.2 FIRST APPROACH FOR EARLY USABILITY EVALUATION: INJECTION OF THE MECHANISM OF TRACES BY ASPECT-ORIENTED PROGRAMMING

In this part, we begin by presenting the basic principles of aspect-oriented programming. Then we explain how the trace mechanisms are introduced by using the concept of aspect.

12.2.1 Aspect-Oriented Programming

Aspect-Oriented Programming (AOP) originated from Xerox PARC investigations on new programming paradigms. AOP is an as an extension of Object-Oriented Programming: indeed, complementary generic mechanisms significantly come to improve the separation of concerns within the applications (Filman et al., 2005).

In a traditional approach (see Figure 12.1), the business objects manage their technical constraints locally (identification/authentication, security, transactions, data integrity). The duplication of these crosscutting elements in methods of classes leads to a phenomenon of dispersion and interlacing of the level system concerns and increases the complexity of the code. AOP allows the modularization of these elements by the addition of a new dimension of modularity, the *aspect*. The scope of the crosscutting concerns supported by AOP exceeds that of the current solutions such as the EJB.

Join point, advice, aspect, and cut point are the principal concepts introduced by AOP. A join point represents a particular location in the flow of the program instructions (beginning or end of method execution, field's read or write access, ...). An advice is a method which is activated when a precise join point is reached: the weav-

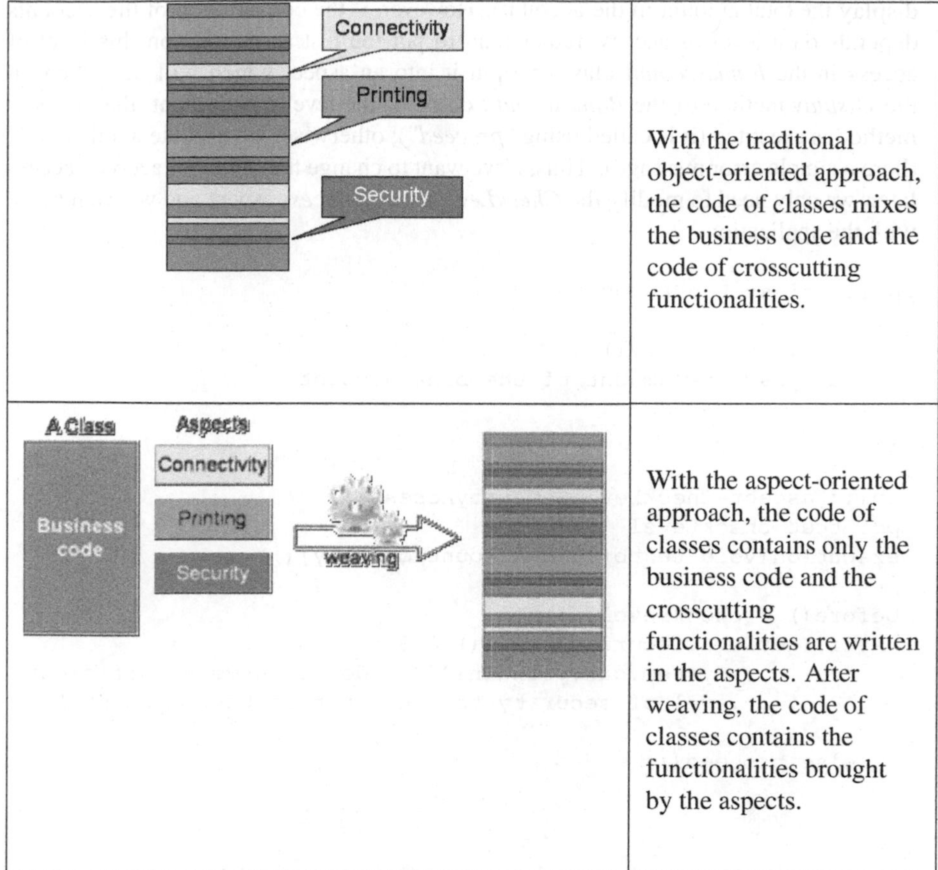

Figure 12.1 AOP basic principles compared to traditional object oriented-approach

ing mechanism inserts the advice calls in the initial code either in a static way (at compile-time) or in a dynamic way (during execution). Advice can execute before, after, or around the join point. An aspect is a module which allows the association between advices and join points by means of cut points. Cut points are used to define a set of join points at which an advice will have to activate. Furthermore, a cut point makes it possible to capture the execution context of join points. For a method call, this context includes the target object, the arguments of the method, and the reference of the returned object, all of which is most useful information when a trace mechanism is to be injected.

Based on the principle of inversion of control (IOC), AOP thus extracts the dependencies on the technical concerns from the business code by locating them in the aspects and by managing them from outside by the mechanism of weaving. It consequently becomes possible to focus on business logic.

The code below shows an example of bank account consultation. In this example, the *BankAccount* class has business methods directly associated to it (for example, to display the total amount in the account). However, if the consultation of the accounts depends on a level of access, rather than to put the test associated on this level of access in the *BankAccount* class, we put it into an aspect which will be woven on the *Display* method of the *BankAccount* class. If the level is sufficient, the business method is executed (it is called using "*proceed*"); otherwise, we execute another code (here a simple error message). Thus, if we want to change the policy of account access later, we only need to modify the *CheckLevelSecurityAccess* aspect and weave it again with the application.

```
public class BankAccount {
...
 public void display() {
  // display the amount of the bank account
 }
...
}
public aspect CheckLevelSecurityAccess {
 pointcut checkLevel ():
 execution(void textbf{BankAccount.display}()) ;

 before() : checkLevel (s) {
    if (getLevelSecurityAccess() $<$ 5)
           { System.out.println(''You do not have a sufficient
            level of security to consult this bank account.'');
           }
    else proceed();
 }
}
```

Moreover, AOP proposes the mechanism of introduction. This mechanism allows the modification of classes, interfaces, or even of existing aspects: it is possible to inject a method or an attribute into a class, to add a relation of heritage, to specify that a class implements a new interface. A classical use of the mechanism of introduction is the implementation of design patterns (for example, the Observer pattern, Gamma et al., 1995) in classes that did not possess them before.

12.2.2 Traces by Aspects

Thanks to the principle of separation of concerns, AOP can inject trace mechanisms in existing applications (see Figure 12.2, step 1) by writing aspects (step 2) which on the one hand listen for user actions, method calls, changes in data values, etc., and on the other hand produce the traces. These aspects are then woven with the initial code (step 3) which remains intact. The code produced by weaving then contains the initial code and code of aspects (step 4). The initial application can be used in an absolutely normal manner without the aspects or be traced with them (step 5). The trace mechanism can thus be disengaged with no effect on the initial code.

Our trace technique uses a sequence of aspects and is implemented through an Eclipse plug-in that we developed. This plug-in generates two sets of files. The first set

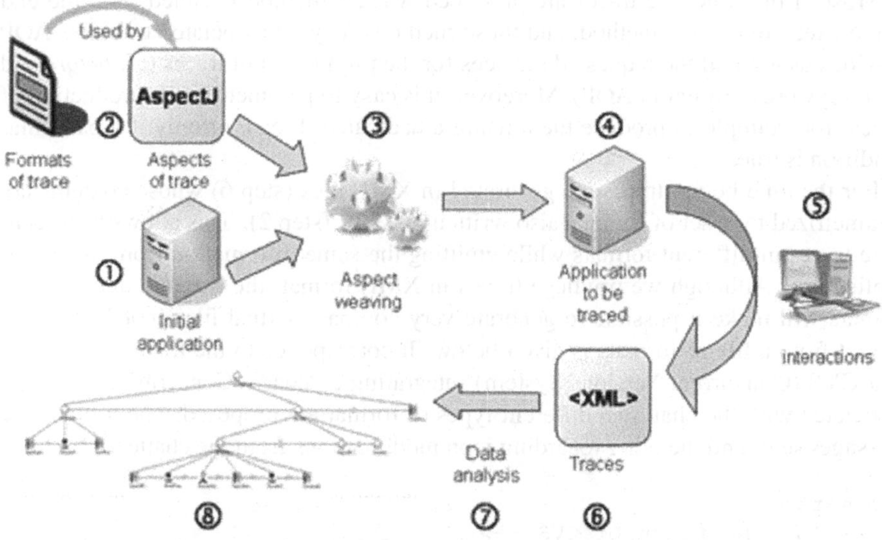

Figure 12.2 Injection of mechanism of traces by aspects

contains the aspects related to the traces which are to be recovered; the content of these aspects is thus specific to the traces to be produced. Each aspect of this set specifies the method to be traced, when the trace must be produced (mainly at the beginning or the end of the method), and the parameters to recover; at the end, after the weaving of aspects, we injected only one line of code by trace to be produced into the application. The second set of files is an invariant package, composed of files whose contents are immutable, whatever the traces are to be generated. The role of this second set is, for each trace, to intercept the execution of the line of code inserted by the first set, and to process this interception by recovering the parameters that it returns. These parameters then make it possible to generate the XML code of trace. The aspects generated by our plug-in are then woven with the initial code (step 3) which is not modified at all in its contents. The code produced by weaving then contains the initial code and the code of the aspects (step 4). The initial application can be used in an absolutely normal manner without the aspects or be traced thanks to them (step 5). The trace mechanism can thus be disengaged with no effect on the initial code.

To produce a trace, we need three types of information: data to be traced, when to produce the trace, and where to store it. Traced data mainly relate to the functional core (and consequently the associated tasks) and the user interface (actions from the user, but also displayed data, ...). For example, it is possible to trace the beginning, the end, or the interruption of a task, the opening of a window, the selection in a drop-down list, etc. Because our work is use-oriented, it is easier to trace the actions of the user when the functional core and the user interface are built from a task-oriented design method. Thus, if the application is designed with an evaluation-oriented approach as presented in Tarby (2006), it is easy to recover other data such as the context of execution of the tasks, the role of the user (in CSCW for example), etc.

Most of the time, the traces are produced when a method is called or at the end of the execution of the method, and these methods may be associated to tasks. AOP provides us with all the requested services for the production of traces (cf. *before* and *after* keywords present in AOP). Moreover, it is easy to parametrize the production of traces, for example to produce them using a dedicated thread, or only if a particular condition is true.

For the time being, traces are generated in XML files (step 6) whose contents are parametrized by a set of formats also written in XML (step 2). This allows us to generate traces in different formats while emitting the same information from the traced application. Although we privilege traces in XML format, the external definition of formats will make it possible to generate very compact textual files (not XML). An extract from a file of formats is given below. It corresponds to the tracing of the use of a CVS (Concurrent Versions System) integrating a "chat". Concerning the traces associated with the chat, two different types of format are proposed: one to trace the messages sent, and the other regarding icon modifications from the chatters.

```
<formats>
 <!-- for the trace of CVS -->
 <format name=''chat_CVS''>
  <comment>Traces of CVS chat</comment>
  <type name=''dated_message_sending''>
   <comment>Dated sending of
                        message</comment>
   <attr>sender</attr>
   <attr>receivers</attr>
   <attr>message</attr>
   <attr>time</attr>
  </type>
  <type name=''icon_change''>
   <comment>Change the icon</comment>
   <attr>new_icon</attr>
   <attr>pseudo</attr>
  </type>
 </format>
 <format name=''ftp''>
  <comment>Traces of FTP</comment>
  <type name=''upload''>
   <comment>Sending of files</comment>
   <attr>sender</attr>
   <attr>file</attr>
   <attr>time</attr>
  </type>
 </format>
</formats>
```

An extract of traces obtained during the use of the CVS is shown below:

```
<appli start="14:52:35.439" id=''CVSChat''>
```

```
<chat_CVS type=``icon_change''
                        new_icon=``Bruce Lee''
                        pseudo=``arnaud''
          />
<ftp  type=``upload''
                        sended=``arnaud''
                        file=``projet.zip''
                        time="14:56:45.23"
          />
<chat_CVS type=``dated_message_sending''
                        sended=``JC''
                        receivers=``all''
                        message=``Hello! How are u ?"
                        time="14:57:44.612"
          />
```

With our approach the exploitation of traces is facilitated because we choose the data we want to trace, as well as the format for the result, unlike approaches based on "log" files. The analysis of traces (step 7) produces statistics, task models (step 8), filtered information, etc. This side of our work is not presented in this paper. At the moment, this analysis is done after the production of traces, but we plan to perform real-time analysis in the future (for an adaptation of the application, to advise the user, etc.). Our work is similar to works such as Akşit et al. (1992), Balbo et al. ; Weber and Kindler, (2003), Ducasse et al. (2006), Egyed-Zsigmond et al. (2003), El-Ramly et al. (2002), and Tarby (2006). It uses AspectJ (AspectJ project) but it could be done with other languages which support AOP such as aoPHP, PHPAspect, and JAC (Java Aspect Components project). We currently use our work within the design and the tracing of task-oriented components (Bourguin et al., 2007).

12.3 SECOND APPROACH: INTERACTIVE AGENT-BASED ARCHITECTURE AND EVALUATION MODULE

12.3.1 Agent-Oriented Architecture for Interactive Systems

Several architecture models have been put forward by researchers over the past twenty years. Two main types of architecture can be distinguished: architectures with functional components (Langage, Seeheim, Arch and their derived models) and architectures with structural components (PAC and its derived models (Coutaz, 1987), the MVC model (Model-View-Controller; from Smalltalk) and its recent evolutions, AMF and its variants (Ouadou, 1994), H4 (Depaulis et al., 2006)). The classic models of interactive systems distinguish three essential functions (presentation, control and application). Some models (such as the Seeheim and ARCH models) consider these three functions as being three distinct functional units. Other approaches using structural components, and in particular those said to be distributed or agent approaches, suggest grouping the three functions together into one unit, the agent. The agents are themselves organized hierarchically among composition or communication principles: for instance PAC and its derived models, or the MVC model.

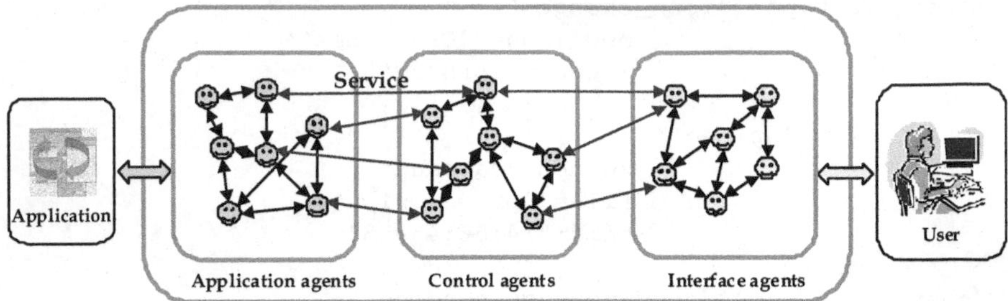

Figure 12.3 Global agent-oriented architecture for interactive systems

These architecture models propose the same principle based on separation between the system (application) and the human-machine interface. Thus, an architecture must separate the application and the interface, define a distribution of the services of the interface, and define an exchange protocol. The interest in separating the interface from the application is to facilitate the modifications to be made on the interface without touching with the application. Figure 12.3 proposes a comprehensive framework for architecture (Ezzedine et al., 2006; Grislin-Le Strugeon et al., 2001), showing a separation in three functional components, called respectively: interface with the application (connected to the application), dialogue controller, and presentation (this component is in direct contact with the user).

These three components group together agents:

1. The *application* agents which handle the field concepts and cannot be directly accessed by the user. One of their roles is to ensure the correct functioning of the application and the real time dispatch of the information necessary for the other agents to perform their task,

2. The *dialogue control* agents which are also called mixed agents; these provide services for both the application and the user. They are intended to guarantee coherency in the exchanges emanating from the application towards the user, and vice versa,

3. The *interactive* agents (or *interface* agents), unlike the *application* agents, are in direct contact with the user (they can be seen by the user). These agents co-ordinate between themselves in order to intercept the user commands and to form a presentation which allows the user to gain an overall understanding of the current state of the application. In this way, a window may be considered as being an *interactive* agent in its own right; its specification describes its presentation and the services it is to perform.

For interactive systems with agent-based architecture, it is necessary to propose new evaluation approaches. A principle of coupling between such architectures and evaluation agents is now described.

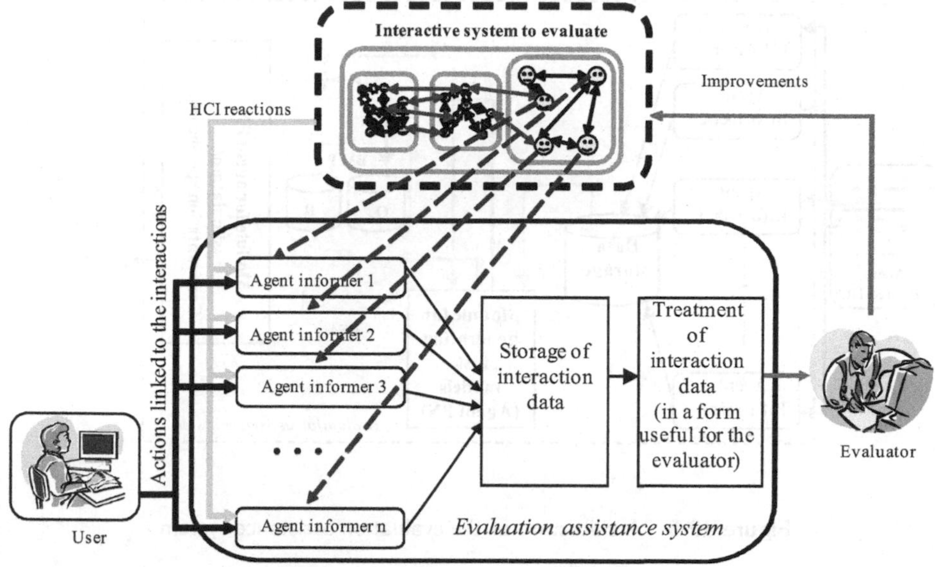

Figure 12.4 Principle of coupling between agent-based architecture of the interactive system and its evaluation (Trabelsi, 2006)

12.3.2 Principle of Coupling Between Agent-based Architecture and Evaluation Agents

Our initial aim was to propose a tool for collecting objective data, adapted to agent-based interactive systems. This tool is, in fact, an electronic informer; it consists of a program, invisible to the user (of the system to be evaluated), which transmits and records all the interactions (user actions and system reactions) in a data base. The exploitation of this data base then aims at providing the evaluator with data and statistics enabling him/her to draw conclusions with regard to various aspects of utility and usability.

As this informer is intended for the evaluation of agent-based interactive systems, it must be closely related to the architecture of the system to be evaluated (Ezzedine et al., 2006; Trabelsi, 2006). We are particularly interested in the *interactive* agents. The electronic informer, Figure 12.4, consists of several *informer* agents which have been deduced using the architecture of the system to evaluate and more particularly starting from the multiagent system concerning presentation. It is based primarily on the acquisition of information and specific data of the system to be evaluated (user actions and system reactions). This information and data will make it possible to rebuild the tasks really performed by the user (*a posteriori* mode) and to confront them with the model of tasks to be carried out (*a priori* mode).

Let us suppose we have a presentation module made up of n *interactive* agents (each one being able to interact with the user); n evaluation agents will be instanced and connected to the *interactive* agents. During the interactions with the user, the n

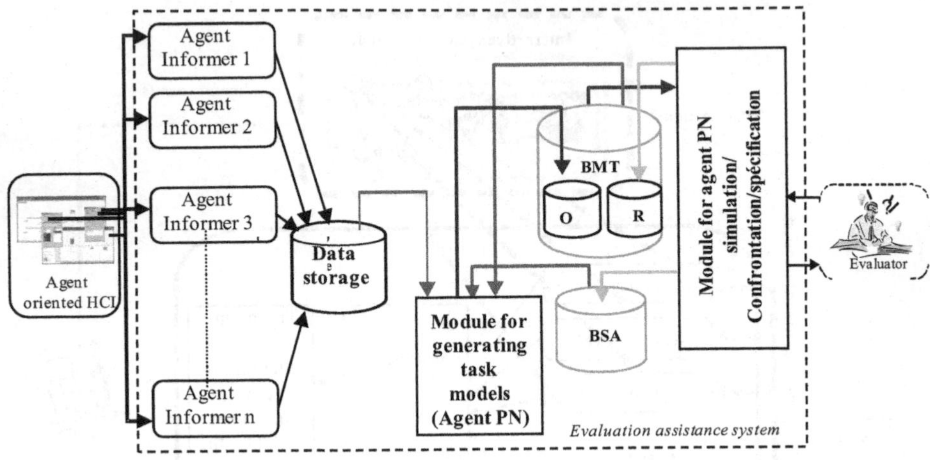

Figure 12.5 Architecture of the evaluation assistance system

evaluation agents memorize in real time the data concerning interaction between the user and the n *interactive* agents. After the tasks have been performed, the data is analyzed automatically; with a user interface specifically intended for the evaluator, the data is presented to the evaluator after a time lapse. The data can range from a bottom level, corresponding to simple user or system events, to higher levels (for example concerning task level). Examples are available in Trabelsi (2006).

In order to assist the evaluator of agent-based interactive systems, in the following section we propose an evaluation assistance system based on such a principle of electronic informer.

12.4 TOWARDS AN ASSISTANCE SYSTEM FOR THE EVALUATION OF AGENT-BASED INTERACTIVE SYSTEMS

The system suggested for helping with the evaluation of interactive systems based on agents is composed of several modules, shown in Figure 12.5 (Trabelsi, 2006).

The *electronic informer* module, directly connected to the interactive system to be evaluated, uses the principles described in the preceding section as regards the association of an informer agent to each agent of the interface. The creation of these informer agents is deduced directly from the architecture of the system which is to be evaluated, more specifically from the presentation multiagent system (cf. example given in figure 12.6).

Once the interaction data has been collected and stored, it is used by a module able to generate a task model. This is based on the exploitation of agent Petri nets, inspired by parametrized Petri nets (Gracanin et al., 1994), selected for their ability to handle entities of the agent type, according to principles described in Ezzedine et al., (2006): the model obtained corresponds to that of the real activity. This module is also able to generate a model corresponding to the task to be performed, whose components are

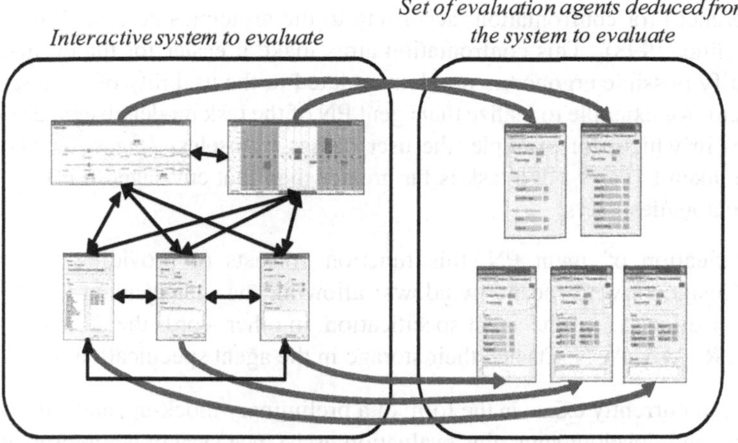

Figure 12.6 Association with each presentation agent of an informer agent

available in a base intended for this purpose (stored in the BMT(R) base, cf. below). Indeed, two bases are available:

1. The Base of Specifications of Agents (BSA) allows the storage of the specifications of the interface agents. It contains the definition (for each agent) of the sets E (set of the possible events), C (set of the conditions), R (set of the resources), Acv (set of the visible actions: such as the action of the user using the mouse or the keyboard, the reaction of the interface by the posting of new windows and/or change of their contents), AcN (set of the actions which are not visible to the user, relating to the interactions between interface agents). The data stored in BSA is intended to be exploited by the module of task model generation (taking the form of agent Petri nets).

2. The Base of Task Models (BMT) is composed of two subbases called BMT(O) and BMT(R). BMT(O) contains the description of the task observed, the models being generated by the module of generation (of agent Petri nets). BMT(R) contains the description of the tasks, also called prescribed or reference tasks (to be realized by the users), such as they are described *a priori* by the designers or evaluators via a module allowing Simulation/Confrontation/Specification of agent Petri nets (cf. below).

The Simulation/Confrontation/Specification module provides the evaluators/designers with the following three functionalities:

1. Simulation of agent PN: this function allows the visualization of agent PN dynamics, and in consequence provides an overview concerning the HCI dynamics; this is because of the exploitation of the task models (modelled by agent PN) and of the formulation which ensures the evolution in agent PN.

2. Confrontation of agent PN: this function exploits the task models (Observed, of Reference) for confrontation (according to the principles described in Abed & Ezzedine, 1998). This confrontation aims make it easier for the evaluators to identify possible ergonomic problems related to the usability of the interactive system; for example to realize that agent PN of the task model observed contains states in which, for example, the user passes by useless stages, or where the time taken to carry out a task is far greater than that envisaged *a priori* by the evaluators/designers.

3. Specification of agent PN: this function consists of providing the evaluators/designers with means (windows) allowing the management (description, modification, ...) of the agent specification, in other words the definition of the E, C, R, ACv, ACN sets and their storage in the agent specification base (BSA).

Although it currently exists in the form of a preliminary mock-up, and still requires various tests and developments, this evaluation assistance system is representative of approaches which can be set up when the interactive system concerned has an architecture based on agents (see Figure 12.7).

12.5 COMPARISON BETWEEN THE TWO APPROACHES

A comparison of the two approaches is given in Table 12.1. Although the methods employed are radically different, they have common objectives: to gather data to compare predicted tasks and activity, and to highlight utility and usability problems. The ways used to obtain this data differ according to the approaches. However, the secondary goals are not the same. With the AOP approach, everything is done so that the initial application is not modified, whereas with the agents approach, the priority is to follow the traces in real time. This can be explained by the domains associated to the works which we have undertaken so far. The approach by agents focuses much more on complex industrial systems (in fact the supervision of collective transport networks) where time is a crucial factor, whereas for the moment, the AOP approach has been used in systems where time does not play such an important part.

Inputs and outputs also differ for the two approaches. Here inputs implies what we must have before beginning the tracing, and outputs what we obtain during and after the tracing. With the AOP, we must have the application code and the aspects code; all of this is generally proposed as packages (the package of aspects also contains the file of trace formats). With the second approach, it is necessary to have specifications of the interface agents, describing their services in terms of visible actions and/or non-visible actions, events, conditions and associated resources (in the BSA database); if one wants to make a confrontation between the model of real human activities, and the model of task to perform, the description of this model (in the form of agent PN) is required.

Concerning the results during or after the tracing, the AOP approach generates an XML file of the traces produced. During the human-machine interactions, the second approach makes it possible to collect all user actions, through the evaluation agents, along with the reactions of the interactive system, and the interactions between agents; this information is stored. With other modules, it is then possible to generate an agent

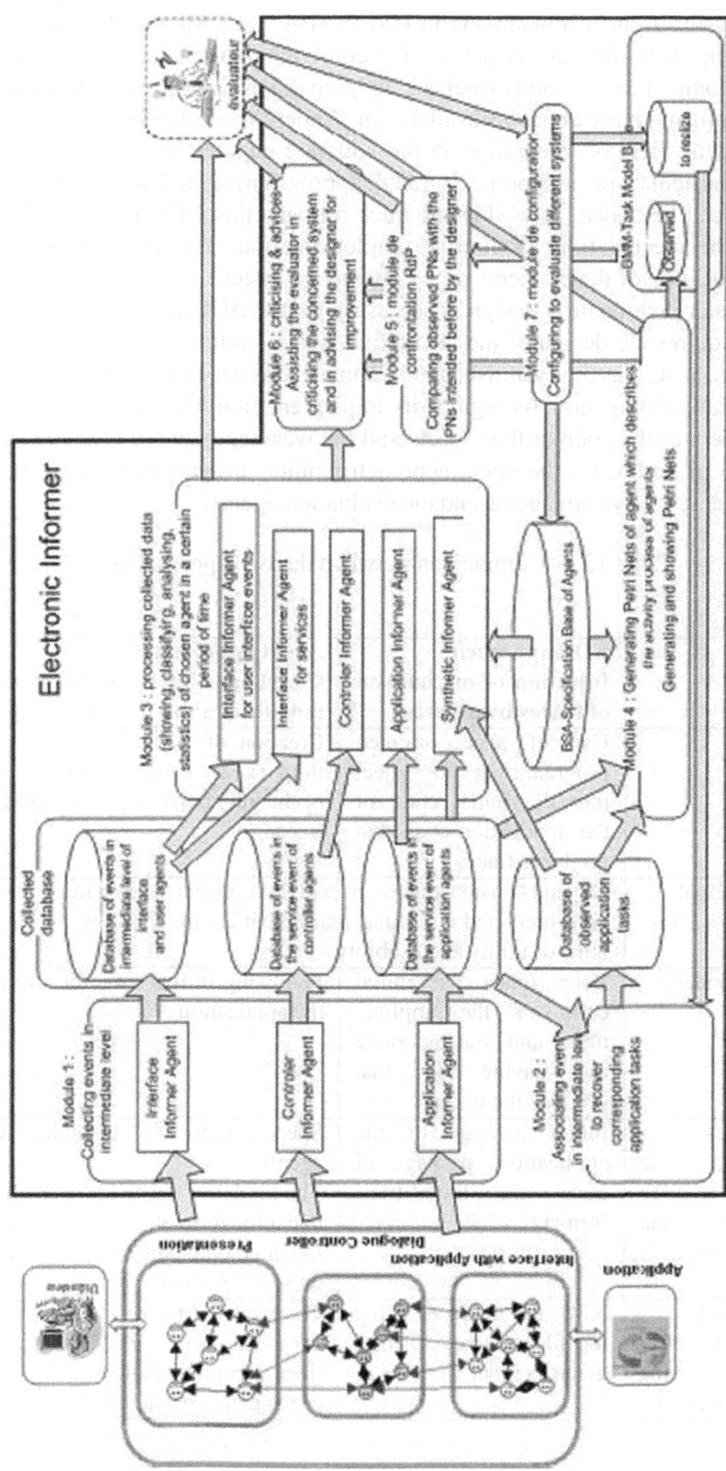

Figure 12.7 Evaluation assistance system

PN of the task, in the form of documents in PNML (Petri Net Markup Language, Weber and Kindler, 2003) format. A perspective consists in automatically generating ergonomic recommendations and criticisms, helping the evaluator to improve the interactive system (using basic concepts available in Vanderdonckt, 1999).

From the point of view of integration in the software engineering, the two approaches require particular specifications. The AOP approach needs to know the methods and data that can be traced, as well as the trace formats; this information can be collected during the specifications or after the implementation. The agent approach requires the specification of the elements of the interactive system, and the evaluation agents. No particular architectural design is necessary for the AOP approach, but the agent approach requires the design of the interactive system architecture to be based on interface agents, as well as the establishment of connections between the interactive agents and the evaluation agents. As regards its implementation, the AOP approach automatically generates the code of the aspects and the weaving with the initial code of the application to be traced; the agent approach requires programming with the services of the interactive system agents and the evaluation agents.

Table 12.1: Comparison between the two approaches

		AOP approach Injection of mechanism of traces by aspects	**Agent approach Coupling of interface agents and module of automatic acquisition**
Method		Use of aspect-oriented programming to inject into the initial code of the application code that produces traces	Creation of evaluation (observation) agents coupled with agents of the interactive application to be traced
Goals	Principal	Depends on how traces are exploited: gathering data to compare predicted tasks and real activities, highlighting problems of utility and usability...	
	Secondary	Keep intact the initial code of the application, and tracing done by weaving code that produce the traces	Following in real time the use of the application
Inputs/ outputs	Inputs (what is necessary to create the traces)	Initial package of the application, package of trace aspects, file of trace formats	Specification of the interactive agents The model of the task to perform, under the form of a PN (in the case in which one aims to compare the prescribed a real human tasks)
	Outputs (after tracing the application)	XML file of traces using the file of trace formats given as input	The model of the real activity, under the form of a PN (in perspective: recommendations and criticisms generated automatically)

Table 12.1: Comparison between the two approaches (continued)

		AOP approach Injection of mechanism of traces by aspects	**Agent approach Coupling of interface agents and module of automatic acquisition**
Traditional stages of software engineering	Preliminary or feasibility study	Explicit consideration in the project of early evaluation by injection of software mechanisms	
	Specification	Specification of: interactive system, parameters to be traced, formats of traces	Specification of: interactive system agents, evaluation agents
	Architectural design	*(empty)*	Design of the interactive system architecture based on interface agents; connections between interactive system agents and evaluation agents
	Coding	Generation of the code of the aspects and weaving between the code to be traced and the aspects	Coding of the services of the interactive system agents and evaluation agents
User-centered evaluation*	Interaction data gathering	Execution of the woven code	Espionage by the evaluation agents of the interactions between interface agents and the user
	Collected data	Any data accessible by a method (in the meaning of object-oriented programming) + Time	User and system events, errors, time of tasks execution, unused objects, number of help requests…
Languages	Current	Java with AspectJ	C++
	Intended	Any language supporting AOP	Java
Types of application	Current	WIMP applications	Information systems used in a context of supervision of network of bus and tramway
	Intended	Information systems, distance learning applications, mobile applications	Information systems
Advantages		No modification of the application initial code. Tracing disengaged very easily	No modification of the initial code of the constitutive agents of the interactive system architecture

Table 12.1: Comparison between the two approaches (continued)

	AOP approach Injection of mechanism of traces by aspects	**Agent approach Coupling of interface agents and module of automatic acquisition**
Current limits	Static weaving of aspects Need to have public object methods to access data to be traced	Difficult to define the optimal number of evaluation agents

*Simultaneously with other possible methods: interviews, eye tracking, questionnaire, etc.

From the user-centered evaluation point of view, in addition to the fact that the two approaches can be coupled with other techniques such as interviews, eye tracking, etc., they also use different modes to gather data: with the AOP approach, data is automatically collected by the execution of the code which comes from the aspect weaving on the initial application code; with the agent approach, data is collected from the evaluation agents by observing the interactions between the interface agents and the user. To be collected with the AOP approach, data must be accessible by a method (with the meaning of the object-oriented programming); this method can be public, inherited, etc. Time is accessible in the same way. Data collected with the agent approach is potentially multiple (see Table 12.1).

In their current version, the approaches use different languages. The AOP approach uses Java and AspectJ; the agent approach is based on C++. In the future, it is expected that the AOP approach will be extended to other languages supporting AOP such as PHP, C++, etc., and that the agent approach will use Java.

Concerning the types of application, the AOP approach currently can trace any application written in Java and supporting AspectJ. However, the traced applications are today mainly interactive applications (WIMP applications). In the future, it is planned that the AOP approach will be applied to information systems, distance learning applications, and mobile applications. The agent approach is currently applied to information systems used in a context of supervision of network of bus and tramway. In the future, it should apply to any type of information system.

The **advantages** of these two approaches are that they provide principles and mechanisms facilitating and prompting evaluation in projects. In addition, the AOP approach allows keeping intact the initial code and thus leading in parallel and/or serially the realization of the application and the realization of the mechanisms of traces.

The **disadvantages** are as follows. With the agent approach, it is difficult to define for the moment the optimal number of evaluation agents (the first version contained an evaluation agent by interaction agent, and the new version will contain only one for the user interface; this aspect is under study). In addition, agent approach lets consider the need for new design methods of user interface envisaging a coupling between interface agents and evaluation agents. To be more effective, the AOP approach needs design methods integrating aspects for the evaluation. That means for example that any potentially traceable data must be accessible by object methods.

12.6 CONCLUSION

The evaluation field is the subject of active research projects in the HCI community. The trace-based approaches are very promising. For our part, we are working on two complementary approaches. The first is based on aspect-oriented programming; it allows the injection of mechanisms of traces in existing applications. The second is based on new possibilities offered by agent-based approaches; it aims at ensuring a coupling between agent-based architectures and evaluation agents. Although turned towards same objectives in terms of evaluation, these two approaches have different characteristics, advantages and disadvantages which have been compared in this paper.

For these two approaches, the research perspectives are numerous.

Thus, concerning the tracing by aspects, our major current limit is related to the fact that we use AspectJ; the produced aspects are consequently *static* aspects, i.e., having to be woven with the application during the compilation. Technologies of *dynamic* aspects such as JAC (Pawlak, 2002), i.e., being able to be woven, modified or even to be removed during the execution, are considered. This will not only make it possible to more easily disconnect the mechanism of traces, but also to propose much more powerful functionalities such as aspects being able to change their behavior during the execution of the application. Another perspective relates to the analysis of the traces generated by the aspects. This analysis is currently performed "manually", or improved as far as possible by dedicated XSLT processes, for example to build models of the users' effective tasks, these models then may be compared with the prescribed tasks models of the applications. We can also transform these traces into scenarios that can be replayed with software environments such as CTTE (Mori et al., 2002) or K-MADe (Kernal Model for Activity Description) for example. For that, we plan to provide process libraries (XSLT, Java, etc.) that automate the transformations, making it possible for example to translate XML files of traces into effective tasks models or scenarios which can be replayed.

The perspectives for the second approach concern the production of an interactive assistance environment for the evaluators of interactive systems with agent-based architecture. This environment should be generic, configurable, automatic, and independent from the application. In addition, we envisage evaluating the durations of communication between the agents of the same module or of different modules in order to improve the global performance of the interactive system.

Although different, the two approaches presented in this chapter can be complementary. We indeed plan to use the AOP to generate and insert the code of the trace agents of the second approach. Thus the AOP approach will make it possible to define the traces (what to trace, where, when, etc.), and the corresponding aspects will be agents able to produce traces whose visualization will be made in real time.

Acknowledgments. The present research work has been supported by the "Ministère de l'Education Nationale, de la Recherche et de la Technologie", the "Région Nord Pas-de-Calais" and the FEDER (Fonds Européen de Développement Régional) during the SART, MIAOU and EUCUE projects. The authors gratefully acknowledge the support of these institutions. The authors also wish to acknowledge José Rouillard,

Philippe Laporte and Thomas Vantroys (LIFL), along with Abdelwaheb Trabelsi and Chi Dung Tran (LAMIH) for their participation in this research.

References

Abed, M. and Ezzedine, H. (1998). Vers une démarche intégrée de conception-évaluation des systèmes homme-machine. *Journal of Decision Systems*, 7:147–175.

Akşit, M., Bergmans, L., and Vural, S. (1992). An object-oriented language-database integration model: The composition-filters approach. In Madsen, O. L., editor, *Proc. 7th European Conf. Object-Oriented Programming*, pages 372–395. Springer-Verlag Lecture Notes in Computer Science.

Balbo, S. Project WAUTER (Website Automatic Usability Testing EnviRonment).

Beirekdar, A. (2004). *Methodology for automating Web usability and accessibility evaluation by guideline*. Ph.D. thesis, UCL, Louvain-la-Neuve, Belgium.

Bourguin, G., Lewandowski, A., and Tarby, J.-C. (2007). Defining task oriented components. In Winckler, M., Johnson, H., and Palanque, P. A., editors, *Task Models and Diagrams for User Interface Design, 6th International Workshop, TAMODIA 2007, Toulouse, France, November 7-9, 2007, Proceedings*, volume 4849 of *Lecture Notes in Computer Science*, pages 170–183. Springer.

Champin, P.-A., Prié, Y., and Mille, A. (2003). MUSETTE: Modeling USEs and tasks for tracing experience. In *ICCBR'03, Workshop 5 'From Structured Cases to Unstructured Problem Solving Episodes for Experience-Based Assistance*, volume 2689 of *LNAI*, pages 279–286.

Coutaz, J. (1987). PAC: an implementation model for dialog design. In *Proceedings Interact'87*, pages 431–436.

Depaulis, F., Jambon, F., Girard, P., and Guittet, L. (2006). Le modèle d'architecture logicielle H4: Principes, usages, outils et retours d'expérience dans les applications de conception technique. *Revue d'Interaction Homme-Machine (RIHM)*, 7:93–129.

Ducasse, S., Gîrba, T., and Wuyts, R. (2006). Object-oriented legacy system trace-based logic testing. In *CSMR 2006. Proceedings of the 10th European Conference on Software Maintenance and Reengineering*.

Egyed-Zsigmond, E., Mille, A., and Prié, Y. (2003). Club [clubsuit] (trèfle): A use trace model. In Ashley, K. D. and Bridge, D. G., editors, *Case-Based Reasoning Research and Development, 5th International Conference on Case-Based Reasoning, ICCBR 2003, Trondheim, Norway, June 23-26, 2003, Proceedings*, volume 2689 of *Lecture Notes in Computer Science*, pages 146–160. Springer.

El-Ramly, M., Stroulia, E., and Sorenson, P. G. (2002). Mining system-user interaction traces for use case models. In *IWPC*, pages 21–32. IEEE Computer Society.

Ezzedine, H., Trabelsi, A., and Kolski, C. (2006). Modeling of an interactive system with an agent-based architecture using Petri nets, application of the method to the supervision of a transport system. *Mathematics and Computers in Simulation*, 70(5-6):358–376.

Filman, R. E., Elrad, T., Clarke, S., and Akşit, M., editors (2005). *Aspect-Oriented Software Development*. Reading, MA: Addison-Wesley.

Gamma, E., Helm, R., Johnson, R., and Vlissides, J. (1995). *Design Patterns: Elements of Reusable Object-Oriented Software*. Addison Wesley Professional Computing Series. `http://www.aw.com`.

Gracanin, D., Srinivasan, P., and Valavanis, K. (1994). Parametrized Petri nets and their applications to planning and coordination in intelligent systems. *IEEE Transactions on Systems, Man and Cybernetics*, 24:1483–1497.

Grislin-Le Strugeon, E., Adam, E., and Kolski, C. (2001). Agents intelligents en interaction homme-machine dans les systèmes d'information. In Kolski, C., editor, *Environnements évolués et évaluation de l'IHM, Interaction Homme-Machine pour les SI 2*, pages 207–248. Hermes, Paris.

Hilbert, D.F. and Redmiles, M.A. (2000). Extracting usability information from user interface events. *CSURV: Computing Surveys*, 32:384–421.

Ivory, M. Y. and Hearst, M.Y. (2001). The state of the art in automating usability evaluation of user interfaces. *CSURV: Computing Surveys*, 33:470–516.

Ivory, M. Y. (2004). *Automated Web Site Evaluation - Researchers' and Practitioners' Perspectives*. Human-Computer Interaction Series, Vol. 4. Springer-Verlag.

Jacko, J. A. and Sears, A., editors (2002). *The Human-Computer Interaction Handbook: Fundamentals, Evolving Technologies, and Emerging Applications*. Lawrence Erlbaum.

Jordan, P., W., Thomas, B., Weerdmeester, A., B., and McClelland, I., editors (1996). *Usability Evaluation in Industry*. London: Taylor & Francis. (paper) 0-7484-0314-0 (cloth).

Mariage, C., Vanderdonckt, J., and Pribeanu, C. (2005). State of the art of Web usability guidelines. In Proctor, R. and Vu, K.-P., editors, *The Handbook of Human Factors in Web Design*. Hillsdale, NJ: Lawrence Erlbaum.

Mori, G., Paternò, F., and Santoro, C. (2002). CTTE: support for developing and analyzing task models for interactive system design. *IEEE Trans. Softw. Eng.*, 28(8):797–813.

Nielsen, J. (1993). *Usability Engineering*. Boston, MA: Academic Press.

Ouadou, K. (1994). *AMF: Un modèle d'architecture multiagents multifacettes pour Interfaces Homme-Machine et les outils associés*. Ph.D. thesis, Ecole Centrale de Lyon.

Pawlak, R. (2002). *La programmation par aspects interactionnelle pour la construction d'applications à préoccupations multiples*. Ph.D. thesis, Conservatoire National des Arts et Métiers (CNAM), Paris.

Sweeney, M., Maguire, M., and Shackel, B. (1993). Evaluating user-computer interaction: A framework. *International Journal of Man-Machine Studies*, 38(4):689–711.

Tarby, J.-C. (2006). Evaluation précoce et conception orientée évaluation. In *ErgoIA'2006*, pages 343–346.

Tarby, J.-C., Ezzedine, H., Rouillard, J., Tran, C. D., Laporte, P., and Kolski, C. (2007). Traces using aspect-oriented programming and interactive agent-based architecture for early usability evaluation: Basic principles and comparison. In Jacko, J. A., editor, *Human-Computer Interaction. Interaction Design and Usability, 12th International Conference, HCI International 2007, Beijing, China, July 22-27, 2007,*

Proceedings, Part I, volume 4550 of *Lecture Notes in Computer Science*, pages 632–641. Springer.

Trabelsi, A. (2006). *Contribution à l'évaluation des systèmes interactifs orientés agents : application à un poste de supervision du transport urbain*. Ph.D. thesis, University of Valenciennes and Hainaut-Cambrésis, Valenciennes, France.

Vanderdonckt, J. (1999). Development milestones towards a tool for working with guidelines. *Interacting with Computers*, 12(2):81–118.

Weber, M. and Kindler, E. (2003). The Petri net markup language. In Ehrig, H., Reisig, W., Rozenberg, G., and Weber, H., editors, *Petri Net Technology for Communication-Based Systems—Advances in Petri Nets*, volume 2472 of *Lecture Notes in Computer Science*, pages 124–144. Springer.

Whitefield, A., Wilson, F., and Dowell, J. (1991). A framework for human factors evaluation. *Behavior and Information Technology*, 10(1):65–79.

Wilson and Corlett (1996). *Evaluation of Human Work: A Practical Ergonomics Methodology (2nd ed.)*. London: Taylor and Francis.

13 ACHIEVING USABILITY OF ADAPTABLE SOFTWARE: THE AMF-BASED APPROACH

Franck Tarpin-Bernard(1), Kinan Samaan(1), and Bertrand David(2)

LIESP, (1) INSA-Lyon, F-69621, France
Bat L. de Vinci - 21, avenue Jean Capelle, 69621 VILLEURBANNE Cedex, France
(2) Ecole Centrale de Lyon

Abstract. This chapter proposes a novel model-based approach for adapting interactive applications to various contexts while ensuring its usability. After a brief overview of the existing software architecture models for HCI and strategies for adaptation, we detail the models we are proposing. This includes task, concept, platform, and user models as well as an interaction model. All these models are linked via an underlying architecture called AMF. It ensures the relationships between all the other models and encapsulates the key usability attributes. We will also show how these models are embedded in a process and a method for building adaptive software.

13.1 INTRODUCTION

Maintaining adaptability between platforms while ensuring usability is one of the major challenges from both the HCI and software engineering perspectives. Designing and implementing interactive applications that are adaptable (manually) or adaptive (automatically) to the context of use requires us to consider the characteristics of the user, the interactive platform as well as the constraints and capabilities of each environment.

Several efforts have been made for tailoring an application to a specific context and especially to the platform constraints. Examples include The Java Pluggable Look and Feel, Web Clipping, and Content Management Systems such PhP Nuke, ZOPE, etc. However, ensuring the usability is still an open research question. This is because the transformation techniques may take into account a specific usability attribute — most of the time cross-platform consistency — rather than considering the overall set of attributes that we generally consider in usability measurement (Seffah et al., 2005; 2006).

A state-of-the-art survey shows us that among the large majority of existing approaches for adaptation, the model-based approach seems to be the most powerful. Such approach uses high level and abstract representations that can be instantiated later on in the development lifecycle to meet specific usability requirements. However, these approaches need to combine apparently independent models such as concepts (e.g., UML), task (e.g., CTT), platform (e.g., CC/PP) or user profiles. The relationships between these models need to be defined at the design step and refined at runtime in order to be able to achieve the overall usability. Our belief is that, what we refer to as an interaction model is the right place to glue together all the other models and usability attributes. This model must support both design stage linking other models and runtime. In addition, because software engineering and HCI show the importance of clearly separate functional core from presentation components, our interaction model is supported by well-structured architecture.

Resulting from the fusion of well-known models either layer-based like Arch (UIMS, 1992) or multiagents like PAC (Coutaz, 1990), our architectural model, called AMF, has been implemented in the format of an engine that at runtime executes the interaction model which links the abstraction and presentation components. AMF combines best architectural practices, such patterns and specification notations, from the software engineering and HCI communities. As an example, we use UML models (from use case to class and sequence diagrams) and user-centered approaches based on task analysis.

13.2 STATE-OF-THE-ART

The architectural model is one of the key elements needed to achieve efficient and good software developments: methods–models–tools. First, it organizes software structure to improve implementation, portability and maintenance. Second, it helps identify the functional components, which is essential during the analysis and design process. Its third role is to help further understanding of a complex system, not only for designers, but also for end-users. For these reasons, the architecture model is the pivot of the lifecycle and we consider that a good model should fulfill four main goals:

- Support specification step (as a formalism);
- Be the skeleton of the implementation (as a framework);
- Insure consistency for executable applications;
- Serve as a representation for dynamic reconfigurations by the user.

Different approaches have been proposed to support various contexts of execution, including a wide range of devices and various user profiles. In order to support plasticity (Thevenin, 2001), that is, the ability to adapt itself to context without compromising usability, different approaches have been proposed.

This set of approaches suggests first revisiting some of the architecture models developed in the early 1980s. This tendency leads to huge improvements, like Arch (UIMS, 1992) or multiagent models like MVC (Krasner and Pope, 1988), PAC (Coutaz, 1990) and PAC Amodeus (Nigay and Coutaz, 1993). Some other researchers suggest also XML-based languages for specifying HCI and rendering engines as a mechanism of adaptation.

13.2.1 Interactive System Architecture in HCI

Most HCI architectural models distinguish at least three main components:

- Presentation or views that manage the direct interaction with the user.
- Controllers, adapters which are in charge of the communication between the other components and/or with the users.
- Abstraction or model which serves as an interface between the functional core and the two other elements.

These various models have been presented differently in the literature and with different names. Here we use the taxonomy that classifies the architectures in three categories: layer-oriented like Seeheim (Pfaff, 1985) and Arch (UIMS, 1992), multiagents like MVC (Krasner and Pope, 1988)), PAC (Coutaz, 1987) and AMF (Ouadou, 1994), and hybrid like PAC-Amodeus (Nigay and Coutaz, 1993) or H4 (Depaulis et al., 1995). Layer-oriented models divide architecture in logical layers. Multiagents models exploit the layer-oriented model and define each layer in the format of a set of agents. Hybrid architectures combine the advantages of the two previous approaches while combining a layered architecture where the dialogue components are structured using agents.

Although most of the existing integrated development environments (IDE) implement some of these architectural models, the Cartesian separation between abstraction and presentation is still not fully achieved. Efforts are needed to support adaptation in particular hardware diversity. Some progress has been made toward this objective especially with the advent of platform independent scripting languages C# and the related standards for describing devices like CDC (SDNa), CLDC (SDNb) or CC/PP (CCPP).

13.2.2 Adaptation Approaches

Adaptation techniques can be classified in four categories ranging from the easiest to implement to the most powerful:

- Translation techniques;
- Markup language-based approaches;

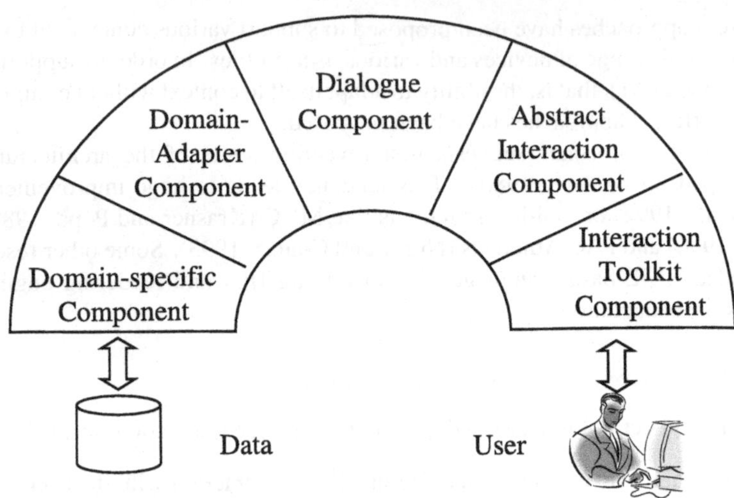

Figure 13.1 Arch model

- Reverse and reengineering techniques;
- Model-based approaches.

User interface translation is a technique widely used in the context of Web pages. There exist also tools for HTML ↔ Java translation. These techniques generally provide insufficient provisions to support usability except in the context where the adaptation contexts are vey similar, nearly the same. New approaches such as graceful degradation (Florins et al., 2004) use the specification of a user interface of the "best" platform — the one with the highest screen resolution and the most powerful graphical toolkit. During the design, adaptation rules called degradation rules are used by developers to adapt the best interface to a specific platform. However, this approach is limited to the translation from one specific language to another available on similar platforms.

Markup language-based approaches define platform-independent descriptions with languages that can be easily reused for a large variety of contexts. During the last five years, many UIDLs (User Interface Description Language) have been introduced. They usually use XML and CSS scripting languages. Rendering engines are proposed to analyze the independent descriptions of UI. They produced platform-dependent description files using specific technologies (HTML, WAP, VoiceXML, etc.). Popular languages include XUL (Hyatt et al., 2001), XForms (Dubinko et al., 2000), AUIML (Azevedo et al., 2000), PlasticML (Rouillard, 2003), RIML (Koskimies et al., 2004). These languages can be classified in two different categories. The first one groups languages that define Abstract Interaction Objects (AIO) which are replaced by Concrete Interaction Objects (CIO). For instance, in UIML, a `<part class=''Button'' id=''MyButton''/>` tag is replaced by a `<Button name= " MyButton''/>` tag in HTML and a `JButton` object in a Java Swing rendering. The other family provides a higher level of abstraction specifying user's interactions like "select element" or "select command". XForms and AUIML use a choice tag that will be concretized by a set of radio button or a scrolling menu according to the device characteristics.

Reverse engineering and interface migration techniques analyze an existing UI description with the perspective to extract abstract representations (language-independent and device-independent). These representations are then instantiated for another platform. First introduced for the migration of text applications to graphical ones (Chikofsky and Cross, 1990), these representations are now generally based on the markup languages presented above (e.g., VAQUITA (Bouillon et al., 2004)).

All these approaches are useful and efficient if and only the initial context used for designing the application and the real contexts have some similaraties. In all other situations, it becomes very hard to warranty the usability of the application. The situation is more drastic in the context of interactive applications that are not form-based like the Web and Wap applications usually modeled.

An answer to these limitations consists of using a set of models (tasks, concepts, presentation, dialogue, platform, etc.) to describe the application at a high level. For example, UIML (Abrams et al., 1999; see also Chapter 7), UsiXML (Limbourg *et al.*, 2004), ArtStudio (Thevenin, 2001), TERESA (Mori et al., 2004), dygimes (Luyten, 2004), and Comets (Calvary et al., 2005). use different models. The abstract Interface, the most abstract model, is transformed step by step into a concrete platform-dependant Interface according to the information stored in the set of models.

Fundamentally speaking, as these approaches considered a very large set of parameters (in the various models), the resulting Interfaces are presumably of better quality with a higher usability. Furthermore, they support a certain level of adaptation when the context of use is evolving (change in the user, the interaction platform, the environment or the activity). However, these techniques are harder to implement mainly because of the difficulty to relate all the models together.

We propose a model-based approach and an underlying software architecture model as both a way to achieve usability and to maintain the same level of adaptability. In the next section, we present the AMF model, its extensions for adaptation in the context of a model-based approach.

13.3 AMF AND ITS RELATIONSHIPS WITH OTHER MODELS

13.3.1 AMF Fundamentals

AMF extends multiagent models like PAC while generalizing the concept of facet while embedding a set of coherent behaviors and functionalities. AMF proposes also a graphical formalism mainly dedicated to the representation of control using standardized UI elements. The number of new facets can be unlimitedly defined (such as Help, Error, Distribution, Rights, etc.) in addition to the classical PAC's facets (Presentation and Abstraction). Similar to Object-Oriented approaches, AMF eases top-down analysis through an iterative decomposition of the application into facets at different levels.

The agent is the basic element for structuring an AMF-based application. Each agent can contain other agents and several instances of the same agent class can coexist.

Thus, an application is composed of a hierarchy of agents, which root is the main application manager agent.

Each agent is composed of several types of **facets** that group a set of services. Each service can be reached through a **communication port**. Three kinds of communication ports exist: input (I), output (O) and I≫O. Input ports represent services offered by the facet. In contrast, an output port represents a required service. An I≫O port first serves as an input port and then as an output port.

To model the control facet, AMF defines special elements called **administrators**. These administrators play three major roles:

- The interconnection between the ports,
- The execution of a treatment on the data exchanged by the ports,
- The handling of activation rules that determine the listened sources and with an eventual listen order (e.g., first, then second, then ...) and the targets to notify.

Depending on their types, the administrators can have several source ports and/or several target ports. AMF formalism contains several types of administrators; we describe here the three most used ones (Figure 13.2). The basic administrator is used to build a unidirectional link without any special treatment. The *Return administrator* is like the Simple administrator but it carries back the result returned by the activation of the targets ports. The result can have several forms depending on the number of targets connected to the administrator (Single result or Array). The *Filter administrator* allows handling the activation of the target ports of a collection of Agents and to select the most appropriate ones to activate. This allows using multiple instances of an Agent, especially useful when a collection of items (each one represented by an Agent) is dynamically managed (e.g., Appointments of a Schedule) or where only some targets must be activated depending on activation conditions (e.g., the window having the focus).

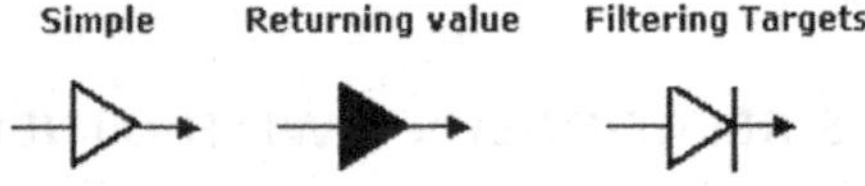

Figure 13.2 The main AMF administrators

The **control propagation** is done according to the AMF tree and can be done only between ports of facets owned by the same agent, or of ports of facets of subagents. In this last case, the propagation is done by the administrator of the same agent, the one containing the facet of the source port. The set of administrators with their links that owns an agent constitutes its Control Facet as defined in PAC.

Figure 13.3 presents a simple interactive agent using the AMF formalism. This agent aims to provide feedback to the user when s/he uses a particular functionality of the application. This user event is represented by the bolt entering the facet and it leads to the activation of the 'Start_Action' *output port* of the *facet* 'Presentation'.

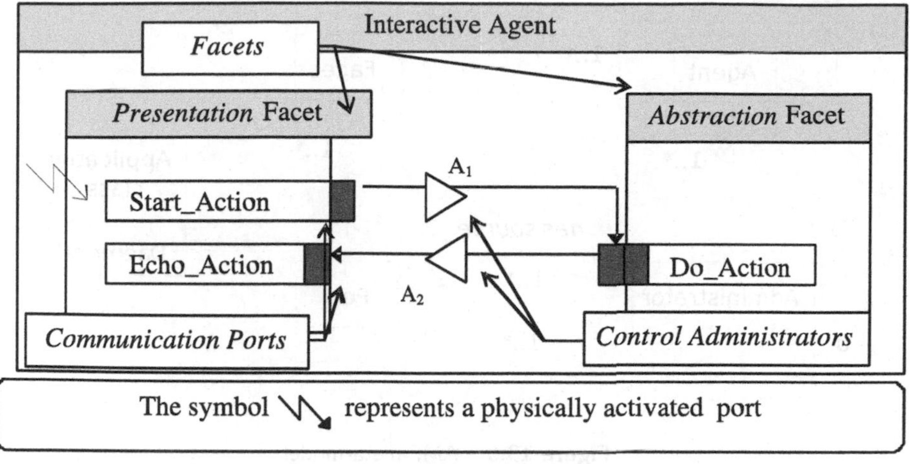

Figure 13.3 A simple interaction described with AMF

The *Simple administrator* 'A1' which has this port as a source dispatches the event to its unique target port 'Do_Action'. As soon as the service has been executed, the 'Do_Action' I≫O *port* sends an event as a result of its activation. Being connected to 'A2' *Simple administrator*, the message it sent is thus dispatched to activate the 'Echo_Action' *input port* that will provide the feedback to the user.

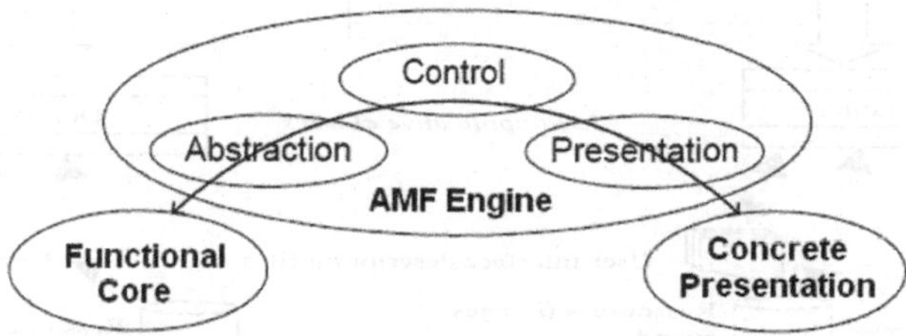

Figure 13.4 The AMF and the Arch models links

13.3.2 AMF Implementation

Hybrid Architecture. AMF is supported by several tools including an editor (or more exactly a graphical development environment) and an execution engine. To implement the AMF architecture, the AMF facets play the role of adapters (in the meaning of Arch, Figure 13.4; Samaan and Tarpin-Bernard, 2004). Thus these classes are concrete facets whereas AMF facets are abstract.

The application control and the adapter facets are finally described within the AMF formalism. The concrete facets like the concrete presentation and the functional core are developed in applicative code. The link between AMF facets and the applicative classes is materialized by the communication ports. Indeed, the ports are associated to

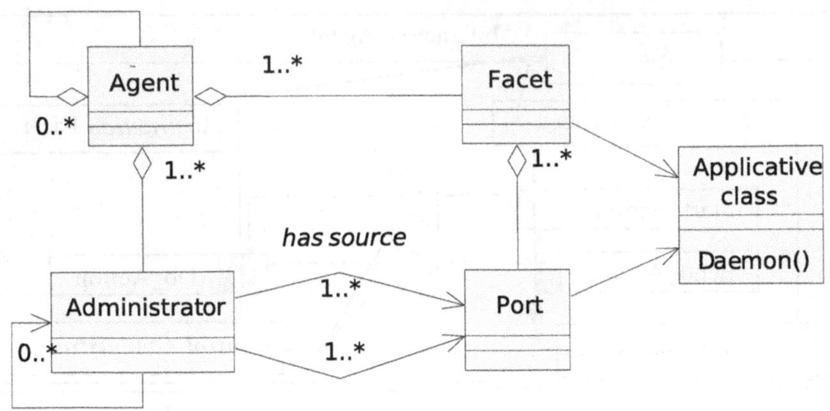

Figure 13.5 AMF meta-model

functions of the applicative classes. We call these functions *daemons*. The activation of a port triggers its daemon. Figure 13.5 synthesizes the meta-model of AMF in hybrid architecture.

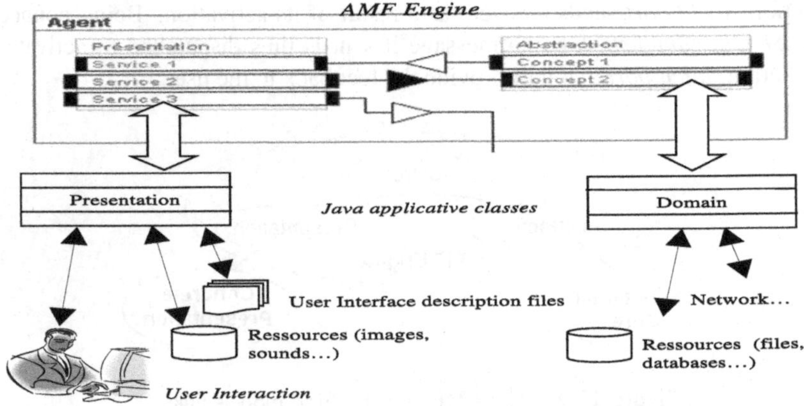

Figure 13.6 Links between AMF and the applicative classes (concrete facets)

The AMF Engine. By AMF engine, we are designating a software process that builds the application and ensures its correct behavior. It links the following elements:

- The application functional core objects, whose role consists in handling the data and performing operations (applicative domain objects);
- The application concrete presentation objects (applicative presentation objects);
- The "AMF objects" themselves, used to manage the communications between the applicative objects (administrator, facets, agents, etc.).

Building the application consists in the setup of the agent hierarchy. The instantiation is done in the following order from the application (top-level) agent: subagents, facets, daemons, ports and then administrators, in a recursive way.

The execution of an application built with AMF requires to instantiate and to initialize not only the applicative objects but also the AMF architecture objects (Agents, Facets, Administrators and Ports). One of the roles of the engine is to perform this loading operation. It instantiates and loads all objects required to the application execution. To determine which objects are required, and then to link them, the engine starts by parsing the control facets description files, that are written in XML. The applicative objects are indicated in the XML control files as URLs. Of course, the engine can also build objects on demand during runtime.

Then, when the user interacts with the application, it will trigger an abstract AMF facet. This activation launches the event dispatch process, which normally ends by the activation of an input port of another AMF facet, which triggers the daemon implemented in an applicative object (the concrete facet).

The Editor. The editor is the AMF instrumentation entry point. Indeed, AMF having a graphical formalism, the first step is to elaborate the architecture model. This editor (Figure 13.7) allows building graphically the AMF-based applications, while making possible the description and integration of AMF templates, components, and configurations.

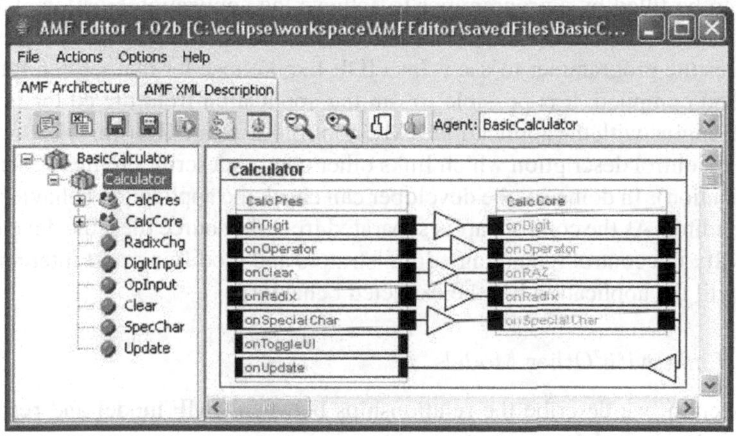

Figure 13.7 The AMF editor (Architecture edition)

In addition to the production of an XML description of the architecture model, the editor fully generates the control of the application (the control facets for a hierarchy of agents), i.e., the links existing between the ports of the facets (Figure 13.8). This functionality is tremendously interesting, as, even if possible, a handmade production of this description is tedious and requires memorizing the description element names to be able to link them.

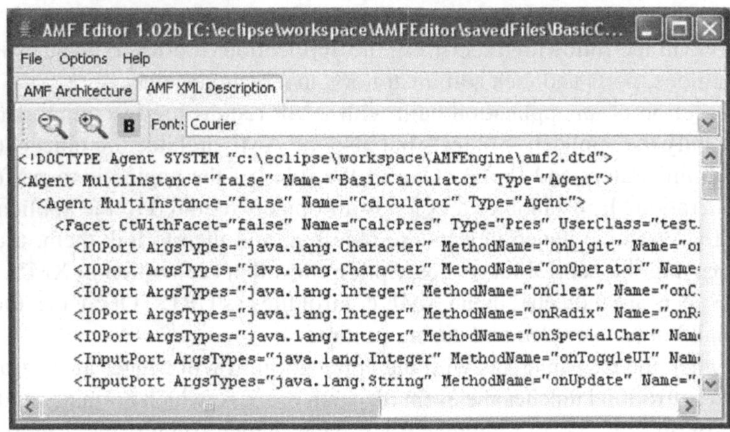

Figure 13.8 The AMF editor (Generated control visualization)

Besides, the editor generates the skeleton of the Java source files of the concrete facets. This process is comparable to a UML MDA process, which creates the structure of the user objects. In our editor, the source files structure generation consists in creating Java packages and classes with public methods that will be the daemons of input and input/output ports. These methods are currently built with an empty body that remains to be filled by a programmer to achieve the application creation. Currently, the editor allows inputting the application source code but in a rudimentary way and we advices the programmer to use a Java IDE like Eclipse for that. When the code is written and compiled, it is possible to run the application from the editor invocating the AMF engine with the application XML control file as a URL (this file contains the root agent control description which links other control description files depending on the application). In doing so, the developer can check the application behavior directly from the editor. As the control part is separated from the source files, the developer can then modify the control (changing administrators and modifying port interconnection paths), until the application has the expected behavior.

13.3.3 Links with Other Models

In this section, we describe the relationships between AMF model and respectively domain and task models.

Interaction Model and Domain Model. The domain model describes all the concepts of the functional core of the application and their relationships. Nowadays, its modeling generally relies on the elaboration of UML models and especially class diagram, which describe the static structure of the application in terms of classes and relations (association, specialization, aggregation, composition and dependence).

We have stated that in AMF hybrid architecture, each facet is associated to a concrete facet called applicative class. This class contains all the methods that are associated to the ports of the abstract facet and additional elements (data and internal functions). As a consequence, the domain model represented by the UML class diagram has usually the same structure as the AMF model; however this is not always the case. To help the designer, we have identified 3 situations:

- Agents are autonomous and each applicative class is associated to an AMF facet. In this common case, there is a bijective relationship and a full symmetry between both models.

- An agent can use specific services realized by a set of applicative classes that are not supposed to be visible and accessible (application of the Facade pattern of Gamma et al., 1995). In this case, these extra classes are not represented in the AMF model. The considered agent is the only element that has a AMF representation and the symmetry is partial.

- Several agents use a complex set of external applicative classes (e.g.,: database access, calculation library, etc.). In this case, the external applicative classes are grouped in a package and a dedicated agent is added to the AMF model to ensure the links between the agents and the external services.

In the first case, the UML relations between classes (association, aggregation, etc.) cannot be maintained. Indeed, the flexibility and the power of AMF require not having direct coupling of applicative classes so that all communications use the AMF engine. Thus, we have proposed rules of translation of the relations between UML classes to AMF model:

- The aggregation of 2 classes is a composition of AMF agents;

- The association between 2 classes leads to the definition of control administrators and communication ports associated to the services that are supposed to be invoked through the association.

- The specialization relations between classes are maintained.

Task Model and Interaction Model. Interaction tasks are naturally associated to the communication ports of Presentation facets. Similarly, computer tasks can be clearly associated to Abstraction facets. Normally, these tasks are also directly linked to the domain model.

In our work, we are using CTT formalism (Paterno et al., 1997) to model tasks. Figure 13.9 represents the relationships between tasks (interaction and computer oriented) and the ports of Presentation and Abstraction facets in a sample application. This application is a music player that provides classic features like Select_Title, Play_Title, Stop_Title, etc.

In model-based approaches, the task model is often the starting model for the design of an interactive application. This model is very flexible in terms of level of details of the modeling. Indeed the specification can be very high (almost functional), e.g., change the volume, or precise, e.g., key ‘up’ / key ‘down’. For this reason, we are considering two versions of the model: the abstract and the concrete models.

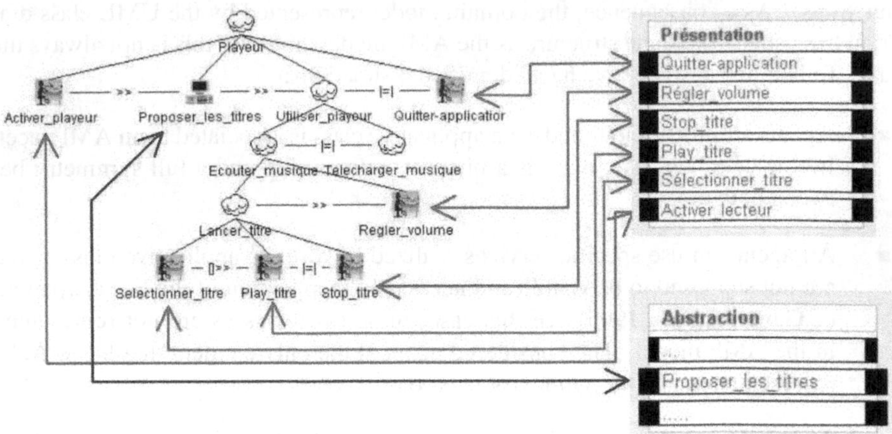

Figure 13.9 Example of relationships between tasks and ports in the interaction model

The abstract task model represents a generic view of the application, which is independent from the context of use and more specifically to the interaction platform. If we go back to our sample, the modelled tasks are abstract tasks because they do not define the elementary interactions. From this model, it is possible to build and abstract AMF interaction model using what we call *abstract ports*. These abstract ports describe services that must be provided without specifying neither how they will be concretely implemented or their relations with other elements. On AMF graphical formalism, abstract ports are represented with a dash border.

In the concrete task model, each leaf of the task tree represents a concrete interaction with objects of the user interface and is generally detailed enough for identifying physical interaction (mouse click, key pressed, etc.). This model is context-dependent. Passing from abstract to concrete task tree supposes making some interaction choices and replacing the abstract task by subtrees of concrete tasks.

In the music player sample, if we consider an interaction platform that only provides a keyboard as interaction mean (it is a very simplified context but sufficient for the illustration), the abstract task *Select_Title* could be replaced (Figure 13.10) by the following subtree:

- *Up/down*: to move into the list of titles.
- *Validate_Title*: to validate the choice.

This concretization operation is a repetitive task that can be assisted by a design tool. Indeed, many tasks are repeated similarly in a design. The next section introduces our vision for the use of task and interaction patterns in the design and implementation process.

Task and Interaction Patterns. AMF interaction model has been designed for supporting a "design patterns" approach (Gamma et al., 1995). Indeed, fragments

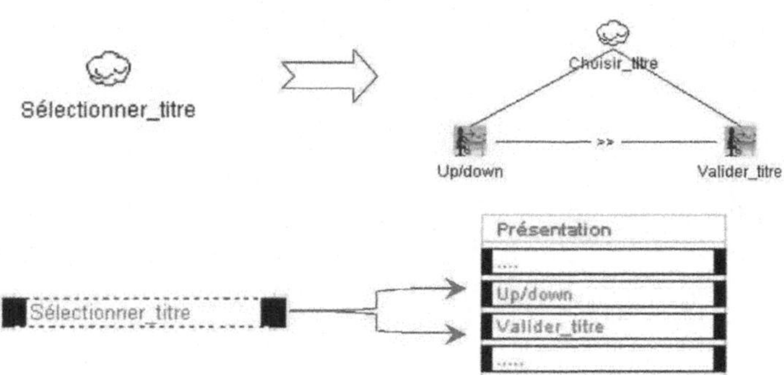

Figure 13.10 Example of concretization of an abstract task and the associated abstract port

of models (agents, facets, ports and administrators) are, by construction, potential patterns when they define a validated solution to a well-defined problem. We call these patterns *interaction patterns.* Thus, several patterns have already been defined (Tarpin-Bernard *et al.,* 1998) but most of them still need to be identified.

In the specific area of interaction adaptation, we have defined several patterns for designing the same generic task in various contexts. For instance, we have modeled the very common task of moving an element inside a container (e.g., an icon in an area, an item in a list, etc.). The design principle is classical: 1) the container object received the notification of a request of selection of an element, 2) the element is identified and the validity of the potential move is checked, 3) the destination is defined, 4) the move is validated, 5) the display is refreshed.

Figure 13.11 shows a pattern that realizes this abstract task and two concrete variants corresponding to two different contexts of use. This interaction pattern has a *Container* agent that contains component agents (multiple instantiations) which can be moved (*Element*). The abstract port (*Select&Move)* of the *Presentation* facet of the composed agent receives the user action events and transmits them to the component agents. The abstract ports and administrators are replaced by concrete elements in the concrete version of the pattern corresponding to different contexts of use (here specific interaction devices).

13.4 A METHOD FOR DESIGNING ADAPTABLE APPLICATIONS

13.4.1 Process

Like most model-based approaches, our method consists in splitting the design and implementation process in several steps (four in our case).

In the first step, the abstract task model and domain model are elaborated. The second step defines the abstract interaction model that represents the general structure using AMF. The third step is a concretization step which leads to a concrete AMF model according to the context of use. Finally, the application is instanciated and

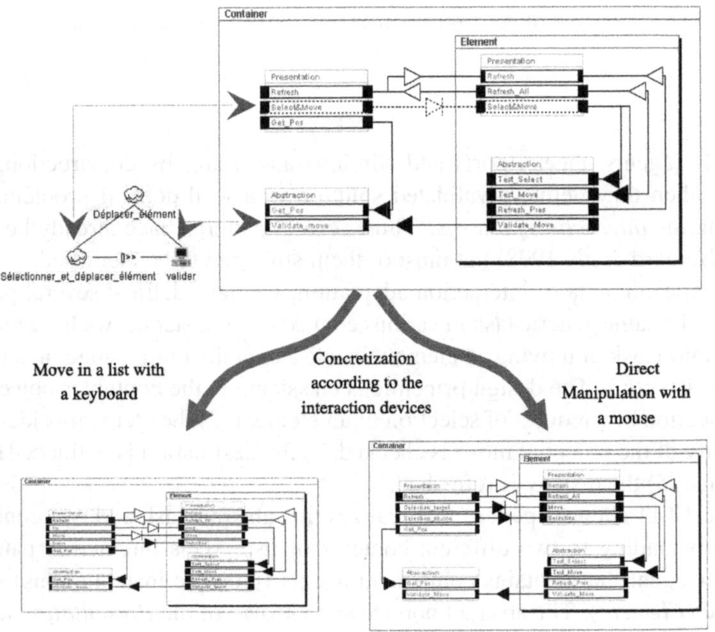

Figure 13.11 A pattern for the abstract task " Select and Move an element "

executed. In the following section, we are going to describe the main techniques we are applying in these steps.

Step 1: Elaboration of Task Model and Domain Model. This step is the most fundamental one. Using techniques generally based on use case identification, it is possible to build UML models (class diagrams, sequence diagrams, activity diagrams) and task diagrams. We will start by building UML or task diagrams. Because many books are dedicated to this first part of the process, we will not detail it. However, we underline that at this stage the task model is abstract which supposes to have generic tasks.

At the end of this step the designer has an abstract task model and a domain model. Some extra models can also be defined at this stage (user model, environment model, etc.). In collaborative situations, it is usual to define at this stage a model for specifying roles and rights.

Figure 13.12 shows a part of the models resulting from this first design step applied to the music player. The abstract task model is on the left side whereas the UML class diagram of the functional core is on the right side. The models are not yet interconnected.

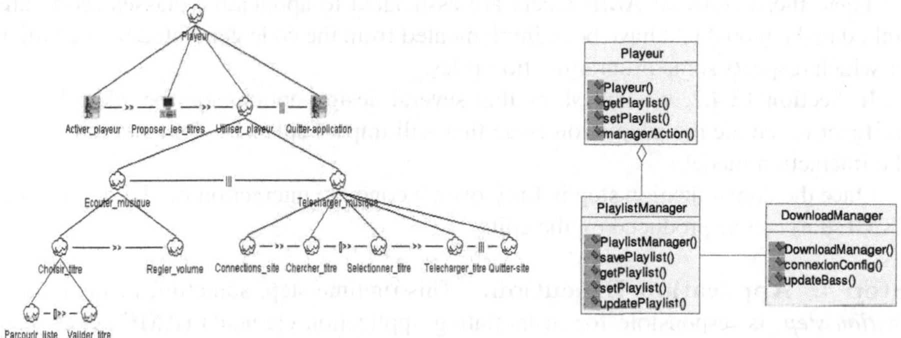

Figure 13.12 Task and domain models after the first design step (music player sample)

This approach is flexible enough to respect designer's habits and culture (software engineering vs. HCI ergonomics). In our own works, we usually start by the task model.

Step 2: Abstract Interaction Design. This step consists in linking previous models building the abstract AMF interaction model.

The temporal logic of the task model usually organizes interactions in a main modal flow defining interaction environmements, which are navigation blocks. Inside each block, the interaction is modal or not (no forced sequence between the tasks).

In order to identify these environments, we currently use the task grouping feature of CTTE. Thus, considering a specific context and thanks to heuristics, the designer can obtain a set of PTS—*Presentation Tasks Set*—which are the tasks that should be accessible simultaneously. These interaction environments are represented in the interaction model by AMF agents that are not naturally identified in the domain model.

However, the domain model is very useful to help organizing the agents. The rules presented in Section 13.3.3 (Interaction model and domain model) lead to structure the hierarchy of agents and define the content of abstraction facets. Then, based on the rules presented in Section 13.3.3 (Task model and Interaction model), the designer can identify abstract ports for each presentation facets postponing any decision about concrete interactions.

As a consequence, the interaction model crystallizes elements from the task models and the domain models. An explicit relationship can be maintained, which will be very useful later if we want to adapt dynamically the application.

The next step consists in concretizing the models to a specific context.

Step 3: Models concretization . The purpose of this step is to replace abstract interactions by concrete interactions. As seen in Section 13.10 (Task and interaction patterns), the designer should be helped in this task by a librairy of interaction patterns related to contexts of use. Once a pattern is chosen, the abstract ports are replaced by concrete ports and administrators. Currently, we have not yet defined heuristics or selection rules but this will be very helpful for the designer.

Then, these concrete AMF facets are associated to applicative classes (ports are linked to daemons) that have been implemented from the code generated by the editor or which respects some programmation rules.

In Section 13.4.2, we will show that several design options can be taken by the designer to handle the adaptation issue that will impact either implementation or just the interaction model.

Once the concretization step is fully over, a concrete interaction model description (XML file) can be produced by the editor.

Step 4: Application Execution. This runtime step, sometimes called *finalization step*, is responsible for instantiating application elements (AMF agents and instances of applicative classes). In our Java implementation, this happens inside a specific component called *AMF engine*. This software component is the heart of an AMF application and ensures 2 main functions:

- Loading the concrete interaction model description files defined in the previous step and instantiating the referenced objects (AMF objects and applicative classes).

- Controling the interaction behavior of the application processing and routing messages between methods of applicative classes through AMF objects (ports, facets, agents and administrators).

The " concrete " facets that are the applicative classes (presentation, abstraction and others) are associated to the AMF engine to provide finalized behaviors. This assembling task is monitored by the AMF engine according to the interaction description files.

Here, we do not directly study the question of the layout of the presentation as this part of the problem is mainly managed by the applicative classes. However, in the next section, we will give some key answers.

13.4.2 Adaptation Options

After having defined a design process and some building rules, we focus our attention on the adaptation options available for the designer. These options depend mainly on the adaptation goals and on the difference between the target contexts. These contexts are defined by the user, the interaction platform, the environment, and the activity. We call distance between two contexts of use the set of differences between both contexts. Even if no metrics are available, this notion is useful to understand when choosing one option or another.

Today, we have identified four strategies for supporting the adaptation. All of them can be combined in a real application according to the required level of adaptation.

First of all, when the distance between two contexts is small, that is, when the adaptation does not require modifying the structuration of the AMF model, it is common to support it inside the presentation applicative classes. For instance, when two interaction platforms own the same input capabilities but have small display differences (e.g., resolution, colors) the adaptation of the size or the layout will not impact the AMF model. Actually, it supposes that the applicative class manages all the possible layouts (which is very similar to the Comet approach) or is able to be parametrized by external description files (see UIDL approaches). In these situations, it is not necessary to modify any connection in the AMF model.

If the target interaction platforms have similar output devices and various input devices but which support similar interaction techniques, the main infrastructure can be maintained but dedicated presentation facets will be inserted. These *Device facets* interact with the real devices. This is particularly useful with non standard devices such as digital gauntlet, eye trackers, or RFID readers (Masserey et al., 2005).

These two first strategies are applied in the last steps of the design process as no significative modifications in the AMF models are required.

When the adaptation implies bigger changes such as another interaction style (e.g., drag-drop with a mouse vs. keyboard interaction) it is necessary to use different communication ports and sometimes new control administrators. As seen earlier, interaction patterns can really ease the designer's task. These patterns can involve one single agent or a small hierarchy.

In the hardest situation, when the adaptation distance is so high that a deep change needs to be done, a total restructuration of the AMF model can occur. Of course, the designer does not need to start from scratch as he can reuse a large part of the interaction model. This kind of adaptation requires making some changes in the second step of our design process using two kinds of actions:

- Filtering tasks that are not achievable in the context (removing abstract tasks in the tree),
- Restructuring interaction environments (grouping differently the remaining tasks).

For this last action, the designer can use tasks grouping heuristics proposed by CTTE (Mori et al., 2002). This way, he can obtain adequate groups of tasks which increase the usability of the resulting application. Indeed, a PC with a large screen is able to display in a single interaction workspace a larger number of tasks than a mobile phone with a small display. Thus, the designer can apply series of grouping steps to reach a satisfying structuration according to the context characteristics, including non platform properties such as user's preferences and abilities.

In the future, we are going to study other techniques to restructure the interaction workspaces. Particularly, we would like to consider the intermediate tasks (virtual/real nodes in the tasks tree).

13.5 FUTURE DEVELOPMENTS AND CONCLUSION

In this paper, we presented a model-based approach organized around AMF, a multiagent model, to achieve adaptability of interactive software as one of multiple aspects of usability. Mainly, we have elaborated an environment composed of a model builder and a runtime engine. These technical tools are associated to a design and implementation process. This helps integrating into an AMF architecture the various models that need to be considered to provide a good adaptation to the context of use (platform, application, and user preferences). Several techniques, mainly based on patterns, can assist the designer in choosing the "best" interaction techniques (in a usability perspective) and easily implement them.

During the description of the AMF model we did not really develop the interest of its multifacet characteristic. As mentioned in several other chapters in this book, usability is not only interaction oriented, but can be concerned by no visible software objects. With AMF, we can consider presentation, control, and abstraction parts, not only at a very large grain, but also at a thinner grain, which allows doing a richer modeling. Indeed, we can collect interesting and reusable behaviors, which can constitute new facets and be reused elsewhere. This way, we allow designers expressing what they consider as new important aspects of the interactive application by creating new facets, which would be reused later by themselves or other designers. The goal of these new facets is also to draw attention during the development process and mainly during usability studies, i.e., answer time for SQL commands which must respect delay constraints to ensure usability of the application. These new facets can be of different natures, i.e., presentation, to create several, alternative presentations for different devices, or different users (mainly in collaborative applications), user's profile, to collect information on user's behavior, presentation preferences, main interactions undertaken and their contexts, in order to be able to determine an appropriate interaction presentation for the user; undo mechanism, in order to indicate the way to stop and undo executed commands, and others, which are explained by creation of new reusable facets. Patterns can be created to express the relation between a new facet and its activation coming from control expressed by appropriate administrators in relation with their ports, can also be created and used in other application designs.

From an architectural point of view, these facets can receive during the adaptation process a particular attention, in order to determine appropriate organizational answer, i.e., specific location of this facet in client-server architecture, location determined by usability requirements as acceptable answer delay. To obtain it, it is possible to locate the facet at the same place as caller and to connect it directly (by procedure call), or to locate it elsewhere and use distant procedure call, soliciting middleware for the call coming from distant facet (see AMF-C; Tarpin-Bernard et al., 1998). This deployment aspect is studied at implementation stage and still open-ended for use (execution) phase adaptations.

Connection between user's actions (interactions) and this new facet and/or between behavior (functional core) facet and this one is expressed graphically at control level with appropriate administrator(s). This visual programming of control can be manipulated by the designer during elaboration process phase as well by the user (in a simplified view to define) during the use (execution) phase. These functionalities are not yet fully operational and constitute interesting future developments.

Finally, we are currently working on the integration of AMF builder into Eclipse environment so that we can enforce the relationships between the AMF model and other views, mainly UML and the visualization of the interface.

References

Abrams, M., Phanouriou, C., Batongbacal, A. L., Williams, S. M., and Shuster, J. E. (1999). UIML: An appliance-independent XML user interface language. *Computer Networks*, 31(11-16):1695–1708.

Azevedo, P., Merrick, R., and Roberts, D. (2000). OVID to AUIML—user-oriented interface modeling. In *Proceedings of Towards a UML Profile for Interactive Systems, TUPIS'2000 Workshop*.

Bouillon, L., Vanderdonckt, J., and Souchon, N. (2002). Recovering alternative presentation models of a Web page with VAQUITA. In Kolski, C. and Vanderdonckt, J., editors, *CADUI, Computer-Aided Design of User Interfaces III, Proceedings of the Fourth International Conference on Computer-Aided Design of User Interfaces, May 15-17, 2002, Valenciennes, France*, pages 311–322. Kluwer.

Calvary, G., Dâassi, O., Coutaz, J., and Demeure, A. (2005). Des widgets aux comets pour la plasticité des systèmes interactifs. *Revue d'Interaction Homme Machine, Europia*, 6(1).

Chikofsky, E. J. and Cross, J. H. (1990). Reverse engineering and design recovery: a taxonomy. *IEEE Software*, 7(1):13–17.

Coutaz, J. (1987). PAC: an implementation model for dialog design. In *Proceedings Interact'87*, pages 431–436.

Coutaz, J. (1990). *Interfaces Homme-Ordinateur, Conception et Réalisation*. Paris: Dunod Informatique.

Dubinko, M., Leigh, L., Klotz, J., Merrick, R., and Raman, T. V. (2003). Xforms 1.0. Technical report, World Wide Web Consortium.

Florins, M., Trevisan, D. G., and Vanderdonckt, J. (2004). The continuity property in mixed reality and multiplatform systems: a comparative study. In Jacob, R. J. K., Limbourg, Q., and Vanderdonckt, J., editors, *CADUI*, pages 321–332. Kluwer.

Gamma, E., Helm, R., Johnson, R., and Vlissides, J. (1995). *Design Patterns: Elements of Reusable Object-Oriented Software*. Addison Wesley Professional Computing Series. http://www.aw.com.

Hyatt, D., Goodger, B., Hickson, I., and Waterson, C. (2001). Xml user interface language (xul) specification 1.0. w3c recommendation. http://www.mozilla.org/projects/xul/.

Koskimies, O., Wasmund, M., Wolkerstorfer, P., and Ziegert, T. (2004). Practical experiences with device independent authoring concepts. In *Advances on User Interface Description Languages, Workshop of AVI 2004*. Expertise Centre for Digital Media.

Krasner, G. E. and Pope, S. T. (1988). A cookbook for using the model-view controller user interface paradigm in Smalltalk-80. *Journal of Object-Oriented Program*, 1(3):26–49.

Limbourg, Q., Vanderdonckt, J., Michotte, B., Bouillon, L., and Lopez, V. (2005). UsiXML: a language supporting multipath development of user interfaces. In *Proc. of 9th IFIP Working Conference on Engineering for Human-Computer Interaction jointly with 11th Int. Workshop on Design, Specification, and Verification of Interactive Systems EHCI-DSVIS'2004*, volume 3425 of *Lecture Notes in Computer Science*, pages 200–220, Springer-Verlag.

Luyten, K. (2004). *Dynamic User Interface Generation for Mobile and Embedded Systems with Model-Based User Interface Development*. Ph.D. thesis, Limburgs Universitair Centrum, School of IT, Expertise Center for Digital Media, Diepenbeek, Belgium.

Masserey, G., Tran, C. D., Samaan, K., Tarpin-Bernard, F., and David, B. (2005). Environnement de conception et développement d'applications interactives selon l'architecture amf. In *IHM 2005: Conférence Francophone sur l'Interaction Homme-Machine*, pages 329–330, New York: ACM Press.

Mori, G., Paternò, F., and Santoro, C. (2002). CTTE: support for developing and analyzing task models for interactive system design. *IEEE Trans. Softw. Eng.*, 28(8):797–813.

Mori, G., Paternò, F., and Santoro, C. (2004). Design and development of multidevice user interfaces through multiple logical descriptions. *IEEE Trans. Software Eng*, 30(8):507–520.

Nigay, L. and Coutaz, J. (1993). A design space for multimodal systems: Concurrent processing and data fusion. In Ashlund, S., Mullet, K., Henderson, A., Hollnagel, E., and White, T., editors, *Proceedings of the Conference on Human Factors in computing systems*, pages 172–178, New York. ACM Press.

Ouadou, K. (1994). *AMF : Un modèle d'architecture multiagents multifacettes pour Interfaces Homme-Machine et les outils associés*. Ph.D. thesis, Ecole Centrale de Lyon, France.

Paterno, F., Mancini, C., and Meniconi, S. (1997). ConcurTaskTrees: a diagrammatic notation for specifying task models. In *Proceedings of IFIP INTERACT'97: Human-Computer Interaction*, pages 362–369.

Pfaff, G., editor (1985). *User Interface Management Systems*. Proceedings of the IFIP/EG Workshop on User Interface Management Systems, Seeheim, FRG, Oct. 1983. Springer-Verlag.

Rouillard, J. (2003). Plastic ML and its toolkit. In *Proceedings of the Tenth International Conference on Human-Computer Interaction*, volume 4 of *Universal Access in HCI : Inclusive Design in the Information Society*, pages 612–616.

Samaan, K. and Tarpin-Bernard, F. (2004). The AMF architecture in a multiple user interface generation process. In Luyten, K., Abrams, M., Vanderdonckt, J., and Limbourg, Q., editors, *Proceedings of the ACM AVI'2004 Workshop on Developing User Interfaces with XML: Advances on User Interface Description Languages*, pages 71–78.

Seffah, A., Donyaee, M., Kline, R. B., and Padda, H. K. (2006). Usability measurement and metrics: A consolidated model. *Software Quality Journal*, 14(2):159–178.

Seffah, A., Gulliksen, J., and Desmarais, M. C., editors (2005). *Human-Centered Software Engineering: Integrating Usability in the Development Process*. New York: Springer-Verlag.

Tarpin-Bernard, F., David, B. T., and Primet, P. (1998). Frameworks and patterns for synchronous groupware: AMf-C approach. In Chatty, S. and Dewan, P., editors, *EHCI*, volume 150 of *IFIP Conference Proceedings*, pages 225–241. Kluwer.

Thevenin, D. (2001). *Adaptation en interaction homme-machine : le cas de la plasticité*. Ph.D. thesis, Universite Joseph-Fourier - Grenoblc I, France.

UIMS (1992). A metamodel for the runtime architecture of an interactive system: the UIMS tool developers workshop. *SIGCHI Bull.*, 24(1):32–37.

IV Reengineering, Reverse Engineering, and Refactoring

14 THE GAINS DESIGN PROCESS: HOW TO DO STRUCTURED DESIGN OF USER INTERFACES IN ANY SOFTWARE ENVIRONMENT

Martha J. Lindeman

Agile Interactions, Inc., 1933 E. Dublin-Granville Road #125, Columbus, OH 43229.

(Published by permission of Agile Interactions, Inc.)

Abstract. This paper describes a user-interaction design process created and used by a consultant to solve two challenges: (1) how to decrease the need for changes in the user interface by subsequent system releases without doing big design up-front and (2) how to apply a structured user-interaction design process no matter when brought into a project or what software methodology was being used. The four design levels in the process parallel Beck and Fowler's four planning levels described in their book *Planning Extreme Programming*. The design process is called "GAINS" because the user-interaction designer has only Attraction, Information and Navigation to connect users' Goals with the project sponsors' criteria for Success. Thus there are five questions, one for each letter of the acronym GAINS, asked at each of four levels of design: The first two design levels, Rough Plan and Big Plan, focus on business-process actions and objects that define users' goals. The next two levels, Release Planning and Iteration Planning, focus on the user interface objects that support the tasks necessary to achieve those goals. Release Planning identifies the displays the user sees for each goal included in that release, and also the across-display navigation for the proposed functionality. Iteration Planning focuses at a lower level of interaction, such as the within-display navigation among controls. For a voice system, the word "sees" would be changed to "hears," but the design process and the levels of focus are the same for user interfaces that are vision output (e.g., GUIs), voice output (e.g., IVRs), or multimodal.

14.1 THE COSTS OF CHANGING USER INTERFACES

Any introduction of new functionality for users, or any modification of functionality currently available to users, requires one or more changes to a user interface. Consequently, it is a given that a new system or a new release of an old system will require users to change some of their mental models and physical behaviors. However, changing part or all of a user interface often has negative consequences as measured by decreases in users' productivity and satisfaction. Although productivity and satisfaction could increase after users make the necessary changes, often first reactions become permanent and the positive effects are never experienced.

The user interface change(s) may seem trivial to developers—such as moving a button to make room for a new button—but changes in a user interface can cause two major types of "user costs":

1. Conceptual changes in a user interface require changes to users' subconscious "mental models" of how to interact with the system, which can be very difficult to change; and

2. Changing interactions that users already have stored in "muscle memory" from a previous version require making errors to change those behaviors.

In an agile development environment such as eXtreme Programming (XP), the user interface frequently changes with each release. However, user interface changes occur in non-agile development environments, just less frequently. For example, Microsoft made major changes in the user interface of its Office suite with the introduction of the new Vista interface.

14.1.1 User Costs of Conceptual Change

An "intuitive" user interface is one in which a user can take a current mental model and immediately apply it to successfully interact with a new system, Web page, etc. The physical behaviors may be very different but the conceptual model is very similar—such as filling out a computerized form that previously required writing on paper. The conceptual model, 'remember this information and put it there,' is the same in both instances.

However, conceptual models are learned during experience and are rarely expressed. For example, when going to a new doctor's office, the receptionist simply says, "Please fill out these forms," without any detailed instructions. The new patient is expected to apply the model for filling out forms even when the patient has never seen those forms.

Similarly, users apply old mental models to new user interfaces without additional instructions. Only when part of an old model does not apply does it become necessary to think about the differences and consciously decide what to do next. The difficulty of deciding what to do next is what makes a user interface difficult to use—the more effort required to decide what to do next, the less intuitive the user interface!

From a developers' perspective, the users' negative reactions to changes will often seem out of proportion. On the other hand, from a cognitive-science perspective the users are correct—people become experts by 'chunking' information and building higher levels of knowledge on the lower-level chunks. Thus changing a single fundamental concept can disrupt a user's entire mental model for how to interact with a system.

For example, early releases of a system might be built around 'account' as a primary interaction concept. When customer stories are written for a later release, they indicate (1) there is a many-to-many relationship between accounts and customers, and (2) that the concept 'customer' is more important than the concept 'account.' A change in the user interface design at this conceptual level can cause major havoc in users' minds as they attempt to adjust their mental models to a different way of thinking. This is true even when the new model is like their original way of thinking prior to the introduction of the first system. What developers may think is a simple reorganization of user interface widgets may seem like a whole new system to users!

Consequently, the three to seven fundamental concepts that underlie the entire system functionality need to be defined at the beginning of the design process, even if it requires some quick research to discover major issues not addressed by the current stories. For example, the fundamental concepts can often be identified from one or more business documents that originally justified the initiation of the project.

14.1.2 User Costs of Logical or Visual Change

Even simple visual changes can have high user costs of change. As a worst-case scenario, imagine users have been frequently using a Confirm button at a particular location in a user interface. During the next release, the need to add buttons at that point causes the Confirm button to be moved 40 pixels to the left and a Delete button is put in the old location of the Confirm button. Users will now repeatedly click on the Delete button when they start using the new release.

There is a simple reason for the decrease in users' productivity because of a seemingly trivial button relocation—any action stored in muscle memory, such as where to move a cursor for a button, can only be unlearned by making mistakes. To see an easy example of automated muscle memory, have a Windows® user move the location of the taskbar to a different location and watch how many times the cursor is moved toward the old location before the user learns the taskbar is no longer there.

People automate physical movements for frequent behaviors to save cognitive resources, and doing it is hard-wired into our brains—verbal training does not unlearn automated actions, which is why expert users have great difficulty with new systems. Automated actions are typically unlearned through errors.

Consequently, the "user costs" of moving the button are the time and effort it takes for the user to (a) unlearn the old location, (b) learn the new location, and (c) correct any errors resulting from the old habits. Depending on the results of the errors, user costs for the physical relocation of one button can be very high, and user costs can rapidly increase as changes are larger. The time and effort taken to change the automated behavior is a function of how long and frequently the behavior is done.

The GAINS approach to user-interaction/interface design was created during 15 years of UI consulting as a way to help decrease users' costs of change while not impacting the project schedule. The project starting point for the use of GAINS has ranged from early project initiation to shortly before a product was to be delivered, and about every possible point in between those two extremes. The software engineering methodology contexts for the projects where GAINS has been applied have ranged from formal methodologies enforced in detail to almost no methodology at all.

14.2 OVERVIEW OF THE GAINS PROCESS

The GAINS process for user interface design, which parallels the XP planning process, has been used for more than 15 years in successful consulting projects for small and large systems in many different content domains. It has been used for many types of hardware, software platforms, and development methodologies. Applying this process for agile user-interaction/interface design may accomplish two goals for the developer/designer: (1) increase system usability, and (2) decrease project risk. A bulletin-board system is used in the remainder of this paper to briefly explain the GAINS design process.

GAINS is an acronym that captures the following statement:

"The user interface designer has only Attraction, Information and Navigation to connect users' Goals with sponsors' criteria for Success."

There is nothing else, and they typically occur in that sequence. Users are attracted to a specific part of a user interface, find information in that location, and then navigate to another location to repeat the sequence.

GAINS can also be expressed as the following five questions that should be answered for any point in an interaction or for any part of a user interface:

G What is the other person's (e.g., user's) goal?

A What will attract the person?

I What information does the person want or need?

N What determines the person's next action?

S How do you (or the project sponsors) define success?

These questions apply to any type of interaction, whether person-to-person or person-to-machine.

When GAINS is applied to user interface design, the questions are asked and answered in four levels of design: Architecture, Goals, Tasks and Aesthetics. Separating the design process into these four levels does two things. First, it 'clears out the underbrush' so that the designer can concentrate on only what is important at each level and thus get usability feedback much faster at each level of design. In that sense GAINS is a top-down approach. Second, it is easy to identify the appropriate level for relevant information gathered from any source at any time. Thus design can run bottom-up and/or middle-out when that type of information is first available. As a consultant, a good UI designer needs to be able to start from any point in a project and work in whatever direction is most efficient and effective for that particular project.

The parallels between the four design levels of the GAINS process and the eXtreme Programming (XP) planning process are shown in Figure 14.1. These are explained in more detail in the following sections of this paper.

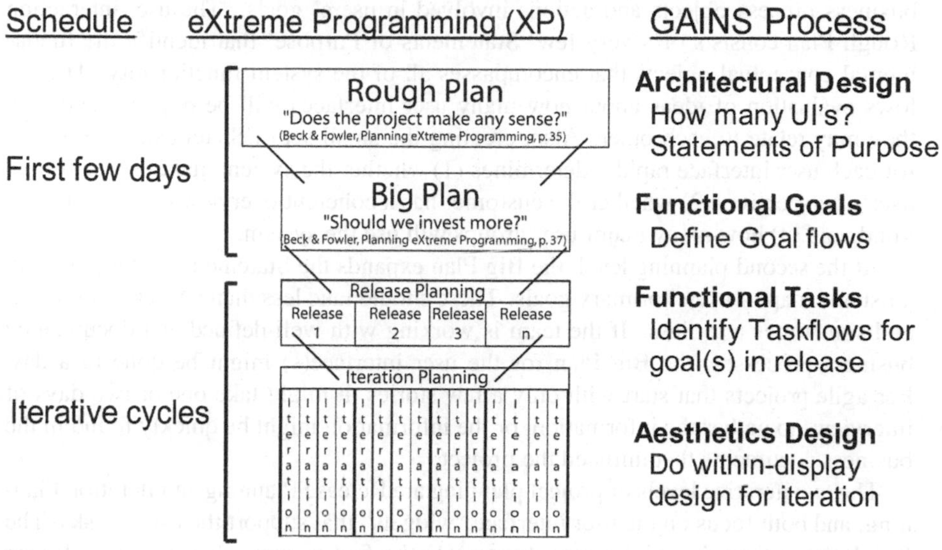

Figure 14.1 Users' goals and roles for the bulletin-board example

There are two higher levels of GAINS design not discussed in this paper: the Organizational level, which focuses on an enterprise-wide view of user interfaces, and the Project level, which applies the enterprise-wide view to a specific project. These two levels define user-interaction design management, and the decisions made at those levels strongly impact what may or may not happen at the four design levels shown in Figure 14.1. However, those two levels are outside the scope of this paper and will be discussed in a forthcoming book on the GAINS design process.

14.3 OVERVIEW OF XP'S PLANNING LEVELS

In *Planning Extreme Programming*, Beck and Fowler (2001) describe project planning at four levels: (1) a "rough plan," (2) a "big plan," (3) "release plans," and (4) "iteration plans." Although the first two may be treated as one, the Rough Plan and Big Plan have been described separately to clearly distinguish how to apply them to user-interaction/interface design. The largest return on investment typically occurs at these higher levels. In most cases, all of the planning prior to release planning takes only a few hours or days. The determining factors will be the complexity of the system, how well the customer knows what she or he wants, and whether there is truly only one customer voice.

Each XP planning level addresses a single question:

Planning Level Question (based on Beck and Fowler)

Rough Plan:	Will this system make sense to its users?
Big Plan:	Should additional money be invested?
Release Planning:	How will project be synchronized with the business?
Iteration Planning:	What development tasks are to be done by whom?

For user interactions, the Rough Plan and Big Plan focus on the few most-important business-process objects and actions involved in users' goals. The user-interaction Rough Plan consists of a very few 'Statements of Purpose' that identify the fundamental conceptual objects that encompasses all of the system functionality. This allows evaluation of ideas about how many user interfaces will be required and how they may relate to each other. Also, creating the small set of Statements of Purpose for each user interface rapidly determines (1) whether the system makes sense from a user's perspective, (2) whether the customer has a coherent overview of the system in mind, and (3) how many major user groups will use the system.

At the second planning level, the Big Plan expands the Statements of Purpose into a list and map of users' primary goals. These should take less than a week to produce, and sometimes a lot less. If the team is working with well-defined and documented business processes, the Big Plan for the user interface(s) might be done in a day. For agile projects that start with only a few stories, it might take one or two days of interviews to gather the information, or the information might be quickly found in the business documents that initiated the project.

The two iterative levels of project planning are Release Planning and Iteration Planning, and both focus on the user interface "widgets" that support the users' tasks. The first Release Plan focuses on two things: (1) the first primary display for each user interface, and (2) the across-display navigation for the first release. Later Release Plans integrate new primary displays into the navigation map for the existing displays. Iteration Planning focuses on secondary displays and within-display navigation.

14.3.1 Rough Plan

The first question that must be answered for any interactive system is, "Will this system make sense to its users?" This is true for all technologies, all types of systems, and all development methodologies. Someone, somewhere, needs to have a single coherent view of the system as it will be presented to the users. As Tom Poppendieck (personal communication, January 4, 2003) expressed it, someone needs to understand "the external conceptual integrity of the whole product." If a system has a user interface with low usability, users will look for other ways to achieve their goals, even when the system uses the best technology or has the best functionality. Thus technically better systems may fail in the marketplace while mediocre systems with a better user interface may succeed.

The highest level of planning, the "Rough Plan," allows the project team to quickly create a coherent overview for interaction design. At this level, the project team creates a set of three to seven "Statements of Purpose" for the system as a whole. Multiple sets of Statements of Purpose are appropriate if, and only if, the system has multiple complex user interfaces. For one set of Statements of Purpose, it is usually better to try to limit the project to five or fewer Statements—difficulty in creating a good set of Statements of Purpose is an early warning of major difficulties that can cause the project to fail.

A bulletin-board system will be used as the example for the rest of this paper. Each completed Statement of Purpose defines one or more fundamental user goals (e.g., manage bulletin board), the associated user profile or profiles (e.g., system administrator), and when, where and how the users will be able to access the system to work on that goal (e.g., through the Internet). Thus one Statement of Purpose for a bulletin-board system might be, "The system administrator will use a control panel to manage all aspects of the bulletin board at any time and from anywhere s/he can use a Web browser supported by the system."

If all of the information for a Statement of Purpose is not known, then the designer starts by identifying the users' goal for a statement and later expands from that. It is also important to define the user characteristics, particularly if they are controversial. Differences in user characteristics can significantly change how the user interface would be designed to achieve greater usability.

Creating a set of "Statements of Purpose" for a system can be done in a few hours if a project makes sense and the information is available. Starting with whatever information is known, first define a set of fundamental "user concepts." They are called "user concepts" because they may not exist as physical objects in the system. For example, in a customer-service system for a utility company, the developers chose to recreate a customer's "bill" each time it was requested by doing joins in the database. Thus the monthly bills for a customer were not permanent objects in the database, but "bill" was a fundamental object in the users' mental models.

Often the fundamental concepts can be identified from the information used to justify the initial project budget or in contracts used to hire consultants. However, when drafting the list of fundamental concepts, make sure to include often initially forgotten user groups such as system administrators and maintenance technicians. Then shorten the list to the fewest concepts with good usability that cover all of the planned functionality of the system.

If there are more than five or perhaps six fundamental concepts in the first list, search for ways to simplify them—particularly for ways they can be made easier to learn and use. Also consider whether the fundamental set defines multiple user interfaces for the same system. For example, some concepts may be fundamental for the system administrator (e.g., "user") and others fundamental for end-users (e.g., "customer"). Then, in essence, you design two different interfaces, and link them together appropriately for the system administrator.

The words chosen for fundamental concepts can make a major difference in usability design! For example, the design of the most important primary display for a call-center GUI will significantly differ if the concept "call," "account," "customer," "stakeholder" or "service" is considered most important.

Also, the highest-level of planning is when to work out relationships among the proposed fundamental concepts—for a GUI, the opening display for each user interface ultimately will have to integrate all of the system functionality appropriate for its users. For a voice-response system, all of the functionality will have to be accessed through a single menu (keypad input) or top-level vocabulary (voice input). Thus for any interactive system, all navigational paths start with a user's first primary display/presentation and then go to whatever depth (number of choices) necessary to complete a task. If it is difficult to define a single list of fundamental concepts, think how interesting it will be to integrate the access points for all navigational paths included in the one top-level display or voice menu!

After identifying each of the fundamental concepts, expand each one into its "Statement of Purpose" by identifying the user profiles, actions and constraints for that concept (if they are known). For example, one statement of purpose for a customer-service system could be "Any authorized user will be able to manage appropriate accounts using any Web browser supported by the system."

1. The words "Any authorized user" identifies the 'who' for that statement of purpose.
2. The interactive verb "manage" will later expand to any defined user action such as access, create, read, edit, delete, print, etc., that will be supported for the concept.
3. The fundamental concept "appropriate accounts" identifies the 'what.'
4. The words "any Web browser" identify the 'means of access.'

The process of creating the set of Statements of Purpose often reveals that the customer is speaking with many voices rather than just one. This needs to be discovered at the beginning of a project rather than when a release causes controversy within the customer's organization. Past projects have revealed that even customers that have spent millions on business-process redesign may not have created a single coherent overview of why the system is being built. But without that coherent overview, either pure luck or genius-level skill will be needed to pull the functionality of a large system together into a user interface with high usability.

Creating Statements of Purpose also often reveals (a) how many user interfaces must be provided for user access, and (b) how various user access-points relate to each other. For example, in a print-shop control system there may be one user interface for shift supervisors and a different user interface for operators. Understanding this early in a project can help developers determine whether stories that appear to be independent actually interact strongly in the user interface. Then the team can plan, or choose not to plan, appropriately.

The set of Statements of Purpose for a bulletin-board system might be the following three statements:

1. All identified users will be able to browse forums, start threads, and manage their posts at any time and from anywhere they can use a Web browser supported by the system.
2. All unknown users may browse forums open to them at any time and from anywhere they can use a Web browser supported by the system.

3. The system administrator will use a control panel to manage all aspects of the bulletin board at any time and from anywhere s/he can use a Web browser supported by the system.

Note that these three simple statements have identified the following requirements: (a) three types of user profiles or status states, (b) the four fundamental goals of non-administrator users, (c) that not all Web browsers will be supported, and (d) that two separate user interfaces will be needed. The first display after a user logs in as a system administrator would contain the application control panel. The first display for another user would contain the list of available forums. These two first displays are so different that they need to be considered as two different user interfaces that must integrated together. In this case the integration is as simple as putting a link to the forums-page on the control-panel page. In other types of systems the integration may be much more complicated and thus require more effort to design.

When the team agrees on the Statements of Purpose, then it becomes obvious that the system "makes sense." At that time the question for the Rough Planning level is answered. Until that happens, it has not been clarified (1) that the customer speaks with only one voice, and (2) that the 'voice' knows at the highest-level what the system is to provide to its users. From experience, these issues must be resolved at this level or the project has a high risk of severe problems and perhaps even failure. It is well worth the few days (or hours) necessary to complete the Rough Plan!

14.3.2 Big Plan

The second level of XP planning is Big Plan, which asks the question, "Should additional money be invested?" For user-interaction design, at this level the team identifies the users' primary goals. These can be expanded and used to assess the user-interaction risks of assigning features to particular release dates, developers, etc.

For the Big Plan, the concepts and actions in the Statements of Purpose are expanded into a list of users' primary goals and a map showing how the goals relate to each other. Although this often cannot be done as quickly as the Statements of Purpose (assuming the team agreed on them), the list and map should take less than a week to produce. If the team is working with well-defined and documented business processes, the list of users' primary goals might be done in a few hours.

When the interaction design is being done within an agile methodology, there may be less pressure to get the list and map exactly right than there is within more traditional methodologies. However, having a more complete and accurate primary-goals list and map very early in the project decreases project risk because it decreases the probability of large changes to the organization of the user interface when it is tested by users or for later releases.

For the bulletin-board example, the three Statements of Purpose identify the list of user goals and roles shown in Table 14.1. That list is then expanded in Table 14.2 so that each row, when read from left to right, states one primary user goal for the user group identified in the first column. Thus, Table 14.2 identifies the first-draft set of primary goals for all users. (Note: Excel is an excellent tool for doing these types of

Table 14.1 List of users' goals and roles identified in the Statements of Purpose

Users' Goals		**User Role(s)**
Action	**Concept**	
Browse	Forums	Registered Users, Guests
Start	Thread	Registered Users
Manage	Posts	Registered Users
Manage	Board	System Administrator

lists. The functionality in Word tables is not as adequate for the sorting of rows needed to design complex systems.)

Table 14.2 First-draft set of primary goals for all users of the bulletin-board system

Primary User Role(s)	**Action**	**Concept**
Registered Users, Guests	Browse	Forums
Registered Users	Start	Thread
Registered Users	Manage	Post(s)
System Administrator	Manage	Board
System Administrator	Manage	Users
System Administrator	Manage	Categories
System Administrator	Manage	Forums
System Administrator	Manage	Threads
System Administrator	Manage	Environment

This first-draft list of users and their primary goals covers every user's goal that the system functionality will support. The concept "board" has been associated with the concepts "users" and "categories" (groups of forums), two concepts that were not included in the Statements of Purpose. [Note: Identifying the users of a system is not the same as including them in the system as objects to be manipulated by the system administrator!] The system "environment" of the board has also been included because, for example, the board may require specific releases of PHP and MySQL to be loaded on the server. Thus managing the environment is a user-interaction goal to be considered by the designer even when it is not included in any user interface of the application.

The dependency map for this set of primary goals is simple and can be expressed in words rather than pictures:

The board must be installed within an appropriate supporting environment before creating any forums or categories of forums. Forums must be created prior to threads, and threads are created by the first post with a new subject. End-users may be registered as soon as the control panel is operational.

In a more complex system, the dependency map can be done with post-it notes on a wall or with informal drawings. The key is to determine the sequence and dependencies among the primary user goals. For example, a window for the administrator's control panel is necessary to support the first user interaction that occurs after the application is installed. Thus the control-panel display and some of the user tasks it supports would be planned for the first release to be used by users. In an agile development environment, other user tasks to be supported by the panel could be identified and their implementation deferred until a later release.

When the team agrees on the draft list and dependency map of users' goals, it is time to begin release planning. The list and dependency map of users' primary goals puts a 'stake in the sand' that, although it can be moved, provides a base for later defining the details of the user-interaction features to be included in each release. To this point, the team has been able to "travel light" while taking about a week to obtain a conceptual overview of interaction design that can be very useful for release and iteration planning.

14.3.3 Release Planning

The third level of XP planning is Release Planning, which asks the question, "How do we synchronize the project with the business?" For user-interaction design, at this level the team plans across-display navigation flows so that the project is less susceptible to high user costs for later changes. Continuing the bulletin-board example, the primary concepts identified in the Big Plan would be expanded to include all the users' goals relevant to the first release and a few later releases. For example, "managing users" for the administrator's control panel would be expanded to include the user goals of "adding/finding/deleting/... user", "editing user profile," "adding/modifying/removing avatars," etc. The first two of these goals might be included in the first release, and "adding/modifying/removing avatars" deferred until later. Beck and Fowler recommend making 3–4 month release plans (p. 128), and these could be used to store deferred items.

Other user goals under "managing users," such as "adding/modifying/removing user title" and "adding/modifying/removing a user-profile field," might not be defined at this time unless they were specifically included in a customer story. Other possible user goals, such as "create user profile," might be discussed and resolved. For example, "create user profile" might become a system action that creates a default profile as soon as a user becomes a registered user.

Notice that a new concept, "user profile," was introduced in the expansion of "manage users" for the first release. The question would arise whether users could edit their own profiles. This is the kind of dynamic change that can be difficult to handle in traditional methodologies but easy to incorporate when using the XP methodology.

New user types of profiles may also be introduced. For example, if the individual forums are moderated, then "moderators" is a type of user group. A board might even have a "super moderator" who can moderate all forums on the bulletin board. New user states might be defined so that a user is always in one of the following states when visiting the board: unregistered, awaiting email confirmation, not logged in, awaiting validation, or registered. Again the customer may not define these changes until the team is well into the development process.

Many kinds of changes frequently occur when defining interaction requirements because users rarely know what they really want until they experience it. There are three mutually exclusive ways software-development projects attempt to handle these kinds of changes:

1. Completely design the physical user interface before beginning to code.

2. Completely define all conceptual and logical user interactions before beginning to code.

3. Use an interaction process that is flexible enough to change while also (a) decreasing the risk of significant rework for the team and (b) decreasing the number of user interface changes that have significant user costs.

The first alternative was successfully used to design and prototype a system in the United States and then the prototype was sent overseas as part of the requirements for system coding. The second alternative is when a project calls for completion of a big up-front design before handing the requirements off to developers for coding.

The third alternative is provided by the XP development methodology when it is integrated with user-interaction design as described in this paper. The Statements of Purpose, list of users' primary goals and goal-dependency map provide a top-down overview. This can be very practical when compared to the bottom-up approach in which there is no interaction design other than choosing and placing user interface widgets while writing code.

It is useful to define the first display for each user interface because there is a limited amount of display space. Thus it can be difficult to assure that everything for a planned first-display will fit on a single screen. If goals and/or tasks planned for the opening display have to be split into multiple displays, the effects may flow throughout the entire user interface. For example, the need to create one or more new displays for an interaction may necessitate redesign of other related interactions.

In Release Planning, primary windows are associated with the users' primary goals and the expected navigational flow is mapped for the primary windows. It is best if all the primary goals can be mapped so that (1) the consequences of release assignments can be considered, and (2) the team can get feedback on whether the task flow for a release makes sense to users.

After Release Planning, the focus should switch from navigating across displays to selection and placement of content (controls, text, links, etc.) within the displays. In this approach, that change of focus indicates a change from Release Planning to Iteration Planning.

14.3.4 Iteration Planning

Iterative planning addresses the user-interaction design question, "What are the details of how users do the tasks?" During "Iteration Planning," user interface controls are selected and placed on user interface displays. This is the most visible level of interaction design, called the "physical design" of the user interface. If no interaction design has been done before this point, developers may have little other than their own experience to guide the choice of a widget and its placement. Then when usability issues show up in the implemented system, it is much more painful than addressing usability issues earlier in the development process. This is particularly true if no one is coordinating widget appearance and behavior to maintain consistency across the displays.

Much could be written about how to select user interface widgets and place them appropriately, but this is not the place to do that. For example, in the Microsoft® Windows visual guidelines for the Vista operating system, there are 18 widgets described as common controls in user interfaces (Microsoft, 2007). Of these, ten can be used to select from a set of alternatives (check boxes, radio buttons, drop-down combo boxes, sliders, spin controls, etc.). It is not enough to know the user has to select among a set of alternatives; it is important to consider, for example, the size of the set, whether the set is dynamic or fixed, whether all of the options are binary and/or mutually exclusive, etc.

14.4 EVALUATIONS OF USABILITY

Usability "testing" done near the time of system release to the customer is important as part of customer acceptance, but it is the least useful of the many different ways of doing usability evaluations. Because the perceptual presentation of the user interface is complete at that point, users often focus only on physical-design issues. For example, users may focus so strongly on colors and widget choices that no one notices an optional step was left out of a task flow.

The GAINS design process embeds usability evaluations throughout the development process, especially when novice and expert end-users are available. For example, if the users cannot agree on the specific terms for fundamental concepts or on a small set of Statements of Purpose, the concepts or statements do not have good usability. Similarly, if users cannot agree on a set of primary goals and/or the dependencies among them, the usability of the entire system is in question. The stronger the disagreements, the more probable it is that the entire development project will fail. Thus usability issues provide an early warning detection of problems that normally surface much later in the development lifecycle.

It also is important to distinguish between verifying and validating a user interface. To **verify** a user interface is to evaluate whether the developers correctly instantiated their conceptual model of the users' tasks. For example, a quality-assurance person might compare the user interface to the system specifications (or customer stories) to verify they are accurately represented. This is often the focus of acceptance testing.

In contrast, **validating** a user interface is to have end-users interact with a representation of the system to test its usability for the real-time work environment. The representation may be a low-fidelity prototype, such as paper-and-pencil drawings, or a high-fidelity prototype, such as a partially functional implementation. Using low-fidelity prototypes to validate usability can save developers hours or even days of time by preventing rework. This is particularly true when customers have failed to report steps in a work process, usually because the experts providing the stories have forgotten to include common muscle-memory actions.

14.5 DIFFICULTIES WITH TWO XP ASSUMPTIONS

The XP methodology includes two assumptions that may be hard to keep valid for user interface design, particularly for large systems. The first assumption is that customer stories should be independent; the second assumption is that the cost of change remains relatively flat during the entire development cycle.

In XP, the customer writes "stories" that identify the features to be included in the system. It is a basic tenet of XP that the stories should be independent in the code. However, stories that are independent in the code may interact in a user's mind, particularly when they are used close together or they are similar in some way; independent stories from a developer's perspective may be very interdependent from a user's perspective.

Also, a system's features must be integrated into a coherent whole at the user interface if the system is to be highly usable. If not, user interactions with the system will feel piecemeal, unpredictable, and perhaps even chaotic. This greatly increases the risk that end-users will reject the system, especially when someone who will not actually use the system does the customer acceptance tests.

The other XP assumption that may be difficult to apply to user interface design is that the cost of change does not greatly increase later in the development cycle. While this may be true for changes that only impact how the code is processed by a computer, it is definitely not true for the user interface. With each subsequent release, users form more complete and automated models of how to interact with the system. As time passes, those models become more difficult to change. Thus, the same change to the user interface will have different users costs of change when it occurs early or late in the overall development cycle.

14.6 CONCLUSIONS

GAINS can be, and has been, successfully used in a wide variety of project and software development environments. Even when a user-interaction/interface consultant is called into a project late in the development lifecycle, it is typically easy to quickly establish the design context of the previous planning levels. In fact, the ease or difficulty of doing so is an excellent indicator of how well the project team understands what they have been asked to build. Thus the designer can often within hours discover hidden issues that are being ignored or deliberately not resolved because of the difficulty in addressing them. It is much better to identify those issues when first starting a project than finding them later.

Interaction design in general and the GAINS process in particular are appropriate for XP projects because it fits into the four levels of planning defined by Beck and Fowler. The Rough Plan and the Big Plan take a very short period of time and can successfully replace big up-front design. Release Planning involves primary display definition and mapping, and Iteration Planning involves secondary displays and selection and placement of the internal content of displays.

References

Beck, K. and Fowler, M. (2001). *Planning Extreme Programming*. Reading, MA: Addison-Wesley.

Microsoft Corporation (2007). Windows Vista user experience guidelines. Retrieved July 19, 2007, from http://msdn2.microsoft.com/en-us/library/aa511456.aspx.

15 LEGACY SYSTEMS INTERACTION REENGINEERING

Mohammad El-Ramly [1,2], Eleni Stroulia[3], and Hani Samir

[1]Faculty of Computer Science and Information, Cairo University
5 Ahmed Zwail St., Orman, Giza, EGYPT
[2]Department of Computer Science, University of Leicester
University Road, Leicester, LE17RH, UK
[3]Department of Computer Science, University of Alberta
2-21 Athabasca Hall, Edmonton, Canada T6G 2E8
{mer14@le.ac.uk, stroulia@cs.ualberta.ca, hanirr@yahoo.com}

Abstract. We present a lightweight approach for reengineering the human computer interaction (HCI) and/or interaction with other software systems. While interaction reengineering can be achieved by changing the source code and design (e.g., library replacement, refactoring, etc.) resulting in a different user interface (UI), we limit the discussion to interaction reengineering methods that do not involve changing the source code or internal design of the system. Instead, we focus on methods and techniques for wrapping and packaging the existing interaction layer to reproduce it in a different format, e.g., on a different platform or to integrate the legacy system services in another application possibly under a different architecture paradigm, e.g., service-oriented architectures (SOA).

15.1 INTRODUCTION

In this chapter we present a lightweight approach for reengineering software systems that we call interaction-reengineering. As the name suggests, interaction reengineering is concerned with reengineering the way the users interact with a software system, i.e., reengineering the human computer interaction (HCI) and/or interaction with other software systems. While this can occur by changing the source code and design (e.g., library replacement, refactoring, etc.) resulting in a different user interface (UI), we limit the discussion here to interaction reengineering methods that do not involve changing the source code or internal design of the system. So, interaction reengineering is concerned with methods and techniques for wrapping and packaging the existing interaction layer to reproduce it in a different format, e.g., on a different platform or to integrate the legacy system services in another application possibly under a different architecture paradigm, e.g., service-oriented architectures (SOA). We use the term *interaction layer* instead of *presentation layer* because (1) interaction layer is not limited to the user interface but may include other sublayers like Data Description Specifications (DDS) source files for iSeries systems, for example and (2) interaction here is not limited to human-accessible interaction layer but it also includes interaction with other software systems. For example, it is possible to reengineer the way an application can be interacted with by other applications in order to integrate it with other applications on a different platform, e.g., Web services. The key points in interaction reengineering are (1) the access point of the legacy system is its interaction layer, (2) no code or design alteration or transformation takes place, and (3) the why the users and other systems interact with the legacy system will be reengineered somehow. In other words, the old legacy presentation is not going to be accessed as is on the target platform (e.g., using emulation), but it will be optimized, remodeled, reengineered, etc. to a small or large extent.

Interaction reengineering was successfully applied in a number of areas, e.g., reengineering character-based user interfaces (CUI) to websites and mobile platforms (Stroulia et al., 2003; Stroulia et al., 2002), reengineering websites to Web services (Jiang and Stroulia, 2004) and reengineering form-based CUI applications to Web services (Canfora et al., 2006). These applications are discussed in Section 15.4.

In this chapter, we consolidate the various works done under interaction reengineering into a bigger framework that draws a generic methodology for interaction reengineering, which can be applied to various current and future instances of the problem. This chapter starts with an introduction to the topic, followed by a section on the motivation for interaction reengineering. Sections 15.3 and 15.4 describe a generic methodology for interaction reengineering and some specific instances of this approach as developed in different research projects. Section 15.5 briefly presents some industrial tools for interaction reengineering. Section 15.6 concludes by a discussion of the limitations and advantages of interaction reengineering.

15.2 MOTIVATION FOR INTERACTION ENGINEERS

Over years of development and investment, business software systems, such as bank finance systems, customer-relationship management (CRM) systems, and airline-reservation systems, grew in size and value. They constitute one of the most important assets for many companies (Liu et al., 1994). Corporations have invested substantially in developing these mainframe-based legacy systems and making them Y2K and Euro compliant (Sneed, 2000). In return, mainframe-based legacy systems have proven reliability and scalability in providing business-critical processing needs, especially for applications involving huge numbers of transactions and simultaneous users like banking and airline-reservation applications. Moreover, many of the business processes and policies of companies are encapsulated in the logic of legacy systems. For many corporations, legacy systems will remain their Information Technology (IT) backbone for years to come.

While the term *legacy system* may invoke the image of a 25 years old application running on a mainframe system, it actually applies to a wide variety of systems. The same argument above now applies to large websites that were built over years of development and investment and became vital to the business of their owners, but yet have to keep up with new technologies. So, every new generation of software technology almost turns the applications developed with the previous generation into legacy systems. For example, the invention and widespread of object-oriented (OO) software development paradigm initiated the development of methods for reengineering programs written in Cobol, C, etc. to modern OO languages (Mossienko, 2003). Also, the invention of the Web led to developing methods for reengineering existing software systems for Web accessibility (Sneed, 2000). The wide spread use of PDA devices created a demand for opening existing systems, particularly Web systems, to PDA-access (Canfora et al., 2006). Distributed objects technology and later components and frameworks technology created a need to reengineer or wrap existing legacy systems as objects or components (Comella-Dorda et al., 2000; Zou and Kontogiannis, 1999). And so on and so forth. This situation led to a continuous evolution and development of reengineering methods by academia and industry.

Broadly speaking, reengineering techniques can be classified into two categories: *invasive reengineering techniques* and *non-invasive reengineering techniques.* The first includes techniques that involve significant modification and alteration to the system code, e.g., program transformation, refactoring, database reengineering, etc. The second includes techniques that interface with the existing system via one of its layers (data, logic, and interaction) without changing or altering the internals of this layer, e.g., wrapping and interaction reengineering.

While many of these activities require program understanding (code, design, etc.), interaction reengineering primarily requires an understanding of how the users (or other systems) currently interact with the system. In this regard, it is a black box reengineering approach. Work in this area is relatively recent and was pioneered by the CelLEST project at the Department of Computer Science, University of Alberta, Canada.

15.3 GENERIC METHODOLOGY

While invasive reengineering technology has matured over time and found its way to industry through heavyweight scalable reengineering artillery, e.g., DMS (Baxter et al., 2004), it is not suitable for all situations. In many cases, it is not possible to use invasive reengineering approaches, leaving no choice other than interaction reengineering approaches. Three perfect examples of such situations are listed below:

- There is no access to the source code, e.g., because it is lost or because it is developed by a third party and there is no license to use it. For example, a government department has a contract management system for managing contracts and contractor relations and they also have access to a central government system for contract management that includes the general rules that they have to adhere to. This resulted in some duplication of data entry and difficulty in managing one task on two separate systems. It was required to integrate both systems and reengineer their interaction layers, but this was only possible using interaction reengineering due to the limited access they had to the central system.
- It is required to integrate the interaction layer of existing applications together in a mega application (Grechanik et al., 2002) or within a newly developed system, while it is also required to keep the original applications running with no alteration. This can happen due to mergers or acquisitions.
- It is required to open the system for access via a different platform, e.g., the Web, mobile devices, or SOA. (Berman and Bregar, 2001)

In these cases, the assumption is that it is required to continue to use the legacy system(s) as is on the original platform without altering the structure or code, either because its performance is adequate and/or because it is too risky, expensive, and/or impossible to change it. In other words, the legacy system is under control and exhibits satisfactory performance but its main weakness is its interaction layer and its inability to be integrated with other systems. This usually occurs due to the legacy interaction layer falling short in one or more of these three areas: user access, usability, and navigation (Berman and Bregar, 2001):

1. **User Access.** The existing system access methods are inadequate. For example, the system is a legacy mainframe system with a character-based user interface and it is now required to open some of its services for public access via the Web. Or the system is a web-based one but the market now demands accessing it as well via mobile devices or repackaging it in the form of Web services.

2. **Usability.** For example, legacy CUIs are non-intuitive and hard to learn. The old-looking "dumb" terminals, e.g., IBM 3270 and VT series, were quite adequate for their time in spite of being quite limited in their display capabilities. Their CUIs dissatisfy today's users, who are used to graphical user interfaces and Web interfaces. Additionally, the learning curve of new users is slow and the training costs are high.

3. **Navigation**. The mode of navigation varies from one platform to another. And with the advent of new platforms, the way an older system is navigated becomes legacy for the new platform. And the old workflows become outdated and time-consuming. For example, due to their limited presentation capabilities, legacy

CUIs offer tedious navigation patterns to accomplish user tasks. For example, flipping a multipage report may require using function keys or issuing some commands to move forward and backward between the many screens containing the report. Instead, in a GUI environment, a scroll bar enables instant access to any page of the report with a mouse click. The same applies to Web applications, if we look at them from a mobile perspective.

4. A Methodology for Interaction Reengineering

In this section we present a methodology for interaction reengineering. This methodology generalizes the different existing interaction reengineering methods and captures their commonalities, while hiding their implementation and technology details. This methodology can be summarized in the following steps which are detailed afterwards.

1. **Step One:** Modeling the legacy interaction layer.
2. **Step Two:** Modeling the services (user tasks) to be reengineered.
3. **Step Three:** Developing (buying) middleware for deriving (interacting with) the legacy system.
4. **Step Four:** Reengineering the service models produced in step 2.
5. **Step Five:** Generating a new interaction layer.

Figure 15.1 shows this methodology in a schematic diagram along with the artifacts produced. Note that the words *model, modeling* and *reverse engineering* in the steps above are used in a very broad sense, i.e., without reference to specific models or modeling techniques. These details are left to the next section and are specific to each instantiation of the methodology.
1. Modeling the legacy interaction layer. In this step, it is required to build a model of the legacy user interface. This can be done manually, automatically, or semi-automatically using reverse engineering techniques. Primarily, this model describes the different units of the interface and the necessary action required to move from one unit to another. You can think of this model as a state-transition model. A state represents a screen, a window, a form or whatever units the user interface consists of. A transition from one state to another is related to some event or user action, e.g., menu selection, button pressing, text typing, hyperlink selection, or whatever user actions are available in the source platform. The attributes of a state and the richness of its description are dependent on the platform under study. The same applies to transitions.
2. Modeling the services (user tasks) to be reengineered. In this step, models of the legacy system services are built. Legacy system services and user tasks are two faces of one coin. A task from a user's point of view is a service that the system offers. So, we will be using both terms interchangeably. In interaction reengineering, it is possible to reengineer only specific services of interest. Hence, not all services need to be modeled. Modeling a user task means defining the task in terms of the states and transitions involved and the specifications of the data to be inputted and outputted. Modeling can occur manually, i.e., by someone who defines these ingredients by hand

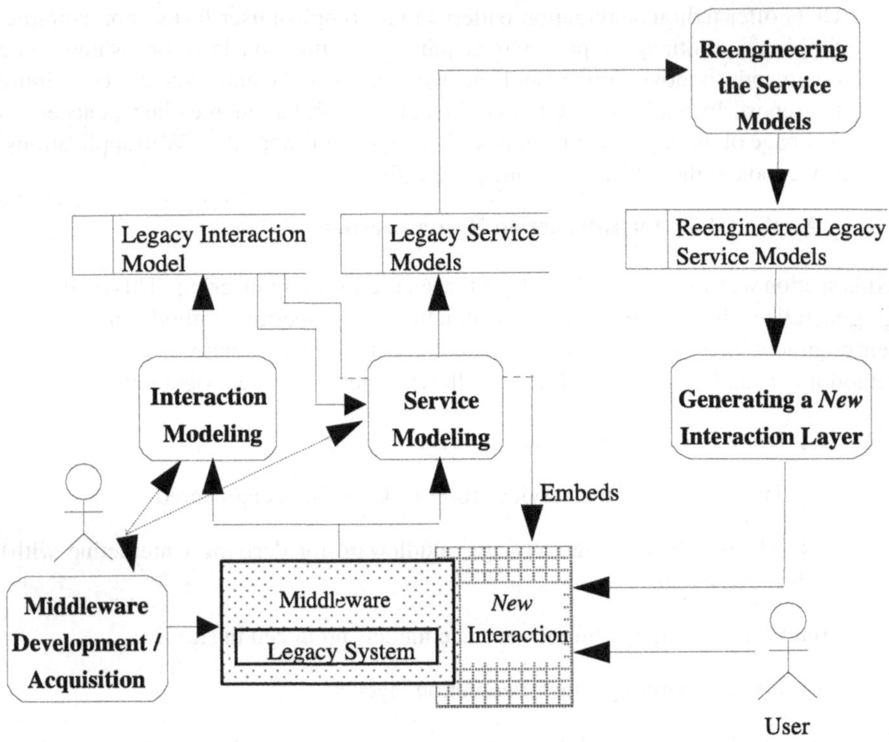

Figure 15.1 A general methodology for interaction reengineering

based on experience or using system documentation and use case models. Or, it can be done semi-manually by observing or recording users' behavior and then using pattern mining methods to infer some draft models of what the users do with the system. Then, these models can be completed and verified manually

3. Developing (buying) middleware for deriving (interacting with) the legacy system. Middleware is needed for the new interaction layer to interact with the legacy system to derive it in order to execute the reengineered system services offered on the target platform. Each service will have a task plan that needs to be executed on the legacy system via the middleware and the relevant pieces of data are passed back and forth between the legacy system and the new reengineered interaction layer.

4. Reengineering the service models produced in step 2. In this step, if needed, the way the legacy systems services are offered or the way the users do their tasks is remodeled and reengineered to optimize the old workflows and to take advantage of the new features available on the target platform. For example, the limitations of character-based user interfaces are lifted when we move to GUI or Web-based interfaces. Tasks that are accomplished via multiple screens can be done in one Web-form. This step can be done manually or semi automatically.

5. Generating a new interaction layer. In this step, a new interaction layer is created on the target platform for the legacy system. This can be done by crafting it from scratch or by generating it from UI specifications. In the latter case, the system services or user-task models are translated to abstract UI specifications that are then translated to a concrete UI implementation, e.g., to XHTML for Web access or WML (Wireless Markup Language) for WAP (Wireless Application Protocol) access.

One can look at the five steps above as divided into two phases. The first phase is a reverse engineering that includes the first two steps and the second is a forward engineering phase that includes the last three steps. The weight and importance of each of these steps in each instantiation of the methodology depends on the source and target platforms.

15.4 APPLICATIONS OF INTERACTION REENGINEERING

This section describes three instantiations of the general methodology described above; each is applied to a different source and target platforms pair. It implicitly explains how the five steps of the generic methodology are implemented for each source and target platforms pair. It is important to note that the weight and depth of each of the five steps in each instantiation depends on the source and target platforms. In other words some steps may be difficult, others may be trivial and yet others may be pointless on certain platforms. This will become clear as we explain the three instantiations below. This section is fully derived from the cited references for the works presented here. It is not a comprehensive description for the works in this area, but it is meant to cover, to a good extent, the breadth of the area.

15.4.1 From Character-Based UIs to Web and WAP Interfaces

The CelLEST project is a pioneer project on interaction reengineering (Kapoor and Stroulia, 2001; Stroulia et al., 2003; Stroulia et al., 2002). It developed a set of tools and methods for task-centered semi-automated reverse engineering and reengineering of legacy CUIs of IBM legacy mainframe systems that use IBM 3270 data stream transfer protocol to Web and WAP interfaces. IBM 3270 is a block-mode data transfer protocol, which pushes one screen at a time to the user (as opposed to scroll-mode data transfer protocols, which interact with the user line by line). Task-centered here means that only the system services (or user tasks) of interest are reengineered. It was an industrial project between the University of Alberta, Canada, and Celcorp, funded by the Canadian National Science and Engineering Research Council (NSERC). An overview of the CelLEST approach is shown in Figure 15.2.

In CelLEST, a mixture of artificial intelligence, data mining, and software engineering and other methods was used to automate the process of "learning" and reengineering legacy mainframe CUIs as much as possible. The objective was to develop an intelligent semi-automated lightweight method for legacy system UI reengineering, Web and WAP-enabling, and front-end integration. The project resulted in a suite of methods and tool prototypes that were verified by reengineering several medium-size applications. The premise of this approach is that monitoring the legacy system users while working with the legacy application and recording traces of their interaction (dialog) with the legacy UI can provide the basis for learning how the legacy UI behaves. The recorded traces are used to build, semi-automatically, the models and artifacts required for interaction reengineering. This includes a behavioral model of the legacy UI (state-transition model), models of the frequent user tasks of interest, an abstract GUI specification, and an automatically generated Web-based GUI and/or WAP-based GUI for the interesting tasks. User feedback is used to ensure the correctness and completeness of the models generated. So, the interesting user tasks are reengineered into abstract GUI specifications, represented in XML-based syntax. These specifications are then translated to XHTML for Web access or WML (Wireless Markup Language) for WAP (Wireless Application Protocol) access, using the appropriate CelLEST interpreter. Hence, the CelLEST approach can accomplish simultaneous reengineering of the same legacy UI to different platforms, using the platform-independent abstract GUI specifications.

The CelLEST approach consists of the following tasks, which are briefly explained and related to the five steps described earlier in Section 15.3.

1. Trace Recording. An IBM 3270 emulator is instrumented to record long traces of the interaction between the legacy system UI and its users while performing their regular tasks.

2. User Interface Modeling. In this task (Task T1 in Figure 15.2), the behavior of the legacy user interface is modeled as a state-transition model using a variety of carefully selected features. A tool called LeNDI (Legacy Navigation Domain Identifier) extracts a vector of syntactic, semantic, and visual features for all screen snapshots recorded in the traces and then applies clustering methods to group them in clusters and finally identifies the unique feature vector (called screen signature) of each legacy screen that uniquely identifies its instances (snapshots). A similar approach is applied using learning by example to model user actions, i.e., transitions between states.

3. Modeling Frequent User Tasks. In this task (Task T2 in Figure 15.2), a novel sequential pattern mining family of algorithms, IPM and IPM2 (El-Ramly et al., 2002b; El-Ramly et al., 2002a), is used to extract the frequent interaction patterns from the recorded traces according to a user-defined criterion that defines the minimum length, minimum number of occurrences, and maximum permitted level of noise for a pattern to qualify for discovery. An interaction pattern consists of a sequence of states frequently traversed in the recorded traces, representing a sequence of legacy screens. This is assumed to represent a user task of interest that s/he does often. Noise is allowed up to a certain limit, in the form of additional states that may exist randomly in the instances of a pattern, representing spurious navigation, error screens, etc.

4. Modeling Frequent User Tasks. In this task (Task T3 in Figure 15.2), the interaction patterns discovered in T2 are augmented with the user actions necessary to execute an instance of the pattern and with models of the data exchanged with the legacy system to accomplish the task. This latter part is done semi-manually. A tool called Mathaino (Kapoor and Stroulia, 2001) tries to learn by example from the pattern instances what type of data was needed for each input. An engineer manually validates and completes this process. Additionally, the engineer manually defines which outputs are of interest in the resulting UI units to include them in the reengineered interaction layer. For example, one might be retrieving information from a legacy library system and only the information concerning book records is needed in the reengineered task, so the

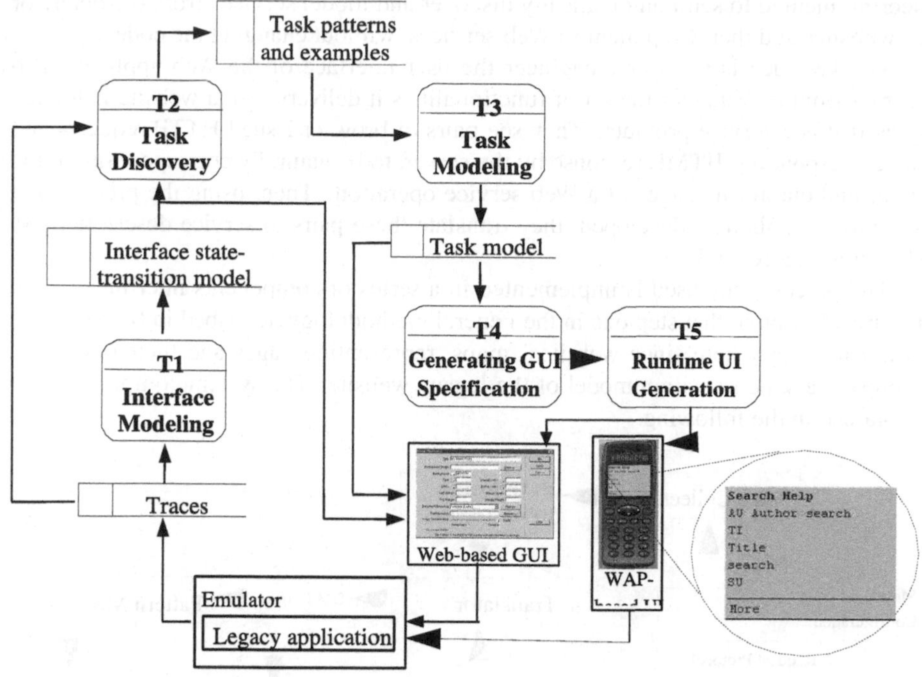

Figure 15.2 The CelLEST UI reengineering process

engineer marks the area where this information is in order to include it in the task model.

5. *Generating Abstract GUI Specifications.* In this task (Task T4 in Figure 15.2), Mathaino automatically translates the completed models of the frequent user tasks to abstract GUI specifications in XML. This step enables simultaneous interaction reengineering for multiple platforms.

6. *Runtime UI Instantiation.* In this task (Task T5 in Figure 15.2), the abstract GUI specifications are instantiated at runtime either as an XHTML interface or a WAP interface using the appropriate interpreter. Obviously, due to the big differences between the two target platforms, the interpretation and implementation of various abstract GUI items will differ depending on the platform.

15.5 FROM WEBSITES TO WEB SERVICES

Web Services and Service-oriented Architectures at large are the hot architectures of the current days. Many organizations are migrating to Web services. But building services from scratch can be expensive and may waste a lot of already existing resources, especially when the required services already exist in current websites. This necessitates the development of automated reengineering tools to reengineer existing websites to Web services and produce the corresponding WSDL (Web Services Description Language) specifications. Jiang *et al* (2004) developed an interaction reengineering method to semi-automatically discover and model services from the behavior of websites and then wrap them as Web services, without changing the code.

The key idea is to reverse engineer the user interface of the Web application to extract from its behavior the set of functionalities it delivers. So, a website is looked at as if it is a service provider. They see pairs of browser-issued HTTP requests and the corresponding HTML response by the server, to be naturally corresponding to the input and output messages of a Web service operation. Then, using the process and supporting tools they developed, they translate these pairs to service descriptions as shown in Figure 15.3.

The process they used is implemented in a series of components interlinked as in Figure 15.3. Note that step one in the general methodology described in Section 15.3 is not necessary here since websites' maps, representing pages and their interlinks, represent a state transition model of the legacy website. The system components are explained in the following.

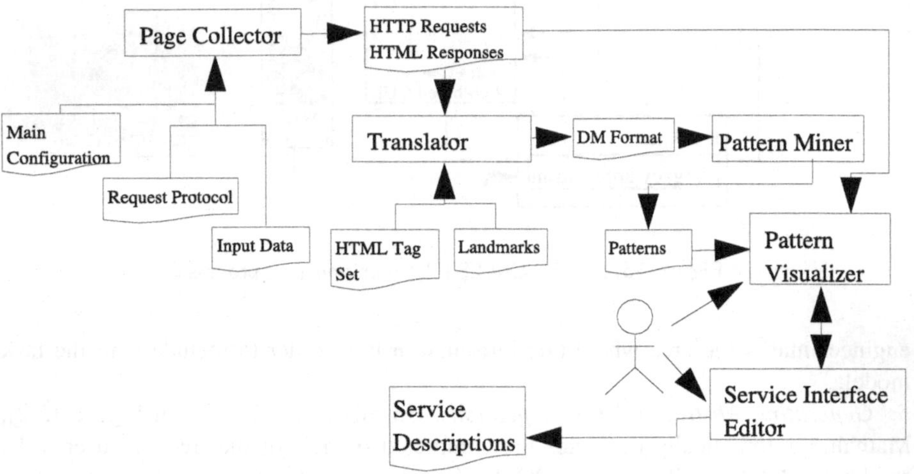

Figure 15.3 Interaction reengineering of websites to web services (Jiang and Stroulia, 2004)

1. The Document Collection Component. This component collects examples of the behavior of the website, from which the potential services will later be mined. This is done by exercising the website by sending to it several HTTP requests with various input values and storing the resulting HTML response in pairs.

2. The Translator Component. This component first "cleans" the HTML documents using JTidy (JTidy) and then the "important" parts of the HTML file are extracted and translated into sequences of numbers to be in a format suitable for pattern mining. The "important" parts of the HTML files are the parts that are expected to convey the main response information to the user and they depend on two configuration parameters:

- A set of "interesting delimiters." These are HTML elements that are of importance. For example, information within HTML tags, such as <b> or <tr> or

<td>. These elements can be good indicators to information that is designed to convey output information to the user.

- "Landmark set." A landmark is defined as a word or phrase frequently used in a specific application domain. These landmark phrases are expected to be used as labels in close proximity to the output information of the website HTML responses.

3. The Pattern Miner Component. This component applies pattern mining (using Sequitur (Jiang and Stroulia, 2004) and IPM (El-Ramly et al., 2002a) algorithms) to produce a set of "good" patterns, which together cover the parts of the website response documents that contain the information of interest to the user of the website. Hence, each pattern corresponds to a frequently occurring sequence of HTML tags and domain specific landmarks, which have a possibility to be the main response information that is expected by the user.
4. The Pattern-Visualizer Component. This component allows the user to examine the patterns and filter out the ones that are not actually useful response information.
5. The Service Description Component (The Service Interface Editor). This component takes as input the filtered patterns and the corresponding HTML response documents in which they appear. It automatically calculates the locations of the patterns' instances in these pages as XPATH expressions and generates a relative XPATH within the pattern for each piece of data selected by the user. Using an editor, the user can designate a name and a data type to each piece of data. This specifies the set of data types that the reengineered Web service will deliver as parameters of the output messages of its operations. Based on the data types defined, this component also provides support for specifying the messages, operations and port types of the Web service.

These specifications, together with the information about the website's URL, request protocol and input parameters—originally contained in the configuration files, constitute a WSDL description of the reengineered Web service, which can be reused in a Web services application. This specification is implemented by a runtime component capable of executing the original website when it receives the input message—corresponding to the original HTTP request—and producing the output message by parsing the website HTML response. Given this WSDL specification, a remote client application can correctly access the website through this runtime component and receive the desired output information.

15.5.1 From Form-based User Interfaces to Web Services

Canfora *et. al.* (2006) developed an interaction reengineering method for migrating form-based user interfaces. Form-based user interfaces are a special case of block-mode data transfer protocols, e.g., IBM 3270, where the flow of data between the system and the user is described by a sequence of query/response interactions or forms with fixed screen organization. This method produces a wrapper that interacts with the legacy system as though it were a user. It does so with the help of a Finite State Automata (FSA) that describes the interaction between the user and the legacy system as shown in Figure 15.4. Unlike the method described in Section 15.4.1 which only reengineers the interesting functionality for access via Web and mobile interfaces, this method aims to wrap the entire system functionality for access as Web service. The idea is that each use case of the legacy system will be reengineered to a Web service. A use case represents all the possible interaction scenarios between the user and the legacy UI and is represented as an FSA as in Figures 15.4 and 15.5. In this FSA (1) a *state* is a *screen template* plus a *set of actions* to be performed on its fields and (2) a *transition* is a user action, e.g., set input field, get output field and submit button. There is an *initial state* where the interpreter starts and a *final state* where the use case ends. A screen template is composed by a set of input fields, output fields and labels, each is associated with a location on the screen. A screen template does the job of the screen signature described in Section 15.4.1 but is much simpler, since the method described here is limited to form-based legacy CUIs. Finding use cases, developing the FSA, and building the screen templates are done completely manual.

(a) Form-Based Systems Flow of Data	**(b) Web Services Flow of Data**
(c) Changing the Interaction Paradigm of Form-based Legacy Systems Web Services	

The FSA is non-deterministic; given a starting state and an input action, (and there is more than one possible transition) one cannot tell which transition will be made. This is because the approach is a black box technique and this information is in the source code. FSAs are stored in an *FSA description document*, which is a repository that stores the XML files containing the specification of the FSA associated with each service (use case) offered by the legacy system.

System Architecture

The organization of the system developed to implement this method is shown in Figure 15.5. Its components are explained in the following.

1. *The Wrapper and the Automaton Engine.* The main goal of the wrapper is to drive the execution of the uses cases on the legacy system by providing it with the needed flow of data and commands using the FSA of that use case. This is mainly done by the automaton engine component, which is responsible for interpreting the FSA associated with a given service offered by the legacy system. The automaton engine's operation can be summarized in the following activities:

   - *Start Activity*
     - A request of the Web service is received.
     - The automaton engine is initialized and the corresponding FSA of the use case of the Web service request is loaded.
     - The legacy application is started and the wrapper intercepts the form received.
     - The current state of the FSA is found. This is done by comparing the returned form by the form template of each state in the FSA model.

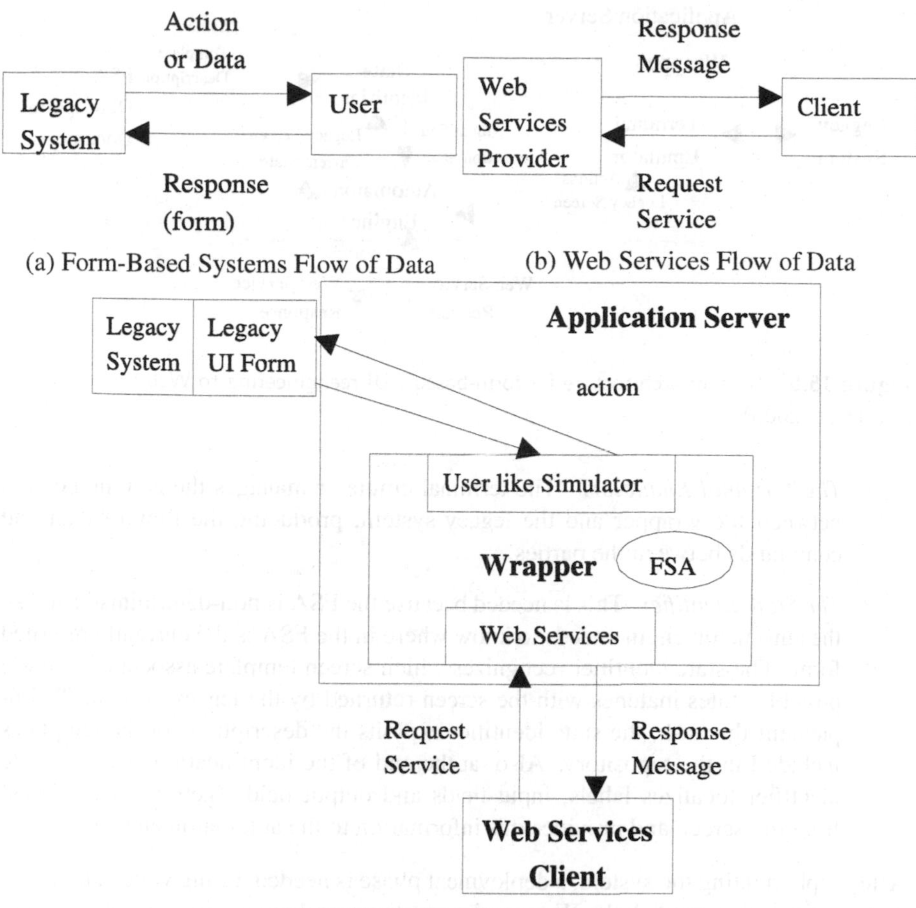

Figure 15.4 Interaction reengineering of form-based CUIs to Web services

- *Interception Activity*
  - While the Current state is not the final state of the interaction, the engine submits the new input and commands to the legacy system, and waits for the new screen returned indicating that a new interaction state has been reached. The current interaction state is updated using screen analysis.
  - When the current state is the final state, the wrapper leaves the interception activity and enters the final one.
- *Final Activity*
  - The wrapper composes the Web service Response Message on the basis of the data values stored in the automaton variables.

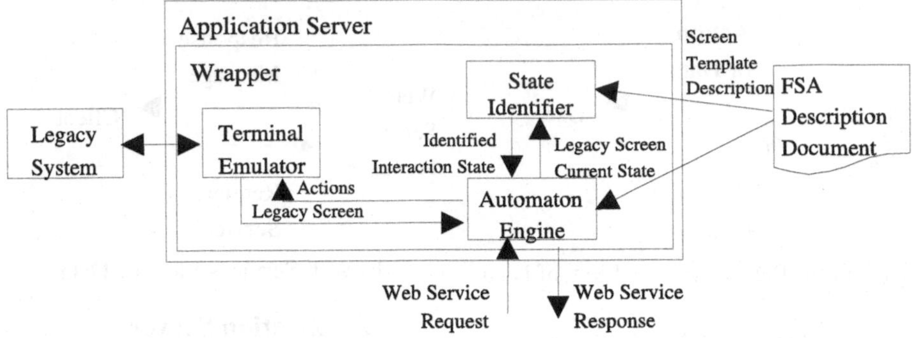

Figure 15.5 System architecture for form-based CUI reengineering to Web services (Canfora et al., 2006)

2. *The Terminal Emulator.* "The terminal emulator manages the communication between the wrapper and the legacy system, producing the flow of data and commands between the parties.

3. *The State Identifier.* This is needed because the FSA is non-deterministic and so the automaton engine needs to know where in the FSA is the currently returned form. The state identifier recognizes which screen template associated to these possible states matches with the screen returned by the legacy system. To implement this task, the state identifier exploits the descriptions of the templates included in the repository. Also, at the end of the identification task, the state identifier localizes labels, input fields and output fields (getting their values) from the screen and provides this information to the automaton engine.

After implementing the system, a deployment phase is needed during which all the operations needed to publish the Web services and export them on an application server have to be performed. That is, the WSDL specification for each service is made.

1. The Industrial Perspective

So far, we described progress in interaction reengineering from a research perspective. It is important to briefly touch on the state of the practice in industry. We do so by briefly describing an interaction reengineering tool from IBM for iSeries and zSeries applications to see what is actually doable in industry using interaction reengineering. This is the IBM Host Access Transformation Services (HATS) (Hartung et al., 2006). This is by no means an endorsement for this product. It was not chosen for any particular reason other than the availability of very good technical documentation that describes how it works. It is important to notice that most products in the market for interaction reengineering are for reengineering CUI systems running on mainframes and the like for access as Web services and through the Web.

IBM Host Access Transformation Services (HATS)

IBM WebSphere Host Access Transformation Services (HATS) (Hartung et al., 2006) is an interaction reengineering tool for Web-facing IBM applications that use

3270 and 5250 data transfer protocols (iSeries and zSeries applications). HATS implements an instance of the general methodology described in Section 15.4.1. HATS uses an interceptor to catch the 3270 or 5250 data stream and transforms it into HTML pages based on preconfigured rules. HATS support user task reengineering and optimization by combining data from multiple host screens that can be navigated using a repeatable system of navigation. Using a wizard and an editor, the engineer defines screen recognition criteria for the beginning and ending screens, how to navigate from screen to screen, the screen region containing the data to gather, and the component and widget to use to recognize and render the gathered data. It is possible to do further development work on the output of the rules by creating a JSP for that specific screen transformation.

HATS allows some flexibility in user task reengineering to accommodate uncertainty and unexpected events on the host, e.g., it allows defining:

- Global Screens, i.e., screens that are intermittently or randomly displayed and always require the same action, e.g., error screens, system messages, etc.
- Data Looping, which allows repeating an action, e.g., displaying the next page of a query result, until a condition is met.
- Landmarks, i.e., specific labels on a legacy screen that are used for relative identification of information elements (inputs or outputs) on the screen, instead of relying solely on the coordinates of the elements.
- Alternative Paths, i.e., auxiliary navigational paths that may exist for a user task.

HATS can consolidate multiple existing applications, without modification, into one single integrated view. It can combine multiple back-end resources, e.g., 3270 and 5250, under one Web front-end. Thus, new user tasks can be created/automated to eliminate the need to manually transfer data between various back-ends to accomplish a task. This is useful for integrating similar legacy systems at the front-end level due to business merger for example.

15.6 ADVANTAGES AND LIMITATIONS

In this chapter we presented a general methodology for interaction reengineering and discussed some instantiations of this methodology. The methodology consists of two phases. The first is a reverse engineering phase, during which, a map or model of the legacy user interface is built and also models of the services to be reengineered and migrated. The second is a forward engineering phase, in which, a reengineered interaction layer is built that derives the legacy system to perform user tasks while interacting with him/her through the new target platform. Legacy system access middleware is built or bought to mediate between the legacy system and the new interaction layer. In these concluding remarks we emphasize the advantages and limitations of interaction reengineering.

The primary advantage of interaction reengineering is that it is a lightweight, risk-free non-invasive approach. It is the only reengineering option when source code is unavailable and is a very viable option when it is highly undesirable to change or alter the source code. It is lightweight in the sense that it is a cheap and quick solution and also in the sense that the skills required are not sophisticated. It is a non-invasive solution that can be implemented and used in parallel to normal operation of the legacy system.

On the other hand, interaction reengineering is limited in a number of ways. First, the reengineered interaction is restricted by what is available through the legacy interaction layer. In other words, no service can be offered through the reengineered interaction layer unless it is already offered through the legacy interaction layer, either as a whole or as an aggregation of different subservices. Second, the reengineered interaction layer is vulnerable to the unexpected events on the legacy system, e.g., system or administrator messages. However, there are technologies that limit the effect of this issue. Third, if the legacy system is subject to frequent changes to its interaction layer, it can be laborious, costly, and error-prone to keep changing the reengineered interaction layer accordingly. But again some technologies offer batch changes and other facilities that limit the effect of this issue. Finally, in interaction reengineering we actually add a new layer on top of an existing system that may affect performance and create, in some cases, an extra level of complexity

Despite these limitations, we think that interaction reengineering is an emerging viable and promising reengineering methodology that can offer high-quality cost-effective solutions particularly in cases, where no other options are available. We laid down the foundation for this area and briefly described some of the major works and we hope that future research and practice will strengthen and further validate this methodology.

References

Baxter, I., Pidgeon, C., and Mehlich, M. (2004). DMS: Program transformations for practical scalable software evolution. In *ICSE*, pages 625–634. IEEE Computer Society.

Berman, D. and Bregar, K. (2001). *Don't Replace – Extend: Why Leveraging Your Legacy Systems Is the Way to Go*. Enterprise Systems.

Canfora, G., Fasolino, A., Frattolillo, G., and Tramontana, P. (2006). Migrating interactive legacy systems to Web services. In *Conference on Software Maintenance and Reengineering (CSMR06)*, pages 24–36. IEEE Computer Society.

Comella-Dorda, S., Wallnau, K., Seacord, R., and Robert, J. (2000). A survey of legacy system modernization approaches. Technical Report CMU/SEI-2000-TN-003, Software Engineering Institute.

El-Ramly, M., Stroulia, E., and Sorenson, P. (2002a). From runtime behavior to usage scenarios: An interaction-pattern mining approach. In Hand, D., Keim, D., and Ng, R., editors, *Proceedings of the Eighth ACM SIGKDD International Conference on Knowledge Discovery and Data Mining (KDD-02)*, pages 315–324, ACM Press.

El-Ramly, M., Stroulia, E., and Sorenson, P. (2002b). Recovering software requirements from system-user interaction traces. In *Proceedings of the* 14th *International Conference on Software Engineering and Knowledge Engineering (SEKE)*, pages 447–454. ACM Press.

Grechanik, M., Batory, D., and Perry, D. (2002). Integrating and reusing GUI-driven applications. In Gacek, C., editor, *Software Reuse: Methods, Techniques, and Tools, 7th International Conference, ICSR-7, Austin, TX, USA, April 15-19, 2002, Proceedings*, volume 2319 of *Lecture Notes in Computer Science*, pages 1–16. Springer.

Hartung, G., Klaedtke, R., Lowery, E., McCarty, E., Motmans, E., and Nartovich, A., editors (2006). *IBM System i Application Modernization: Building a New Interface to Legacy Applications*. IBM Redbooks Series. IBM.

Jiang, Y. and Stroulia, E. (2004). Towards reengineering websites to web-services providers. In *Proceedings of the Conference on Software Maintenance and Reengineering (CSMR)*, pages 296–308. IEEE Computer Society.

JTidy. JTidy: Java port of HTML tidy. http://sourceforge.net/projects/jtidy/.

Kapoor, R. and Stroulia, E. (2001). Mathaino: Simultaneous legacy interface migration to multiple platforms. In *Proceedings of the Ninth International Conference on Human-Computer Interaction*, Volume 1, pages 51–55.

Liu, Z., Ballantyne, M., and Seward, L. (1994). An assistant for reengineering legacy systems. In *Proceedings of the 6th Innovative Applications of Artificial Intelligence Conference*, pages 95–102.

Mossienko, M. (2003). Automated COBOL to Java recycling. In *Proceedings of the 7th European Conference on Software Maintenance and Reengineering (CSMR)*, pages 40–50. IEEE Computer Society.

Sneed, H. (2000). Accessing legacy mainframe applications via the Internet. In *Proceedings of the 2nd Int. Workshop on Web Site Evolution (WSE'2000)*.

Stroulia, E., El-Ramly, M., Iglinski, P., and Sorenson, P. (2003). User interface reverse engineering in support of interface migration to the Web. *Automated Software Engineering*, 10(3):271–301.

Stroulia, E., El-Ramly, M., and Sorenson, P. (2002). From legacy to Web through interaction modeling. In *Proceedings of the 18th International Conference on Software Maintenance (ICSM)*, pages 320–329. IEEE Computer Society.

Zou, Y. and Kontogiannis, K. (1999). Enabling technologies for web-based legacy system integration. In *Proceedings of the 1st International Workshop on Web Site Evolution (WSE'99)*.

16 USING REVERSE ENGINEERING FOR AUTOMATED USABILITY EVALUATION OF GUI-BASED APPLICATIONS

Atif M. Memon

Department of Computer Science, University of Maryland, College Park, Maryland, USA

Abstract. Graphical user interfaces (GUIs) are important parts of today's software and their usability ensures the usefulness of the overall software. A popular technique to check the usability of GUIs is by performing usability evaluations either manually or automatically using tools. While manual evaluation is resource intensive, performing automatic usability evaluation usually involves the creation of a model of the GUI, a significant resource-intensive step that intimidates many practitioners and prevents the application of the automated techniques. This chapter presents "GUI ripping," a new process that automatically recovers models of the GUI by dynamically "traversing" all its windows and extracting all the widgets, properties, and values. The usefulness of this process is demonstrated by recovering a *structural model* called a GUI forest and *dynamic models* called event-flow graphs and integration trees. Results of case studies show that GUI ripping is effective and requires very little human intervention.

16.1 INTRODUCTION

Graphical user interfaces (GUIs) are one of the most important parts of today's software (Memon, 2002). They make software easy to use by providing the user with highly visual controls that represent everyday objects such as menus, buttons, lists, and windows. Recognizing the importance of GUIs, software developers are dedicating large parts of the code to implementing GUIs (Memon, 2001). The usability and correctness of this code is essential for the usefulness of the overall software. This chapter leverages techniques previously developed for GUI testing (Memon et al., 2001a; Memon, 2001; Memon, 2002; Memon, 2003; Memon et al., 1999; Memon et al., 2003,), and applies it to improve the usability of GUIs. Borrowing the terminology used in ISO9241, *Ergonomic requirements for office work with visual display terminals*, we note that usability is "... the extent to which a computer system can be used by users to achieve specified goals effectively and efficiently while promoting feelings of satisfaction in a given context of use ...." A popular technique to measure the usability aspects of a GUI and identify specific problems is by conducting usability evaluations (Nielsen, 1994; Dix et al., 3 19; Nielsen, 1993).

A large number of usability evaluation techniques have been proposed (Nielsen and Molich, 1990,; Baker et al., 2002,; Wixon, 2003,; Pinelle and Gutwin, 2002,; Morley, 1998,; Marsh, 1999,; John, 1996,) and are in use (Wixon, 2003,; Rohn et al., 2002,; Perlman, 1996,). Many techniques are manual and require performing human-intensive tasks. To reduce the cost of usability evaluations, several automated techniques have been proposed (Kieras et al., 1995,; Castillo et al., 1998,; Hilbert and Redmiles, 2000,) to complement the manual techniques. Examples include systems such as GLEAN (Kieras et al., 1995) that generates quantitative predictions from a supplied GOMS model and a set of benchmark tasks, and USAGE (the UIDE System for semi-automated GOMS evaluation) (Byrne et al., 1994) that takes the application model necessary to drive the UIDE system and generates an NGOMSL model of the interface.

While the above types of systems require the development of a usage model for the software, other systems take an alternative approach—they provide some limited platform-specific support to extract information from the interfaces at a level of abstraction that is useful for evaluating usability. Hilbert and Redmiles (Hilbert and Redmiles, 2000) provide an excellent survey of computer-aided techniques/tools used to extract usability-related information from user interfaces and develop a framework to help compare the approaches that have been applied to this problem.[1] These tools are useful in that they assist in usability evaluation but require considerable human intervention (Ivory and Hearst, 2001). A typical example is the SHERLOCK tool suite developed by Mahajan and Shneiderman (Mahajan and Shneiderman, 1996), which includes a translator program to convert Visual Basic form and resource files into a canonical format. The canonical form is not general, i.e., it has limited applicability and the translator works on Visual Basic sources. Similarly, most other automated techniques developed so far are also either restrictive in their scope or require the development of a complex usage model of the GUI—a significantly resource intensive task that intimidates many practitioners and prevents the application of the techniques. There is a need for techniques/tools that can obtain both structural and behavioral in-

[1] Note that a discussion of tools for Web applications (Brinck and Hofer, 2002,; Winckler et al., 2000,) is beyond the scope of this chapter.

formation automatically from the GUI and allow usability engineers to fine-tune it to their needs.

This chapter presents two general-purpose models that can be automatically derived from the GUI—a *structural* and a *behavioral* model. A technique called *GUI ripping* is used to obtain these models directly from the *executing* GUI. Once verified manually, these models are then used for automatic usability evaluation. GUI ripping has numerous other applications such as testing, porting and controlling legacy applications to new platforms (Moore, 1996), and developing model checking tools for GUIs (Dwyer et al., 1997). For space reasons this chapter will provide details relevant to the usability evaluation process.

GUI ripping is a dynamic process that is applied to an executing software's GUI. Starting from the software's first window (or set of windows), the GUI is "traversed" by opening all child windows. All the window's *widgets* (building blocks of the GUI, e.g., buttons, text-boxes), their *properties* (e.g., background color, font), and *values* (e.g., red, Times New Roman, 18pt) are extracted. Developing this process has several challenges that required us to develop novel solutions. First, the source code of the software may not always be available; techniques that extract information from the executable files had to be developed. Second, there are no GUI standards across different platforms and implementations; all the information had to be extracted via low-level implementation-dependent system calls, which are not always well-documented. Third, some implementations may provide less information than necessary to perform automated usability evaluation; heuristics had to be developed to determine missing parts. Finally, the presence of *infeasible paths* in GUIs prevents full automation. For example, some windows may be available only after a valid password has been provided. Since the GUI Ripper may not have access to the password, it may not be able to extract information from such windows. New processes and tool support to manually add parts to the extracted GUI model had to be developed.

GUI ripping is used to extract both the structure and execution behavior of the GUI – both essential for automated usability evaluation. The GUI's structure is represented as a *GUI forest* and its execution behavior as *event-flow graphs* and an *integration tree* (Memon et al., 2001b). Each node of the GUI forest represents a window and encapsulates all the widgets, properties, and values in that window; there is an edge from node x to node y if the window represented by y is opened by performing an event in the window represented by node x, e.g., by clicking on a button. Intuitively, event-flow graphs and the integration tree represent the *flow of events* in the GUI. Details of these structures are provided in Section 16.2.

The GUI ripping algorithm has been implemented in a software called the *GUI ripper*. Details are provided of two instances of the GUI ripper, one for Microsoft Windows and the other for Java Swing applications. The performance of the ripper is evaluated on four Java applications with complex GUIs, Microsoft's WordPad, Yahoo Messenger, and Microsoft's Notepad. The results of the evaluations show that the ripping process is efficient, in that it is very fast and requires little human intervention. The evaluation also shows that ripping consumes very little resources.

The specific contributions of the work include the following.

- An efficient algorithm to extract a software's GUI model without the need for its source code.
- New structures called *GUI forests*, *integration tree*, and *event-flow graphs*.
- New usability metrics for the above new structures.
- Implementation details of a new tool that can be applied to a large number of MS Windows and Java Swing GUIs.

It is important to note that the work presented in this chapter is viewed as a valuable addition to the usability engineer's tool-box, not a substitute to manual usability evaluation. There are many goals of usability evaluation and many of them require significant human opinion, such as satisfaction. However, automated usability evaluation can help to save significant manual effort.

The next section formally presents the GUI models that are obtained by the GUI ripper. The design of the ripper and an algorithm that can be used to implement the ripper follow. Section 16.4 discusses the MS Windows and Java implementations of the GUI ripper. Empirical evaluations of the algorithms are done on several large and popular software. A discussion of related, ongoing, and future work concludes the chapter.

16.2 GUI MODEL

During GUI ripping, a representation of the GUI that models its structure and execution behavior is created from the executing GUI. Since developing general model extraction solutions for all types of GUIs is difficult, this research focus on an important subclass of GUIs is described next.

16.2.1 What Is a "GUI"?

GUIs, by their very nature, are hierarchical. This hierarchy is reflected in the grouping of events in windows, dialogs, and hierarchical menus. A GUI user focuses on events related by their functionality, e.g., by opening a particular window or clicking on a pull-down menu. For example, all the "options" in MS Internet Explorer can be set by interacting with events in one window of the software's GUI.

The important characteristics of GUIs include their graphical orientation, event-driven input, hierarchical structure, the widgets they contain, and the properties (attributes) of these widgets. Formally, the class of GUIs of interest may be defined as follows:

Definition: A *Graphical User Interface (GUI)* is a hierarchical, graphical front-end to a software system that accepts as input user-generated and system-generated events, from a fixed set of events and produces graphical output. A GUI contains graphical *widgets*; each widget has a fixed set of *properties*. At any time during the execution of the GUI, these properties have discrete values, the set of which constitutes the state of the GUI. □

The above definition specifies a class of GUIs that have a fixed set of events that can be performed on widgets with discrete-valued properties. This definition would need to be extended for other GUI classes such as web-user interfaces that have synchronization/timing constraints among objects and movie players that show a continuous stream of video rather than a sequence of discrete frames. This chapter focuses on techniques to evaluate the class of GUIs defined above.

16.2.2 GUI Forest

The first GUI representation that is obtained during the ripping process is called a GUI forest. Intuitively, the GUI forest represents the structure of the GUI's windows as nodes of the forest, and the hierarchical relationship between windows as edges. Each node encapsulates the state of a window that constitutes the window's widgets, their properties, and values.

A GUI window is modeled as a set of *widgets* (e.g., buttons, labels, text fields) that constitute the window, a set of *properties* (e.g., background color, size, font) of these widgets, and a set of *values* (e.g., red, bold, 16pt) associated with the properties. Each window will contain certain types of widgets with associated properties. At any point during its execution, the window can be described in terms of the specific widgets that it currently contains and the values of their properties. More formally, a window is modeled at a particular time t in terms of:

- *widgets* $W = \{w_1, w_2, ..., w_l\}$, i.e., the widgets that the window currently contains,
- *properties* $P = \{p_1, p_2, ..., p_m\}$ of the widgets, and
- *values* $V = \{v_1, v_2, ..., v_n\}$ of the properties.

For example, consider the `Open` window shown in Figure 16.1(a). This window contains several widgets, two of which are explicitly labeled, namely, `Button1` and `Label1`; for each, a small subset of properties is shown. Note that all widget types have a designated set of properties and all properties can take values from a designated set.

The set of widgets and their properties can be used to create a model of the *state* of the window.

Definition: The *state* of a window at a particular time t is the set S of triples $\{(w_i, p_j, v_k)\}$, where $w_i \in W$, $p_j \in P$, and $v_k \in V$. □

A description of the *complete state* would contain information about the types of *all* of the widgets currently extant in the window, as well as *all* of the properties and their values for each of those widgets. The state of the `Open` window, partially shown in Figure 16.1(b), contains all the properties of all the widgets in `Open`.

The windows of the GUI form a hierarchy — once the software is invoked, the user is presented with a *top-level* window (or set of windows). All other windows of the GUI are invoked from one of the top-level windows or from their descendants. In general, the relationships among windows may be represented by a set of directed

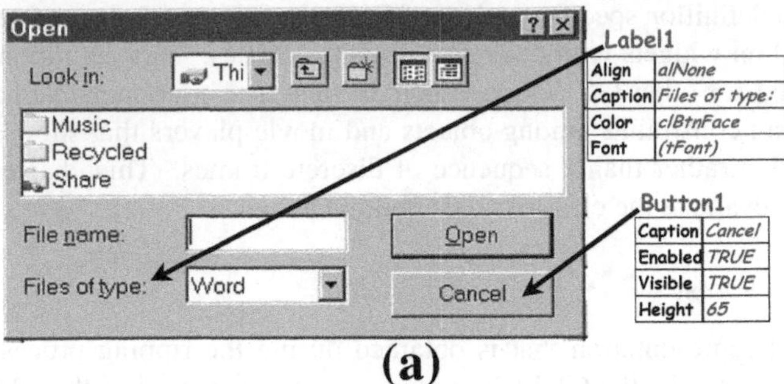

State **= {(Label1, Align, alNone), (Label1, Caption, "Files of type:"), (Label1, Color, clBtnFace), (Label1, Font, (tfont)), (Form1, WState, wsNormal), (Form1, Width, 1088), (Form1, Scroll, TRUE), (Button1, Caption, Cancel), (Button1, Enabled, TRUE), (Button1, Visible, TRUE), (Button1, Height, 65), …}**

(b)

Figure 16.1 (a) `Open` window, (b) its Partial State

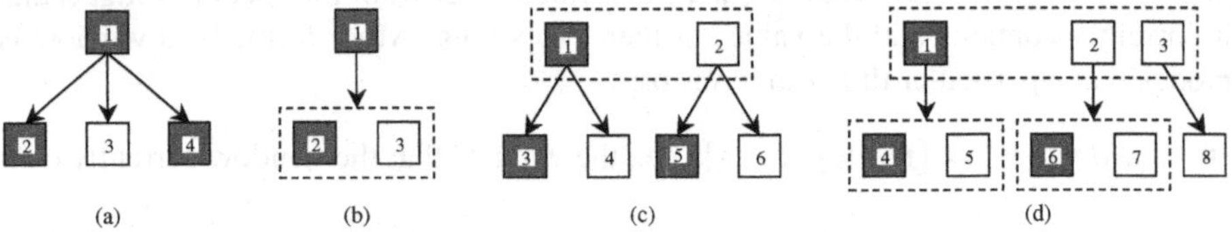

Figure 16.2 Examples of GUI forests

acyclic graphs (DAGs), since multiple windows may invoke a window. However, each DAG can be converted into a tree by copying nodes. A tree model simplifies the algorithms based on tree traversals. Note that since most GUIs have a single top-level window, in most cases, the forest reduces to a single tree. Formally, a GUI forest is defined as:

Definition: A *GUI forest* is a triple $< \mathcal{W}, \mathcal{T}, \mathcal{E} >$, where $\mathcal{W}$ is the set of windows and $\mathcal{T} \subseteq \mathcal{W}$ is a designated set of windows called the `top-level` windows. $\mathcal{E}$ is the set of directed edges: there is an edge from node x to node y if the window represented by y is opened by performing an event in the window represented by node x. □

Different types of GUI forests may be obtained depending on the types of windows that the GUI contains. For the purpose of modeling, two types of windows are important: *modal* windows and *modeless* windows.

Definition: A *modal window* is a GUI window that, once invoked, monopolizes the GUI interaction, restricting the focus of the user to a specific range of events within the window, until the window is explicitly terminated. □

The language selection window is an example of a modal window in MS Word — when the user performs the event `Set Language`, a window `Language` opens; the user spends time selecting the language, and explicitly terminates the interaction by either performing `OK` or `Cancel`.

Other windows in the GUI are called *modeless windows* that do not restrict the user's focus; they merely expand the set of GUI events available to the user. For example, in the MS Word software, performing the event `Replace` opens a modeless window entitled `Replace`.

Figure 16.2 shows some examples of GUI forests. The shaded nodes represent modal windows and unshaded nodes represent modeless windows. Dashed boxes group windows that open simultaneously. Figure 16.2(a) shows the simplest case of a GUI in which window 1 is a modal window; three events in window 1 are used to open three windows 2, 3, and 4, where 2 and 4 are modal, and 3 is modeless. Figure 16.2(b) shows a more complex case of a GUI in which window 1 contains an event that opens two windows 2 and 3 simultaneously, where 2 is modal and 3 is modeless. Figure 16.2(c) shows a case where the software presents two top-level windows to the user. Window 1 is modal and 2 is modeless. Figure 16.2(d) shows another case with multiple top-level windows, i.e., 1, 2 and 3. Windows 1 and 2 contain events that open two windows ($\{4, 5\}$ and $\{6, 7\}$ respectively) simultaneously.

Figure 16.3 shows the GUI forest (in this case a single tree) for MS WordPad. Note that the window that is presented to the user when WordPad is launched is called the "top-level" window and forms the root of the tree. All other windows are either invoked from the top-level window or from one of the child windows. For example, the window "connect to printer" is invoked from "page setup-2" which in turn is invoked from "page setup-1."

The GUI forest represents the static structure of the GUI. For usability evaluation, a usability engineer may choose to associate additional attributes with each entity in the GUI forest. Common examples (and the ones used in Section 16.5) include *depth of a node*, which is the "distance" of a window from a top-level window; *branching factor*, which is the number of windows that can be invoked from a given window; *number of events per window*, which indicates the complexity of each window. Note that by default, the forest contains values of properties for each widget in each window of the GUI, allowing the usability engineer to compute any structural usability metric.

16.2.3 Flow of Events

Additional information is collected during ripping to develop new structures that model the GUI's execution behavior called its *flow of events*. Moreover, for usability evaluation, *units of interaction*, i.e., parts of the GUI that can be evaluated in isolation are defined. The ripping process extracts additional information from the GUI such as event types to develop these structures. To develop units of interaction, the GUI's hierarchy is exploited to identify groups of GUI events that can be analyzed in isolation. One hierarchy of the GUI and the one used in this research is obtained by examining the structure of modal windows in the GUI.

At all times during interaction with the GUI, the user interacts with events within a modal dialog. This modal dialog consists of a modal window X and a set of modeless

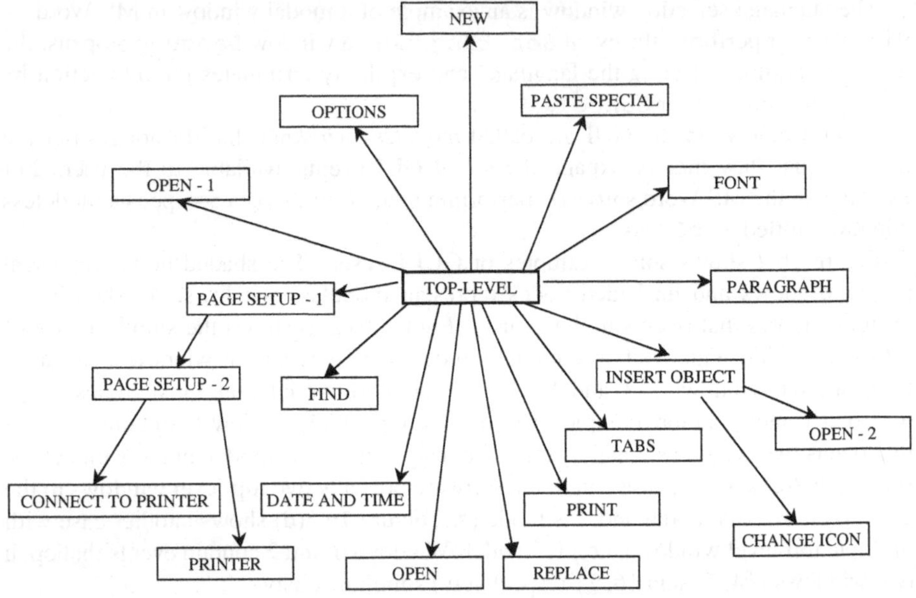

Figure 16.3 GUI Forest (Tree) for MS WordPad

windows that have been invoked, either directly or indirectly by X. The modal dialog remains in place until X is explicitly terminated. Intuitively, the events within the modal dialog form a *GUI component*.

Definition: A *GUI component* C is an ordered pair $(\mathcal{RF}, \mathcal{UF})$, where $\mathcal{RF}$ represents a modal window in terms of its events and $\mathcal{UF}$ is a set whose elements represent modeless windows also in terms of their events. Each element of $\mathcal{UF}$ is invoked either by an event in $\mathcal{UF}$ or $\mathcal{RF}$. □

Note that, by definition, events within a component do not interleave with events in other components without the components being explicitly invoked or terminated. Since components are defined in terms of modal windows, a classification of GUI events is used to identify components. The first class of events, called **restricted-focus events**, open *modal windows*. For example, `Set Language` in MS Word is a restricted-focus event. The second class, called **unrestricted-focus events**, open *modeless windows*. For example, `Replace` in MS Word is an unrestricted-focus event. **Termination events** close modal windows; common examples include `Ok` and `Cancel`.

The GUI contains other types of events that do not open or close windows but make other GUI events available. These events, called **menu-open events**, are used to open menus. They expand the set of GUI events available to the user. Menu-open events do not interact with the underlying software. Note that the only difference between menu-open events and unrestricted-focus events is that the latter open windows that

Component	Term.	Rest. Focus	Unrest. Focus	Sys. Int.	Menu Open
WordPad					
Main	1	11	2	69	6
FileNew	2	0	0	2	0
FileOpen	2	0	0	18	0
FilePrint	2	0	0	3	0
Yahoo Messenger					
Main	1	15	2	66	4
Login	1	0	0	12	0
Send File	1	1	0	9	0
Join Room	1	0	0	22	0
Notepad					
Main	1	4	1	13	4
FilePageSetup	2	1	0	25	0
PageSetUpFaxProps	2	0	0	3	0
TerpPaint					
Main	1	7	0	101	6
ImageStrech	2	0	0	12	0
ImageRotate	2	0	0	6	0
ImageAttribute	2	0	0	9	0
TerpSpreadSheet					
Main	1	3	1	54	6
FormatFormatCell	2	2	0	13	0
FmttCellBackColor	2	0	0	35	0
FileSave	1	0	0	19	0
TerpWord					
Main	1	4	3	35	4
EditGoto	1	0	0	3	0
ChangeFont	2	0	0	2	0
TerpCalc					
Main	1	3	0	44	4
About	1	0	0	1	0

Table 16.1 Event types in some GUIs

must be explicitly terminated. The most common example of menu-open events are generated by buttons that open pull-down menus. For example, in MS Word, `File` and `SendTo` are menu-open events.

Finally, **system-interaction events** interact with the underlying software to perform some action; common examples include the `Copy` event used for copying objects to the clipboard. Table 16.1 lists some of the components of some of the subject applications used in the empirical study. Each row represents a component and each column shows the different types of events available within each component. `Main` is the component that is available when the application is invoked. Other components' names indicate their functionality. For example, `FileOpen` is the component of WordPad used to open files.

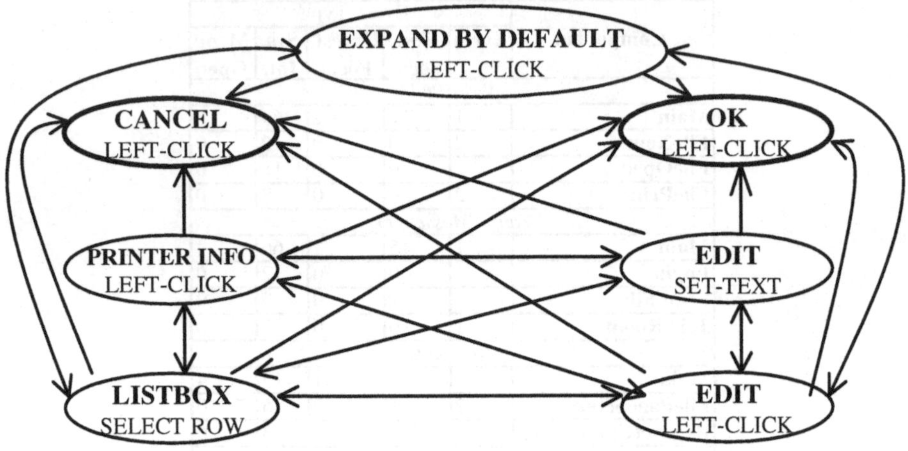

Figure 16.4 Partial event-flow graph of MS WordPad

16.2.4 Event-Flow Graphs

A GUI component's flow of events may be represented as a flow graph. Intuitively, an *event-flow graph* represents all possible interactions among the events in a component.

Definition: An *event-flow graph* for a component C is a 4-tuple <**V**, **E**, **B**, **I**> where:

1. **V** is a set of vertices representing all the events in the component. Each $v \in \mathbf{V}$ represents an event in C.
2. $\mathbf{E} \subseteq \mathbf{V} \times \mathbf{V}$ is a set of directed edges between vertices. Event e_j **follows** e_i iff e_j may be performed immediately after e_i. An edge $(v_x, v_y) \in \mathbf{E}$ iff the event represented by v_y **follows** the event represented by v_x.
3. $\mathbf{B} \subseteq \mathbf{V}$ is a set of vertices representing those events of C that are available to the user when the component is first invoked.
4. $\mathbf{I} \subseteq \mathbf{V}$ is the set of restricted-focus events of the component.

□

An event-flow graph is created by identifying the events in a GUI component. For every event *e*, the events that can be performed immediately after *e* are identified. They are linked with *e* using the **follows** relation. An example of an event-flow graph for the "connect to printer" component of MS WordPad is shown in Figure 16.4. The nodes represent events in the component and the edges show the `follows` relationship.

16.2.5 Integration Tree

Once all the components of the GUI have been represented as event-flow graphs, the remaining step is to identify event flows among components. A structure called an *integration tree* is constructed to identify interactions (invocations) among components.

```
PROCEDURE DFS-Trees(DFS-Forest F)
  R /* Set of all root nodes in the forest F */
  FORALL root ∈ R DO
    DFS-Tree-Recursive(root)

PROCEDURE DFS-Tree-Recursive(Node n)
  W = get-child-nodes(n)
  W /* Set of child nodes of the node being visited */
  FORALL w ∈ W DO
      DFS-Tree-Recursive(w)
```

Figure 16.5 Visiting each node of a forest

Definition: Component C_x **invokes** component C_y if C_x contains a restricted-focus event e_x that invokes C_y. □

Intuitively, the integration tree shows the invokes relationship among all the components in a GUI. Formally, an integration tree is defined as:

Definition: An *integration tree* is a triple $< \mathcal{N}, \mathcal{R}, \mathcal{B} >$, where $\mathcal{N}$ is the set of components in the GUI and $\mathcal{R} \in \mathcal{N}$ is a designated component called the `Main` component. $\mathcal{B}$ is the set of directed edges showing the invokes relation between components, i.e., $(C_x, C_y) \in \mathcal{B}$ iff C_x **invokes** C_y. □

Note that a software's integration tree is very different from its GUI forest; each node in a GUI forest represents a window whereas a node in an integration tree represents a group of windows (called a component, as defined earlier).

The event-flow graphs and integration trees can be used to obtain a wealth of usability metrics for the GUI. Some of these metrics (used in Section 16.5) include *average number of nodes in an EFG*, *average number of outgoing edges per node*, and *average number of edges in an EFG*; these metrics define the usability complexity of each modal dialog; nodes and edges in an integration tree define the usability complexity of the entire GUI.

16.3 DESIGN OF THE GUI RIPPER

The process of GUI ripping consists of two steps. First, the GUI of the application is automatically traversed and its structure is extracted by an automated tool called the **GUI ripper**. However, for reasons described later, the automated tool may miss some parts of the GUI. A usability engineer has to manually inspect the model and add these missed parts using additional tools.

16.3.1 GUI Traversal and Extraction Algorithm

As discussed earlier, the GUI of an application is structured as a forest. This structure is obtained by performing a **depth-first traversal** of the hierarchical structure of the GUI. A generalized depth-first search algorithm is shown in Figure 16.5. The procedure `DFS-Trees` takes as input a forest, represented as a set of trees. It performs a DFS traversal starting from the root of each tree (lines **2–3**). The procedure `DFS-Tree-Recursive` visits the tree rooted at node n. A list $\mathcal{W}$ of all the child nodes of the node n is obtained (line **4**). Then a recursive visit for the subtrees rooted at each of the child nodes is performed (line **6–7**).

The algorithm of Figure 16.5 is tailored to handle GUI traversal. The resulting algorithm is shown in Figure 16.6. Two procedures `DFS-GUI` and `DFS-GUI-Recursive` traverse the GUI of the application and extract its structure. The function `access-top-level-windows` (line **1**) returns the list of **top-level windows** in the application. Recall that top-level windows of an application are those windows that become visible when the application is first launched. A tree is constructed for each of the top-level window by invoking the procedure `DFS-GUI-Recursive`. The trees are constructed in the set $\mathcal{GUI}$. At the termination of the algorithm, $\mathcal{GUI}$ contains the GUI forest of the application.

Note that lines **4–7** of Figure 16.5 has been replaced with lines **5–12** in Figure 16.6. This is because, for a directed tree, the children of a node can be obtained by invoking the procedure `get-child-nodes`. However, for a GUI application, a node is a GUI window. It may contain several widgets, which, in turn, may invoke one or more GUI windows. To obtain a list of all GUI windows that can be invoked from a GUI window g, each of g's constituent widgets is queried.

The procedure `DFS-GUI-Recursive` performs a depth-first search of the GUI tree rooted at the GUI window g. In line **5** the call to `get-widget-list-and-properties` returns a list $\mathcal{W}$ of the constituent widgets in the GUI window g. The function `identify-executable-widgets` in line **6** searches the set $\mathcal{W}$ and returns a list of widgets which invoke other GUI windows. This is because not all of the widgets in $\mathcal{W}$ invoke other GUI windows.

A widget e that invokes other GUI windows is executed by `execute-widget` in line **8**. When executed, e may invoke one or more GUI windows. The function `get-invoked-gui-windows` in line **9** returns the list of GUI windows invoked by e. Note that each of the GUI windows c in the set $\mathcal{C}$ is a child nodes of the node g in the GUI tree. The GUI tree $\mathcal{GUI}$ is updated in line **10**. This is done by inserting each GUI Window c from $\mathcal{C}$ as a child node of the GUI window g. Lines **11–12** performs a recursive search of the subtree rooted at each of the invoked GUI windows c.

When the procedure `DFS-GUI-Recursive` returns to `DFS-GUI`, the tree rooted at the top-level window t is constructed. At the completion of the procedure `DFS-GUI`, the complete GUI forest of the application is available in $\mathcal{GUI}$.

The algorithm described in Figure 16.6 is general and can be applied to any GUI defined earlier. Later sections describe how the high-level functions used in the algorithm may be implemented using Windows and Java API.

16.3.2 Manual Inspection

The automated ripping process is not perfect. Different idiosyncrasies of specific platforms sometimes result in missing windows, widgets, and properties. For example, there is no automatic way to distinguish between modal and modeless windows in MS Windows; the structure of the `Print` dialog in Java Swing cannot be extracted. Such

```
   GUI /* GUI tree of application */
   PROCEDURE DFS-GUI(Application A)
1    T = access-top-level-windows(A)
2    GUI = T
     /* T is set of top-level windows in the application */
3    FORALL t ∈ T DO
4      DFS-GUI-Recursive(t)

   PROCEDURE DFS-GUI-Recursive(Window g)
5    W = get-widget-list-and-properties(g)
     /* W is the set of all widgets in the Window */
6    E = identify-executable-widgets (W)
     /* From W identify executable widgets */
7    FORALL e ∈ E DO
8      execute-widget(e)
       /* Execute the widget e */
9      C = get-invoked-gui-windows(e)
10     GUI = GUI ∪ g
11     FORALL c ∈ C DO
12       DFS-GUI-Recursive(c)
```

Figure 16.6 Traversing and extracting the GUI of an application

platform-specific differences require human intervention. Tools to edit and view the extracted information have also been developed. A process called "spy" allows a usability engineer to manually interact with the application, open the window that was missed by the ripper, and add it to the GUI forest at an appropriate location.

16.3.3 Generating the Event-Flow Graph and Integration Tree

During the traversal of the GUI, the event type (discussed in Section 16.2) is determined by using low-level system calls. Once this information is available, the event-flow graphs and integration tree are created relatively easily using algorithms described in Memon (2001). Details of the algorithms are omitted here due to lack of space.

16.4 IMPLEMENTATION

This section describes the platform-specific details of two implementations of the GUI ripper, one for MS Windows GUIs and the other for Java Swing GUIs. The discussion will frequently refer back to the line numbers and high-level functions invoked in the algorithm of Figure 16.6.

16.4.1 Windows Applications

The Windows Operating System provides a **handle** for all GUI windows and widgets. The handle is an identifier, which uniquely identifies the GUI window or widget. Using the Windows API (*Application Programmers Interface*) it is possible to perform GUI operations such as enumerating the visible GUI windows, enumerating the widgets embedded in a GUI window and detecting the invocation of a new window.

Lines 1–2: The Windows ripper needs to identify the top-level windows of an application. This is a manual process, where the usability engineer points-and-clicks on the top-level windows. The GUI ripper, which executes as a background process, records the windows handle of the top-level windows. **Lines 3–4:** A Recursive depth-first search is initiated for each top-level window using its window handle.

Line 5: The procedure `get-widget-list-and-properties` returns the list of *all* the widgets in the specified GUI window and their state. It uses the Windows API *EnumChildWindow*, which takes a handle to the GUI window and returns a list of widgets (handles) embedded in it. The handles are then queried for state information of the widgets, such as visibility state, caption, etc. **Line 6:** 'Executable' widgets are those that represent restricted-focus events, i.e., those that invoke other GUI windows. The *caption property* of a widget is examined to see if it ends with three dots '...'. For Windows applications, this signifies that the widget is executable.

Lines 7–8: An 'executable' widget is executed by emulating a user's left-click mouse action. The Windows API *SendMessage* is used to send a message to the widget to emulate it. **Line 9:** The procedure `get-invoked-gui-windows`, returns the list of GUI windows that are actually invoked by an executable widget. This is implemented using a Windows *hook*. A hook is a mechanism by which a predefined user level function is called by Windows, whenever a specified GUI event occurs. This event is the invoking of one or more GUI windows. If the widget invokes GUI windows, C, the handles of C are sent by Windows to the hook procedure. This handle is then used to analyze the new window. **Line 10:** GUI windows that appear in response to executing a widget are child windows of the window containing the widget. The GUI tree being traversed is updated with this structural information. **Lines 11–12:** The windows opened by the widget are traversed. Each window is analyzed by the DFS-GUI-Recursive using its unique Windows handle.

The Windows implementation of the GUI ripper may miss some widgets during the process of ripping. This happens when a widget does not have a Windows handle. Widgets created by the application that bypass the Windows drawing functions usually do not have handles and are missed by the GUI ripper. As described earlier, after ripping is complete, the usability engineer may manually add the missed widgets.

16.4.2 Java Applications

Java applications do not have a handle and hence cannot be ripped using the Windows ripper. The Java implementation (**Java ripper**) is used to rip the GUI structure of applications developed using Java Swing. In such applications, GUI windows and widgets are instances of Java classes. They are analyzed using Java APIs.

Lines 1–2: From the executable class file(s) of the software, the GUI ripper locates the file containing the `main` class. Using this class, it launches the software as an object. The Java API *java.awt.Frame.getFrames()* is used to identify all visible GUI windows (ripper's and those belonging to the application). The ripper ignores the windows belonging to itself. The remaining windows are the top-level windows of the application. **Lines 3–4:** A recursive search is initiated for each top-level window of the application using two threads. These are the `Controller` and `Spy` threads. The `Spy` thread analyzes individual GUI windows and their widgets. The `Controller` thread monitors the ripping process and identifies the window to be analyzed by the `Spy` thread. **Line 5–6:** The `Spy` thread analyzes each window of the application and at the end of the analysis disposes the window. The analysis of the window involves extracting its constituent widgets and their properties. For this we used methods *getComponents()* of class *Container* and *java.awt.Frames.getJMenuBar()* of class *MenuBar*. These methods are then used recursively to get all the widgets (buttons, menu items) that belong to the window. From this array a set of clickable/executable widgets are identified. This is achieved by selecting the widgets that belong to the *AbstractButton* class family. **Lines 7–8:** For analyzing all the windows that belong to the application they need to be invoked. A `click` event is executed on the executable widgets. This is done by triggering the `click` event using the Java API *doClick()* of class *AbstractButton*. For example, clicking the menu item `New` on an application will launch *New* window. **Lines 9–10:** The new windows that are visible as a result of event are detected using Java API method *java.awt.Frame.getFrames()*. This method returns an array of windows that are tracked by the `Controller` thread. The GUI tree being traversed is updated with this information.

Lines 11–12: With the help of the `Controller` and `Spy` threads the analysis is recursively performed untill all the windows of the application are analyzed. Once all the windows of the application have been analyzed, the Java Ripper generates the GUI forest.

16.5 EMPIRICAL EVALUATION

This section empirically demonstrates that the ripping process is *efficient* in that it is fast and requires very little resources and manual effort, and *effective* in that it automatically produces GUI structures that are very close to complete. Examples of metrics that can be derived directly or indirectly from the models are also evaluated via a study involving several students.

16.5.1 Ripped Structures

The performance of the GUI rippers is evaluated on several subject applications, including MS Windows and Java Swing applications. The MS Windows applications include Microsoft WordPad, Yahoo Messenger, and NotePad. The Java applications are part of an open-source office suite developed at the Department of Computer Science of the University of Maryland by undergraduate students of the senior Software

Application	Rip Time (Sec)	Ripped Windows	Missed Windows	Manual Effort (mins)	Size (KB)
TerpCalc	29	4	0	5	15.1
TerpPaint	42	7	3	7	24.5
TerpWord	40	10	2	6	53.8
TerpSpreadSheet	89	7	1	7	72.8
WordPad	5	22	2	8	148
Notepad	6	14	2	7	90
Yahoo Messenger	6	18	4	10	159

Table 16.2 Time for ripping windows and Java applications

Engineering course. It is called TerpOffice[2] and includes TerpWord (a small word-processor), TerpCalc (a calculator), TerpPaint (a Java clone for MS Paint), and TerpSpreadSheet (a simple spreadsheet application).

The first step of the ripping process, i.e., extracting the GUI model from the GUI application, was done fully automatically. It did not require any human intervention. As expected, some GUI windows were missed by the ripper. These windows were identified manually; the ripper automatically ripped and added them at the appropriate place in the GUI forest.

Table 16.2 shows the results of ripping the applications. The time taken to rip Java applications is significantly more than Windows applications, although the total time in almost all cases is less than a minute. The time taken to rip an application is directly proportional to the number of windows it contains. This is because rendering windows is a time-consuming process. For example, clicking `File` → `Open` causes a delay launching the *FileOpen* dialog.

Note that the ripper was able to extract a large fraction of the total number of windows in all applications. Very few windows were missed that had to be manually added later. This process took several minutes. The size of the resulting structures is also shown.

16.5.2 Aid to Usability Evaluation

This study consisted of two parts. The first part involved human subjects (15 undergraduate/graduate students), who evaluated the subject applications manually. The second part was to develop metrics for the GUI ripper to evaluate the usability automatically.

All the students were very familiar with all applications. They were asked to note down why they felt that some applications were (more) usable than others. The results showed that (1) most applications were easy to use since at most four windows had to be opened simultaneously to perform a task, (2) TerpCalc was the easiest to use because it gave the maximum flexibility of use, (3) TerpPaint was complex since it

[2]http://www.cs.umd.edu/users/atif/TerpOffice

Applications	Nodes	Edges	Max Depth	Max Children per Node	Avg. Widgets/ Window	Max. Windows
Wordpad	19	18	4	2	19	3
Yahoo Messenger	20	19	3	2	22	3
Notepad	11	10	4	2	20	2
TerpPaint	8	7	2	1	30	1
TerpSpreadSheet	7	6	3	2	29	1
TerpWord	6	5	2	1	18	1
TerpCalc	4	3	2	1	13	1

Table 16.3 Structural attributes (GUI forest)

contained a large number of widgets per window, and (4) WordPad and Yahoo Messenger had too many windows; although the users had used these two applications for years, they were not familar with some of the features.

The human study suggested the computation of several metrics from the structural and behavioral models. Some of the structural attributes are summarized in Table 16.3. The results show that Yahoo Messenger and WordPad have the largest number of windows whereas WordPad and NotePad GUIs have the largest depth. Note, however, that the depth of all GUIs is less than 4. From each window, the user can go to at most two more windows. The average widgets per window is approximately 20 except for TerpPaint which provides a color selection palette and a wide array of tools. The maximum number of windows per modal dialog is 3. The average edges per node in TerpCalc's event-flow graphs was 35, showing increased flexibility.

The dynamic aspects of the GUIs are shown in Figure 16.4. The numbers are averaged for event-flow graphs. The average number of nodes, i.e., events in each event-flow graph, is small (less than 30). The average number of edges per node indicates the number of widgets that can `follow` a given widget. This number was also small, except for the calculator application, TerpCalc, which allows a lot of flexibility. The average number of edges per event-flow graph was also small. Although informal, there seems to be a strong correlation between the metrics computed automatically by the GUI ripper and the observations of the human study. For example, the metric "average edges per node" may be used as an indicator of GUI's flexibility; the number of nodes, depth, "widgets per window" may be used to measure the complexity of the GUI.

16.6 RELATED WORK

Ivory and Hearst (Ivory and Hearst, 2001) and Hilbert and Redmiles (Hilbert and Redmiles, 2000) provide excellent discussions of automated techniques for usability evaluation. This section summarizes the efforts that have been made to recover models of software automatically.

Applications	Avg. Nodes	Avg. Edges/Node	Avg. Edges
Wordpad	26	17	908
Yahoo Messenger	23	14	780
Notepad	20	14	367
TerpPaint	28	22	1319
TerpSheet	25	19	583
TerpWord	23	17	464
TerpCalc	13	35	1676

Table 16.4 Usability attributes for event-flow

Reverse engineering has been used to generate representations of software applications. One popular representation is UML (Unified Modeling Language).[3] There are a number of reverse engineering tools available that make use of this representation. One such tool is Reveal (Matzko et al., 2002) that constructs a UML class diagram representation by parsing the input program's source code. Similarly other tools such as Rational Rose[4] and Together ControlCenter[5] generate class diagrams from the source code. Our GUI ripper is different from these tools in that it uses the executable software to generate the representation, not the source code.

Moore (Moore, 1996) describes experiences with manual reverse engineering of legacy applications to build a model of the user interface functionality. A technique to partially automate this process is also outlined. The results show that a language-independent set of rules can be used to detect user interface components from legacy code. Developing such rules is a nontrivial task, especially for the type of information that we need for usability evaluation.

Systä has used reverse engineering to study and analyze the runtime behavior of Java software (Systä, 2001). Event trace information is generated as a result of running the target software under a debugger. The event trace, represented as scenario diagrams, is given as an input to a prototype tool SCED (Koskimies et al., 1998) that outputs state diagrams. The state diagrams can be used to examine the overall behavior of a desired class, object, or method.

16.7 CONCLUSIONS AND FUTURE WORK

Usability evaluation of software that have a GUI has become extremely important as GUIs become increasingly complex and popular. Usability evaluation may either be done manually or automatically from a model of the software. Experience with GUIs has shown that such models are very expensive to create manually and software spec-

[3] `http://www.uml.org`
[4] `http://www.rational.com`
[5] `http://www.togethersoft.com`

ifications are rarely available in a form to derive these models automatically. A new technique called GUI ripping to obtain models of the GUI's structure and execution behavior automatically was presented. The GUI's structure was represented as a *GUI forest* and its execution behavior as *event-flow graphs* and an *integration tree.* The GUI ripping process, which is applied to the executing software, was described. The process opens all the software's windows automatically and extracts all their widgets, properties, and values. The execution model of the GUI was obtained by using a classification of the GUI's events. Once the extracted information is verified by a usability engineer, it is used for automatic usability evaluation. Empirical evaluations showed that this approach requires very little human intervention. Examples of metrics that may be used for usability evaluation were presented.

High-priority future work includes a more comprehensive usability study coupled with the definition of several new usability metrics. Implementation of the GUI ripper will be extended to handle more MS Windows GUIs, Unix, and Web applications. The integration of the GUI ripper with SHERLOCK will also be explored.

References

Baker, K., Greenberg, S., and Gutwin, C. (2002). Empirical development of a heuristic evaluation methodology for shared workspace groupware. In *Proceedings of the 2002 ACM conference on Computer supported cooperative work*, pages 96–105. ACM Press.

Brinck, T. and Hofer, E. (2002). Automatically evaluating the usability of websites. In *CHI '02 Extended Abstracts on Human Factors in Computer Systems*, pages 906–907. ACM Press.

Byrne, M. D., Wood, S. D., Foley, J. D., Kieras, D. E., , and Sukaviriya, P. N. (1994). Automating interface evaluation. In *Proceedings of the SIGCHI Conference on Human Factors in Computing Systems*, pages 232–237.

Castillo, J. C., Hartson, H. R., and Hix, D. (1998). Remote usability evaluation: can users report their own critical incidents? In *CHI 98 conference summary on Human factors in computing systems*, pages 253–254. ACM Press.

Dix, A., Finlay, J., Abowd, G., and Beale, R. (2002-03-19). Human computer interaction (booksite).

Dwyer, M. B., Carr, V., and Hines, L. (1997). Model checking graphical user interfaces using abstractions. In Jazayeri, M. and Schauer, H., editors, *Proceedings of the Sixth European Software Engineering Conference (ESEC/FSE 97)*, pages 244–261. Springer–Verlag.

Hilbert, D. M. and Redmiles, D. F. (2000). Extracting usability information from user interface events. *ACM Computing Surveys*, 32(4):384–421.

Ivory, M. Y. and Hearst, M. A. (2001). The state of the art in automating usability evaluation of user interfaces. *ACM Comput. Surv.*, 33(4):470–516.

John, B. E. (1996). Evaluating usability evaluation techniques. *ACM Computing Surveys*, 33(4):139.

Kieras, D. E., Wood, S. D., Abotel, K., and Hornof, A. (1995). GLEAN: a computer-based tool for rapid GOMS model usability evaluation of user interface designs. In

Proceedings of the 8th Annual ACM Symposium on User interface and Software Technology, pages 91–100. ACM Press.

Koskimies, K., Männistö, T., Systä, T., and Tuomi, J. (1998). Automated support for modeling OO software. *IEEE Software*, 15:87–94.

Mahajan, R. and Shneiderman, B. (1996). Visual and textual consistency checking tools for graphical user interfaces. Technical Report CS-TR-3639, University of Maryland, College Park.

Marsh, T. (1999). Evaluation of virtual reality systems for usability. In *CHI '99 Extended Abstracts on Human Factors in Computer Systems*, pages 61–62. ACM Press.

Matzko, S., Clarke, P. J., Power, J. F., and Monahan, R. (2002). Reveal: A tool to reverse engineer class diagrams. In *Proceedings of the Conference in Research and Practice in Information Technology*, pages 13–21.

Memon, A. M. (2001). *A Comprehensive Framework for Testing Graphical User Interfaces*. Ph.D. thesis, Department of Computer Science, University of Pittsburgh.

Memon, A. M. (2002). GUI testing: Pitfalls and process. *IEEE Computer*, 35(8):90–91.

Memon, A. M. (2003). Advances in GUI testing. In Zelkowitz, M. V., editor, *Advances in Computers*, 58:149–201. Academic Press.

Memon, A. M., Banerjee, I., Hashmi, N., and Nagarajan, A. (2003). DART: A framework for regression testing nightly/daily builds of GUI applications. In *Proceedings of the International Conference on Software Maintenance 2003*.

Memon, A. M., Pollack, M. E., and Soffa, M. L. (1999). Using a goal-driven approach to generate test cases for GUIs. In *Proceedings of the 21st International Conference on Software Engineering*, pages 257–266. ACM Press.

Memon, A. M., Pollack, M. E., and Soffa, M. L. (2001a). Hierarchical GUI test case generation using automated planning. *IEEE Transactions on Software Engineering*, 27(2):144–155.

Memon, A. M., Soffa, M. L., and Pollack, M. E. (2001b). Coverage criteria for GUI testing. In *Proceedings of the 8th European Software Engineering Conference (ESEC*, pages 256–267.

Moore, M. M. (1996). Rule-based detection for reverse engineering user interfaces. In *Proceedings of the Third Working Conference on Reverse Engineering*, pages 42–48. IEEE.

Morley, S. (1998). Digital talking books on a PC: a usability evaluation of the prototype DAISY playback software. In *Proceedings of the Third International ACM Conference on Assistive Technologies*, pages 157–164. ACM Press.

Nielsen, J. (1993). *Usability Engineering*. Boston, MA: Academic Press.

Nielsen, J. (1994). Heuristic evaluation. In Nielsen, J. and Mack, R. L., editors, *Usability Inspection Methods*. New York: John Wiley.

Nielsen, J. and Molich, R. (1990). Heuristic evaluation of user interfaces. In *Proceedings of the SIGCHI Conference on Human Factors in Computing Systems*, pages 249–256. ACM Press.

Perlman, G. (1996). Practical usability evaluation. In *Conference Companion on Human Factors in Computing Systems*, pages 348–349. ACM Press.

Pinelle, D. and Gutwin, C. (2002). Groupware walkthrough: adding context to groupware usability evaluation. In *Proceedings of the SIGCHI Conference on Human Factors in Computing Systems*, pages 455–462. ACM Press.

Rohn, J. A., Spool, J., Ektare, M., Koyani, S., Muller, M., and Redish, J. (2002). Usability in practice: alternatives to formative evaluations-evolution and revolution. In *CHI '02 Extended Abstracts on Human Factors in Computer Systems*, pages 891–897. ACM Press.

Systä, T. (2001). dynamic reverse engineering of java software. Technical report, University of Tampere, Box 607, 33101 Tampere, Finland.

Winckler, M.A. Carla, M.D.S., and Valdeni de Lima, J. (2000). Usability remote evaluation for WWW, CHI'00 extended abstracts on Human factors in computer systems, pages 131–132.

Wixon, D. (2003). Evaluating usability methods: why the current literature fails the practitioner. *Interactions*, 10(4):28–34.

17 TASK MODELS AND SYSTEM MODELS AS A BRIDGE BETWEEN HCI AND SOFTWARE ENGINEERING

David Navarre, Philippe Palanque, and Marco Winckler

LIIHS-IRIT, Université Paul Sabatier Toulouse 3
118, route de Narbonne,
31062 Toulouse Cedex, France
navarre, palanque, winckler@irit.fr

Abstract. This chapter claims that task models per se do not contain sufficient and necessary information to permit automatic generation of interactive systems. Beyond this, we claim that they must not contain sufficient and necessary information otherwise they could no longer be considered as task models. On the contrary we propose a way of exploiting in a synergistic way task models with other models to be built during the development process. This chapter presents a set of tools supporting the development of interactive systems using two different notations. One of these notations called ConcurTaskTree (CTT) is used for task modeling. The other notation called Interactive Cooperative Objects (ICO) is used for system modeling. Even though these two kinds of models represent two different views of the same world (a user interacting with an interactive system), they are built by different people (human factors specialist for the task models and software engineer for the system models) and are used independently. The aim of this chapter is to propose the use of scenarios as a bridge between these two views. On the task modeling side, scenarios are seen as a possible trace of user's activity. On the system side, scenarios are seen as a trace of user's actions. This generic approach is presented on a case study in the domain of Air Traffic Control. As both CTT and ICO notations are tool supported (environments are respectively CTTE and PetShop) an integration tool based on this notion of scenarios is presented. Its use on the selected case study is also presented in detail.

17.1 INTRODUCTION

In the Human-Computer Interaction domain (HCI), when dealing with interactive systems it is widely agreed upon that user information has to be taken into account and that this must be done through task analysis and task modeling. During the design process of interactive systems, user goals have to be analyzed as part of the specification phase, while task analysis is conducted during the design phase.

Classically formal notations are meant to guarantee certain quality of the models. For instance, they are used to ensure completeness or non-ambiguity of the descriptions. We try to demonstrate in the following that they can also be used to ensure consistency among the various models that are build in the various phases of the development process of an interactive system. As models built using formal notations are non-ambiguous, they can be analyzed automatically by inspection tools.

Even though formal notations are used for task modeling, it is not possible to generate, from the task models, the interactive application supporting those tasks. The justification of this claim comes from the following argument we develop hereafter: "it is impossible because there is not enough information in the task models to generate code." It is possible to extend the task models with additional information, but in that case we claim that the resulting model is not anymore a task model but a merging of both a task model and a model of the behavior of the system. Another alternative is to use generic information about interactive application and to use them in order to generate the code of the final interactive system. In that case we claim that the application generated is very stereotyped and that this is only possible for a very small number of applications.

We take as an example the Trident project (Bodart et al., 1994) that was dedicated to the generation of form-based interactive applications from task models and data models. Even for this kind of "simple" interactive application a data model was mandatory and was actually the core of the generation process (the task model was only used for the dialogue part of the application and the structure of the various windows of the application). Instead of generating the code from a task model, we propose to use the task model as a means for checking that the system model is compliant with it (Palanque and Bastide, 1997).

In the chapter, after a short discussion of related works, we recall the basic concepts of the approaches and tools that we aim to integrate. Then, we discuss the architecture of the solution identified. An example of application of the integrated set of tools is discussed before drawing some concluding remarks. The case study presented is extracted from the European Project MEFISTO which is a long-term research project dedicated to the definition and use of formal method for the design of safety-critical interactive systems. In particular, the project has focused on the air traffic control application domain from which this case study has been drawn.

17.2 RELATED WORK

The use of models has often been criticized for the effort required to develop them and the difficulties in using the information that they contain to support design and evaluation. When introducing a new notation, after having carefully evaluated the opportunity and the needs of doing it, the first concern should be providing users also with tools making the use of such notation more effective and easier. The problem is that getting used to another notation involves a significant amount of effort and time spent by the potential users in order to understand features, semantics, and meaning of the notation's conventions. In addition, even when users have understood the main features of the notation, there is still the risk that their effort might be wasted if they find that using it is difficult and not really feasible or appropriate for intensive use and real case studies.

Indeed, one of the strengths of a notation is the possibility of supporting it through automatic tools. Developing a formal model can be a long process, which requires a considerable effort. Automatic tools can ease such activity and can help designers to get information from the models, which is useful for supporting the design cycle.

Some research prototype was developed years ago to show the feasibility of the development of such tools, but the first prototypes were rather limited in terms of functionality and usable mainly by the people who developed them. Only in recent years have some more engineered tools been developed, and in some cases they are also publicly available. For example, Euterpe (van Welie et al., 1998) is a tool supporting GTA (Groupware Task Analysis) where task models are developed in the horizontal dimension with different panels to edit task, objects, actors. A simulator of task models of single user applications has been given with the support of an object-oriented modeling language (Biere et al., 1999).

Mobi-D (Puerta and Eisenstein, 1999) and Trident (Bodart et al., 1994) are examples of tools aiming to use information contained in models to support design and development of user interfaces. In particular, in Mobi-D the designer can choose different strategies in using the information contained in task and domain model to derive the user interface design.

In our work we envision a solution based on the use of two tools (CTTE and PetShop) developed to support two different types of models. The former is a tool for task modeling supporting a unique set of functionality (simulation of models of cooperative applications, comparison of task models, support of use of scenarios to develop task models, etc). The latter supports system models described using Petri nets in an object-oriented environment. PetShop is able to support editing of a Petri net controlling the dialogues of a user interface even at runtime thus allowing dynamic change of its behavior. Their integration allows thorough support to designers since early conceptual design until evaluation of a full prototype.

17.3 WHY A TASK MODEL IS NOT ENOUGH

Tasks correspond to actions that are to be performed by a user in order to reach a goal. The relationships between tasks and goals are clear as described in Norman's theory of action (Norman, 1986). Indeed, each time a task is performed the user has to compare the perceivable state of the system with respect to the goal.

Various notations are currently available for modeling tasks. They range from very abstract to concrete. The representation of an abstract task model requires a declarative abstract notation. The notation must be able to describe actions and qualitative temporal relationships among actions. A notation belonging to this category is ConcurTaskTree (Lecerof and Paternò, 1998). A concrete task model requires a procedural notation describing both quantitative and qualitative temporal relationships among actions but also to represent the data needed in order to perform the actions (see for instance Palanque et al., 1995).

17.3.1 Example: The Game of 15

We consider a simple (and somewhat silly) game that requires two players. The rule is as follows: the numbers from 1 to 9 are initially available to any of the two players. The players play in turn. At each turn, the player chooses one of the remaining numbers (thus making it unavailable). If the player possesses three numbers that add up to exactly 15, she wins the game. You might want to try this game with one of your colleagues, without the help of any external tool (paper, pencil, or other). It turns out, rather unexpectedly, that this game is almost impossible to play this way, because the user task is extremely complicated, as we will show by constructing a task model for it. We will later show that, although you may not be aware of it, you have almost certainly played this game.

17.3.2 An Abstract Task Model

Both players share a common goal: "win the game", and subgoal: "if I cannot win, don't let the other player win." The task of someone playing the game of 15 can be described as follows:

- I wait for my turn.
- When my turn comes, I choose a number among the remaining numbers (here, I must apply some form of strategy to decide which number to take). Within this activity the player might also check whether or not the other player is about to win.
- I then evaluate if I win the game. This operation is especially difficult, because I need to compute all combinations of 3 numbers among the numbers I have already chosen, and decide if this combination adds up to 15.
- If I do not win, I let the other player take her turn.

This task requires some "background activities": remember the numbers I have already taken, remember the remaining numbers (or alternatively remember the numbers taken by my opponent), and remember who is next. These background activities are very demanding to the short-term memory of the player, and contribute to making it actually impossible to play without adequate support.

17.3.3 A Concrete Task Model

Figure 17.1 presents a concrete task model for playing the game of 15.

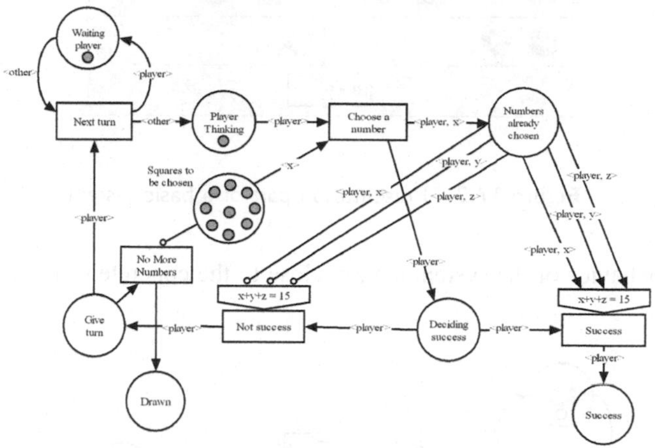

Figure 17.1 Petri net representation of the concrete task for playing the game of 15

Several simpler models could be built for instance including random selection of numbers. We have already considered these aspects in a previous paper (Moher et al., 1996) and we focus our discussion here on the more efficient task models. In this Petri net model of tasks we can note that:

- Information is stored in places thus representing what the user has to remember.

- Actions are represented by transitions; as there is no support all the actions are to be performed directly by the user. Two transitions feature preconditions (namely, transitions *"Not Success"* and *"Success"*), which means that the transition can occur only if the precondition is true. Transition *"Not Success"* is related to place *"Number Already Chosen"* by means of inhibitor arcs. This type of arc has an effect on the preconditions i.e., the transition "Not Success" can occur only if there is no combination in the place *"Number Already Chosen"* that matches the precondition.

17.4 A CLASSICAL SYSTEM MODEL

Figure 17.2 presents an interactive system for playing the game of 15. The behavior of this system is modeled using the same formalism as for task model. However, in order to model an interactive system more information needs to be represented such as activation (how the user can act on the interactors) and rendering (how the system renders information to the user).

Figure 17.3 presents the behavior part of the system. The proposed system fully supports all the actions that were left to the user in the unsupported game. For this

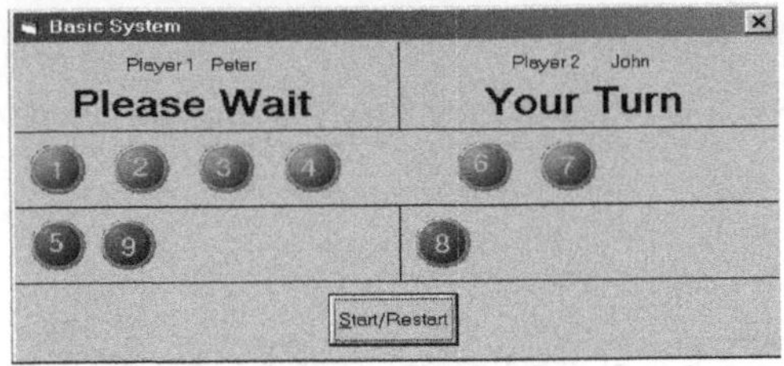

Figure 17.2 Presentation part of a basic system

reason, the behavior of the system is very close to the concrete task model presented in Figure 17.1.

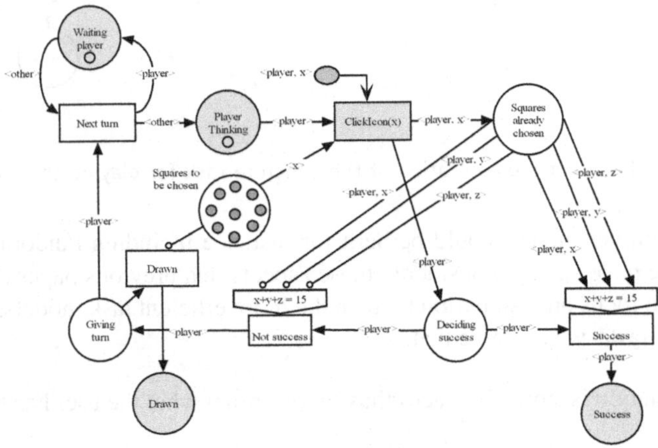

Figure 17.3 Behavior of the basic system for the game of 15

Some places are grayed-out, which means that there is some kind of rendering associated to them (not detailed here but for instance when a token enters place *"Success"* the player who won is displayed on the user interface). Transition *"ClickIcon(x)"* is grayed-out, which means that this transition is related to the user interface and responsible for triggering transitions according to user's actions on the interactors.

17.5 THE IMPROVED SYSTEM MODEL

Another system model for playing the game is presented in Figure 17.4c. This system model is based on magic squares and Tic-Tac-Toe games.

A magic square (see Figure 17.4a) is made up of a set of cells each cell being filled in by a number. A 3×3 magic square is made up of 9 cells and the valid numbers are from 1 to 9. A specific feature of magic squares is that the sum of the numbers in each row equals the sum of the numbers in each column equals the sum of the numbers in each diagonal. In the case of a 3×3 magic square, the sum is always 15.

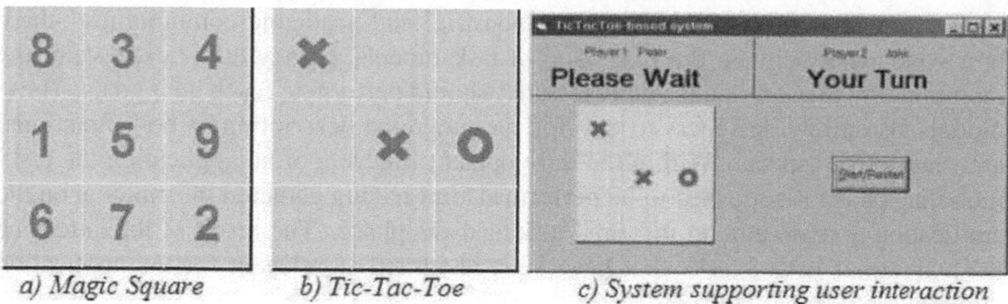

Figure 17.4 Examples for the improved system model

The user interface for playing the game is thus exactly the same as the one for playing Tic-Tac-Toe (see Figure 17.4b). This interface supports very well most actions in the task model:

- It shows the numbers still available (the empty cells).
- It shows the numbers already chosen for each player (for instance a cross for player 1 and a circle for player 2).
- It shows if a player has won (a row, a column or a diagonal is filled-up with the same symbol).
- From a strategy point of view, this user interface provides very relevant information:
  - It shows if a player is about to win and this might influence the behavior of the other player.
  - It shows that some numbers are more important than others (for instance number 5 in the center of the magic square).

The paper version of the Tic-Tac-Toe does not support turn taking between the players but this is easily done using a computer-based version of the game. Now Figure 17.3 also can be used to explain the behavior part of the system model of the Tic-Tac-Toe application. This system model is the same as for the previous system. The question is then why we call this an improved system model? If you try to play the game using one system after the other, it is immediately noticeable that the second one is much easier that the first one. The answer lies in the concrete task model presented in Figure 17.1. This model features a transition *"Choose a Number"* representing the selection made by a player from the set of remaining numbers. This user activity is highly demanding from a cognitive point of view, as it requires strategic computation.

17.6 SCENARIOS AS A BRIDGE BETWEEN TASKS AND SYSTEM MODELS

Various models have been proposed in the Human-Computer Interaction field. When designing and developing interactive software systems, task and system models are particularly important. In HCI—both industrial and academic communities—there is a wide agreement on the relevance of task models as they allow expressing the intentions of the users and the activities they should perform to reach their goals. These models also allow designers to develop an integrated description of both functional and interactive aspects. Within the development lifecycle of an application the task-modeling phase is supposed to be performed after having gathered information on the application domain and an informal task analysis phase. The result of the latter one is an informal list of tasks that have been identified as relevant for the application domain.

After this step, designers should develop a task model that forces them to clarify many aspects related to tasks and their relationships. In some cases task models are first developed and then used to drive the system design. In other cases designers have to address an existing system and need to develop a task model to better understand and evaluate its behavior (Palanque and Bastide, 1997).

System models describe important aspects of the user interface. In this work we pay particular attention to the dialogue supported by the system: how user actions and system feedback can be sequenced. Scenarios (Carroll, 1995) are a well-known technique in the human-computer interaction area. They provide a description of one specific use of a given system, in a given context. Their limited scope is their strength because they can easily highlight some specific aspect and are easily understood and remembered. Thus, they can also be considered as a useful tool to compare different models and analyze their relationships.

One point is that we can quite easily check if the task models fulfill the expected requirements, and we can check if the system model matches the planned behavior. However, what cannot be missed is checking if both models are consistent, which means if both specifications really refer to the same system. This requires checking if for each user action assumed in the system model there is an actual counterpart in the task model, and each system output provided to the user has been foreseen in the task model specification.

Another relevant point is that these two models can be specified by different people and in distinct moments of the design cycle of the user interface development process. Indeed, especially in real case studies it happens that sometimes the task models will be performed at first, sometimes they might be specified after the system model has already been obtained. So, we need an approach that does not have specific constraints and requirements on what is assumed to be available at a certain phase of the system design, as they can be equally used efficiently in both cases.

In our approach we decided to check this correspondence and completeness by means of abstract scenarios, which can be the common "lingua franca" useful to ensure and show whetehr there is an actual correspondence between what has been specified within the task models and what has been specified in the system model. The idea is to focus attention on specific examples of usage either on the system side or on the task side and to check if on these simple examples of the system use such correspondence exists.

We used the ConcurTaskTrees notation for specifying tasks. This notation provides the users with the possibility to explicitly express how the allocation of the different tasks has been assumed in the system design: on the user alone (user tasks), on the application alone (application tasks), on the interaction between the user and the application (interactive tasks), or if the activity is too general to be specifically allocated on each of them (abstract task). This explicit mention of the allocation of tasks is one of aspects which characterises the notation as very supportive and suitable to express the behavior of interactive systems, because for each task it is possible to define from which part of the system (user, application, interaction between them) the task is assumed to be undertaken.

This aspect is effective especially when both comparison and integration with different models have to be carried out, as in our case. The possibility of explicitly mentioning in the task models when a system support is requested on the user interface allows comparison and cross-check if the specification of the task models reflects and is adequately supported by the correspondent system model. More specifically, the points that have to be carefully checked in the task model specification are the application tasks, with which has been emphasised that at a certain point during a user session a specific behavior of the system is expected.

This behavior can be expressed for instance in terms of a specific feedback of an action the user has performed while interacting with the system, or in terms of a result that the system has produced after some elaboration, or in terms of availability of a specific input which is needed by users in order to perform their tasks. All those possibilities have to be carefully supported especially if the considered domain is vast and complex, such as in the air traffic control domain which is considered in our case study. Such a case study is composed of a number of entities maintaining a complex relationship structure, because of their internal structure or because of the dynamic behavior they follow, which has to be appropriately presented to the users (air traffic controllers).

17.7 A CASE STUDY

Our case study is extracted from the European Project MEFISTO which is a long-term research project dedicated to the definition and use of formal method for the design of safety-critical interactive systems. This project is focused on the air traffic control application domain from which this case study comes. This section presents the various models built in order to represent both predictive user activities and the system under consideration. Section 17.7.2 presents the use of CTT and its support environment for tasks modeling and simulation as well as the extraction of scenarios from the task models. Section 17.7.3 presents the use of the ICO formalism and its support environment PetShop for modeling and executing interactive systems.

17.7.1 Informal Description of the Case Study

This example comes from an En-route Air Traffic Control application focusing on the impact of data-link technologies in the ATC field. Using such applications air traffic controllers can direct pilots in an airspace sector. The radar image is shown in Figure 17.5. On the radar image each plane is represented by a graphical element providing air traffic controllers with useful information for handling air traffic in a sector. In the simplified version of the radar image each graphical representation of a plane is made up of three components: (a) a label (providing the plane ID, speed, cleared flight level, etc.), (b) a dot (representing the current position of the plane in the sector), and (c) a speed vector (a graphical line from the dot which represents the envisioned position of the plane in 3 minutes).

An Air Traffic Control is in charge simulating the arrival of new planes in the sector while in reality they would be instantiated on the user interface by calls from the functional core of the application processing information provided by physical radars. The user can interactively control the simulator triggering the arrival of a plane by clicking on a NewPlane button. The ATC simulator user interface can be found on the right-hand side of Figure 17.28. On the top of the window the button New Plane allows for introducing a new plane in the sector.

Initially the radar image is empty. Each time a new plane is randomly generated it is graphically represented on the radar image. The user can select planes by clicking on their graphical representation. The selection of a plane will change its state to the *"Assume"* state meaning that the air traffic controller is now in charge of the plane. Assuming the plane changes its graphical representation as can be seen on the left-hand side of Figure 17.5. Once a plane is assumed, the controller can send clearances (i.e., order to this plane). In this case study we only consider the change of frequency functionality corresponding to the controller's activity of transferring a plane to an adjacent sector. When the plane is assumed the corresponding button *"FREQ"* becomes available (see plane 1123 on the left-hand side of Figure 17.5). Clicking on this button opens a menu allowing the controller to select the new value for the frequency as shown on the bottom of Figure 17.28.

17.7.2 The ConcurTaskTrees Notation and Environment Used in the Case Study

There are various approaches that aim to specify tasks. They differ in aspects such as the type of formalism they use, the type of knowledge they capture, and how they support the design and development of interactive systems. In this chapter we consider task models that have been represented using the ConcurTaskTrees (CTT) notation (Paternò, 1999). In CTT, activities are described at different abstraction levels in a hierarchical manner, represented graphically in a tree-like format (see Figure 17.6 for an example).

In contrast to previous approaches, such as Hierarchical Task Analysis, ConcurTaskTrees provides a rich set of operators, with precise meaning, able to describe many possible temporal relationships (concurrency, interruption, disabling, iteration, and so on). This allows designers to obtain concise representations describing many possible evolutions over a user session. The notation also gives the possibility of using icons or geometrical shapes to indicate how the performance of the tasks is allocated.

For each task it is possible to provide additional information including the objects manipulated (for both the user interface and the application) and attributes such as frequency. Automatic tools are needed to make the development and analysis of such task models easier and more efficient. In addition, as in the design of complex cooperative environments more and more attention is being paid to the horizontal mechanism

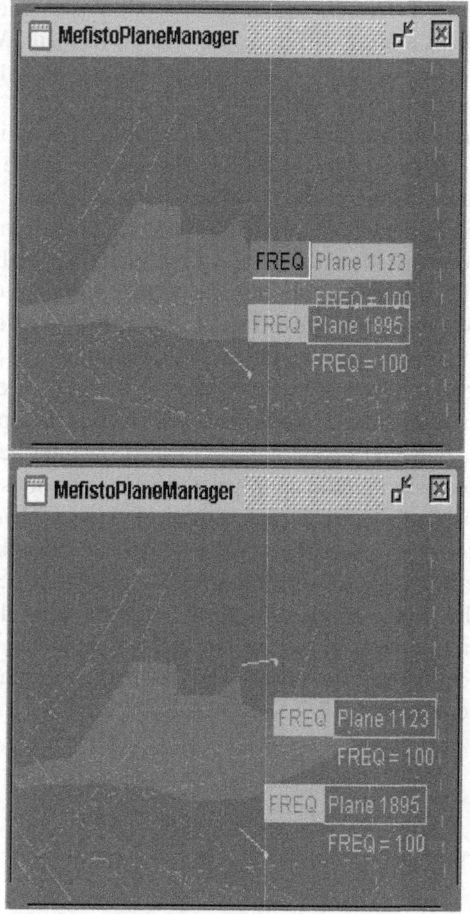

Figure 17.5 A screen-shot of the radar screen with planes (left-hand side, one of the planes 1123 is assumed)

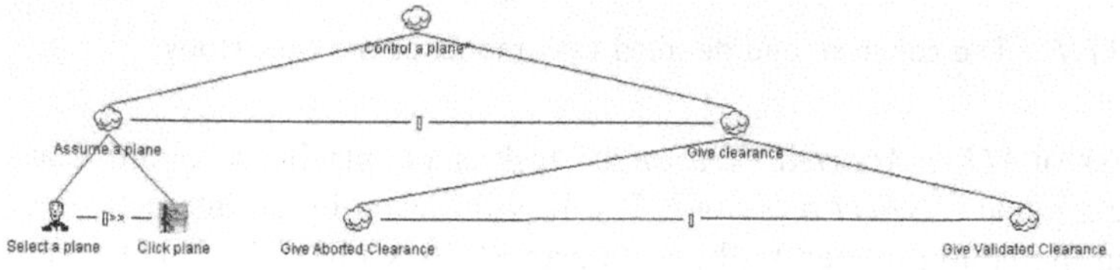

Figure 17.6 The abstract task model of case study using CTT notation

of coordination between different roles, and CTT allows designers to specify explicitly how the cooperation among different users is performed. We give hereafter an overview of the main features of the notation by commenting on two excerpts of specification from the considered case study.

The activity of controlling a plane (*"Control a plane"*) is an iterative task (see the iterative operator *) which consists of either assuming a plane (*"Assume a plane"* task) or giving clearance to the plane (*"Give clearance"* task). These two activities are mutually exclusive, as you can see from the choice operator []. The activity of assuming a plane is composed of deciding which plane has to be assumed (Select a plane task, the associated icon emphasizes the cognitive nature of this so-called user task). Once this activity has been performed it is possible to select the button related to the plan (see the Enabling operator with information passing []≫, which highlights that only after the first activity has been carried out and delivered information to the second task, the latter can be performed). In addition, the Click plane task requires an explicit action of the controller on an element of the user interface so it belongs to the category of interaction tasks and the appropriate icon has been used. The *"Give clearance"* task is composed of two different activities: *"Give Aborted Clearance"* and *"Give Validated Clearance"*, depending on whether the clearance has been aborted or not. Each of these two activities is a high-level one, whose performance cannot be entirely allocated either to the application alone, or to the user alone, or to an interaction between the user and the system: this is expressed by using the cloud-shape icon associated to the so-called abstract tasks. The detailed specification of each of these two tasks is described in Figure 17.7.

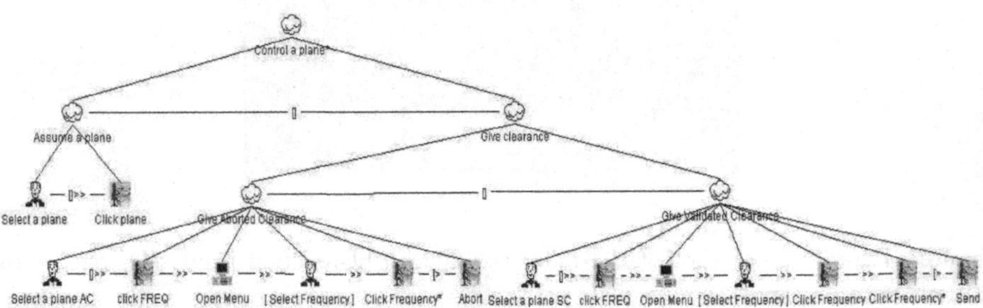

Figure 17.7 The concrete and detailed task model of the case study

The first subtask of *"Give Aborted Clearance"* task is a controller's cognitive activity of selecting a plane (*"Select a plane AC"*). It is followed by an interactive activity for selecting the button related to the frequency ("Click FREQ"). This triggers the opening of a correspondent menu on the controller's user interface (i.e., *"Open Menu"*; notice the special icon representing an application task), then the controller can think about a specific frequency (in the task model the possibility of performing or not performing this task is expressed by the option operator expressed by squared brackets [T], see the task *"Select Frequency"*). Then, controllers choose the appropriate value of frequency within the user interface (*"Click Frequency"* task, which can be performed more than one time since it features the iterative operator *) until they decide to interrupt the entire activity (see the *"Disabling"* operator "[>" which refers to the possibility for the second task to disable the first one), by selecting the related object in the user interface (*"Abort"* task).

In case of a clearance that is really sent to the pilot (*"Give Validated Clearance"*), the sequence of actions is mainly the same, apart from the last one ("Send" task), with which the controller sends the clearance to the pilot.

A set of tools, namely, CTTE, have been developed to specify task models for co-operative applications in ConcurTaskTrees, to analyze their content and to generate corresponding user interfaces. The CTTE tool has various features supporting editing of task models. It can automatically check the syntax of the specification, give statistical information, compare task models, simulate their behavior and give examples of scenarios of use. The CTTE editing environment is intended as a computer-based support tool for CTT, and is freely downloadable from http://giove.cnuce.cnr.it/ctte.html.

With this tool, it becomes very intuitive and effective to exploit the graphical and hierarchical nature (tree-like format) features of the notation by providing all the necessary operations (cut, paste, insert) that are usually possible on tree-like structures. In addition, even the specific layout selected for the tool conveys further useful information about the notation. For instance, the relative positions of the user interface objects presenting the operators within the tool convey information about their priorities (sorted top to bottom from highest to lowest priority operator). In addition, it is possible to recall the meaning of any operator by means of useful tool tips available within the environment (such feature was found very useful especially by users who are rather new to the notation and unable to recall the meaning of the operators). Finally, the ability to structure the specification with some tasks that can be referenced in both the single-user and cooperative parts well supported by the environment because it allows easy switching between these different views. These simple examples, relative to the case of the CTT notation, serve to highlight the extent to which the use of a suitable tool can support users while building the task specifications.

Figure 17.8 presents a screenshot of the simulator provided by CTTE tool. When this tool is activated, in the left-hand part of the window it is possible to have highlighted (by means of a different colour) all the tasks that are active at any moment of the simulation. This means all the tasks that can be performed at a specific time, depending on the tasks that have been previously carried out. The execution of a task can be performed either within the graphical panel on the left (a task can be executed by double-clicking on the related task icon), or by selecting the task name within the list of *"Enabled Tasks"* panel on the right and then selecting the *"Next task to be performed"* button. In addition, in the *"Scenario to be performed"* list it is possible to have the list of tasks which have been carried out until now: this sequence of tasks can be saved in a separate file and executed later on.

As an example of scenario we have chosen to extract from the task model of Figure 17.7 the following trace of low-level tasks (this scenario has been extracted using CTTE and is displayed on the right-hand side of Figure 17.8):

- The controller selects (in her head) one of the planes not assumed yet (this is a user task)

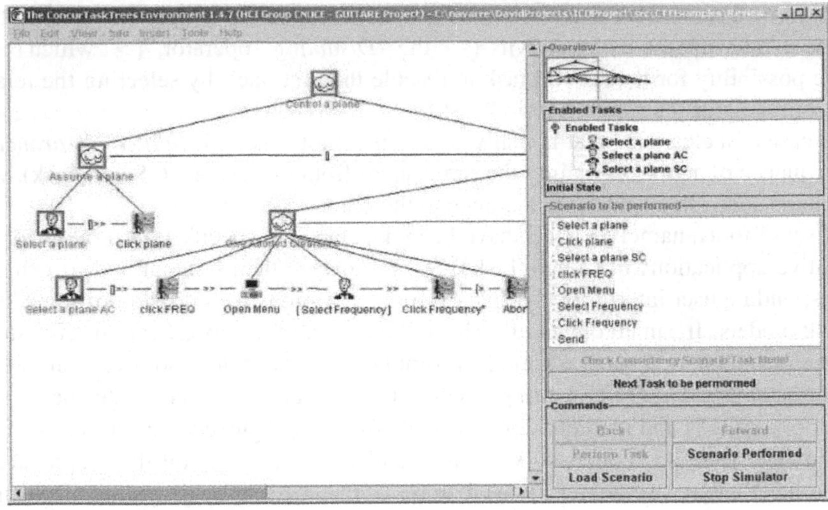

Figure 17.8 CTTE for extracting scenarios

- The controller clicks on this plane to assume it (this is an interactive task)
- The controller decides (in her head) to change the current frequency of one of the flights assumed (this is a user task)
- The controller clicks on the label FREQ to open the data-link menu (this is an interactive task)
- The controller selects (in her head) a new frequency for this plane (this is a user task)
- The controller clicks on one of the available frequencies for this plane (this is an interactive task)
- The controller clicks on the SEND button to send the new frequency to the aircraft (this is an interactive task)

17.7.3 ICOs and PetShop used in the Case Study

System modeling is done using the ICO formalism and its development environment called PetShop. Both of them are presented hereafter using the case study as support. The ICO formalism is the continuation of early work on dialogue modeling using high-level Petri nets (Bastide and Palanque, 1990). The various components of the formalism are introduced informally in subsection 17.7.3 and all of them are fully exemplified on the case study in subsection 17.9. Section 17.7.3 presents the PetShop environment and the design process it supports.

ICO Formalism. The Interactive Cooperative Objects (ICO) formalism is a formal notation dedicated to the specification of interactive systems. ICOs use concepts borrowed from the object-oriented approach (dynamic instantiation, classification, encapsulation, inheritance, client/server relationship) to describe the structural or static aspects of systems, and use high-level Petri nets to describe their dynamic or behavioral aspects. ICOs were originally devised for the modeling and implementation of event-driven interfaces. An ICO model of a system is made up of several communicating objects, where Petri nets describe both behavior of objects and communication protocol between objects. In the ICO formalism, an object is an entity featuring four components: behavior, services, state, and presentation.

Interface: The interface specifies at a syntactic level the services that a client object can request from a server object that implements this interface. The interface details the services supported and their signature: a list of parameters with their type and parameter-passing mode, the type of the return value, the exceptions that may possibly be raised during the processing of the service. For describing this interface we use the CORBA-IDL language (OMG, 1990). An ICO offers a set of services that define the interface (in the programming language meaning) offered by the object to its environment. In the case of user-driven application, this environment may be either the user or other objects of the application. The ICO formalism distinguishes between services offered to the user (user services) from those services offered to other objects.

Behavior: The behavior of an ICO states how the object reacts to external stimuli according to its inner state. This behavior is described by a high-level Petri net called the Object Control Structure (ObCS) of the object. The state of an ICO is the distribution and the value of the tokens (called the marking) in the places of the ObCS. This allows defining how the current state influences the availability of services, and conversely how the performance of a service influences the state of the object.

Presentation: The Presentation of an object states its external look. It is made up of three components: the widgets, the activation function, and the rendering function. This Presentation is a structured set of widgets organized in a set of windows. The user–system interaction will only take place through those widgets. Each user action on a widget may trigger one of the ICO's user services. The relation between user services and widgets is fully stated by the activation function that associates to each couple (widget, user action) the service to be triggered. The rendering function is in charge of presenting information according to the state changes that occur. It is thus related to the representation of states in the behavioral description i.e., places in the high-level Petri net.

ICO are used to provide a formal description of the dynamic behavior of an interactive application. An ICO specification fully describes the potential interactions that users may have with the application. The specification encompasses both the "input" aspects of the interaction (i.e., how user actions impact on the inner state of the application, and which actions are enabled at any given time) and its "output" aspects (i.e., when and how the application displays information that is relevant to the user). An ICO specification is fully executable, which gives the possibility to prototype and test quickly an application before it is fully implemented. The specification can also be validated using analysis and proof tools developed within the Petri nets community.

ICO Environment (PetShop). Figure 17.9 presents the general architecture of PetShop. It is composed of a set of rectangles and documents-like shapes. The button-like rectangles represent the functional modules of PetShop. The documents-like shapes represent the models produced and used by the modules.

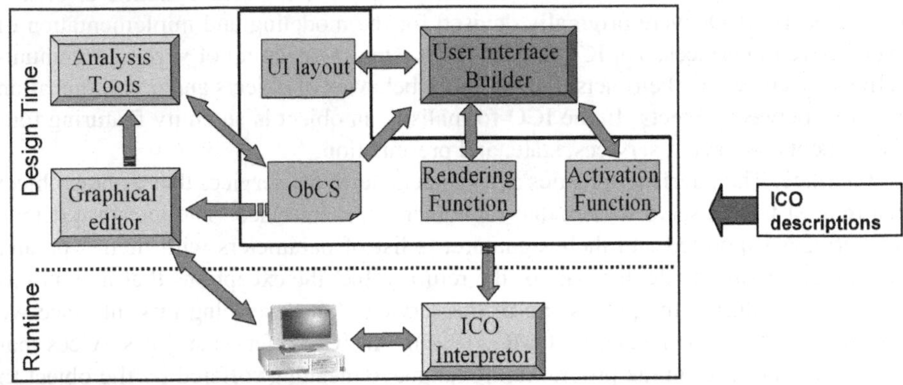

Figure 17.9 Tools available for designers in PetShop environment

Since this tool is not the main topic of the chapter its precise functioning is not presented here. For a detailed description of PetShop features see Bastide et al., 1999.

Presentation of ICOs and PetShop on the Case Study. This subsection only presents a subset of the set of classes and objects that have to be built in order to fully implement the case study. The complete description of the case study can be found in David et al. (2005)(David et al., 2005).

As presented in this chapter the case study is modeled as a set of three cooperating classes: *"MefistoPlaneManager"*, *"MefistoPlane"* and *"MefistoMenu"*. These three classes are fully-fledged hereafter.

The class *"MefistoPlaneManager"*. The class *"MefistoPlaneManager"* is in charge of handling the set of planes in a sector. Each time a new plane arrives in the sector the *"MefistoPlaneManager"* instantiates it from the class *"MefistoPlanes"*. There is only one instance of this class at running time. The set of services offered by this class is described in Figure 17.10.

```
interface MefistoPlaneManager {
void closePlane(in MefistoPlane p);
void terminatePlane(in MefistoPlane p);
void addPlane(in MefistoPlane p);
};
```

Figure 17.10 IDL description of the class "MefistoPlaneManager"

This IDL description (above) shows that the class offers three services dealing with the managing of the planes in a sector: adding a plane, terminating a plane (when it leaves a sector), and closing the menu of a plane.

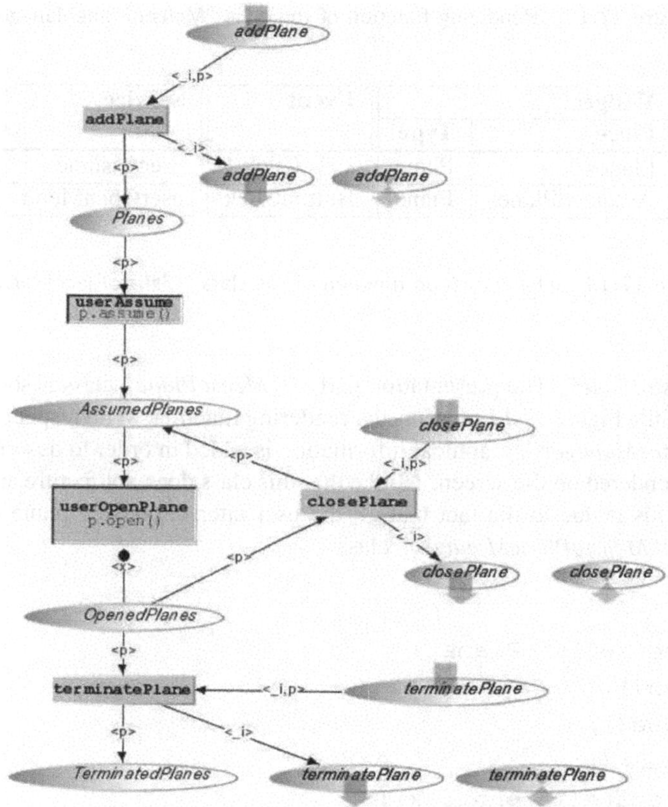

Figure 17.11 ObCS description of the class "MefistoPlaneManager"

Figure 17.11 presents the behavior of the class and, according to the current state, what services are available to the other objects of the application. The transition *"UserOpenPlane"* has an input arc from place *"AssumedPlanes"* meaning that a controller can only open a menu on a plane that has previously been assumed. The inhibitor arc between that transition and the place *"OpenedPlanes"* states that only one plane at a time can have the data-link menu opened.

Figure 17.12 and 17.13 describe the presentation part of the ICO *"MefistoPlane-Manager"*. From the rendering function it can be seen that this class only triggers rendering through the class *"MefistoPlane"* as each time a new token enters in the place Planes the graphical function Show is triggered on the corresponding plane.

The class "MefistoPlane". The class *"MefistoPlane"* is also an ICO class. Figure 17.14 shows its IDL description. Figure 17.15 describes the behavior of the

ObCS Element	Feature	Rendering method
Place Planes	token <p> entered	p.show()

Figure 17.12 Rendering function of the class "MefistoPlaneManager"

Widget		Event	Service
Place	Type		
Planes	Plane	LabeClick	userAssume
AssumedPlanes	Plane	ButtonClick	userOpenMenu

Figure 17.13 The activation function of the class "MefistoPlaneManager"

class *"MefistoPlane"*. The presentation part of *"MefisoPlane"* class is shown in Figure 17.16 while Figure 17.17 presents the rendering function. With respect to the class *"MefistoPlaneManager"*, graphical information is added in order to describe how the planes are rendered on the screen. Notice that this class does not feature an activation function. This is due to the fact that all the user interaction on a plane takes place through the *"MefistoPlaneManager"* class.

```
interface MefistoPlane {
void open();
void close();
void assume();
void validate(in short x);
};
```

Figure 17.14 IDL description of the class "MefistoPlane"

The class "MefistoMenu". This class is in charge of the interaction taking place through the data-link menu that is opened by clicking on the button FREQ on the plane label.

Similarly to the other classes, Figure 17.18 shows the set of services offered to the other objects of the application. Figure 17.19 describes the corresponding behavior. Figures 17.20, 17.21 and 17.22 give the presentation part of the class *"MefistoPlane"*.

Notice that some of the information given above is only required in order to provide full excitability of the models. However this description still lacks the code of the functions given in Figure 17.20 and in Figure 17.16 for describing precisely the graphical behavior of the classes. This is not given here due to space limitation, but a complete demo of the case study is available.

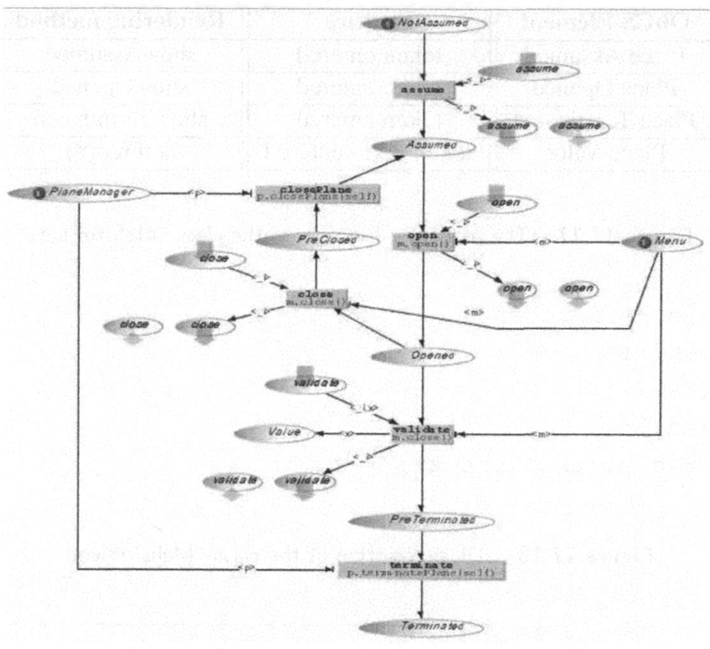

Figure 17.15 ObCS of the class "MefistoPlane"

```
public class WidgetPlane {
//Attributes
//A button to open the menu for the change of frequency
Button freqButton;  //A label to display the name of the
plane
Label label;  //Rendering methods
void show () { } //show plane
void showAssumed () {  } //show plane as assumed
void showOpened () { } //show plane as opened
void showTerminated () { }//show plane as terminated
void setFreq(short x) {  } //show the new frequency
}
```

Figure 17.16 The presentation part of the class "MefistoPlane"

17.8 THE INTEGRATION OF THE MODELS: CTT-ICO

The integration framework we have followed takes full advantage of the specific tools that we have developed initially in a separate manner. One advantage of this separation

ObCS Element	Feature	Rendering method
Place Assumed	token entered	showAssumed
Place Opened	token entered	showOpened
Place Terminated	token entered	showTerminated
Place Value	token <x> entered	setFreq(x)

Figure 17.17 The rendering function of the class "MefistoPlane"

```
interface MefistoMenu {
void open();
void close();
void send();
void setValue(in short x);
};
```

Figure 17.18 IDL description of the class "MefistoMenu"

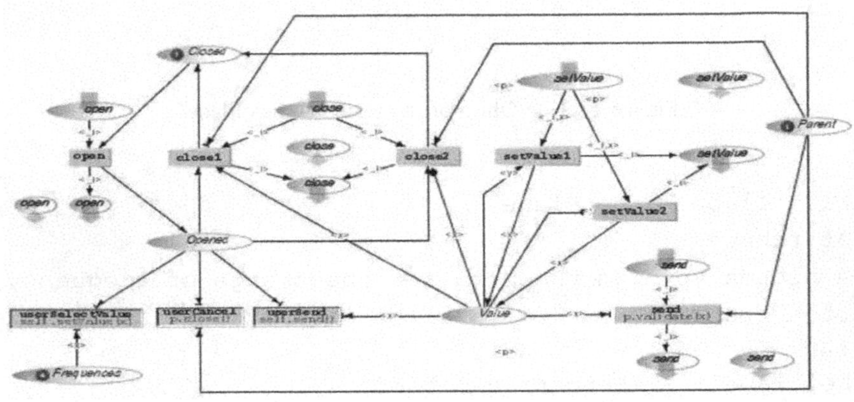

Figure 17.19 ObCS of the class "MefistoMenu"

is that it allows for independent modification of the tools, provided that the interchange format remains the same.

We have previously investigated the relationship between task and system models. For instance in Palanque et al. (1995) we proposed a transformation mechanism for translating UAN task descriptions into Petri nets and then checking whether this Petri net description was compatible with system modeling also done using Petri nets. In (Palanque et al., 1997) we presented the use of CTT for abstract task modeling and high-level Petri nets for low-level task modeling. In that chapter the low level task model was use in order to evaluate the "complexity" of the tasks to be performed, by means of performance evaluation techniques available in Petri net theory.

```
public class WidgetMenu {
//Attributes
//Button to validate or cancel the current choice for
frequency
Button sendButton, cancelButton ;
//A comboBox to show the set of possible frequency
ComboBox freqComboBox;
//Rendering methods
void show () {   } //show menu as opened
void hide () {   } //hide menu
}
```

Figure 17.20 The presentation part of the class "MefistoMenu"

ObCS Element	Feature	Rendering method
Place Opened	token entered	show()
Place Closed	token entered	hide()

Figure 17.21 Rendering function of the class "MefistoMenu"

Widget		Event	Service
Place	Type		
sendButton		actionPerformed	userSend
abortButton		actionPerformed	userCancel
freqComboBox		select	userSelectValue

Figure 17.22 The activation function of the class "MefistoMenu"

17.8.1 CTT Environment

Parts 1 and 2 of Figure 17.23 highlight the outputs provided by the CTT environment and processing. The CTT environment provides a set of tools for engineering task models. For the purpose of integration we only use the interactive tool for editing the tasks and the simulation tool for task models that allows scenario construction from the task models. Thus the two main outputs are a set of task models and a set of scenarios. These two sets are exploited in the following way:

- A set of interaction tasks is extracted from a CTT model. This set represents a set of manipulations that can be performed by the user on the system (part 1 of Figure 17.23).

- The set of scenarios is used as inputs (part 2 of Figure 17.23).

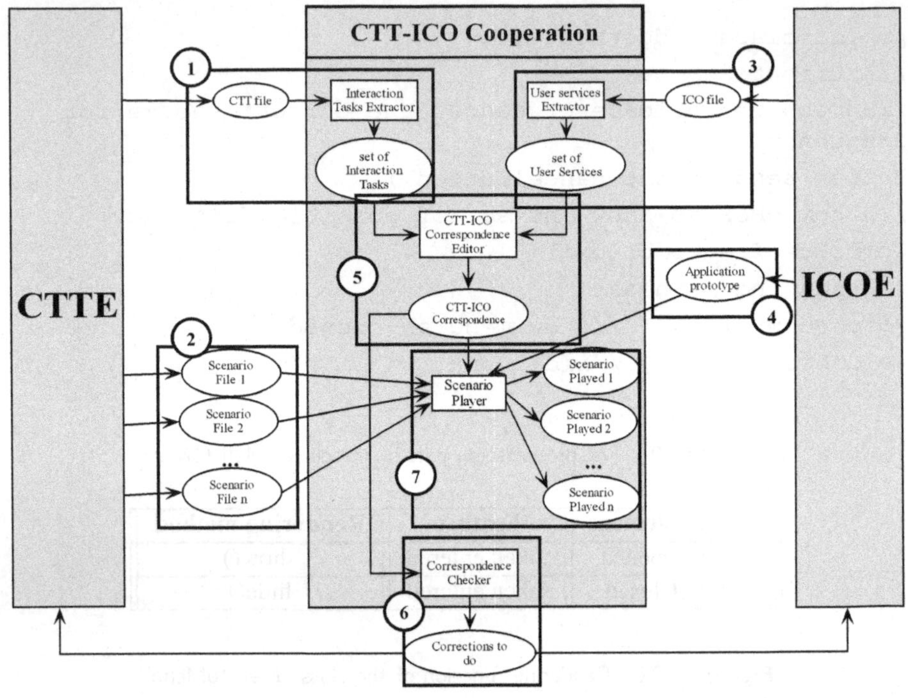

Figure 17.23 The framework for CTTE – PetShop integration

17.8.2 ICO Environment

The outputs of the ICO environment and their processing are highlighted by parts 3 and 4 of Figure 17.23. From the ICO environment (PetShop) we only employ for the integration the tool for editing the system model. It allows executing the system model as follows:

- From the ICO specification we extract a set of user services (part 3 of Figure 17.23).
- From the ICO environment we use the prototype of the system modeled (part 4 of Figure 17.23).

A user service is a set of particular transitions that represents the functionalities offered to the user by the system. These transitions are performed when and only when they are fireable and the corresponding user actions are performed (which is represented by the activation function in the ICO formalism).

The Correspondence Editor. The activities that are managed by the correspondence editor correspond to parts 5 and 6 of Figure 17.23. The first component of the correspondence editor relates interaction tasks in the task model to user services in the system model (part 5 of Figure 17.23). When the task model is refined enough, the leaves of the task tree represent low-level interaction on the artifacts. It is then possible to relate those low-level interactive tasks to user action in the system model that are represented, in the ICO formalism, by user services.

In order to check that this correspondence is valid we have developed a model checker (part 6 of Figure 17.23). The properties checked by the model checker correspond to the verification and validation phase in the development process. Validation phase relate to the question "do we have modeled the right system?" while the verification phase address the question "do we have modeled the system right?". In the context of ICO-CTT integration for the verification phase the model checker addresses the following two questions:

1. Are there at least as many user services in the ICO specification as interaction tasks in the CTT model?

2. Are all the possible scenarios from the task model available in the system modeled?

In the context of ICO-CTT integration for the validation phase the model checker addresses the following two questions:

1. Are there more user services in the ICO specification than interaction tasks in the CTT model?

2. Are there scenarios available in the system model that are not available in the task model?

If the answer is yes for one of these two subrules, the system modeled offers more functionalities than expected by the task model described with CTT. This leads to two possible mistakes in the design process. Either the system implements more functions than needed or the set of task models built is incomplete. In the first part of the alternative the useless functionalities must be removed. In the second part either task models using this functionality are added or the use of this functionality will never appear in any of the scenarios to be built.

The role of the correspondence checker is to notify any inconsistency between the CTT and the ICO specifications. We can imagine it could provide recommendations on how to correct these mistakes; however, this has not been implemented yet. After having put the task model and the system model into correspondence, we produce a CTT-ICO correspondence file.

Execution: the Scenario Player. As a scenario is a sequence of tasks and as we are able to put a task and a user service into correspondence, it is now possible to convert the scenarios into a sequence of firing of transitions in the ICO specification.

An ICO specification can be executed in the ICO environment and behaves according to the high-level Petri net describing its behavior. As the CTT scenarios can be converted into a sequence of firing of transitions, it can directly be used to command the execution of the ICO specification.

To this end we have developed a tool dedicated to the execution of an ICO formal description of a case study driven by a scenario extracted from a task model (see part 7 of Figure 17.23).

Application on the Case Study. This section presents the application of the integration framework presented in Section 17.8 to the Air Traffic Control case study presented in section 17.7.1.

Figure 17.24 presents the correspondence editor introduced above. The left-hand side of the window contains the task model that has been introduced in Section 17.7.2 and loaded into the correspondence editor. In the case study under consideration, only one task model can be loaded. However, if cooperative task models are considered, the correspondence editor makes it possible to include several task models. In such a case, the *"Task Tree"* panel includes tabs widget for each task model. In this panel the set of interactive tasks are displayed. On the right-hand side of Figure 17.24 the panel *Set of User Services* displays the set of user services in the ICO specification that has been loaded. Here again it is possible to load several ICOs. The set of user services of each ICO appears in a separate tab widget.

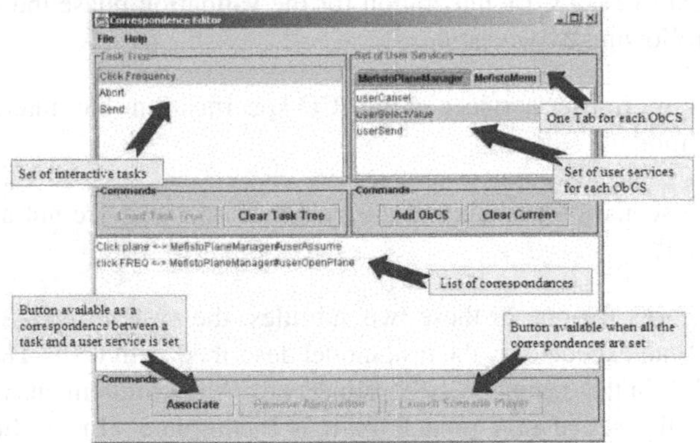

Figure 17.24 Association of interactive tasks and user services

The lower part of the window in Figure 17.24 depicts the set of associations that have been performed when all user services in the ICOs that have been loaded have been associated with all the interactive tasks loaded in the *"Task Tree"* panel the *"Launch Scenario Player"* button is available.

Clicking on this button opens the window presented in Figure 17.25 corresponding to the scenario player. This tool allows for loading a scenario (produced using CTTE tool presented in Figure 17.8) and executing it in PetShop. The scenario can thus be considered as a driver replacing user interaction that would normally drive the execution of the ICO specification.

The right-hand side of Figure 17.25 presents the set of actions in the selected scenario. The first line in the scenario represents the current task in the scenario. In Figure 17.25 the current task is *"Select a plane"* and is a user tasks, i.e., the task is performed entirely by the user without interacting with the system. Clicking on the *"Perform Task"* button triggers the task and the next task in the scenario becomes the current task.

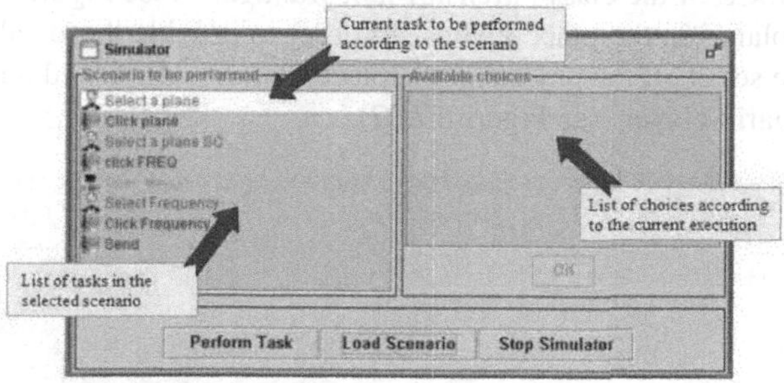

Figure 17.25 The scenario player

Figure 17.26 shows the scenario player in use. The right-hand side of the figure shows the execution of the ICOs specification with the two main components: the Air Traffic Control application with the radar screen and the ATC simulator allowing for test purpose to add planes in the sector.

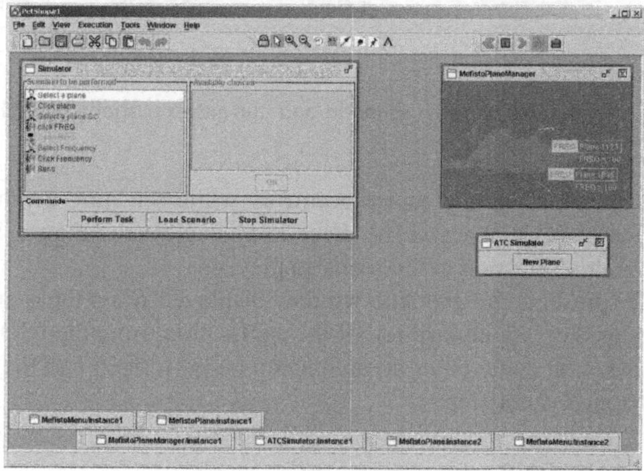

Figure 17.26 Execution of the scenario of the system

Some tasks of *"interactive"* or *"application"* type require runtime information to be performed. This is the case for instance of interactive task *"Click plane"* that correspond to the user's action click on a plane. Of course, the click can only occur on one of the *"current"* planes in the sector and thus, the identification number cannot be known at design time and thus cannot be represented in the task model.

Figure 17.27 gives an example of this aspect. Triggering the action *"Click plane"* in the task model requires a parameter, i.e., a plane identifier. As this interactive task has been related to the user service *"UserAssume"* (in the correspondence editor) the triggering of this task triggers the corresponding user service. However, the triggering of this service requires one of the values in the input place of the transition *"UserAssume"* in the ObCS of the class *"MefistoPlaneManager"* (see Figure 17.11), i.e., one of the objects planes in the place Planes. In order to provide those values to the scenario player the set of all the objects in the place Planes is displayed on the right-hand side of the scenario player (see Figure 17.27).

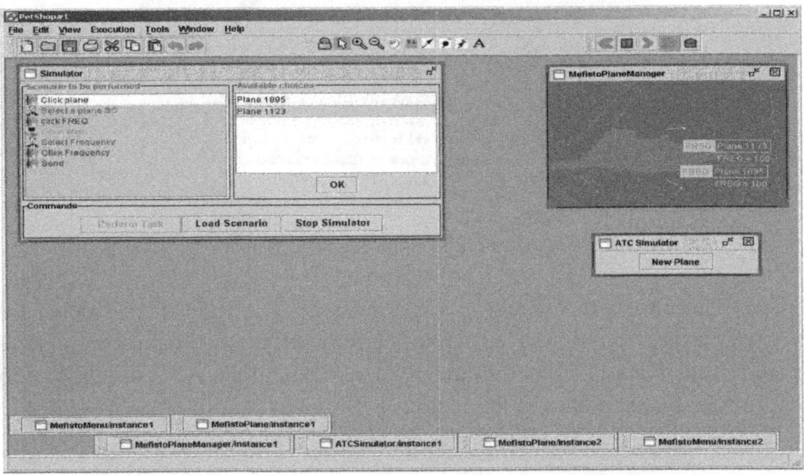

Figure 17.27 Interaction between scenario and current execution: plane IDs are selected at runtime

Figure 17.28 shows the interaction occurring while selecting a value for the frequency. The set of frequencies in the place Frequencies (see Figure 17.19) are displayed for the user's selection in the scenario player.

Figure 17.29 presents the dialogue window displayed when the scenario has been successfully played on the description of the application using the ICO formalism. A scenario fails when at some point no action can be performed and the list of actions still to be performed is not empty.

17.9 CONCLUSIONS

In this chapter we have used a very simple example to show that creativity must remain an explicit phase in the design process of interactive systems and thus that generation of interactive systems from task models cannot lead to efficient interactive systems.

In contrast to related work in the field such as Paterno et al. (1999), we have tried to show here that the generation of an interactive system from task models is not a valid use of a task model as:

- Either you need to add information in the task model in order to be able to generate the interactive system from it and in that case this is not a task model anymore (this is done for instance in the work from (Bodart et al., 1995).

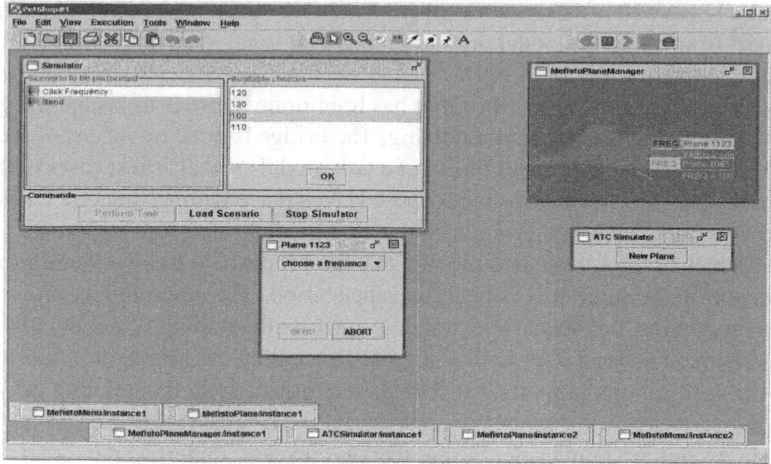

Figure 17.28 Interaction between scenario and current execution: values for frequency are selected at runtime

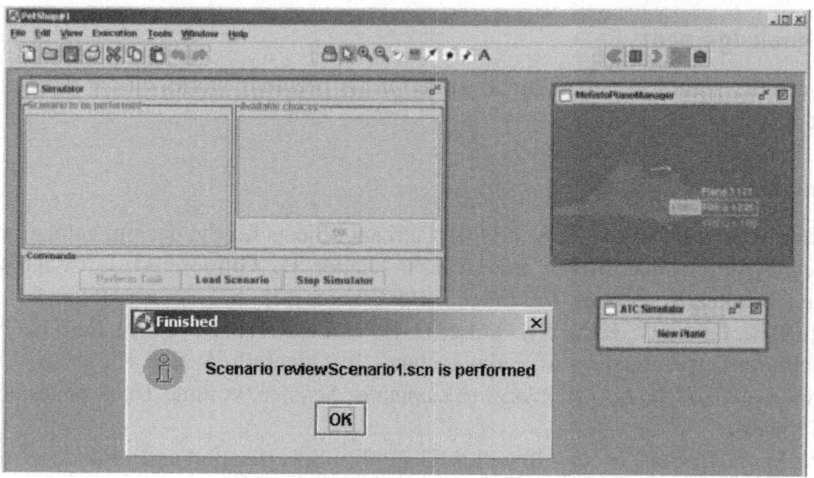

Figure 17.29 End of the execution of the scenario on the system model

- Or you can generate a basic interactive system that does not cover efficiently users' activities. This has been shown in the example above where the Tic-Tac-Toe application supports users' strategy in selecting the best number. This strategic part of users' activity was not represented in the task model, as this kind of model is not meant to encompass this kind of information.

We also believe (but we have not shown it here for space reasons) that generating a task model from a system model does not bring a lot to interactive systems' design, as this is advocated in Lu et al. (1999).

This chapter has presented work that has been done in order to bridge the gap between task modeling and system modeling. The bridge is done by means of scenarios that are considered here as traces of use of a task model as well as test cases of the system model. The use of scenarios we proposed takes place within a generic framework. This generic framework is thoroughly supported by dedicated software tools.

The chapter has not presented the fact that the proposed framework and its related tools support in the same way cooperative application. The environment proposed for both task modeling and scenario extraction supports the editing of cooperative tasks. The environment proposed for both editing and executing the formal description of the interactive applications supports distributed execution of models according to CORBA standard.

On the system modeling side, further work is currently undertaken in order to make the editing of the presentation part of the ICO models easier. Indeed, currently both activation and rendering functions are edited in a textual way while graphical edition with a direct manipulation style would make this task easier. This integration framework based on scenario can be generalised to other task models provided they make explicit the distinction between system tasks, user task, and interactive tasks.

Acknowledgements

The authors want to thank Rémi Bastide for his previous works on the draft of this topic.

References

Bastide, R. and Palanque, P. A. (1990). Petri net objects for the design, validation and prototyping of user-driven interfaces. In Diaper, D., Gilmore, D. J., Cockton, G., and Shackel, B., editors, *INTERACT 1990*, pages 625–631. North-Holland.

Bastide, R., Palanque, P. A., Sy, O., Le, D.-H., and Navarre, D. (1999). Petri net based behavioral specification of corba systems. In Donatelli, S. and Kleijn, H. C. M., editors, *ICATPN, Lecture Notes in Computer Science*, volume 1639, pages 66–85. Springer.

Biere, M., Bomsdorf, B., and Szwillus, G. (1999). Specification and simulation of task models with vtmb. In *CHI'99 extended abstracts on Human factors in computing systems*, pages 1–2. ACM Press.

Bodart, F., Hennebert, A. M., Leheureux, J. M., and Vanderdonckt, J. (1995). A model-based approach to presentation: A continuum from task analysis to prototype. In Bodart, F., editor, *Focus on Computer Graphics Series*, pages 77–94. Springer-Verlag.

Bodart, F., Hennebert, A.-M., Provot, I., Leheureux, J.-M., and Vanderdonckt, J. (1994). A model-based approach to presentation: A continuum from task analysis to prototype. In Paternò, F., editor, *DSV-IS*, pages 77–94. Springer.

Carroll, J. M., editor (1995). *Scenario-based design: Envisioning work and technology in system development*. New York: Wiley.

David, N., Philippe, P., and Bastide., R. (2005). Specification of middles touch screen using interactive cooperative objects.

Lecerof, A. and Paternò, F. (1998). Automatic support for usability evaluation. *IEEE Trans. Softw. Eng.*, 24(10):863–888.

Lu, S., Paris, C., and Linden, K. V. (1999). Toward the automatic construction of task models from object-oriented diagrams. In *Proceedings of the IFIP TC2/TC13 WG2.7/WG13.4 Seventh Working Conference on Engineering for Human-Computer Interaction*, pages 169–189.

Moher, T., Dirda, V., Bastide, R., and Palanque, P. A. (1996). Monolingual, articulated modeling of users, devices, and interfaces. In Bodart, F. and Vanderdonckt, J., editors, *DSV-IS*, pages 312–329. Springer.

Norman, D. A. (1986). Cognitive engineering. In Norman, D. A. and Draper, S. W., editors, *User centered system design: New perspectives on human-computer interaction*, pages 31–61. Erlbaum, Hillsdale, NJ.

OMG (1990). The common object request broker: Architecture and specification.

Palanque, P. A. and Bastide, R. (1997). Synergistic modeling of tasks, users and systems using formal specification techniques. *Interacting with Computers*, 9(2):129–153.

Palanque, P. A., Bastide, R., and Paternò, F. (1997). Formal specification as a tool for objective assessment of safety-critical interactive systems. In Howard, S., Hammond, J., and Lindgaard, G., editors, *IFIP Conference Proceedings*, volume 96, pages 323–330. Chapman & Hall.

Palanque, P. A., Bastide, R., and Sengès, V. (1995). Formal specification as a tool for objective assessment of safety-critical interactive systems. In Bass, L. J. and Unger, C., editors, *IFIP Conference Proceedings*, volume 45, pages 189–212. Chapman & Hall.

Paternò, F. (1999). *Model-Based Design and Evaluation of Interactive Applications*. Springer-Verlag, London, UK.

Paternò, F., Breedvelt-Schouten, I. M., and de Koning, N. (1999). Deriving presentations from task models. In *Proceedings of the IFIP TC2/TC13 WG2.7/WG13.4 Seventh Working Conference on Engineering for Human-Computer Interaction*, pages 319–337. Kluwer.

Puerta, A. R. and Eisenstein, J. (1999). Towards a general computational framework for model-based interface development systems. In *Intelligent User Interfaces*, pages 171–178.

van Welie, M., van der Veer, G. C., and Eli`ens, A. (1998). An ontology for task world models. In Markopoulos, P. and Johnson, P., editors, *Design, Specification and Verification of Interactive Systems '98*, pages 57–70. Springer-Verlag.

Author Index

Subject Index